P9-ASK-598

NAVAJO
ARCHITECTURE

Cribbed-log hogan, Hubbell's Trading Post, Arizona, 1970; R.F.

NAVAJO ARCHITECTURE

FORMS, HISTORY, DISTRIBUTIONS

STEPHEN C. JETT
and
VIRGINIA E. SPENCER

UNIVERSITY OF ARIZONA PRESS
TUCSON, ARIZONA

About the Authors . . .

STEPHEN C. JETT, professor and chairperson of the Department of Geography at the University of California, Davis, has a distinguished reputation as an expert on the cultural and historical geography of the Navajo and other southwestern native peoples. His numerous publications include co-authorship of the award-winning book *Navajo Wildlands* (Sierra Club) and of *House of Three Turkeys* (Capra).

VIRGINIA E. SPENCER, Indian Housing Specialist with the Housing Assistance Council, has worked as a housing expert in New Mexico and in Washington, D.C. Her master's thesis of 1969, written under Dr. Stephen Jett at the University of California at Davis, sparked the cooperative venture that resulted in the writing and publication of *Navajo Architecture*.

THE UNIVERSITY OF ARIZONA PRESS

This book was set in 10/12 point Times Roman on a Videocomp 830.

Library of Congress Cataloging in Publication Data

Jett, Stephen C   1938–
    Navajo architecture.

    Bibliography: p.
    Includes index.
    1. Navaho Indians—Architecture. 2. Indians of
North America—Arizona—Architecture. I. Spencer,
Virginia E., joint author. II. Title.
E99.N3J39   722'.91   80-39684

ISBN 0-8165-0688-4
ISBN 0-8165-0723-6 (pbk.)

*Dedicated to
David M. Brugge,
authority on
Navajo history and archaeology
and valued friend.
For us, he opened many doors.*

CONTENTS

FIGURES

MAPS

TABLES

PREFACE

The most obvious and distinctive features of the cultural landscape of the Navajo Country of Arizona, New Mexico, and Utah are the dwellings and other structures of the Navajo people*—the subject of this study. Vernacular or folk architecture has had a small but significant place in cultural geography and has received attention from ethnographers, architects, art historians, folklorists, and others, and this book continues that tradition.†

The Navajo culture region is unique in the United States. It is inhabited by the nation's largest Indian tribe (over 150,000), and it represents the country's largest geographical area of single-tribe occupance (approximately 25,000 sq mi, or 64,750 sq km)—an essentially non-Western enclave the size of West Virginia set in the midst of "Anglo-America" (Young 1961: v; Harmon, O'Donnell and Henniger, Associates 1969: 15; Jett 1978a: 351). The Navajos' retention of a substantial portion of their non-Western culture is reflected in the cultural landscape, particularly by the distinctive Navajo dwelling, the hogan. Although all hogans share certain characteristics, they nevertheless display considerable variation in form and materials. These variations represent, in part, different lines of hogan evolution and also reflect areal differences in availability of specific building materials. As a result of these areally varying historical and environmental factors, certain patterns of distribution of the various types have developed over time. Major aims of this study are the classification and description of the different forms of hogans, the determination of their histories, and an outlining of their geographical distributions.

Although a large number of Navajos were still living in hogans in the 1970s when this study was being made, the influence of Anglo-American architecture was being increasingly felt; the proportion of hogans relative to houses appeared to be declining rapidly. A variety of house forms occurred, but rectangular plank shacks in particular were so rapidly replacing the traditional round, polygonal, or subrectangular hogan that the opportunity of studying the latter might soon have passed. Therefore, it was important that hogan forms and distributions be described and analyzed before this unique cultural tradition was modified beyond recognition or was entirely submerged by that of the majority culture. Too, the study of Navajo housing during the period

---

*For early general works on native American dwelling forms, see Morgan 1881 and Waterman 1925.
†For representative bibliographies, see Rickert 1967: 212–15; Rapoport 1969a: 136–46.

of transition could be revealing of the process of acculturation. One could still find the most ancient Navajo forms in the 1970s, as well as modified "traditional" forms and the completely derivative "modern" forms reflecting acculturation. The unusually complete historical and archaeological record of Navajo culture provided a rare opportunity for discerning the sequence of evolution of dwelling forms, and comparative methods could help reveal the diverse sources of the many kinds of Navajo architecture.

Despite the fact that the Navajo are probably the most studied of tribal peoples anywhere and although a number of significant works have dealt with Navajo architecture, most such works are descriptive and no truly systematic and comprehensive survey and analysis of the Navajo's unique architectural forms and their histories have previously been made. In particular, Navajo houses, being nontraditional, largely have been ignored. In this book we have tried to fill these gaps. It is based upon a very broad survey of the vast literature and archives relating to the Navajo and on extensive field investigation by both authors beginning in 1968 and extending over a dozen years. Intensive investigation was carried out by Spencer in Black Creek Valley, Arizona–New Mexico (Spencer 1969; Spencer and Jett 1971), and by Jett in Canyon de Chelly–Canyon del Muerto, Arizona (for place names see Hyde and Jett 1967: map). Thousands of structures were examined, many in detail. Additional research involved many interviews and much correspondence with Navajos and Navajo specialists.

This book certainly goes far beyond any earlier work on Navajo structures. It may well be the most thorough and comprehensive single study of the architecture of *any* tribal society. But even though we feel that structure types of the 1970s are reasonably well described herein, there has not as yet been enough intensive work done in most areas of the vast Navajo Country to be sure that all important variations have been discovered, nor is it possible to draw a fully satisfactory map of dwelling-type distributions. We have also found that, every time we thought we must certainly have recorded every possible detail or minor structure, we discovered the disconcerting—though refreshing—fact that the seemingly limitless Navajo imagination and ingenuity had come up with something we had not yet seen or anticipated. Sometimes it almost appeared as though an effort had been made expressly to frustrate our attempt to classify structures into neat categories. (See, for instance, Fig. 5.51.)

A great deal is also still unclear about the origins and histories of certain types of Navajo structures; we hope that analysis of Navajo Land Claim records as well as future archaeological and comparative work will clear up some of the questions which we have not fully answered. We believe, nevertheless, that this work provides a framework that will facilitate the collection and correlation of data by future workers.

ACKNOWLEDGMENTS

Dozens of individuals have contributed to this book in one way or another. Not all can be mentioned, but we would like particularly to thank the persons listed below (titles and affiliations given are those held at the time aid was provided). We have received particularly great assistance as well as useful critical suggestions from David M. Brugge of the U.S. National Park Service (formerly with the Navajo Land Claim) and the late J. Lee Correll, Research Section, Navajo Tribe. We are also grateful to the following for their help and encouragement: Dave Bohn and Clyde Childress (for field assistance); James Charles (consulting archaeologist); Roy Farber, Barbara Frierson, and Mary F. Jett (for field assistance); Charlotte Johnson Frisbie (Anthropology, Southern Illinois University, Edwardsville); Charles D. James III (archaeologist, U.S. National Park Service); Jerrold E. Levy (Anthropology, University of Arizona); William Morgan (Navajo translator; Navajo Community College); Chauncey Neboyia (Navajo informant, Canyon de Chelly, Arizona); Gordon Page (New Mexico State Planning Office); the late Editha L. Watson (Research Section, Navajo Tribe, retired), Roscoe Wilmeth (Archaeological Survey of Canada); and Robert W. Young (Linguistics, University of New Mexico).

We wish to thank the research, library, and archives staffs at the American Museum of Natural History (Anthropology Department), Arizona Historical Society, Arizona State Museum, Bancroft Library, Canyon de Chelly National Monument, Cleveland Public Library, Huntington Library, Library of Congress, Museum of New Mexico, Museum of Northern Arizona, National Archives (Still Picture Branch), Navajo Tribal Museum, New York Public Library, St. Michael's Catholic Mission, Smithsonian Institution (National Anthropological Archives), Southwest Museum, University of California (Berkeley, Davis, Los Angeles), University of Arizona, and University of New Mexico (Maxwell Museum of Anthropology). Note should also be made of the usefulness of the *Navajo Bibliography with Subject Index* (Correll, Watson, and Brugge 1969, 1973).

The authors' respective contributions to this book may be summarized as follows: assembly and synthesis of the basic published descriptive sources, initial organization of the book, devising of a dwelling taxonomy, and the early field work were accomplished mostly by Spencer. Later field work (including work with informants), description of nondwelling structures, archival research and historical synthesis, linguistics, cross-cultural comparisons, and writing were done primarily by Jett.

Unless otherwise indicated, all photographs are by Jett and were printed from slides by various members of the Illustration Services photographic staff, University of California, Davis. Photographs by Farber, Spencer, or Milton S. Snow (late of the U.S. Soil Conservation Service) are indicated by the initials R.F., V.E.S., or M.S.S. The Snow photographs have accompanying numbers, representing their places in photo group 114-G-ARIZ, Still Picture Branch, U.S. National Archives. Graphics and drafting were contributed by Stanley Wells, Susan Leyba, Celeste Wardin, Kenneth Duffy, Virginia M. King, and Hidechiro Horiuchi. Typing was done by Sarah Blair, Mary Moore, Judy Riddle, and Carolyn Simmons.

Finally, we wish to thank the University of Arizona Press—especially our editor, Marie L. Webner—for effecting publication.

Stephen C. Jett
Virginia E. Spencer

ORTHOGRAPHY
of Navajo Words

Although there are alternative systems of spelling the Navajo language, in this work the Young-Morgan system is used since it has become increasingly standard in the linguistic and ethnographic literature (see Young and Morgan 1980 for a complete explanation).

Most Navajo sounds symbolized by Roman letters are pronounced in a fashion similar to the pronunciation of the sounds represented by the same letters or digraphs in the same orthographic contexts in standard American English. However, some Navajo phonemes are absent in English or are not differentiated in English spelling. These sounds are symbolized as follows:

1. An apostrophe, ', represents a glottal stop (as between the two parts of the English "huh-uh").

2. In a syllable-final position, *h* represents an unvoiced spirant similar to the English letter. In a syllable-initial position it is an unvoiced spirant pronounced like the Greek letter *chi* or the Spanish letter *jota*. *H* is understood to occur between *t* and any following vowel but is not written.

3. *Gh* is voiced velar spirant, equivalent to the syllable-initial *h* and like the Greek *gamma*. The sound occurs, but is not written, before *w* and *y*.

4. *Ł* is an unvoiced lateral like the Welsh "ll".

5. "A" is pronounced as in the English "father," "e" as in "bet," "i" either as in "bit" or, when doubled, as in "beet," and "o" as in "oh." Doubling of a vowel indicates a lengthened pronunciation of that vowel sound.

6. Nasalization of a vowel is indicated by a hook beneath it (e.g., ǫ). All vowels following *n* are nasalized but are not marked. Pronunciation of nasal vowels is similar to that in French.

7. Tonality is relatively low unless an accent is present: ´ = high tone; with respect to long vowels and diphthongs, ´ on the first of two vowels = falling tone, ´ on the second of two vowels = rising tone.

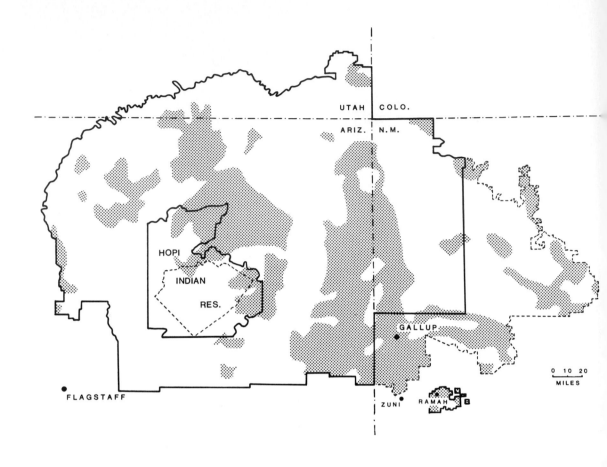

Map 1.1. The Navajo Country (excluding the Cañoncito and Alamo reserves), showing wooded areas (stippled). Solid lines represent 1978 reservation boundaries, dashed lines the limits of organized Navajo occupance in 1977.

Chapter 1

INTRODUCTION

PHYSICAL GEOGRAPHY OF THE NAVAJO COUNTRY

Estimates of the extent of past and present Navajo occupance vary from approximately 30,000 square miles (77,700 sq km; Hester 1962: 7) to perhaps 50,000 square miles (129, 500 sq km; Littell 1967: 692–93). The Navajo Country lies primarily in northeastern Arizona, northwestern New Mexico, and southeastern Utah (Map 1.1), with extensions having taken place, during certain periods, into parts of southwestern Colorado (Map 13.1; Keur 1941: 3; Littell 1967: 692–93).

The Navajo Country is part of the Colorado Plateau physiographic province and is characterized by sedimentary strata—mostly of sandstone and shale—which have been uplifted more or less as a unit, with only local deformation; thus, the strata remain, for the most part, horizontal or gently dipping. The high elevation of the Plateau (averaging perhaps 6,000 ft [1,829 m] above sea level) has permitted the cutting of deep canyons, with subsequent cliff retreat. The characteristic topography is a series of approximately flat, stripped surfaces bounded by cliffs, dissected by sheer-walled canyons, and studded with mesas and buttes. The generally dry climate

accounts for the little-weathered angularity of the landforms. Igneous landforms also occur, including cinder and composite cones, necks, dikes, flows, and laccolithic mountains such as the Carrizo Mountains, Arizona; Navajo Mountain, Utah; and Ute Mountain, Colorado (Gregory 1917: 83–108, 128). Although most of the region lies between 5,000 and 7,000 feet (1,524 and 2,134 m), extreme elevations range from 2,800 feet (853 m) at the mouth of the Little Colorado River in the Grand Canyon, Arizona, to the 11,301-foot (3,445-m) summit of Mount Taylor, New Mexico.

The Chuska-Carrizo mountain chain, straddling the Arizona–New Mexico border, separates the two major physiographic divisions of the Navajo Country—the Navajo and San Juan structural basins, to the west and east, respectively. The floors of these are of low relief for the most part, although a few shallow canyons and low mesas and buttes occur; the major exception to this generalization is the extensive highland known as Black Mesa, in the central portion of the Navajo Basin. The Navajo Country also extends into a third major physiographic division of the Colorado Plateau, the Canyonlands. Here, adjacent to the Colorado and lower San Juan rivers, are innumerable deep and narrow canyons cut into the sandstone, as well as many striking buttes and mesas (Fenneman 1931: 309–19).

> Mesa, butte, volcanic neck, canyon, wash, repeated indefinitely are the elements of the Navajo landscape. Alcoves, recesses, and miniature erosion forms of great beauty stand as ornamental carvings on the larger architectural features, and over all is spread an unevenly developed sheet of wind-blown sand. [Gregory 1916: 21–22]

Permanent streams of major importance (and of exotic origin) include the Colorado, the San Juan, and a few right-bank tributaries of the latter; permanent springs and seeps are not uncommon in certain areas. Smaller streams are generally intermittent or ephemeral but do provide soil moisture for crop raising in the drier regions. Since the mid-nineteenth century, channel trenching (at least in part attributable to overgrazing) has affected most drainages. Concentration of flood waters in these deep, narrow arroyos now prevents overflow onto the former floodplains and has resulted in a decrease in permanent surface water and soil moisture, with a consequent shift to more xeric edaphic conditions and vegetation and a reduction of the areas suitable for floodwater farming (Bryan 1925, 1928; Leopold 1951; Jett 1964: 285–89; Cooley 1962; Cooke and Reeves 1976). Occasionally, however, arroyo-cutting has exposed the local water table, resulting in more permanent streamflow (e.g., Moenkopi Wash and Laguna Creek; Gregory 1915: 114–15; Gregory 1916: 100). In recent years, available water supply has been greatly increased by the construction of small dams and water tanks and the drilling of wells (see chapter 9). The primary effect of this has been to allow expansion of sheep- and goat-raising into areas without permanent natural water supplies.

The Navajo Country is part of the great belt of arid and semiarid climates of interior North America. It is characterized by great meteorological contrasts, experiencing marked seasonal and diurnal fluctuations in temperature as well as seasonal and annual variation in precipitation. Both temperature and precipitation vary a good deal with elevation as well, temperature decreasing and precipitation increasing with altitude. In the region as a whole, July temperatures average about 70 degrees Fahrenheit (21 degrees Celsius), and January temperatures average about 30 degrees Fahrenheit (ca. −1 degree Celsius); extremes range from above 100 degrees (38 degrees Celsius) to well below zero. Daily temperature ranges may be as great as 40 to 50 degrees Fahrenheit (23 to 28 degrees Celsius). Precipitation averages approximately 10 in. (25.4 cm) annually. Late spring and autumn are relatively rainless, while in summer violent convectional and orographic storms are fairly frequent (sometimes supplemented by cyclonic rainfall); in winter, frontal storms occur, not uncommonly in the form of snowfall (Kangieser 1966: 1–2; Sellers and Hill 1974).

As noted, altitude greatly influences local climatic conditions, which in turn influence vegetation (Map 1.1). The lower elevations (less than 5,500 ft; 1,676 m) of the southwestern and northwestern portions of Navajoland are truly arid. Vegetation, if present, is characterized by xerophytic shrubs, cactus, and sparse grass and forbs. Tamarisk (*Tamarix pentandra*) and scrub willow (*Salix lasiandra*) dominate the riparian flora. Areas between 4,000 and 7,000 ft (1,219 and 2,134 m)—which comprise the majority of the Navajo Country—are generally semiarid. The major semiarid plant associations are, beginning at the lower elevations: bunchgrass (often very reduced by overgrazing); sagebrush (*Artemesia* spp.), usually located in valleys, on plains, and on slopes; and juniper (*Juniperus* spp.) and mixed juniper and pinyon pine (*Pinus edulis*), often found on mesas and in foothills (usually stunted below 5,000 ft [1,524 m]). Cottonwoods (*Populus acuminata*) frequently occur along watercourses, with scrub oak (*Quercus gambelli*) being common in many canyons. At higher elevations (particularly in the Chuska Mountains and on the Defiance Plateau) in the central area, relatively open forests of ponderosa pine (*Pinus ponderosa*) occur, interspersed, in the Chuskas,

Map 1.2. Distribution of Athapaskan speech in aboriginal times.

with groves of quaking aspen (*Populus tremuloides*) as well as grassy "parks." In the few areas above 8,000 feet (2,438 m)—and in shaded canyons or on north-facing slopes at somewhat lower elevations—Douglas fir (*Pseudotsuga menziesii*), spruce (*Picea* spp.), and fir (*Abies* spp.) are commonly found (Kearney and Peebles 1951: 13; Arnberger 1962: 10, 12, 15; Bohrer and Bergseng 1963).

Large mammals of the Navajo Country—now mostly extirpated—included mule deer (*Odocoileus hemionus crooki;* recently reintroduced), pronghorn ("antelope"; *Antilocapra americana americana*), bighorn sheep (*Ovis canadensis*), elk (*Cervus canadensis*), coyote (*Canis latrans mearnsi*), gray wolf (*Canis lupus*), mountain lion (*Felis concolor*), bobcat (*Lynx rufus baileyi*), black bear (*Euarctos americanus amblyceps*), and grizzly bear (*Ursus horribilis*). Some smaller mammals of former economic importance are blacktailed

jackrabbit (*Lepus californicus texianus*), porcupine (*Erethizon dorsatum conesi*), and Gunnison's prairie dog (*Cynomus gunnisoni zuniensis;* Halloran 1964). Among game birds, the wild turkey (*Meleagris gallopavo*) should be mentioned. Eagles were ceremonially important.

NAVAJO CULTURE HISTORY[1]

Origins and Dinétah Phase (1500–1696)

The Navajo (Diné) are relative newcomers to the Colorado Plateau. The primary ancestors of the people now known as the Navajo were Athapaskan-speakers who migrated southward from western Canada (see Map 1.2; Sapir 1916; Jett 1978a, 1979). We have little direct knowledge of their early culture, although it is assumed that the proto-Navajo subsisted by hunting, fishing, and gathering in prehistoric times, as did the northern Athapaskans in historic times; fishing was eventually abandoned by the Navajo and most other Apacheans, apparently owing to the acquisition of a Puebloan-Plains taboo (Brugge 1964a: 16–17). At an unknown date, but before 1600 (and probably at least a century or two earlier), the proto-Navajo had entered the Southwest. There they seem to have adopted some of the cultivated plants and farming techniques, as well as ceremonial lore, of their close neighbors, the Puebloans. (Spicer 1962: 210; Hester 1962: 70; and Brugge 1964a: 17 suggest the possibility that rudimentary agriculture was acquired by the proto-Navajo while living in the western Plains prior to their penetration into the Southwest.) The earliest identifiable area of settlement is known as Dinétah ("Navajo Country"); it lies in northwestern New Mexico and adjacent Colorado, particularly along the San Juan River and extending to the upper Chama, Gobernador, and Largo drainages, New Mexico. The culture of this period is known as the Dinéth Phase (ca. 1500–1696).

Gobernador, Cabezon, del Muerto, and de Chelly Phases (1696–1864)

Following the arrival of Spaniards, who first settled in the upper Rio Grande Valley in 1598, Rio Grande Puebloans gradually acquired small numbers of sheep, horses, and cattle; Navajos probably also acquired the horse at this time. During the four years following the return of the Spanish in 1692, after their expulsion during the Pueblo Revolt of 1680, many Puebloan refugees fled to the canyons of Dinétah. For some fifty years (Refugee Period), Navajos and Puebloans lived together, exchanging various culture traits through trade, intermarriage, and other mechanisms. Sheepherding, weaving with wool, additional food plants and techniques of cultivation, certain pottery-making methods, and elaborate ceremonies were probably among the traits acquired by the Navajo during this period, as was the use of stone ma-

sonry. Settlement in the east was often associated with defensively sited and constructed pueblitos. Despite massive Puebloan influences, the Navajo language remained dominant, and the Puebloan refugees who did not return to the Rio Grande eventually died and their progeny was absorbed by the Navajo (Forbes 1960: 270–72; Spicer 1962: 212; Jett 1977: 684–87. This phase (ca. 1696–1770), during which territorial expansion to the south and west took place, is known as the Gobernador; in the west, the less Puebloan-influenced del Muerto Phase has been recognized (James 1976: 100–01).

Utes and Comanches advanced into the Dinétah region between 1716 and 1720, and a shift of the center of Navajo occupance from the San Juan valley south into the Gobernador Canyon area of New Mexico occurred. By the 1740s Utes had begun a continuing series of raids on Dinétah, and the Navajo gradually abandoned the region. Some experimented with living in pueblos under Spanish protection, but this proved to be unworkable. Most Navajos chose to retain a seminomadic lifeway, and hostilities with the Spanish and native tribes increased. Cultivation continued to be practiced, but the need for defensive mobility seems to have resulted in farming being deemphasized in favor of increased gathering, hunting, and especially the raising of mobile livestock such as horses, sheep and goats (but see Kemrer and Graybill 1970). As game declined, sheep and goats became an increasingly important food source; some raiding of European and Puebloan settlements for food, livestock, and slaves also occurred. Navajo population increased, and, with their sheep and horses, the Diné spread beyond northwestern New Mexico into eastern Arizona and southern Utah, becoming widely established. Cultural manifestations were the Cabezon and de Chelly phases (ca. 1770–1863), in the eastern and western sections, respectively. The period was characterized by the disappearance of some Puebloan traits, such as pueblitos and painted pottery, "Navajoization" of others (as in religion), and more dispersed settlement.

Bosque Redondo (1864–68)

After the hegemony of the United States was established in the Southwest in 1846, treaties between various bands of Navajo and the United States government were made and broken, until in 1864 the Navajo were definitively defeated following destruction of many of their fields, orchards, and flocks (McNitt 1972; Jett 1975). About 8,500 Navajos eventually surrendered and were marched to the Bosque Redondo Reservation at Ft. Sumner in east-central New Mexico. This first reservation experiment was a total failure, but significant cultural contact took place, and the Navajo acquired some Anglo-American techniques. In 1868 the final treaty was signed, the Navajo accepting the authority of the United States in order to return home.

Reservation Period (1868 to present)[2]

From 1868 to 1900 the Navajo tried to rebuild their former economy in the reservation assigned them in their homeland. The government encouraged farming and issued the Navajo sheep; and, except for raiding, the old social and economic patterns were reestablished. The curtailment of warfare among both the Navajo and their enemies allowed an ever increasing emphasis on farming as well as more sedentary and conveniently located settlement.

With the arrival of the Atcheson, Topeka, and Santa Fe Railroad (originally, the Atlantic and Pacific) in 1880, a new phase in Navajo economic and cultural history began, for the possibility of large-scale Anglo-Navajo trade was created as well as the opportunity for wage work. Navajo maize, wool, mutton, hides, and crafts were exchanged for packaged foods and manufactured goods. At the same time, food-gathering activities declined as store-bought food became available, and hunting largely disappeared as the use of firearms caused the elimination of almost all the larger game. Trading posts sprang up, and the trader (usually Anglo-American) played an important role in interpreting for the Navajo the alien way of life that now surrounded them. He presided over the Navajo's adoption of manufactured tools, weapons, yard goods, and foods, which took place roughly between 1870 and 1920, and he guided the Navajo into the market system. The trading post also served as a center for news from the outside world, and government notices were posted on the store's bulletin board—although Indian agents and specific government policies changed frequently, and the Navajos remained confused about government affairs (McNitt 1962).

The 1930s saw several important events, including the Indian Reorganization Act; although the act was not accepted by the Navajo, they felt some of its effects. The Navajo Tribal Council was reorganized, and Indian cultural differences and values were officially recognized by the federal government. Material improvements were made on the Reservation, including irrigation and soil-conservation programs, the restoration of alienated Indian lands, establishment of day schools, and the designation of a "Navajo Capital" to be set up at Window Rock, Arizona. A particularly significant event resulted from a study of range lands in the Navajo Country which found the Reservation to be 100 percent overstocked. The Department of the Interior imposed grazing regulations and forced reduction of the number of livestock on the Reservation by over two-thirds, an action neither understood nor appreciated by the Navajo and considered by them an appalling act of senseless destruction. "Stock reduction more than any other issue, served to retard the institutionalization of a modern Indian government in Navajo society" (Shepardson 1963: 16). A direct result of stock reduction was the forcing of many Navajos to seek wage work to compensate for the loss of income from sheep. World War II provided many job opportunities, and this became one of the most significant periods in Navajo history from the point of view of acculturation. Wage work has become an increasingly important source of income, particularly as tribal income from oil, gas, and mining developments has permitted

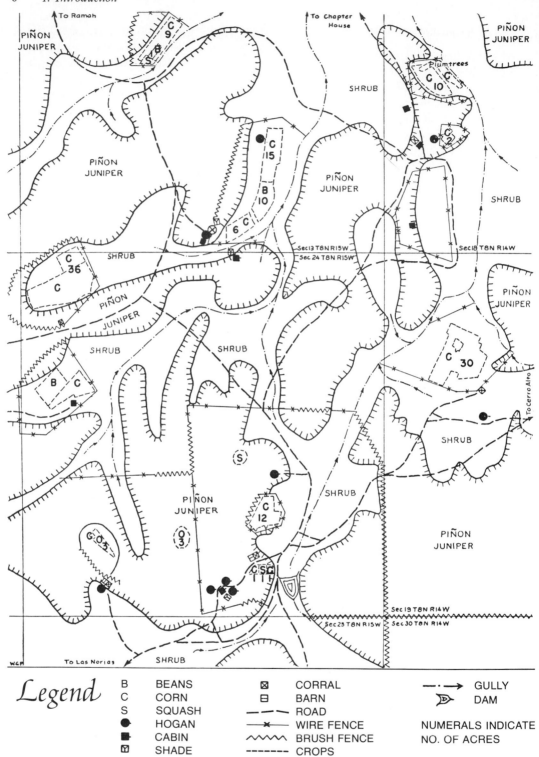

Map 1.3. The Patricio Coho establishment, Ramah district, New Mexico, ca. 1941, showing settlement features (Landgraf 1954: 48–49).

the initiation of many tribal programs. In recent years, tribal and federal welfare programs have become significant sources of income in cash, kind, and services.

World War II proved to have been an important turning point for the Navajo. Many had left the Reservation to work for wages, and over 3,600 had joined the armed forces. This helped to broaden their view of the world, and they became better acquainted with the customs and language of the majority society. When the war was over, however, many Navajos returned home jobless. Welfare programs became necessary, and bitterness was widespread; alcohol problems worsened. The social and economic situation of the Navajo was such that the government finally initiated a long-range rehabilitation program, including relocation of numbers of tribal members to off-Reservation areas where jobs could be obtained; but relocation efforts have had only partial success. On-Reservation improvement included programs for better land management, new schools and roads, and the development of business and industry; but in the 1970s many Navajos continued to live by low-income traditional means and welfare, although more and more individuals were becoming trained for various types of wage work. Schooling for Navajos had been very greatly extended since the 1950s, and culture change gathered momentum during the 1960s and '70s.

Four major authority systems operate on the Navajo Reservation: traditional Navajo, modern Navajo, federal government, and state government. The U.S. Bureau of Indian Affairs and the tribal government, both headquartered at Window Rock, are currently the most important political forces. The more acculturated Navajos are becoming increasingly dominant, although there remains a deep cleavage between educated, relatively highly acculturated Navajos, and traditionalists who lack formal education. Even among traditionalists, there is considerable enthusiasm for modern medicine and education, and acculturation appears to be ever accelerating.

NAVAJO SETTLEMENT PATTERNS

Dispersion

Navajo settlement is dispersed, as was that of the Navajo's Northern Athapaskan ancestors (Jett 1978a: 358–59). Urbanization is not a Navajo characteristic (McIntire 1967); agglomerations tend to be confined to homesteads occupied by extended families and usually containing only one or a few dwellings (see below).

Socioterritorial Groups

The smallest socioterritorial group is the "nuclear household," consisting of a biological or nuclear family (occasionally, a single individual) which occupies a dwelling and its immediate environs. A "homestead group" is an extended family—usually a nuclear family plus its married daughters' families—which occupies a territory or territories including the homestead and the farm and/or pasture land. A higher unit of socioterritorial organization is sometimes present, the "resident lineage." It consists of related homestead groups occupying contiguous territories (Map. 1.3). The "community", comprising a number of not necessarily related homestead groups and resident lineages oriented toward a single trading center or school or mission, is the descendant of the historic "band" or "semiband," which occupied a territory based upon subsistence resources. Finally, the various communities make up the "tribe," which occupies the Navajo Country (reservations and allotted and purchased lands). (For a fuller description of Navajo socioterritorial groups, see Jett 1978a: 355–58.)

Homesteads ("Camps")

Any isolated dwelling or cluster of dwellings and appurtenant structures may be called a homestead or, in local parlance, a "camp" (Fig. 1.1). Each homestead group has at least one camp, and the homesteads of the families comprising resident lineages may be in fairly close proximity and appear to form a single

Fig. 1.1. Hastin Bekini's homestead. From left: firewood pile and wagon; water drum; hay-storage platform; storage platform supporting the wagon box, which contains crates; two drying racks holding pelts; wall-less ramada (with fodder stored on top?); conical forked-pole hogan (see Fig. 5.3); cooking fire, two partially collapsed drying racks, holding the wagon seat, harness, etc.; part of a storage platform. Dinnehotso area, Arizona, 1935; M.S.S. (881).

Fig. 1.2. Homestead. From left: flat-roofed shade (ramada), flag pole (?), conical forked-pole hogan, wagon with water drum. Paiute Farms, Utah, 1962.

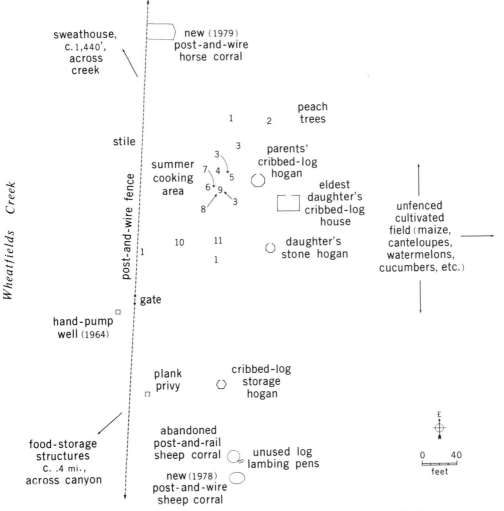

Map 1.4. Chauncey and Dorothy Neboyia's summer-farm homestead, Zuni Trail, Canyon de Chelly, Arizona, 1978. Riparian cottonwoods extend from the upper left to the lower right. Numbers refer to structures, as follows:

1. Chicken house or roosting platform (log-dugout or plank)
2. Firewood pile
3. Drying rack (one end attached to a tree)
4. Rug loom
5. Homemade food cupboards attached to a tree
6. Grill (built by National Park Service)
7. Masonry summer fireplace
8. Homemade tables
9. Crate utensil cupboards
10. Beehive oven
11. Maize-grinder shelf on a tree

straggling agglomeration. It is very rare that such collections of buildings include as many as twenty dwellings; more nearly typical would be a homestead consisting of a hogan, a house or two, and a shade, placed so as to leave plenty of space between structures. In addition, one or more corrals are likely to be present, as well as, in many cases, animal shelters, root cellars, privies, beehive ovens, and sudatories (Figs. 1.1, 1.2, 1.3, 1.4, 1.5, 4.17, 5.7, 7.1, 7.12). There is seldom any patterned arrangement of buildings (Map 1.4).

Homesteads are situated with reference to resources, specifically farm land, stock water, pasturage, and firewood supply. Traditionally, preferred sites were flat, in sheltered and inconspicuous locations. In recent times, concentration of principal camps along main

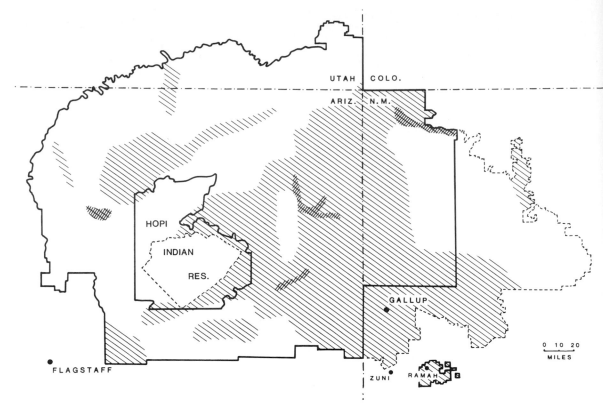

Map 1.5. The Navajo Country, showing subsistence activities in 1930 (modified from Young 1961: 310). Sheepherding dominates in the unshaded areas, mixed herding and farming in the hatched areas, and farming in the cross-hatched areas (which are, clockwise from the northeast, San Juan Valley, Chinle Valley–Canyon de Chelly, Pueblo Colorado Valley, and Tuba City area; for explanation of boundaries, see Map 1.1).

roads has become pronounced in some areas, in response to increased orientation toward stores, schools, and employment opportunities in the settlements, and upon the pickup truck as the principal means of transportation. (These matters are treated more fully in Jett 1980.)

Seasonal Migrations

Most Navajo homestead groups maintain at least two camps with permanent structures, a summer one and a winter one. Some or all of the members of the group move seasonally between these camps. Permanent or temporary dwellings may also be built at other sites, for use during activities of limited duration or involving one or a few individuals for longer periods.

Although many variant patterns exist, different degrees of emphasis of farming and herding (Map 1.5) generate the two principal types of seasonal migrations (for details, see Jett 1978b).

Where farming is more important, the summer camp is typically near the lowland farm; the winter homestead is at somewhat higher elevation where firewood is available. If grazing is paramount, families tend to move to the mountain meadows in summer and to lower elevation pasturage in wintertime. [Jett 1978a: 361]

[10]

Fig. 1.3. Homestead, Canyon de Chelly, Arizona, opposite The Window: (top) view from above, showing (from left) a rectangular stake-and-rail sheep corral against the cliff, a polygonal flat-roofed shade with horizontal-log walls, a polygonal leaning-log hogan with corbeled-log roof, and a circular stone hogan with corbeled log roof; beyond the post-and-wire fence, at the upper right, is the maize field; also visible are sites of now dismantled structures; (bottom) view from ground level. 1971.

Fig. 1.4. Homestead. From left: frame outhouse by a post-and-wire fence; cribbed-log house with ramada extensions; L-shaped cribbed-log house with a gabled roof, two chimneys, and a small porch; planted saplings surrounded by salvaged snow fencing; cribbed-log hogan with a pyramidal roof; firewood pile and corral; beam-roofed cribbed-log house. Black Creek Valley, 1968.

Fig. 1.5. Homestead. From left: picket fence, frame house with a gabled roof, firewood pile, cribbed-log/palisaded house with low-pitched roofs, beehive oven, cribbed-log hogan with a corbeled-log roof, cribbed-log hogan with a pyramidal roof. East of Ft. Defiance, Arizona, 1968.

Chapter 2

NAVAJO DWELLINGS
General Characteristics

TEMPORARY AND SUMMER DWELLINGS

In addition to the more substantial and permanent dwellings described below, the Navajo construct a variety of temporary and summer shelters, although these appear to have declined proportionately to permanent structures in recent times. Unlike hogans and houses, these are not designed to protect their users against precipitation and low temperatures but serve, rather, as shelters from the summer sun and/or from wind and windblown sand. Their walls and roofs are usually not solid as are those of hogans but instead normally consist (with the exception of tents) of poles and/or boughs; juniper, pinyon, cottonwood, oak, willow, and other boughs or brush, or even weeds or grass, are used, according to local availability, and use of boards is increasingly common (Vestal 1952: 12–13, 22; Roberts 1951: 30; Ostermann 1908: 863; and personal observations). (For details of building materials, see "Hogans," below.) In camps where substantial trees cast good shade, summer arbors may be dispensed with. Sometimes, particularly during journeys, blankets or the canvas covering of a covered wagon is used instead of brush (although such wagons are fast disappearing today), and a blanket or piece of canvas or stitched-together flour sacks may simply be thrown over a tree branch or shrub to provide shade during a brief stop on a journey (James 1905: 642; Johnston 1972: 259, 288, plate; Johnson 1977: 61; Frisbie and McAllester 1978: 30). Shelters of these various sorts are more or less equivalent to the Navajo category *chaha'oh* or "shades".[1] Tents, though commercially made, are used in contexts similar to those of shade use, and are included in this category.

In addition to the aforementioned habitations, Navajos have occasionally utilized natural rock shelters as temporary dwellings, particularly during the wars of the mid-nineteenth century.[2] Too, while employed at the Bellmont munitions depot west of Flagstaff during World War II, some Navajo workers reportedly lived in discarded crates, while others built hogans (Boyce 1974: 119–20).

HOGANS

The word "hogan" *(hooghan)* is a combination of two stems: *hoo,* "place" or "area," and *-ghan,* "dwelling" or "home," and thus

Fig. 2.1. Double hogan, with a shared wall. The left-hand structure is cribbed-log, the right-hand unit palisaded. Both roofs are corbeled-log; erosion of part of the earth covering reveals what appear to be wood chips, maize stalks, and sheets of tarpaper and metal. On the right-hand structure, horizontal boards act as sole plates for the roof. Note the homemade door and the chicken-wire-screened windows as well as the brackets for support of the eave boards. South of Burnt Water, Arizona, 1970; R.F.

can be translated as "home place" or "dwelling area." Hogans are ordinarily circular, sub-circular, polygonal, or subrectangular in plan,[3] and normally contain a single room. Rarely, two hogans share a wall, forming "double" or "twin" hogans (Brugge 1976: 43; Malcolm, 1939: 10–11; see Fig. 2.1); a house and a hogan may, in some instances, be similarly joined, and brush-covered shades are sometimes attached directly to hogans or houses, usually on the doorway side (Fig. 1.4, 7.17). Hogans are thought of as traditional Navajo dwellings, although Puebloan, Spanish, and Anglo-American building materials, tools, methods, and styles have influenced all contemporary hogan types to a significant degree (Jett 1981).

Ceremonial Role

Living in hogans is sanctioned by the Emergence and Blessingway myths, and hogans play a ceremonial role which cannot be filled by houses: "In spite of current changes in housing, most Navajo still regard their hogans as places of worship, and the only proper place in which to hold ceremonials and chants" (Frisbie 1968: 34; see also Frisbie 1970; Haile 1942: 45–46; Correll 1965a: 29; Platero 1967: 164). Ceremonial requirements include a central hearth and a smoke hole (Wyman 1936: 635; Coolidge and Coolidge 1930: 83). "Even families that prefer to live in a cabin or modern house usually build a hogan in which to have ceremonies. Many nuclear units have two hogans, one for storage"

(Downs 1972: 48; but see Tremblay et al. 1954: 216–17). Hogans—usually of larger-than-average size—are also sometimes built expressly for Navajo ceremonials, and some are built today for exclusive use as churches for peyote (Native American Church) ceremonies (Wagner 1974: 272–73, 333).

Site Preparation

When a site is prepared for the erection of an ordinary hogan, a flat area is sought and the ground is cleared and smoothed. In many cases, the floor area is excavated to a depth usually not exceeding 2 feet (.61 m). Such excavation has the following effects: increasing the interior height of the structure; creating a 6- to 12-inch-wide (15.24 to 30.48 cm) peripheral bench or shelf on which household items may be placed; locating the floor on the firm subsoil or, occasionally, bedrock; and leveling any slope or irregularities in the original surface of the site. When the structure or its roof is to be earth-covered, the excavated dirt is used for this purpose. The floor may be packed with sand or clay, although usually it is not. A few hogans have flagstone floors, and in recent times poured concrete or planks have been used on occasion (e.g. Kluckhohn et al. 1971: 147).

In some instances, "dugout" hogans and houses were built, although these seem to be uncommon today. In such cases, the floor excavation, either into a hillslope or into flat ground, was much deeper than normal, and the sides of the excavation formed all or most of the wall. Dugout hogans were used particularly in areas lacking in timber for normal wall construction (see chapter 3 and this chapter, below).

Building Materials and Procedures

Logs *(tsin),* juniper ("cedar") bark *(dilk'is bizhííh),* and earth *(łeezh)* are the most widely utilized traditional building materials. Some informants state that timbers used in building a dwelling should be from vigorous, living trees and that they should not have been previously used. Specifically proscribed are wind-felled and lightning-struck trees (Haile 1952:

5, 7)[4] and timbers from prehistoric ruins or from hogans deserted because of a death (Newcomb 1940a: 26; Mindeleff 1898: 487). Some or all of a dwelling's sound timbers and stones may be reused when a new structure replaces it at the same or another location (Jett 1980b), and old, no longer functional notches are sometimes observed near the ends of reused wall logs (Fig. 5.38).

Larger timbers are most often of pinyon pine *(chá'oł),* although ponderosa pine *(ń dísh-chíí')* is often used where available; the latter is said to rot more rapidly and to be more vulnerable to wood-eating beetles, although its length and straight grain have advantages for construction (Elmore 1943: 19, 22; Vestal 1952: 12–14; Coolidge and Coolidge 1931: 77; Kluckhohn et al. 1971: 144). Branches of these trees and logs of juniper *(gad; dilk'is* when dry) usually serve as the smaller timbers, including those of the roof. Juniper logs are less straight than those of pinyon, although juniper wood has even greater resistance to rotting and insects. One-seed juniper *(J. monosperma)* is the most commonly used juniper species (Vestal 1952: 13). Aspen *(T'iisbáí)* was reportedly preferred by some in the Sanostee, New Mexico, area (Johnson 1977: 128). Where the aforementioned trees do not occur within a convenient distance, logs from cottonwood trees *(t'iis)* along watercourses may be used. The last are not popular, perhaps because they are less durable. Where all timber is scarce, slender poles, brush, corn and weed stalks, and the like may be substituted for smaller logs.

Bark is ordinarily removed from logs to retard rotting (Roberts 1951: 30), and logs are sometimes squared (planked or hewn); these practices appear to be post-steel-ax, and of Hispano origin in the Southwest (Gritzner 1971: 60), although bark-stripping has been recorded among some Northern Athapaskans (Honigman 1946: 50). Before steel axes became generally available in the latter nineteenth century, full-grooved polished stone axes (Kluckhohn et al., 1971: 173–75) were used in procuring timber, and tree trunks were sometimes burned to release the branches

Fig. 2.2. Homemade sleds for hauling logs and stones: (top) small, crude sled of logs and boards secured with nails and wire (Yazhe Clark's camp above Middle Trail Canyon, Canyon del Muerto, Arizona, 1972); (bottom) a large, more elaborate sled made by Chauncey Neboyia of poles, planks, and steel strips held together by nails, bolts, and wire. Neboyia homestead, north of Canyon de Chelly, Arizona, near head of Beehive Trail, 1972.

(Keur 1941: 23). Both steel axes and D-saws are standard today. One "way we got posts was to ask a group of [about ten] men who were known for carrying posts or hauling heavy things to bring them.... [They] brought the wood on their shoulders" (Frisbie and McAllester 1978: 30). However, ordinarily logs and rocks are hauled singly or several at a time behind horses, mules, or donkeys; on homemade hand- or animal-drawn sleds (Fig. 2.2; see Kluckhohn et al. 1971: 103; for comparison with Anglo sleds, see Owen 1980); in wagons; and in pickup trucks. Logs may be left to dry before hauling (Roberts 1951: 30; Newcomb 1966: 65; Kluckhohn et al. 1971: 103).

Log hogans and houses are usually chinked with tree limbs, poles, splints, brush (especially rabbitbrush, *Chrysothamnus*), twigs, chips, or other pieces of wood, and then with juniper and sometimes other bark; grass and weeds, sod, corn husks, reeds, etc. may also be used; stones, cloth, and sheet metal and plastic have also been recorded. Tamped damp earth is the final chinking (Ostermann 1908: 863). Some hogans have earth-covered roofs or are entirely covered with earth. Branches may be placed over the damp earth to protect it while it dries. These branches are usually eventually blown away or used as fuel but may be maintained to keep livestock off the roof (David M. Brugge, personal communication); wire fences are occasionally erected around hogans to perform the same function (Figs. 5. 23, 7.29). Russell (1977: 5) found that at Shonto, Arizona, hogans built exclusively for summertime use employed less earth and perhaps lighter timbers than hogans intended for winter or year-round occupation.

Masonry hogans and houses (usually of sandstone) are also constructed. Stone (*tsé*) is obtained from blocks naturally weathered from the bedrock, small quarries, and sometimes Anasazi or abandoned Navajo masonry structures (Reher 1977: 62, 68).

In modern times, planks (*tsin neheshjíí'* = saw log)—mostly from the tribal sawmill, Navajo Forest Products Industries—nails, tarpaper and roll roofing, chicken wire, and cement have come into widespread use in dwelling construction. Adobe bricks, fired bricks, and cinder blocks are also occasionally employed.

Traditionally, dwellings are normally built by the current or prospective head-of-household and his kinsmen,[5] But some semi-professional hogan builders were recorded by 1952 (Kluckhohn et al. 1971: 148; denied by Chauncey Neboyia, 1971; Bertha Dutton, personal communication, 1972, spoke of a specialist in the construction of peyote hogans). Although gratis aid in hogan-building is traditional, for many years some men have earned a bit of cash by helping others build their hogans (e.g., Frisbie and McAllester 1978: 226), and in any case etiquette requires that the owner feed the helpers. In the Newcomb, New Mexico, area before 1936, building was a cooperative effort, overseen by "The Builder," some local man who was acknowledged to be expert in such matters. Laying of the logs had to be completed in one day's time (Newcomb 1966: 66–67; Coolidge and Coolidge 1931: 77), but such time limits are often ignored today. Tradition dictates the desirability of a Navajo House Blessingway rite being performed prior to a home's being occupied, to ensure the future well-being of its inhabitants (Haile 1954: 10; Frisbie 1968, 1970; McAllester and McAllester 1980).

Traditionally, dwelling ownership was seldom an issue among the Navajo, and the hogan is considered to belong to all who use it; if any individual can be said to own the hogan, however, it is probably the wife, at least when matrilocal residence is involved (Coolidge and Coolidge 1930: 299; Haile 1937: 8; Reichard 1928: 92), as is true among Puebloans and at least some Northern Athapaskans (Osgood 1940: 324). If significant investment of labor and materials is required, however (as in the case of modern houses), ownership is in the hands of the person(s) who supplied or paid for these requirements (Haile 1954: 11–12). This would ordinarily be the husband (Haile 1942: 49).

Entry Orientation

A hogan has a single entry, which is normally oriented toward the direction of the first appearance of the rising sun (at the time of construction), to catch the blessing of the first rays (Newcomb 1940a: 18, 23; Wilmsen 1960; James 1905: 643; Brugge 1968a: 19) and to accommodate the dominance of east in ritual activities (Franciscan Fathers 1910: 56; Haile 1952; Stephen 1890); this also puts the entry away from prevailing southwest winds and accompanying storms, and from cold north winds of winter. Most other Navajo structures are also given an eastward orientation,[6] although shades and certain other structures follow this rule less strictly than do hogans (Mindeleff 1898: 495). Although Vestal (1957: 3) attributed eastward orientation to Mackenzie Basin tribes, the authors have not found references to that effect in monographs on Northern Athapaskan groups, and they have found some denials of directional orientation (e.g., Osgood 1936: 49; Clark 1974: 121). Eastward orientation does occur on the Great Plains (Laubin and Laubin 1957: 34–36) and among some Siberian groups (Levin and Potapov 1964: 262, 478), and eastward or southward orientation seems to be common among Apaches.[7]

Brugge (1968a: 19) considered orientation to be a "local innovation [in Dinétah] in the Puebloan tradition of orientation of buildings." Eighth-century Basketmaker pithouses in the Durango, Colorado, area had entries oriented toward the southeast (Carlson 1963). Gallina Phase houses in the Dinétah area about 1100–1250 were given north-south orientation (Blumenthal 1940: 11). Although Parsons (1939:98) stated that "there is no general rule of orientation for Pueblo buildings," Fewkes (1906a: 89–90) noted a supposedly solar, southerly-to-easterly orientation of Hopi pueblos, and Hough (1906: 450) contended that eastward orientation of pueblos was both to intercept the early sunlight and "on account of the importance of the rising sun in heliolatry." Most Rio Grande pueblo house blocks are oriented on east-west axes (Stubbs

1950), and the ventilators of the round kivas or ceremonial chambers were usually placed toward the east or south (Wendorf 1954: 207, 209, 211, 214); perhaps this latter usage was transferred to the hogan—which is a ceremonial structure as well as a dwelling—as one of the many results of Puebloan influences on Navajo religion. Entries toward the east are also characteristic of the Ute (Stewart 1942: 257–58), many Shoshonean gatherers of the intermontane West (Lowie 1924: 218–21; Steward 1941: 283; Stewart 1941: 378; Ellis 1974: 74), and the Pima, Papago, Cocopah, Maricopa, Yavapai, and Walapai of southern and northwestern Arizona (Spier 1933: 87; Gifford 1940: 108; Drucker 1941: 105).

To the extent that orientation is determinable, the entries of eighteenth-century hogans are not consistent, but northeasterly orientation is apparently most frequent, although easterly orientation is also common. Northerly orientation is known as well.[8] Keur (1941: 29) concluded that topographic obstructions resulted in northeastward orientation, but this orientation may also reflect the fact that the point on the horizon of the solar rising is toward the northeast during the summer (but toward the southeast during the winter [e.g., James 1976: 61]); a number of southeasterly orientations *are* found (e.g., Keur 1944: 76). It is also of interest that among most Puebloan groups, north rather than east is the prime direction (Parsons, 1939: 205, 365), kiva ventilator position notwithstanding. More work will be required to determine whether there is any preferred building season. Since hogans are especially for winter use, however, it seems likely that they would most often be built during summer or early autumn.

Entry Coverings

Hogan entries (for Navajo terminology, see Fig. 2.6) are rectangular and not overly high. Door jambs, lintels, and sills (if any) originally were trimmed logs (the verticals often forked and sometimes doubled or tripled),

but today plank door frames usually supplement or replace the logs.

The hogan doorway seems originally to have been covered with hides—apparently a northern legacy (e.g., Honigman 1946: 50; Clark 1974: 123)—or a twined or checkerwoven yucca, grass, juniper-bark, cliffrose, or willow-withe mat (*dáátááń* = entrance thick or stiff closer).[9] The Western Apache also formerly used doors of "laced boughs" (Opler 1973: 59), skins, or blankets (Reagan 1930: 290; Gifford 1940; 108: Mails 1974: 94), and many Shoshoni and Paiute groups used woven brush, bark, or grass door coverings (Steward 1941: 283; Stewart 1941: 378–79; 1942: 257), and the Gila River Yumans employed willow-bark or rabbit-skin blanket doors (Spier 1933: 87). Among the Navajo, hides and mats were largely replaced, after weaving of wool became prevalent, by old handwoven blankets (*dáá [di]níbaal* = entrance [closure] fabric hanging linearly) or canvas or other commercial cloth (*naak'a'at'ą'í dah sibaalígíí* = cloth hung from above), hung from pegs or nails inside or outside the hogan (Figs. 5.7 and 5. 12). The southern side of the blanket would be raised when entering the hogan (Haile 1937: 2), and the northern side attached to the northern doorpost (Haile 1942: 44).

Most modern hogans have homemade or commercially made doors (*dáá[ń]dilklał* = entrance [closure] repeatedly shut) of vertical, horizontal, or diagonal planks, or of plywood, or of combinations of these, the blanket replacing the door usually only on ceremonial occasions. Aluminum-frame screen doors are still very rare. Doors have long been used on hogans by some Navajos (Goddard 1909–11: 14483; Ostermann 1917: 3), but until the latter 1920s blankets were usual. The transition from blankets to doors seems to have taken place primarily during the 1930s, being more or less completed during the 1940s.[10] Commercially manufactured steel hinges are the rule on doors today, but formerly strips of leather or metal were used (Page 1937b: 49). Hasps or chains that can be padlocked are usual; Roberts (1951: 41) noted that locks were universal on doors in the Ramah area, although "smoke holes were never closed or locked."

The ground immediately in front of the doorway is occasionally covered with flagstones. We have also seen a stoop faced with vertical slabs and filled with earth. "In front of one . . . hogan an earth platform faced with logs serves as a porch" (Kluckhohn et al. 1971: 147).

Extended entryways sometimes occur; they are discussed below in connection with descriptions of individual hogan forms. One or two low, short masonry walls extending out from doorways have also been noted (e.g., Platero 1967: 167).

Windows

Hogans were originally windowless, although each had a smoke hole at, or just entryward of, the center of the roof, allowing some light to enter from above (Haile 1937: 2; Newcomb 1940a: 24). Anglo influences—including governmental promotion for health reasons (Lockett 1952; Jones et al. 1939: 84)—have resulted in many contemporary hogans having one or more square or oblong windows, usually small ones; the authors have observed them in all varieties of hogans other than leaning-log and corbeled-log types (we have seen only one example in a conical forked-pole hogan). To construct a window, a gap is left in —or, more commonly, sawed out of—the wall, and a plank frame or a commercially made window and frame is built or installed. The window may be left entirely open, be screened, or be glazed with or without glazing bars. Steel bars have also been observed over windows, and boards or pieces of canvas are sometimes used to close off window openings. Sometimes the window is attached by hinges to the top, bottom, or side of the frame so that the window is allowed to open inward; it may then be held in place by chains or some other arrangement. In one case, a Navajo removed a car door and incorporated it into the hogan wall so that the car window became a

hogan window that could be rolled up and down in response to changes in the weather (David M. Brugge, Martin Link, Barton Wright, personal communications). According to Newcomb (1940a: 23), a "set rule says that there shall never be a window that opens to the north," the direction of the spirits of the dead and of storm winds, and that windows (if any) are placed on the southern, southeastern, or southwestern sides of the hogan (exceptions occur, however). Windows have always been used in houses in modern times and were early glazed, but it is not clear just when they became common in hogans. The earliest reference of which we know is Hollister (1903: 71).[11]

Hearths, Stoves, Smoke Holes, and Chimneys

In archaeological hogans (and occasionally in more recent ones), the usual hearth (*kǫ'k'eh* = fireplace) is a shallow round or oval, usually basin-shaped pit, sometimes stone-rimmed. It is located at the center of the hogan or, more commonly, somewhat off-center toward the entry, under the smoke hole (*ch'íláyi'* = interior out-point), or, rarely, against a wall; Western Apache practice is similar (Mails 1974: 94). Square, slab-lined fire pits were occasionally used in early times.[12] Keur (1941: 32, 34; 1944: 76) recorded the occasional eighteenth-century occurrence of vertical stone-slab deflectors adjacent to fireplaces on the entryway side, as in Puebloan kivas. Although retaining their central or east-of-center position (c.f. Newcomb 1940a: 24), hearths and smoke holes have often been much modified in recent times. "The family hearth in a Navajo hogan is right on the ground under the smoke hole; neither stone nor anything else marks its place, and when the fire is not burning it can only be distinguished by the ashes or the burnt appearance of the floor" (Ostermann 1917: 8).

Flues, which were made with such materials as cans, old buckets, or rolled sheet metal, and which often were connected with adobe or vertical-slab fireplaces, were widely adopted early in the century, to supplement the simple

Fig. 2.3. Interior of a stacked-log dugout, showing a niche in the earth wall, in which a fire burns beneath a flue made of sheet metal, cannisters, a bucket, a kettle, and a coffeepot. Mexican Water, Arizona, 1935; M.S.S. (1010).

Fig. 2.4. Remains of the fireplace in a ruined turn-of-the-century stone hogan (Chauncey Neboyia's birthplace in 1909). A chimney extends out from the wall, behind the visible masonry. Above Big Cave, Canyon del Muerto, Arizona, 1972.

smoke hole (Figs. 2.3 and 8.8).[13] At present, the common heating and cooking device is a commercial or homemade wood-burning stove (*béésh bii' kǫ'í* = iron within which fire) whose stovepipe protrudes through the smoke hole. (Stovepipes and chimneys are given the same name as smoke holes: *ch'íláyi'.*) Homemade stoves—primarily for heating—are commonly made from cutoff oil drums (Fig. 5.6; Franciscan Fathers 1952); bottomless milk cans have also been used (e.g., Leighton and Leighton 1949: 94), as have steel tanks and other contraptions (Roberts 1951: 19). The time of adoption is unclear; Verplanck (1934:

7, 22) stated, based on 1913 and 1925 observations, that stovepipes (flues?) were unusual. Landgraf (1954: 47) found only one stove at Ramah in 1941, and more unadorned hearths than hearths with flues. But Roberts (1951: 41) reported that stoves were universal in the area in 1946. Bottled gas is now used for cooking and heating in some localities. Commonly, the smoke hole is framed with logs or boards to retain the roof's earth covering. Occasionally, a cribbed-log, plank, wooden-box, or even oil-drum pseudo-chimney may extend above the smoke hole; or, the roof may be built up on the windward side alone (Haile 1942: 55). True

Fig. 2.5. Hexagonal cupola (with commercially made [?] ventilation louvers) in place of a smoke hole, atop a hexagonal pyramidal hogan roof (see Figs 5.26 and 8.11). Mexican Springs, New Mexico, 1972.

chimneys with wall-side fireplaces were used in some stone and perhaps leaning-log hogans in Canyon de Chelly, Arizona, around the turn of the century (Chauncey Neboyia, personal communication; see Fig. 2.4), and a 1908 Vernon Bailey photograph (No. 2422-C-5, National Anthropological Archives) shows what appears to be a conical forked-pole hogan with a mud-covered chimney rising from the base of the wall north of the doorway. Fired-brick chimneys have replaced smoke holes in a few contemporary hogans (Fig. 5.49).

Smoke holes were and are usually left open to the weather, although Gifford (1940:

107) reported that their size might be reduced during the winter. If a ceremonial sandpainting was made in the hogan, pinyon branches might be laid across the opening to keep out precipitation (Matthews 1902: 49). When modern heating devices are installed, or when a hogan is built for, or converted to, storage use, the smoke hole may be partially or wholly capped with blankets, boards, or wooden "hatch covers" (Fig. 5.45), replaced by a cupola (Fig. 2.5), or eliminated entirely (Landgraf 1954: 50; Downs 1972: 48).

In both archaeological and modern sites, ashes are most commonly deposited in a pile (*łeeshch'ih nehekaah* = ashes are carried [in an open container], *łeeshch'ih nehe'nííł* = ashes are placed, *łeeshch'ih sinil* = ashes lie) a short distance from the structure, commonly northeastward, eastward, or southeastward. Trash was deposited in trash heaps—sometimes with the ashes—after Puebloan fashion in Dinétah, but after the mid-eighteenth century it came to be disposed of more or less randomly, though usually downslope from the dwelling (Fig. 7.1). Today it is sometimes thrown into a small gully.[14]

Other Floor Features

Occasional floor features of archaeological hogans, particularly during the eighteenth century, include (1) mealing bins (usually consisting of a slightly sunken rectangle or hollow rectangle bounded by three or four upright stone slabs and floored with small stones or clay to form a sloping floor for a metate); (2) storage bins (similar, but built against a wall and lacking floor stones and a metate); (3) jar-shaped excavated storage pits; (4) jar-shaped cooking pits; and (5) holes to receive loom posts, normally in the northern half of the hogan (Keur 1941: 32–34; 1944: 76–77; Vivian 1960: 15–16, 19–20, 23–24; Hester and Shiner 1963: 10–11, 47–49; James 1976: 4, 26, 29). All of these traits, with the possible exception of cooking pits, were apparently introduced by Puebloan refugees but except for loom posts were gradually abandoned.

Today, the earth floor between the stove and the furnishings is often covered with sheep and goat pelts, canvas, old saddle blankets (Roberts 1951: 41), or pieces of pasteboard or linoleum.

Social Division of Interior Space

Hogans are one-room structures, and interiors are never physically subdivided. A strategy of multiplication of structures rather than division of interiors is followed when additional space units are desired. Nevertheless, Navajo tradition divides hogan interiors into distinct functional sectors (for terminology, see Fig. 2.6):

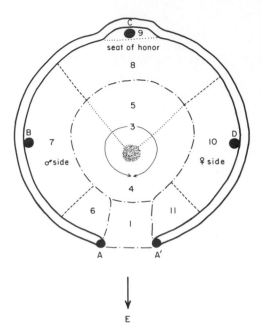

Fig. 2.6. Structural framework and conceptual sectoring of a conical forked-pole hogan (sources: Mindeleff 1898; Franciscan Fathers 1910; Haile 1942, 1950, 1951; Robert W. Young). Black circles represent the principal timbers; double lines indicate the walls.
Framework (*sahdii* = main alone)

    A, A'. Entry pole(s) (*ch'é'étiindęę' náá'áí* = [slender-ridged objects] slanted from the exit path; *ch'é'ét-iin bii'ni'nílii* = those lying on the ground inside the exit path [?]; *Nahasdzáán bijáadii* = Earth World's* leg)

    B. Southern pole (*shádi'ááhdéé' náá'áí* = [slender ridged object] slanted from the south; *Dził'isdzáá* [or *Dzi-łisdzáán*] *bijáadii* = Mountain World's* leg)

    C. Western pole (*'e'e'aahdéé' náá'áí* = [slender ridged object] slanted from the west; *biyi'jį' 'anilkaad* = fell into it's interior [fork]; *Tóísdzáán bijáadii* = Water World's* leg)

    D. Northern pole (*náhookosdéé' náá'áí* = [slender ridged object] slanted from the north; *Dá'asdzáán bijáadii* = Corn World's* leg) (Note: *-jí,* toward, is sometimes substituted for *-déé'* in the above terms.)
Interior (*hooghan góne'* or *wóne'[é]* = hogan interior) floor (*łeeshta'* = between earth)

    1. Entryway (*ch'é'étiin* = exit path; *ya'abitiin* [or *yah 'e'etiin*] = entry path)

2. Hearth(*ko[n]k'eh* [or *konik'eh*] = fireplace)
3. Fireside (*honbah,* [or *konibah, honibaah[gi], konibaahgi*] = [at] fireside)
4. Ceremonial fireside (*honishghah* or *konishghah; honishbaahgi* = fireside)
5. Farther center (*ya'ałníí'* [or *yahałníí(n)*] = under [or sky?] center; *'ayayi'* = underneath inside)
6. Eastern recess (*ha'a'aahjí ńtsístł'ah* = small eastern stop-forward recess)†
7. Southern recess (*shádi'ááhjí* [or *shádi' ááhjí' ńtsítł'ah* = southern stop-forward recess)
8. Western recess (*'e'e'aahjí ntsítł'ah* = western stop-forward recess (*yóniid* or *wóniid* [= far inside] apparently refers to the area along the western wall)
9. Mask recess (*jish binástł'ah* = mask's curved recess; *ńtsístł'ah[gi]* = [at] small stop-forward recess)
10. Northern recess (*náhookosjí ńtsítł'ah* = northern stop-forward recess)
11. Small northern recess (*náhookosjí ńtsístł'ah* = small northern stop-forward recess†
Not shown: peripheral shelf (*bitát'ah* = its forehead ledge)

*These "worlds" or realms are personified as women. Earth Woman and Mountain Woman symbolize the sources of the building materials, while Water Woman and Corn [Maize] Woman represent the sources of sustenance of the hogan's inhabitants.

†The areas to either side of the entry, 6 and 11 above, are also called *báhástł'ah* = recesses for.

. . . custom still dictates that upon entering the hogan, women go to the right or the north side where the kitchen supplies and utensils are maintained, and the loom erected, and the men go to the left or south side [although this is commonly ignored today]. The rear of the hogan is the place of honor and is usually reserved for the patriarch or matriarch of the family. In a sense, this method is actually a partitioning of the hogan into separate rooms. [Correll 1965a: 31][15]

A "mask recess" is sometimes found at the base of the western wall. During a ceremony, people entering a hogan must pass south of the hearth; upon exiting, the individual passes to the north of the fireplace—i.e., a sunwise course is followed (Mindeleff 1898: 493, 517; Ostermann 1917: 26; Haile 1942: 50–51).

That this sexual, honorific, and ceremonial subdivision of interior space (and possibly eastward orientation as well) is ancient and was brought by Athapaskans from the north is suggested by the exact same social layout in the dwellings of the Siberian Altai, Tuvans, and Tolalars (Levin and Potapov 1964: 316, 400, 478), among the Mongols (Huc 1900: 47), and probably among other groups in Eurasia, and at least the equivalent position of the "seat of honor" in parts of northern North America (Paulson 1952), including among some Athapaskans (Morice 1909: 593; Honigman 1954: 62). (Among the Sioux, the male-female division is the reverse of the Navajo's; Laubin and Laubin 1957: 3, 91–92.) This social-division pattern is not a Puebloan trait. The sunwise ceremonial circuit has also been recorded in the north, among the Kaska (Teit 1956: 100), as well as among Puebloans.

Other Interior Features

It is beyond the scope of this book to deal with nonstructural hogan furnishings; inventories may be found in Roberts (1951: 15–24; 41).[16] Belongings are typically arranged around the perimeter of the hogan and may include trunks for clothing and other possessions, beds, a food-preparation table, and so forth. The central area is kept clear as a sitting, eating, and working space, in the approximate center of which is the cooking or heating stove, or both, or the hearth. Sheets of cloth are occasionally hung around the walls and under the part of the roof over the food preparation area (e.g., Anderson 1973: 51), for esthetic reasons and to keep out chinking dirt. Wooden shelves and cupboards, frequently made from boxes and crates, are often nailed to the interior walls of hogans and other dwellings. Wooden pegs for hanging things may be driven into interstices in the walls, or nails be pounded part way into the logs. Limbs are occasionally left to project from wall logs for the same purpose. Frequent, too, are horizontal strings or wires, or metal rods or wooden poles secured in wall interstices or suspended by ropes or wires and run across dwelling corners or parallel to walls (Fig 4.17). These are for hanging bedding, clothing, and other items; this is also a historic-period Puebloan trait and was practiced by Spanish colonial residents of New Mexico (Roberts 1951: 41; Kluckhohn et al. 1971: 181; Boyd 1974: 21). The earliest record for the Navajo is 1898 (James 1913: 217).

HOUSES

Kin is the Navajo word for the square-cornered, rectilinear-plan, vertical-walled house (or pueblo), a dwelling form which is not "traditionally" Navajo.[17] Houses of stone, adobe, or both, have been built continuously in the Southwest by Puebloans since long before the Navajo are known to have lived there, and Hispanos and Anglo-Americans have built house of various materials during their occupance. Gradually, more and more Navajos have adopted such houses, yet few discussions of Navajo *kin* are found in the literature. Anthropologists and cultural geographers often tend to discount "non-traditional," culturally intrusive objects and practices, and contemporary Navajo *kin* are clearly derivative from Puebloan and European modes of building (mainly from the latter) since the late nineteenth century. The only published studies

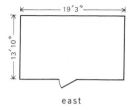

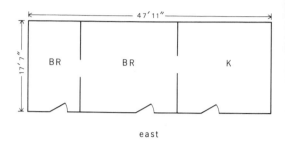

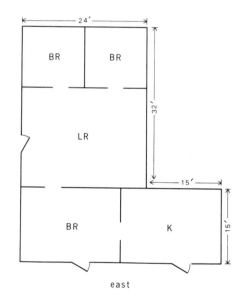

Fig. 2.7. Plans of three stone houses, showing dimensions and room functions. Oak Springs area, Red Valley, New Mexico, c. 1970s (Navajo Environmental Protection Commission Staff, 1980).

Fig. 2.8. Conjoined L–plan frame house and cribbed-log hogan. The house and gabled roof are covered with composition shingling, the hipped-with-ridge hogan roof with mineral-surfaced roll roofing (note the television antenna and two stovepipes). A sort of porch extends between the house and the hogans southeastern wall. The logs are squared and half lap-jointed. The house has a commercially made door (with a Christmas wreath) and double-hung windows with muntins; the hogan's window, door, and screen door are homemade. Note the bottled gas. Other structures include, at left, an apparent large water tank and a frame barn or garage. North of Fort Defiance, Arizona, 1970.

dealing at any length with modern Navajo houses are by Tremblay et al. (1954), who used house types as a measure of acculturation among an off-Reservation group of Navajos, and by Spencer and Jett (1971).

Houses inhabited by Navajos range from square, one-room, Navajo-built cabins to multi-room, complex-plan, commercially constructed tract houses (Fig. 2.7). However, small, single-story, usually one- or two-room dwellings far outnumber the latter, which are largely confined to the few small urban areas in the Navajo Country. Only owner-built housing is described herein (with the exception of tents and house trailers).

Unlike hogans, single-room houses may grow by accretion, as more living space is required: a new unit will be added to the original house, making use of one or more of the existing walls. Thus, a single dwelling may be,

in essence, two or more noncommunicating houses structurally connected. Sometimes, two or more building techniques and/or materials may be combined in a single dwelling, to form a "hybrid" of two house types, and a few cases of hogans physically joined to houses have been noted (Figs. 2.8, 5.41). Some Navajo families that have moved into square-roomed frame houses have retained the idea of traditional round hogan-type living space by using the corners of the square rooms for storage, thus creating an essentially circular living area (Anonymous, 1968a: D-1).

Dugouts and Ruin Use

Hogans and the more traditional house types are occasionally seen in dugout form, in which an excavation is made into flat ground or into a slope or bank. In such cases, the

Fig. 2.9. Remains of a stacked-log dugout house, showing the board-sided entryway and plank door. The beam roof has collapsed and some of the earth walls have been eroded. Black Creek Valley, Arizona, 1968.

excavation sides form part or all of the walls (Fig. 2.3). With respect to houses, log beam roofs are usual on hillslope and bank dugouts, low-pitched gabled roofs on flat-ground dugouts (Figs. 7.4, 7.8, and 7.29). Hillside structures often have entryways set a few feet into the hill; the sides of the cut are then shored with sloping logs or planks, and one enters via a couple of earth-cut steps (Fig. 2.9). Gable-end doors are usual with flat-ground dugouts. Although there is no question that such structures have not infrequently been used as dwellings, their usual function today is as cool food-storage structures ("root cellars"). Reichard (1934: 6–7) temporarily occupied one normally used for winter storage of wool; it was about 5 feet (1.52 m) deep, with a 12-by-15 foot (3.66 X 4.57 m) floor. Ordinary houses also often serve primarily or occasionally as

storage structures (Roberts 1951: 42–43; Lockett 1952: 137; Jones et al. 1939: 82).

Navajos have apparently occasionally refurbished and reoccupied abandoned Puebloan structures (Adams 1959; Vivian 1960), but this is rare, partly because many Navajos consider such ruins to be *ch'įįdii*, or ghost-infested (Newcomb 1940a; 26).

Floors, Doorways, and Windows

The floors of Navajo houses are commonly of dirt or packed sand, but nowadays many houses are built on stone-masonry, concrete, or plank foundations, and may have plank, plywood, concrete or flagstone floors. Doorways are typically framed with nominal 2-by-4 inch (5.08 X 10.16 cm) or 2-by-6 inch (5.08 X 15.24 cm) boards. Doors seem to have been used from the earliest period of modern house building (for example, a Joseph City, Arizona, Mormon made a door frame and installed two locks on Navajo doors in Feburary 1885; Tanner and Richardson 1977: 71). Commercially manufactured doors are more common on houses than on hogans. A frequent feature of Navajo houses is the placing of two (or, occasionally, more) doorways in the facade, usually on one of the long sides (Figs. 7.3, 7.11); this practice dates back at least to the early twentieth century (Fraser 1919: 200; see also Kluckhohn et al. 1971: 149). This sometimes reflects a second unit being added to an exsting one, and even in cases involving a single episode of construction, two adjacent rooms not connected by a doorway but each with its own exterior door may reflect the concept of the single-room dwelling. Note, however, early trading posts with two doorways in the facade, one to the store and one to the trader's living quarters, and early Mormon houses with two front doorways (Forrest 1970: 25–26; Spencer 1945: 448). Too, some Navajo houses have interior, connecting, doorways. When, as is usual, there is but a single doorway, it is ordinarily in one of the longer sides. Sometimes plank, stone, or concrete door steps or stoops, or even porches (recorded as early as Fraser 1919: 200), are constructed (Fig. 7.11). Although many *kin* do not exhibit eastward orientation, most do, in conformity with general Navajo practice regarding structures (e.g., Tremblay et al. 1954: 214–15; Spencer and Jett 1971: 71).[18] Most houses have, and have had since the nineteenth century, small- to medium-sized windows, which (unless commercially manufactured) are typically framed with nominal 2-by-4s or 2-by-6s. Windows are normally glazed; ready-made commercial wood- or aluminum-framed windows are sometimes used and have been for years. As early as 1930, doors and windows manufactured at the government sawmill near Ft. Defiance were "sold on part payments to the Indians" (Coolidge and Coolidge 1931: 84). The Office of Navajo Economic Opportunity (ONEO) subsidized the purchase of commer-

Fig. 2.10. Mud-plastered interior walls, corner fireplace, and corner chimney of the stone house in Fig. 7.24. Note the fireplace opening's pole lintel. Burnham, New Mexico, 1935; M.S.S. (1008).

cially made doors and windows during the 1970s (Jerrold E. Levy, personal communication, 1980).

Fireplaces and Chimneys

Stone, brick, or concrete-block fireplaces and chimneys on exterior walls—Anglo introductions—are not uncommon (Figs. 7.11, 7.27, 7.28; a chimney arrangement was recorded in 1886, and chimneys were also observed in 1902; Shufeldt 1892: 280; Forrest 1970: 115); otherwise, and more commonly, a stove and stovepipe are used, occasionally in conjunction with a plank pseudo chimney (for an unusual stovepipe-chimney combination, see Shufeldt 1892: 280). Corner fireplaces and interior chimneys (Figs. 2.10, 7.24)—of Spanish derivation, probably in part via the pueblos

(Boyd 1974: 10–12)—are known archaeologically and ethnographically (Adams, Lindsay, and Turner 1961: 10; Cassidy 1956: 78; Vivian 1960; Kluckhohn et al. 1971: 149). Bottled gas is being increasingly used (Fig. 7.14).

Other Features

Possessions, such as harness, may be hung on nails in the interior or exterior walls (Fig. 7.5).

Under the rural electrification program of the Navajo Tribal Utility Authority ("A light in every hogan") beginning in 1960, an increasing number of owners of hogans and houses have in recent years installed electric lights (Fig. 5.25), and rooftop television antennas are not infrequently seen (Figs. 2.8, 5.49, 7.28).

DWELLING ABANDONMENT

Because of ghost fear, traditional Navajos desert a hogan or house (and sometimes the entire site) if death (at least from a cause other than old age; Haile 1952: 7) occurs within.[19] An attempt is made to avoid this eventuality, especially in the case of houses, by removing any very sick person to a temporary shelter, an outlying or seldom-used hogan, or, today, to a hospital. A death hogan is popularly known as a "chindi" (ch'íídii = ghost) hogan, or, more formally, a hook'eeghan, "no-hearth home." If the structure is not too massive, a hole may be broken or chopped through the northern portion of its wall (western, according to Marmon 1894: 159; northern or western according to Coolidge and Coolidge 1930: 151, 298), through which the body is removed, and the structure may be pulled down and/or burned; sometimes after barring the entry with logs (Van Valkenburgh 1947a: 16–17). If the body is buried or left uninterred within (especially in winter, when the ground is frozen or if light-ning is the cause of death, and typically against the northwest wall), all openings may be closed with poles, posts, or rocks as a warning and to exclude scavengers (and to confuse the ghost?), or the structure may be torn down over the grave or corpse, and/or burned (except for abandonment, these practices appear to be relatively uncommon today). Any new hogan is sited at least 150 feet (45.7m) away (Lamphere 1976: 23); or, the entire site may be abandoned until the death hogan disintegrates, and the other hogans may be dismantled and moved to a new site at least 0.5 mile (.8 km) away (Downs 1972: 47–48; Roberts 1951: 75; Reichard 1939: 127; Frisbie and McAllester 1978: 283–84, 338).

A dwelling may also be deserted if the occupants are beset with bad luck or quarreling, if lightning strikes the structure, if serious storm damage occurs, or if a bear rubs against it.[20] Lice or bedbug infestation sometimes results in the building of a new hogan and abandonment of the old (Kluckhohn and Leighton 1962: 46–49; Wyman, 1952: 102; Landgraf 1954: 51). One function of the House Blessing Ceremony is prevention of such occurrences (Frisbie 1968: 31). Extreme fear of the dead and the destruction of dwellings where death has occurred are not Puebloan traits (Ellis 1968) but are found among Apacheans and appear to be of Athapaskan origin.[21] Removal of the dying to a temporary dwelling, removing a corpse via a hole broken through a wall, fear of ghosts, and abandonment and destruction of dwellings following a death are all reported for Northern Athapaskans (Brugge 1980; Honigman 1946: 87; 1954: 138–40, McClellan 1975: 234, 342, 372–74).[22] With increasing acculturation, such Navajo practices are becoming less common (Tremblay et al. 1954: 215–16).

Sites may also be abandoned as a result of land conflicts, range depletion, and changing kinship alliances (Landgraf 1954: 51).

Chapter 3

CLASSIFICATION
of Navajo Dwellings

The geographer of dwelling types is concerned with determining the basic physical forms of dwellings, their origins in time and space, their distributions, and the origins of those distributions. None of these goals can be attained without first delineating the significant characteristics of the dwellings and establishing criteria for their classification.

Dwellings are categorized as such on the basis of function: being dwelt in,[1] which is ordinarily thought of as including sleeping, domestic tasks such as food preparation, and day-to-day family and other social life. However, there is no universally accepted system of classification of dwelling types. Systems used are based upon characteristics which one wishes to emphasize, attributes that are most conveniently observed or described, and the goals of study. Single-criterion systems include construction method, building materials, roof type, facade form, general style, plan, or historical period. Multiple-criteria systems may use any combination of these criteria.[2]

Although historical origins are sought in the present study, no truly phylogenetic taxonomy of Navajo dwellings is possible since several of the different types are of basically

different origins and since interinfluence and external influences have resulted in significant modifications. Perhaps these difficulties account in part for the literature's dearth of really systematic attempts at classification.

It appears to the authors that the broadest useful categorization of Navajo dwellings can be based on the Navajo (and English) distinction between (1) *chaha'oh* or shades (relatively insubstantial summer or temporary shelters of various plans and origins which are, more often than not, at least partially wall-less; in this category have also been included, in this book, windbreaks and tents); (2) *hooghan* ("traditional," more or less distinctively Navajo dwellings, of round, polygonal, or subrectangular plan)[3]; (3) *kin* or houses (rectilinear in plan, with vertical walls, and of largely or totally foreign—Puebloan or European—derivation).

Various classification criteria were considered in attempting further to subdivide the above categories. One of these criteria, roof structure and materials, was considered since:

1. There is no distinction between walls and roof in the case of lean-to, conical forked-

pole, and corbeled-log hogans, and such hogans may be thought of as roofs set directly on
the ground.

2. At least the lean-to and conical forked-
pole types preceded the types in which walls
and roof are distinct.

3. Hogans with separable walls and roof
can in some cases be thought of not as hogans
with roofs but as hogans (conical forked-pole,
corbeled-log, etc.) which have been given
added height by being set on walls of any of a
number of possible types.

4. A category used by the Navajo in reference to dwellings is *yaadah['Jaskání* (loosely,
"under the dome"), which apparently refers to
any hogan with a corbeled-log roof, regardless
of wall structure or material (although the latter may be referred to in other classificatory
systems or in subdividing *yaadahaskani;*
Franciscan Fathers 1910: 332; Haile 1937: 3;
1952:4).

This system was eventually rejected, however,
except in partial application to shades.

Stephen (1890) claimed that the Navajo
recognized six hogan types and six forms of
summer shelters. Although no attempt was
made by us to construct a complete taxonomy
of dwelling forms as perceived by the Navajo,
Navajo terms for various types of structures
have been collected from published sources
(especially Mindeleff 1898; Franciscan Fathers 1910: 330–40; Haile 1942, 1950, 1951,
1952; Kluckhohn et al. 1971; and Young and
Morgan 1980); and from William Morgan.
Robert W. Young, Chauncey Neboyia, and a
few other informants.[4] Based on these terms,
as well as upon common English usage in reference to Navajo dwellings, and based on the
features that appeared to be most significant
for the purposes of this study, it was decided
to use wall structure and materials as the basic
criteria of classification of permanent dwellings (Table 3.1). Where walls and roof were
inseparable, they were treated as walls ·(although the term "sides" would be appropriate
for general purposes). Structure is here considered to refer both to form and to the method

TABLE 3.1.

Taxonomy of Navajo Dwellings

A. Temporary and Summer Shelters
1. Windbreaks
   a. Palisaded windbreak or shade
   b. Stacked-bough windbreak
   c. Stone windbreak
   d. Cloth-walled windbreak
2. Conical forked-pole shade
3. Tipi shade
4. Lean-to shade
5. Flat-roofed shade (ramada)
6. Corbeled-log-roof shade
7. Frame shade
8. Tents
   a. Wedge tent
   b. Wall tent
   c. Conical army tent
   d. Pyramidal tent
   e. Tipi

B. Hogans
1. Conical forked-pole hogan
2. Lean-to hogan
3. Vertical-post hogans
   a. Leaning-log hogan
   b. Palisaded hogan
4. Stacked-log hogans
   a. Corbeled-log hogan
   b. Cribbed-log hogan
   c. Abutting-log hogan
5. Plank hogans
   a. Leaning-plank hogan
   b. Post-and-plank hogan
   c. Frame hogan
6. Masonry hogans
   a. Stone hogan
   b. Adobe-brick hogan
   c. Cinder-block hogan
7. Poured-concrete hogan

C. Houses
1. Palisaded house
2. Stacked-log houses
   a. Cribbed-log house
   b. Abutting-log house
3. Frame house
4. Masonry houses
   a. Stone house
   b. Adobe-brick house
   c. Fired-brick house
   d. Cinder-block house

of achieving that form. Although this system is not perfect, it seems to serve its purpose. (We have revised our taxonomy somewhat since it was first proposed [Spencer and Jett 1971]). It would have been less useful, for example, to classify dwellings simply on the basis of external appearance; earth-covered leaning-log, palisaded, corbeled-log, and plank hogans are superficially similar or identical, as are stuccoed plank, stone, and cinder-block houses.

Roof types, being partly independent of dwelling types as defined by the above criteria, are classified separately in chapter 8.

As noted in chapter 2, a number of hogan and house types occur occasionally as "dugout" dwellings (*łeeyi' hooghan* = in-the-earth hogan, and *łeeh hoogeed* = dug-earth place; the latter applied to dugout *kin* and to modern cellars). These structures differ from the standard varieties in that their walls are partly or wholly formed by the digging of an excavation into flat or sloping ground or into a bank. Dugouts are, or were, sometimes used as dwellings, especially in areas where building materials are scarce, but at present the primary function of dugouts is as "root cellars," for the storage of perishable foodstuffs (see "Drying and Storage Structures," chapter 9). Haile (1952: 5; see also Franciscan Fathers 1910: 336) wrote that "dugout shelters are really intended for shade," and are sometimes called *łeeh hoogeed'go chaha'oh,* "dug-earth-place shade."

Field Ramada southeast of Rock Point, Arizona, 1970.

Chapter 4

ORIGINS, EVOLUTIONS, AND FORMS
Of Temporary And Summer Dwellings

We have no direct knowledge of the dwelling forms brought to the Southwest by the proto-Navajo. Nevertheless, some idea of these dwellings may be obtained by (1) determining the kinds of dwellings used by the Navajos' Northern Athapaskan linguistic relatives, (2) seeing what dwellings other Southern Athapaskans have utilized, and (3) examining the archaeological and historical record for the Navajo.

WINDBREAKS

The simplest Navajo dwellings are temporary or seasonally used arcuate windbreaks, of piled or upright boughs or of stones (Figs. 4.1, 4.2). These provide shelter for sleeping and cooking. Such structures are of very ancient origin and are found worldwide. Northern Athapaskans (Curtis 1928: 24; Osgood 1936: 51–52, 55), Shoshoneans (Stewart 1941: 282, 334; 1942: 261; Steward 1941: 377), Pimans, Yumans (Drucker 1941: 106), Puebloans (Mindeleff 1891: 218; Brown 1974: 328–29), Apacheans (Gifford 1940: 23, 110), and many other North American groups employed roof-less arcuate windbreaks of boughs. We assume Navajo use to be of Athapaskan origin, although the occasional employing of stones is presumably southwestern. We know of no published archaeological example of definite windbreaks, although some of the cruder stone "hogans" described (e.g., Keur 1941: 26) may in fact be windbreaks. Early descriptions of bough windbreaks include Rice's for 1851 (Dillon 1970: 68) and Stephen's (1890; 1893: 350). According to Rice, this was "the only refuge they [Navajos] have"—clearly an incorrect assessment.

Detailed descriptions of windbreaks follow:

Diagnostic feature: a simple wall of boughs and/or brush or logs, or of stones, or of cloth, largely or entirely roofless.

Stacked-Bough Windbreak

Navajo name: 'ił názt'i' = [conifer-] bough circular line.

Major features:

1. Wall structure: boughs and/or brush or untrimmed logs, piled horizontally.

2. Plan: arcuate or circular.

Fig. 4.1. A palisaded windbreak, consisting of a circle of boughs, butt ends emplanted into the ground and inclining slightly inward. The foliage has fallen off. North of Cow Springs, Arizona, 1969.

Fig. 4.2. Probable stone windbreak, although possibly a lambing pen. The rough, uncoursed, dry-laid masonry incorporates a boulder. The entry is oriented approximately northeastward. There were other, cruder, arcs of piled stones in the immediate vicinity. A ramada is visible on the skyline. Across the Colorado River from Lees Ferry, Arizona, 1963.

3. Roof: none, or a partial roof made with a blanket or blankets, a canvas wagon cover, a hide, or a few boughs. The natural shade roof of a tree may be utilized.

Minor features and variations:

1. Boulders or living trees may be incorporated into the walls.

2. Snow photographs of 1935 (937, 938) show a "windbreak" east of Red Lake (Tolani Lakes), Arizona, consisting of tumbleweeds (Russian-thistle) held in place by a post-and-wire fence.

Palisaded Windbreak or Shade

Navajo name: 'ił *bee chaha'oh* = with-[conifer-] bough shade (when conifer boughs are used).

Major features:

1. Wall structure: boughs and/or saplings set up as a slightly inward-leaning loose palisade (Fig. 4.1).

2. Plan: arcuate or circular.

3. Roof: none, or a partial roof made with a blanket or blankets, with the canvas covering of a wagon, or with a hide. The natural shade roof of a tree may be utilized.

Minor features and variations:

1. The vertical boughs may be secured by being tied near their tops to an encircling sapling (James 1905: 642).

2. Stones may be piled around the base of the vertical-bough structure.

3. Canvas, boards, and packing crates have also been recorded as supplemental wall materials (Reichard 1934: 1; Leighton and Leighton 1944: 15).

Cloth-Walled Windbreak

Major features:

1. Wall structure: cloth is hung from stringers supported by several vertical posts (Luckert 1979: 162).

2. Plan: polygonal.

3. Roof: none.

Stone Windbreak

Major features:

1. Wall structure: rough dry-laid stone masonry (Fig. 4.2).

2. Plan: arcuate, circular, or rectangular.

3. Roof: none or of "any handy material" (Hollister 1903: 70).

Variations:

1. Boulders may be encorporated into the walls.

Construction and Use

Windbreaks not only cut the wind, they also provide shelter from drifting sand as well as some shade (particularly when built beneath a tree). They are usually temporary shelters for use on journeys and on other occasions (such as when herding, hunting, pinyon gathering, or temporarily occupying a farm), when more permanent shelter is unavailable. In the Ramah area, palisaded windbreaks also served as outdoor working areas at the entries of tents and seem to have filled the role played by the ramada in other areas (see "Flat-Roofed Shade," below; Roberts 1951: 41–42, Fig. 1). Windbreaks are usually constructed of freshly cut juniper, pine, or other boughs set in the ground nearly vertically but leaning slightly inward (Fig. 4.1) or piled horizontally in a near-circle, with a blanket secured at the entrance (the authors have encountered only the former type). Two men with axes can erect one of these shelters 15 to 20 feet (4.6 to 6.1 m) in diameter and 4 or 5 feet (1.2 or 1.5 m) high in about half an hour.[1] Windbreaks stand from hip- to stature-height or more (Kluckhohn *et al.* 1971: 157); the vertical-bough varieties, although sometimes no more than 2.5 to 3 feet (.75 to .9 m) high, are generally the tallest, and are probably primarily for providing shade. Diameters vary according to the number of users; for a single individual, a structure a few feet wide is erected, but for larger parties windbreaks up to 25 feet (7. 6 m) across are sometimes built. The fire is usually made in the circle's center, although Rice, in 1851, described piled-pinyon-bough windbreaks 3 to 4 feet (.9 or 1.2 m) high, carrying "a slight bough roof, with a small fire in its front to keep the wolves and other wild animals out" (Dillon 1970: 68). Blankets or other fabric may be stretched over branches for shade. The entrance of a windbreak for an-telope hunters was in the same direction as that of the corral trap erected (see "Hunting Structures," chapter 7), and not necessarily toward the east.

Hill (1936: 12), describing stacked-bough windbreaks once used by war parties, noted that the growing tips of the boughs used should point eastward. The same was often true of windbreaks for hunting parties, although rearward orientation and sunwise laying were also practiced. The southern half of the circle was built first, working from the eastern end; then the northern half was constructed. Hunters built shelters from front to back or in a sunwise direction (Hill 1938: 102, 114, 118, 124, 146, 163, 189). One of Luckert's (1975: 62–63; also, Johnston 1972: 100) informants described deer hunters' windbreaks as 2 to 3 feet (.6 to .9 m) high, with branch tips facing sunwise and the entry to the east; the fire was built in the center, and branches (tips facing northward) were laid westward of the fire to receive the venison.[2] If women accompanied the hunters, a separate shelter had to be built for them.

Structures of the same form (also *'ił názt'i',* or *'ił náshjin* = [conifer-] bough dark circular line) or the palisaded form are erected for ceremonials such as Nightway, Navajo Windway, Shootingway, and Beautyway, and function as dressing rooms for masked dancers; the single entry gap is on the east, although openings are broken at the other three cardinal points at dawn, after the ceremonies (Frink and Barthelmess 1965: 41 [from 1883]; Franciscan Fathers 1910: 335, 376–77; Haile 1951: 293). Matthews (1902: 50, plate 1) described the Nightway circle as being about 20 feet (6.1 m) in diameter and 12 feet (3.7 m) high, located some 100 paces eastward of the ceremonial hogan. The fire was at the center, the entry to the south. The origin of these ceremonial circles may be northern; brush dance "corrals" were used by many Utes, Paiutes (Stewart 1941: 415; 1942: 321), and Shoshonis (Steward 1941: 323), and fenced dancing grounds are reported for Northern Athapaskans (Honigman 1946: 89; Osgood 1936: 52, 122, 125).

Fig. 4.3. The only conical forked-pole shade observed; there is no evidence that an earth covering ever was applied. Some of the leaners have fallen, exposing the lower two-thirds of the western pole of the tripod frame. Near Hunters Point, Arizona, 1972.

Stone windbreaks (Fig. 4.2) are not common (Hoover 1931: 422; Luomala 1938: 81; Reher 1977: 62). Their use is similar to that of bough windbreaks (Hollister 1903: 70; Goddard 1913: 136). In addition, small, rectangular, dry-laid stone-masonry enclosures with an entry have sometimes been built to shield outdoor cooking areas (Mooney 1970: 21).

The only cloth-walled windbreak of which we have heard is one pictured by Luckert (1979: 160–73), constructed as a Coyoteway dressing room and prayer site east of the patient's hogan (the entry was toward the south).

CONICAL FORKED-POLE SHADE

The common dwelling type among most Northern Athapaskans linguistically closely related to the Navajo was a conical, pole-and-bark-covered hut with a tripod foundation. The Navajo also occasionally construct a conical shade which closely resembles this northern form (Fig. 4.3). Conical forked-pole shades (wikiups) are also made by Western Apaches (Schaeffer 1958: 14, 17), and conical shades were used by the Llanero Apache and the Zuni (Gifford 1940: 110). Although such shades probably are generally of lighter construction than conical forked-pole hogans (see chapter 5), the two are not differentiated archaeologically. The earliest recognizable description, based on an 1849 observation, is that of Simpson (1852: 13). The 1582 report of Espejo setting fire to "Querecho" shacks (Correll 1976: 3) may refer to such dwellings, but this is not provable. These structures seem not to have undergone any significant evolution except in the occasional addition of an extended entryway and, perhaps, in the direction of increased size (for further discussion, see chapter 5).

The conical forked-pole shade may be described as follows:

Navajo name: chaha'oh 'ałch'į' 'adeez'á = converging-points shade.

Diagnostic feature: a tripod frame of poles whose forked ends are interlocked at the apex.

Other major features:

1. Wall structure: Two parallel poles are ordinarily leaned against the tripod frame to form the entryway. The gaps between the main poles are filled with smaller poles leaned against the frame and each other (Fig. 4.3). The leaners are often but not always covered with brush, boughs, bark, corn stalks and husks, canvas, and the like.

2. Plan: circular or oval; possibly D-shaped.

3. Roof: inseparable from the walls.

Variation:

Entries are occasionally extended.

Construction and Use

This type of shade or "summer hogan" (Fig. 4.3) is very rare today and is seldom mentioned in the literature.[3] Many Northern Athapaskans covered their conical dwellings. with bark; a pine-bark-covered shade mentioned by Haile (1950: 15), *'akásht'óózh bee hooghan,* may represent the Navajo equivalent. Brush or bough covering is more common, however. Building procedure was presumably similar to that of the conical forked-pole hogan (see chapter 5).

Although use of the conical shade was similar to that of other shades, conical shades were also built especially for ceremonies, particularly those intended to elicit rain. In such cases, the tips of the covering poles were pointed groundward to cause precipitation; juniper poles were used to elicit male (violent) rain, pinyon for female (gentle) rain, and both kinds of poles for both kinds of rain (Hill 1938: 74).

TIPI SHADE

In the Wheatfields, Arizona, area, one example of a conical shade was seen which had a number of lashed poles rather than a three-forked-pole framework (Fig. 4.4). Although similar to some northern and Apache forms, this unique occurrence among the Navajo may represent an innovation inspired by the Plains

Fig. 4.4. The only tipi-form shade encountered. There are at least eight principal poles, plus many light leaners, some of which appear to be reinforced by horizontals attached about one-third of the way up the sides. The upper two-thirds of the sides have been covered with oak(?) boughs, and a pole-and-plank entry added. We suspect the structure of being connected to Native American Church ceremonies. Part of a ramada is visible behind and to the right of the shade. Wheatfields area, Arizona, 1972.

tipi, which is often used at meetings of the Native American Church.

This idea is supported by the recording of a tipi (see below) near Lukachukai whose upper two-thirds was covered with boughs held in place by poles leaned against the structure (McAllester and McAllester 1980: 63). The tipi shade's characteristics are:

Diagnostic feature: many poles leaned together and lashed below the apex of the resultant conical framework.

Other major features:

1. Wall structure: inclined poles covered with boughs (Fig. 4.4).

2. Plan: circular.

3. Roof: inseparable from walls.

Minor features:

1. Horizontals were attached, running between the main poles about one-third of the way up.

2. A door frame was constructed a short distance inward from the perimeter, facing eastward.

Construction

Ten or twelve poles were debarked, leaned together to form a cone, and lashed near the apex. Horizontals were attached; the smaller poles were leaned against these and the main poles. Foliage was present on the upper two-thirds of the structure's exterior.

LEAN-TO SHADES

Lean-tos exhibit no differentiation between roof and walls and consist of poles leaned against a vertical forked pole, a ridgepole (Figs. 4.5, 4.6, 4.7), or a rock or bank. The poles may then be covered with vegetal material.

Single and double pole-and-brush or -bark or -moss lean-tos are known to the Canadian and Alaskan Athapaskans, and the latter was the principal dwelling among certain tribes. Most or all Apache groups also used lean-tos (Packard and Packard 1970: 21; Spier 1928: 182; Goddard 1913: 134; Gifford 1940: 109). Lean-tos are recorded in the Navajo archaeology of the latter eighteenth century (Dittert et. al. 1961:240; Keur 1941: 37; Farmer 1947: 18). Certain structures referred to in Navajo Land Claims records as "windbreaks" appear to be lean-to shades. One of these was associated with hogans dating to about the 1730s (Navajo Land Claim n.d.b vol. 9, Cebolleta Mesa, site I). Shoshoneans (Steward 1941: 233, 283–84, 334–35; Stewart 1941: 378–79, 430), Picuris Puebloans (Brown 1974: 329), and probably other groups also used lean-tos, but a northern origin among the Navajo is the most economical hypothesis. These forms seem to have remained essentially unchanged over the years. A detailed description follows:

Fig. 4.5. "One-legged" double lean-to shade, with the ridgepole running from the single upright to the ground. Hypothetical reconstruction.

Navajo name: chaha'oh t'ááłá'í (naaki) bijááá = shade's one (two) leg(s); *chaha'oh shichidí* (?) = shade squats (for single, two-legged lean-to?).

Diagnostic feature: boughs, poles, or logs leaned against a support.

Other major features:

1. Wall structure: poles or logs leaned against a support and sometimes covered with any or all of the following: boughs (Fig. 4.6); brush; maize, weed, and reed stalks; grass and weeds; straw; a blanket or canvas. Bark coverings are referred to in legend (Roessel and Platero 1974: 29–36).

2. Plan: semicircular, triangular, subtriangular, rectangular, or subrectangular.

3. Roof: inseparable from the walls.

Minor features and variations:

1. The leaners may be supported by a single forked vertical pole or by a ridgepole resting on the end(s) (usually forked) of one or two vertical or somewhat inclined poles. If there is no ridgepole, the plan is roughly semicircular. If a ridgepole is present (as is usual), it may be inclined, with one end resting in the fork of a single standing pole and the other end on the ground, in which case the plan is approximately triangular (Fig. 4.5); or, the ridgepole may be horizontal, resting on the ends of two standing poles or on the end of one standing pole and in the fork of a tree or on a tree branch or boulder, in which case the plan is

rectangular or subrectangular (Figs. 4.6, 4.7). Sometimes, instead of a ridgepole, a cliff or a boulder or a piled up semicircle of rocks provides the support for the leaners, or an excavation is made in a hillside and walled with leaners, whose ends rest on top of the rear wall (Vivian 1960).

2. The poles may be leaned on only one side (usually the west) of the ridgepole (single lean-to; Fig. 4.6) or on both sides (double lean-to; Figs. 4.5, 4.7), and the ends of the lean-to may be left open or be wholly or partially closed by leaning poles or boughs against the main leaners.

3. One or more of the verticals may be doubled.

4. If built on a slight slope, the floor may be excavated to create both a level surface and a shelf at the rear to hold household articles.

Construction and Use

Lightly constructed lean-to shades (Figs. 4.5, 4.6, 4.7)[4] are most commonly for use near fields distant from the main camp or for occasions when one is herding or traveling. A lean-to or other temporary shelter may be erected to house a person who is isolated from the main dwelling because of critical illness or, formerly, because the individual was engaged in basket-weaving (Newcomb 1940: 37). Keur (1941: 37) described four eighteenth-century

Fig. 4.6. One of two lean-to shades encountered. Two forked vertical poles carry a stringer upon which lean three major poles. Several lesser poles rest across these at right angles and are, in turn, lightly covered with oak and cottonwood boughs. Yazhe Clark's camp in Canyon del Muerto, Arizona, above Middle Trail Canyon, 1972.

Fig. 4.7. "Two-legged" double lean-to shade, with the ridgepole supported by two forked uprights. Hypothetical reconstruction.

Fig. 4.8. A good-sized ramada entirely walled with leaning logs. Closely set roof poles are piled with sticks and other vegetal material. What appears to be a fallen half-door probably is erected when livestock needs to be excluded. A stake-and-rider-fenced corral is visible in the left background. "White Horse's summer hogan, Douglas Mesa," Monument Valley (?), 1936; M.S.S. (1107).

Fig. 4.9. A large ramada, with six uprights. The few leaning wall poles and roof beams are supplemented with quantities of weed stalks and boughs; a sheet of canvas covers part of one wall. "Summer hogan of Hostin T'sosi (Mr. Slim) just east of Dinnehotso Day School," 1935; M.S.S. (859).

Fig. 4.10. Ramada or "summer hogan" with a flat, earth-covered roof. Three walls are of closely set leaning poles. Two forked vertical poles support a stringer at the right-hand wall's approximate mid-height level, but the stringer seems too far from the leaners to be designed to keep them in place; perhaps it is a drying rack. The fourth wall might be termed "stake-and-rail"; it consists of horizontal logs stacked between two of the ramada's main uprights on the interior side, and two exterior verticals near the wall ends. Southern Chuska Mountains, New Mexico, 1972.

Fig. 4.11. Ramada with three walls and the roof covered with brush held in place with wire; the entry wall is of horizontal planks, with a gap at head height. Note the home-made door. This is a summer field shelter. Near Rock Point, Arizona, 1970.

specimens made of pinyon and juniper poles, ranging in height from 3 feet (.9 m) to 6 feet (1.8 m). We have seen only two lean-to-shades, both "two-legged," one single, one double.

FLAT-ROOFED SHADE (RAMADA)

In simplest form, the ramada or flat-roofed shade consists of a flat roof of poles or boughs supported on stringers running between four vertical posts (Figs. 4.8, 4.9, 4.10, 4.11, 4.12). Ramadas are built by most or all Southwestern tribes including the Havasupai (Spier 1928: 178) and Apaches, although it is reportedly "modern" among the western and Chiricahua Apache (Gifford 1940: 23, 110; Schaeffer 1958: 19). It is apparently the only remaining Puebloan vestige of a construction technique once commonly used in the building of pit houses (for exteneded discussion, see "Vertical-Post Hogans," chapter 5). Central Alaskan Athapaskans also built summer

Fig. 4.12. View from the interior of a ramada similar to that shown in Fig. 4.11. Visible are: one of the forked corner uprights carrying a stringer, upon which rest several beams; a single horizontal midwall board on each side, attached to the upright; brush and weed stalks attached to the midwall boards. Near Rock Point, Arizona, 1970.

houses using vertical posts with stringers, but these were roofed with bowed poles (Clark 1974: 130–31). Navajo ramadas probably represent a Puebloan-refugee introduction. The earliest recorded evidence of Navajo use of a shade of this type has been unearthed in the Navajo Reservoir district of New Mexico. This large structure, as indicated by thirty-three post holes, was 56 feet long and 12 feet wide (17.1 by 3.7 m), and trapezoidal in plan. It dates from the Gobernador Phase (1696–1770); the earliest known leaning-log hogan, which was also at this site, seems to predate the shade slightly (Hester and Shiner 1963: 9, 14–15). Farmer (1947: 18) listed ramadas as being used in the Upper Largo drainage, New Mexico, in the period 1700–75. Early documentary evidence of this form includes an 1873 O'Sullivan photograph (Horan 1966: 292) and Stephen's (1890) description.

Temporal changes in ramada construction have been minimal and include the occasional use of some lumber, nails, and wire, and sometimes the use of unforked uprights.

A detailed description of flat-roofed shades follows:

Navajo name: chaha'oh = shade; *ni'í* = at ground (?).

Diagnostic feature: four or more vertical (occasionally slightly inclined) poles connected by stringers upon which rests a flat roof.

Other major features:

1. Wall structure: may be wall-less or have one or more loosely constructed walls of leaning poles and/or leaning planks or slabs, with or without a covering of brush (Figs. 4.8, 4.9, 4.17); half, three-quarter, and full walls of horizontal logs, poles, sawmill slabs, planks, and/or plywood—nailed to the verticals or held in place by supplemental corner verticals —have been observed (Fig. 4.10), as have full walls of brush, willow withes or maize and weed stalks held vertically against the stringers and midwall horizontals by an exterior horizontal wire or wires or by exterior horizontal poles attached with wire (Figs. 4.11, 4.12). Canvas walls have been noted, and partial walls of dry stone masonry have been recorded (Blackwood 1927: 227); partial walls of mortarless cinder blocks were observed in one instance. In another case, the space between the roof and the top of the three-quarters-height front wall was covered with window screening.

2. Plan: rectangular, subrectangular, trapezoidal, subpolygonal, or circular.

3. Roof: flat, with horizontally laid beams which support smaller-diameter poles or boughs; today, planks sometimes replace roof poles. Juniper, oak, cottonwood, or other boughs; brush, reeds, or grass; and/or blankets or canvas or, today, tarpaper or plastic sheeting held down by chicken wire and boughs, are usually laid over the roof poles. In a few cases, the roof is covered with earth (Fig. 4.10); this seems to have been more common in the past (Kluckhohn et al. 1971: 157).

Minor features and variations:

1. Tree crotches may serve in place of one or more of the vertical poles.[5] "When living Pinyon trees are incorporated in the shade house, the stumps of cut branches are sealed with mud to prevent the dripping of resin" (Vestal 1952: 13).

2. The vertical poles may be forked, sawed off square, rabbetted, or have saddle-shaped cuts in which stringers are laid; in one case, short planks were nailed at angles to the tops of the vertical posts to form pseudo-forked poles. The horizontal stringers are sometimes nailed and/or wired to the vertical posts of the frame (for variations, see Fig. 4.-13).

3. If the shade is completely walled, a vertical door frame and entryway may extend from the eastern wall. A sort of "front porch" roof may extend beyond the entry wall of the main shelter in the case of the enclosed shade (such "porches" are sometimes built immediately adjacent to hogans and houses as well).

4. Subpolygonal shades with walls in part cribbed, in part leaning-log, occur in and near Canyon de Chelly, Arizona (Fig. 1.3). Hayes

Fig. 4.13. Eight different means by which vertical posts support stringers.

(1964: 122) mentioned "a brush-covered, five-sided lean-to made by running poles between supporting trees" at Mesa Verde, Colorado.

5. Earth is occasionally piled along wall bases.

6. If only short poles are available, the floor may be excavated (Luomala 1938: 82). Open-fronted hillside dugout shades were mentioned by Hollister (1903: 70).

7. One structure intermediate between a ramada and a frame house was seen. It had walls of spaced horizontal planks, a doorway and a window, and a brush-covered gabled roof (see also, "Frame Shade," below). Another structure was seen near Tuba City, Arizona, consisting of four vertical posts supporting a camper body designed to fit the back of a pickup truck.

Construction and Use

The flat-roofed shade or ramada is by far the most common type of shade encountered today (for descriptions, see Kluckhohn et al. 1971: 157–62; Stephen 1890). The usual number of vertical supports is four, but six or more are common. Page (1937b: plate 7) pictured an example with eleven uprights, and Hester and Shiner (1963: 9, 14–15) recorded an archaeological example with thirty-three posts. Ramadas often occur without walls, but one or more walls or half-walls are commonly added to afford protection from the wind and wind-blown sand. Four-walled "summer hogans" or ceremonial "hogans" of this same genre are not infrequently seen; their leaners are often covered with brush, and they may have plank

Fig. 4.14. Summer fireplace of stone-and-mud masonry, with a sheet of steel over the closed end. Provision is made for the attachment of a stovepipe. A homemade table stands in the right background. Chauncey and Dorothy Neboyia's summer farm homestead, Zuni Trail, Canyon de Chelly, Arizona, 1972.

door frames (Figs. 4.8, 4.9, 4.10, 4.11, 4.12, 4.17). Unlike some Pueblo ramadas, Navajo ramadas seldom have earth-covered roofs today and are not used as above-ground working or lookout platforms, although they are sometimes used as drying and storage areas, keeping produce, fodder, or hay above the reach of livestock (Fig. 10.12). Ramadas are used mainly as summer living, cooking, and working areas, and often shelter rug looms. They often contain wooden-crate cupboards for utensils and may have nails driven into the uprights for hanging clothing and equipment (Landgraf 1954:50). Large ramadas are also constructed for guests at ceremonials. One measured 51 feet (15.54 m) long, 18 feet (5.49 m) wide, and 8 feet (2.44 m) high (Kluckhohn et al. 1971: 157). The number of hearths under such a structure reflects the number of visiting families. If walled, such a structure may have multiple doorways, and the interior may be partitioned with canvas hangings or pole walls. Such shades are typically built just northward of the ritual hogan for Enemyway ceremonials, for the sway dancers (Haile 1950: 153).

Rectangular or narrow horseshoe-shaped, open-ended, dry-laid stone masonry summer fireplaces are often built under or just beyond the northern edge of shades, or under shady trees (Fig. 7.10); once in a while a vertical-slab fireplace is built instead. These fireplaces are occasionally mistakenly called ovens. They frequently have one end covered with sheet metal, from which may rise a length of stovepipe (Fig. 4.14; Anonymous 1970: 21). This fireplace form may derive from similar, all-steel Anglo camp stoves in use around the turn of the century (e.g., a 1906 Charles F. Lummis photograph, Southwest Museum archives). Nevertheless, sheet-metal griddles (*bik'i'it'eesí* = on which cooking is done) are successors to stone-slab griddles (*tsét'ees* = cooking stone; Kluckhohn et al. 1971: 127–28). One case of a steel cannister lid set on four piers of rock for use as a hibachi was observed (Fig. 5.55). Three or four rocks used as pot, griddle, or spit sup-

Fig. 4.15. Presumed octagonal corbeled-log-roof shade. The ends of the eight principal uprights are sawn square, but the supplemental upright at the left has a saddle-cut end. The conical arrangement of logs at the left is probably a firewood pile. Barely discernible behind and to the left of the shade is a high horizontal pole, the visible end of which rests on a limb of the juniper tree. A Manson Apples carton lies on the wagon. Cedar Ridge area, Arizona, 1970.

ports (*tsé bijááh* = rock's leg) in cooking fires were described by Kluckhohn et al. (1971: 129).

CORBELED-LOG-ROOF SHADE

There is a rare shade type which has a corbeled-log roof (for a full description of this roof type, see chapter 9). It is presumably derivative from vertical-post hogans (see chapter 5). Its characteristics are:

Navajo name: yaadahaskánígo chaha'oh = under-the-dome shade.

Diagnostic feature: corbeled-log roof on uprights (Fig. 4.15).

Other major features:

1. Wall structure: appears always to be wall-less between the half-dozen or so vertical-log supports.

2. Plan: polygonal.

3. Roof: corbeled-log, with no covering material.

Construction and Use

This extremely rare form is simply a non-earth-covered corbeled-log roof supported by vertical posts. It looks like an unfinished hogan and is used as a shade (Fig. 4.15). It is mentioned in the literature only by the Franciscan Fathers (1910: 336), Roberts (1951: 42), and Ellis (1974: 261, after Van Valkenburgh), and we have seen only one apparently definite specimen, near Cedar Ridge, Arizona. A second structure in the same area bearing an incomplete but earth-covered roof was not clearly either a shade or an unfinished hogan.

FRAME SHADE

This category was created to accommodate a single structure photographed by Jerrold E. Levy at Tuba City. It was constructed like a wall-less frame house with a balustrade. It was located on a slope, and a masonry platform had been built to provide a level base.

Diagnostic feature: frame roof on uprights.

Other major features:

1. Wall structure: wall-less between corner uprights, or with a "balustrade" of vertical planks between which gaps are left.

2. Plan: rectangular.

3. Roof: low-gabled; other forms may exist.

Minor feature:

1. May be erected upon a stone-masonry foundation platform.

TENTS

A commercially made tent is not infrequently employed as a substitute for, or supplement to, the pole-and-brush shade or "summer hogan," as a temporary dwelling while a hogan is being built, or in cases where frequent moving of flocks is necessary.

Tents were issued to some Navajos at Ft. Sumner (Underhill 1956: 128), and an 1863 photograph of the fort shows a wall tent (Bailey 1964: 160, 178). Wall tents also appear in an 1880s (?) photograph of Ft. Defiance (Frink 1968: 31). Marmon (1894: 157), writing of the 1890 census, noted that "some of the well-to-do [Navajos] buy wall or officers' tents and use them" in summer. Hollister (1903: 72) wrote, "In recent years the common [conical] Sibley tent has been used in summer to some extent,

as it is less work to take it down, move and set up again . . ." Reichard (1928: 7) wrote that "Frequently too when the family can afford it, the brush shade is supplemented by a canvas tent which is pitched behind the shelter." Page (1937b: 48) stated that "if the family is fairly well-to-do, the summer house usually is a tent" but that ramadas are more usual. Wall tents (Figs. 4.16, 4.17) were moderately common during the 1970s, but conical (Fig. 4.17) ones were no longer used. Wall tents and the technique of erection described below have for many years been used by Anglo-Americans (Kephart 1917: 46),[6] and this is no doubt the source of Navajo usage.

The Plains tipi (Fig. 4.18) is not a traditional Navajo dwelling, but it has been observed on occasion among the Navajo (Page 1937b: 48, plates 4 and 27; Spencer and Jett 1971: 168). It is a result of relatively modern contacts with Indians of Plains culture. A ca. 1900 photograph by Carl N. Werntz in the Museum of New Mexico archives shows a crude tipi, supposedly Navajo. Southern Utes, who occupy a reservation adjacent to the Navajo Reservation and with whom Navajos trade and sometimes intermarry, use canvas (formerly hide) tipis (Forrest 1970: 170, 172–73, 177, 184), as do some Apache groups. Brugge (personal communication) was informed of turn-of-the-century tipis of small size and without smoke flaps, used as temporary camp structures among the Aneth-area Navajos in Utah, and he suggests imitation of nearby Ute tipis. The hearths were placed outside and in front of the Navajo tipis. Newcomb (1966: plate opposite p. 39) pictured a small tipi near Newcomb, New Mexico, apparently dating to the 1920s. Some contemporary occurrences may be cases of Plains Indians visiting Navajo friends, but "modern use of tipis seem to be related almost, if not entirely, to religious use for peyote services [Native American Church], although these are also held in hogans" (David M. Brugge, personal communication, 1971).

The principal tent types used by Navajos are described below:

Fig. 4.16. Wall tent, held up by ropes attached to exterior poles and to a guy frame. The lower edges of the walls are held down by being tied to poles lying on the ground, parallel to the canvas. Below Standing Cow Ruin, Canyon del Muerto, Arizona, 1972.

Navajo name: níbaal = fabric hanging linearly.

Diagnostic feature: walls and roof of machine-woven fabric.

Wedge Tent

Major features:

1. Wall structure: vertical fabric (on the ends only) supported by two vertical end-poles and guy lines.

2. Plan: oblong.

3. Roof: Gabled, of the same materials as the end walls; the eaves rest upon the ground. (This type is documented only by one Ben Wittick photograph, in the Museum of New Mexico collection.)

Wall Tent

Major features:

1. Wall structure: vertical fabric supported by two vertical end-poles and guy lines (Fig. 4.16, 4.17).

2. Plan: oblong.

3. Roof: gabled, of the same material as the walls; a ridge pole is often used.

Minor features and variations:

1. A guy frame is characteristic (Fig. 4.-16). This involves a pair of vertical poles supporting a stringer, one on each side of the tent, a few feet from, and paralleling, the wall; the guy ropes are tied to the stringers or cross them before descending to tent pegs (e.g., Roberts 1951: 42; Tremblay et al. 1954: 200, 205).

Fig. 4.17. Navajo camp. Left to right middleground: a wagon with a water drum, a drying rack with airing bedding, a wall tent with external poles supporting the corners (note the stovepipe), a ramada (note the suspended horizontal pole with blankets), a palisade-fence corral beyond the wagon wheels, a conical U.S.A. tent supported by a center pole and guy frames. Just beyond the post-and-wire fence in the foreground is an accumulation of vegetal debris; the ax on the ground suggests a log-debarking or firewood-chopping site. Two miles north of Steamboat, 1935; M.S.S. (1071).

2. Tent sites may be smoothed before use. Reher (1977: 39, 52, 60, 62) observed "semi-subterranean tent bases" in the lower Chaco River, New Mexico, area. These appear to have been rectangular excavations over which tents would be erected. Large rocks sometimes placed around the peripheries may have held the canvas down or may have been used in connection with guy ropes. These "dugout tents" apparently served to improve insulation during autumn use. Often associated is a substantial masonry fireplace with a stone-slab mantle and a 2-meter-high (6.6 ft) chimney, built in one-half of the tent's entry.

3. A hole may be cut in the roof to receive a stove pipe (Tremblay et al. 1954: 205).

4. Roberts (1951: 18, 42) reported that all tents in the Ramah area had windbreak-style shades at their entries.

5. A Snow photograph of 1935 (2281) shows a weaver shaded by blankets strung from the loom to other vertical posts.

Pyramidal Tent

Major features:

1. Wall structure: canvas, supported by a center pole, spreaders, and guy lines tied to vertical poles, and held down at the edges by pegs.

2. Plan: square.

3. Roof: pyramidal (the profile of the whole tent is that of a bent pyramid).

Fig. 4.18. Plains tipi employing twelve poles. Note the smoke flaps. An arrangement of boards temporarily closes the entry. Black Creek Valley, Arizona, 1968; V.E.S.

Conical Army Tent

Major features:

1. Wall structure: canvas, supported by a center pole and guy lines (Fig. 4.17).

2. Plan: polygonal, approaching circular.

3. Roof: pyramidal, but approaching conical.

Tipi

Navajo name: níbaal yadiits'ózígíí = cone-shaped sideways hanging loosely (i.e., tent).

Diagnostic feature: fabric over about eight poles which rest on a conical framework of three or four poles lashed together below the apex.

Major features:

1. Wall structure: canvas over poles (Fig. 4.18).

2. Plan: circular or polygonal.

3. Roof: inseparable from the walls.

Variation:

1. McAllester and McAllester (1980: 63) picture a tipi against which saplings had been leaned to hold in place boughs covering the upper two-thirds of the structure.

Use

Tents are sometimes used as substitutes for ramadas, or serve as temporary dwellings for transients or while a permanent dwelling is being erected or while the family is endeavoring to accumulate funds to build such a dwelling (Tremblay et al. 1954: 204–05; Reher 1977: 39). Reichard (1939: 7) wrote that "Frequently . . . when the family can afford it, the brush shade is supplemented by a canvas tent . . . where food and valuables are stored." A wall tent is occasionally used as a roof (see "Tent Roof," chapter 8).

Sibley (wall-less) and U.S.A. (walled) conical tents (Fig. 4.17) were used by army officers and were acquired by some Navajos in the late nineteenth and early twentieth centuries (Kephard, 1917: 78–81; Marmon 1894: 157; Hollister 1903: 72; Snow photo 1074). They are no longer used.

Plains-style tipis (Fig. 4.18) are rare among the Navajo, and usually occur in association with other, more substantial dwellings (Page 1937b: 48, plates 4 and 27; Spencer and Jett 1971: 166). Although small tipis were once used as ordinary temporary shelters in the Aneth area, tipi use today seems to be mainly in connection with rites of the Native American church.

WAGONS AND PICKUPS AS TEMPORARY DWELLINGS

Among temporary dwellings—if not precisely folk housing—are wagons and pickup trucks. As Wilmsen (1960: 18–19) has written,

another interesting development in living units has occurred on the reservation. When the traders came in force during the 80s one of the items they brought with them was the covered wagon, and the Navaho took to it quickly. . . . The wagon became a home on wheels; it never replaced the permanent, stationary hogan, but many families found that it served very well on the long trips to summer pasture and, indeed, was quite acceptable as a home while at pasture, especially since it allowed free movement to find the best grass. The wagon also allowed the whole family to attend the great religious ceremonials and numerous local fairs. . . . The wagon held its own for 70 years or so but in time it, too, was replaced. Since the end of World War II, and particularly since 1950, the pick-up truck has become the mobile home. . . . Small cabins have sometimes been built onto the bed of the truck and a great deal of ingenuity has been shown in their equipment.

Increasingly, commercially made "camper bodies" are seen installed over the beds of Navajo pickup trucks. Buckboards have nearly gone out of use, and we have not seen a canvas wagon cover in years.

Chapter 5

HOGAN ORIGINS, EVOLUTIONS, AND FORMS

DUGOUT STRUCTURES

The earliest recorded definite description of a Navajo dwelling is that of Benavides (Ayer 1916: 44) in 1630, which mentions a "*vivienda debaxo de tierra*." This expression has been interpreted as meaning a "dwelling under the ground"—that is, a pit dwelling or dugout (Brugge 1968a: 16); however, the phrase could perhaps be equally well translated as "dwelling under earth," that is, an earth-covered dwelling, a description that could apply to any of the more traditional hogan types (particularly if they had excavated floors) without implying a truly undergound habitation. (Whether or not earth covering of dwellings was characteristic of the Navajo at this early date is debatable, however. See below.)

The conical forked-pole hogan (described below) is the type most frequently mentioned in legend and song (Haile 1937: 8),[2] and most Navajos today consider the conical forked-hogan the oldest house type used by their people and the type most intimately associated with their religion. There is a minority opinion, however, that the earliest hogan type was a pit or semi-pit house [see Page, 1937b: 47; Franciscan Fathers, 1910: 327; Johnson 1977: 315] . . . the 'tlehoged' or dugout hogan, may well be a continuation of this tradition. [Brugge 1968a: 16; see also Kluckhohn et al. 1971: 144, 150][3]

However, according to the Franciscan Fathers (1910: 327, 335), this pit dwelling (*łeeh hoogeedgo hooghan* = into-earth-dug-space hogan) was little more than a hole in the ground, roofed with mats and entered by a ladder (see also Parsons 1923: 273–74). The ladder and mats were taken along when a move was made. Navajo archaeology includes, at present, no entirely subterranean dwellings and very few dugouts of any kind (e.g., Littell 1967–6: appendix I). Although conical forked-pole hogans often had excavated floors, particularly when logs were difficult to obtain, the pit-house tradition appears to refer to something other than these hogans. References to dugouts could conceivably relate to the pre-Ft. Sumner period, during which, because of warfare, Navajos were reduced to hiding in caves, crevices, and the like. (Among the Athapaskan Kaska of British Columbia, children were secreted from enemy attack by being hidden under hides [and earth?] in pits. An informant also stated that " 'a long time ago people dug into the side of a hill' for a place to live" [Honigmann 1954: 59–60].) Too, during the Ft. Sumner sojourn, owing to a lack of timber "the latest comers dug round holes in the ground, as deep as possible without the earthen walls falling in. Then they covered these with branches [in conical form in one photograph] and brush . . . canvas . . . and cowhides and even buffalo hides" (Underhill 1953: 169; see also, Link 1968: 3). Or, the tradition about pit habitations could possibly represent a folk memory introduced by Puebloans who joined the Athapaskans, for their ancestors did indeed live in pit dwellings, with rooftop entryways, though not usually as rudimentary as those described in the Navajo tradition (Bullard 1962; McGregor 1965: 312). Too, Ellis (1960: 6) claimed that Acoma and Laguna Puebloan hunters and herders sometimes dug pits into the earth as temporary shelters, and Kluckhohn et al. (1971: 160) reported Navajo travelers digging sleeping pits about 3 by 3 by 7 feet (.9 by .9 by 2.1 m), which would be preheated by burning brush inside, then removing the ashes; heated rocks would be placed under the feet.

Alaska, British Columbia, and California Athapaskans built earth-covered semisubterranean dwellings, as well as, in Alaska, large subsurface caches similar to dugouts, although the linguistically closest known Northern Athapaskan relatives of the Navajo did not.[4] In any case, all of the Alaska and many of the California dwellings had "tunnel" entryways (a term apparently including surface extended entryways; Driver and Massey 1957: 307–09; Osgood 1940: 333). Thus, it does not seem possible to say whether the pit tradition derives from the north or was acquired from Puebloans or was developed spontaneously on the Plains or in the Southwest in response to a lack of timber. In any case, James (1905: 642) mentioned dugout dwellings in timber-poor areas, and a number of Navajos told Hill

in the 1930s (Kluckhohn et al., 1971: 152) of contemporary lean-to-covered pit dwellings up to 7 feet (2.1 m) deep; it is not stated how these were entered (present-day dugouts are entered from the end, not the roof). Informants disagreed as to whether this type of dwelling was early or late in origin. Most contemporary dugouts are rectangular, with gabled roofs; however, Figure 5.1 shows a dugout whose flat roof is essentially flush with the ground.

Although the ultimate sources and antiquity of Navajo dugout dwellings remain obscure, it seems likely that modern dugout houses (see chapter 7), used mainly for storage, represent a fusion of Anglo-American dugout structures with the forms and functions of older Navajo ones. Anglo dugouts date to early Colonial times in the eastern United States and were widely used in the American West during the nineteenth century. They were often used as dwellings until better houses could be built (for example, by the first Mormon settlers of Escalante, Utah, in 1875 [Woolsey 1964: 50], and in West Texas [Jordan 1978: 111, 113, 184, 208])—after which they were used mainly for storing produce ("root cellars"). (For further discussion, see chapter 2.)

CONICAL FORKED-POLE HOGAN

Age

Whatever the situation with regard to dugout dwellings, the Athapaskan ancestors of the Navajo presumably constructed dwellings, including conical forked-pole shades, similar to those used by their close cultural and linguistic relatives who remained in Canada.

The earliest dated archaeological hogans are of the conical forked-pole type, which is similar to the conical forked-pole shade but is earth-covered (Figs. 5.2, 5.3, 1.1, 1.2). This finding may in part reflect the fact that this form is assumed to be earliest and so has often been the only type sought and recognized as being early, but it no doubt also reflects the fact that this type *was* the most common early form. Brugge (1968a: 16), a most experienced worker, flatly stated that "The vast majority of early hogans . . . are the conical forked-pole type."

In regard to dating, Brugge (1968a: 16) wrote:

While a number of Athapaskan sites have produced pre-1700 tree-ring dates, none of the structures in these sites can be conclusively shown to have dated well prior to 1700. This does not necessarily mean that some of these sites may not have had earlier occupation, but the structural remains visible on the surface cannot be shown to be earlier.

(No attempt will be made here to analyze the early tree-ring dating of forked-pole hogans, nor the evidence for the date of initial

Fig. 5.1. Dugout in flat ground, consisting simply of an entry and a flat roof placed over the excavation. Post-and-wire clothesline at the left, a plank privy at the right. Cedar Ridge, Arizona, 1970.

Fig. 5.2. Conical forked-pole hogan with partially eroded earth cover; underlying juniper bark, maize (?) stalks, and broadleaf boughs are revealed. Note the somewhat extended entry and the stones (door slabs?) at the right-hand base of the entry. Teec Nos Pos, Arizona, 1935; M.S.S. (1069).

Fig. 5.3. A conical forked-pole hogan whose earth covering shows evidence of recent renewal. Note the stovepipe emerging from the smoke hole, and the homemade door (which lacks a hasp). A storage platform stands at the right. On the ground in front of the children are a Navajo saddle blanket and, on the goat pelt, three pitch-covered wicker water bottles. "Hostin Bekini's winter hogan, with two [sic] of his children," Dinnehotso area, Arizona, 1935; M.S.S. (880).

Athapaskan penetration into the Southwest.[5]) Almost all explicit early accounts and depictions of Navajo dwellings are of conical hogans exclusively, the earliest being that of Tronosco in 1788 (Worcester 1947: 220).[6] The above considerations suggest that the conical forked-pole hogan was an, or the, initial Navajo type; it was certainly the typical form during the last three-quarters of the nineteenth century and into the early twentieth century (e.g., Mindeleff 1898; Stephen 1893: 350; Ostermann 1908: 862).

Conical Form, Forked Poles, and Earth Covering

In historic times, many Canadian Athapaskans built crude conical huts consisting of a tripod or tetrapod frame of poles, on which additional poles were rested, the whole then being covered with hides, bark, brush, boughs, or combinations of these. The hides and bark were not sewn together; "they were simply laid on like thatch and held down with additional poles tied on the outside" (Driver and Massey 1957: 299, 303–06). The ultimate source of this type of dwelling probably cannot be traced, for it occurred very widely in North America and northern Eurasia in pre-Columbian times. One may hazard the guess, however, that it had a single, very ancient origin somewhere in northern Asia.

Navajo use of forked poles appears to be of northern origin. The Alaskan Athapaskan Kutchin tipi had three foundation poles, one of which was forked and received the other two (McKennan 1965: 43).

The ordinary dwelling of the [Canadian Athapaskan] Beaver was a [hide-covered] tipi of the general Northern or Chipewyan type. It has a three-pole foundation but these poles are usually not tied at the place of crossing as is the case in the Plains, since they are either forked or have projecting limbs so that they interlock. The tops of the remaining poles which make up the foundation rest in the top of this tripod. [Goddard 1916: 210]

The historical Navajo conical forked-pole hogan seems to differ from these Northern Athapaskan huts mainly in having earth as the

external covering; bark, brush, or other vegetal material underlies this covering, and the
earth does away with the need for external
poles to hold down the bark (although boughs
are occasionally laid down to protect the earth
covering from livestock). In the Southwest,
where large sheets of bark and large hides were
not readily available and where the climate is
fairly dry, earth was a logical principal covering (it also improves insulation). Although one
northwestern Navajo told Stewart (1942: 257,
338–39) that earth-covered hogans had been
made only since the introduction of iron shovels, Navajos were described as early as 1786 as
living in "sod huts" (Thomas 1932: 348).
Brugge (1968a: 19) suggested that the use of
forked poles in conical hogans was a local innovation in Dinétah, following the arrival of
Puebloan refugees beginning in 1692, and a
response to the added weight of an earth (as
opposed to a purely vegetal) covering; he considered the earth covering to be of Puebloan
origin, reflecting a Puebloan preference for
more substantial, permanent dwellings than
those originally constructed by Athapaskans.
Navajo construction involving close-set poles
plus vegetal matter plus earth is identical to
that of many Puebloan roofs (e.g., Mindeleff
1891: 149–51) except that hogan sides are inclined, not horizontal (Jett 1981). The use of
interlocking forked poles among certain of the
Navajo's northern linguistic relatives, however, and the not infrequent use of this technique (with four main poles) among the White
Mountain Apache for brush-covered wikiups
(Schaeffer 1958: 14, 17), indicate that the more
parsimonious hypothesis is that Athapaskans
brought this trait to the Southwest.[7] However,
even though use of forked poles by the Navajo
probably preceded contact with Puebloans,
the adoption of earth covering may well have
been a consequence of such contacts and have
resulted in the use of stronger—and less perishable—frameworks, as suggested by Brugge
(1968a: 19).

Another possible origin of the earth covering is the Navajo's having learned its use from
Plains Indians during migrations from the
north. Although too little attention has been
paid to a possible Plains-Southeast origin of
certain aspects of Navajo culture (see Hester
1962: 70), various facts militate against this
hypothesis: (1) pre-Columbian Plains earth
lodges were found mainly in the eastern Plains
(Driver and Massey 1957: 308); (2) non-
Navajo Apacheans, who presumably followed
a similar migration route, seldom use earth
covering but instead retained the usual northern custom of covering their conical wikiups
only with brush, grass, bark, and/or hides;[8]
(3) the Zuni word for "hogan" means "brush
or leaf shelter," implying that the Navajo
dwellings earliest observed by the Zuni lacked
an earthen covering (Cushing 1886: 474); and
(4) most of the earliest conical-forked-pole-
hogan remains are found in Dinétah, where
the most intensive Navajo and Pueblo-refugee
contacts took place—the adoption of earth
covering and stronger frameworks would have
resulted in archaeologically more preservable
structures.[9]

A barely possible origin of the conical
earth-covered hogan is through a survival of
the early Modified Basketmaker (Basketmaker
III) practice of building conical earth-covered
pithouses (Bullard 1962: 127–28). However,
this type of pithouse used four or more principal poles for the structure's framework, and
the poles were probably lashed together,
rather than employing interlocking forked
poles. Too, this sort of pithouse may well have
been extinct by the time the Navajo entered
the Southwest (Wormington 1947: 49–50;
McGregor 1965: 208–10). The slightly excavated floors of conical hogans suggest a possible influence from Anasazi pit dwellings but
other plausible explanations also come to
mind (see below).

Finally, the practice of earth-covering
could conceivably have accompanied the
proto-Navajo on their way southward. Some
Alaskan and Yukon Athapaskan groups covered their rectangular dwellings with sod or
earth (Driver and Massey 1957: 295, 308; Osgood 1940: 295, 304, 313; Vanstone 1974: 34,
36). Although most Northern Athapaskan

conical dwellings were not earth-covered, at least the Kaska and some Sekani of British Columbia sometimes covered their conical habitations with sod (and occasionally used stone foundations; Honigmann 1954: 59, 62). However, most of the arguments against adoption of earth covering from Plains tribes also apply to a possible northern source.

Extended Doorways

Many conical forked-pole hogans possess vestibules known as extended doorways (Figs. 5.2, 5.5, 5.8). The origin of these entryways is problematical. They are attested to in the earliest recognizable description of a conical forked-pole hogan, the Tronosco doucment of 1788: "[the dwelling] is like a field tent, except that it had a small, square room at the entrance" (Worcester 1947: 220). Archaeological extended doorways date to at least as early as the Gobernador Phase (1696–1770) in the Navajo Reservoir district (Hester and Shiner 1963: 10–14; see also Carlson 1965: 9–15). Brugge (1968a: 19) considered the extended entry to be an Athapaskan trait. Modern Western Apaches often build extended doorways of planks on their conical wikiups. These have been said to be recent, dating to about the 1920s (Schaeffer 1958: 18; Baldwin 1965: 71), although a photograph in Curtis (1907: plate opposite p. 15) shows a short extended entryway on a thatched wikiup. There is reason to believe that the plank entry was preceded by longer, curved entryways of natural materials, constructed to keep out the wind (Gifford 1940: 107–08). The extended doorway is apparently not present among those northern groups linguistically most closely related to the Navajo, nor among those whose predominant dwelling was the conical hut. Extended doorways did occur on many Plains earth lodges (Driver and Massey 1957: 295, 298, 308–09) and were found on some kinds of prehistoric Anasazi pithouses (Bullard 1962: 137). Certain California Athapaskan tribes built semisubterranean houses with extended doorways (Driver and Massey 1957: 309), and if Navajo traditions of the clans created by

Changing Woman having migrated to Navajoland from the shores of the western sea (Underhill 1956: 22) have a basis in fact, then California, too, must be considered as a possible source. None of these sources seems particularly likely, however, and extended entries may well be a local innovation intended to keep precipitation out of dwellings having excavated floors, and to provide a vertical doorway for hanging a hide or blanket entry cover. The vestibule may also originally have served a defensive function (Jett 1981).

Excavated Floors

Despite its insulation and other advantages, excavation of floors seems not to have been a Northern Athapaskan trait in those areas geographically and linguistically closest to the Navajo (e.g., Helm and Lurie 1961: 44), but it had been anciently practiced in the Southwest (Bullard 1962) as well as ethnographically in Alaska, California, and on the Columbia Plateau (Driver and Massey 1957: 295–99). It is also recorded for the Western Apache (Gifford 1940: 108), where it is possibly of Navajo origin. The Navajo often excavate hogan floors, leaving a peripheral shelf. Whether the Navajo emulated this practice or developed it spontaneously as a response to a paucity of long timbers and to provide earth for the exterior covering, or for other reasons, cannot be said (see "Dugout Structures," above). In view of the hogan's religious role, however, it is possible that the inspiration was the semisubterranean ceremonial kivas of Puebloan refugees' home villages (Jett 1981).

A detailed description of conical forked-pole hogans follows:

Navajo name: hooghan 'ałch'į' adeez'á (or deez'á[h]í) = converging-points hogan.

Diagnostic feature: a (normally) tripod frame of poles whose (normally) forked ends are interlocked at the apex (Fig. 5.4).

Other major features:

1. Wall structure: Two parallel poles are ordinarily leaned against the tripod frame to

Fig. 5.4. Interlocked forked poles and leaners (eastern ones missing) of a partially ruined conical forked-pole hogan. The main southern pole is received by the main northern pole, and the main western pole receives these two. Artists Point, Monument Valley, Arizona, 1978.

form the entryway. The gaps between the main poles are filled with smaller poles leaned against the frame and each other (*bighą́ą́dę́ę́' bíniizhoozhí* = [rigid] objects that lie parallel leaning against it; *bighą́ą́dę́ę́' bínii'nilí* = [rigid] objects that were placed against it); a second layer of even smaller-diameter poles may be added. Short logs are laid horizontally across the middle parts of the entry poles; the lowest of these horizontals may be supported by the ends of two logs lying atop the lower parts of the entry poles, by branch stubs left on the entry poles, or in some other fashion; a gap of perhaps 3.5 feet (1.07 m) is left between the top horizontal (*ch'ílá[h]dei* and the apex of the hogan, as a smoke hole (an *apical* smoke appears in a ca. 1896 Simeon Schemberger photograph [Museum of Northern Arizona]; a smoke hole in the *side* of the hogan, just north

of the entry pole, is pictured in Kluckhohn et al. 1971: 144). The entire exterior is chinked with sticks, bark (usually from junipers), burlap, or other materials, and an external covering of earth is applied (Figs. 5.2, 5.3, 5.5, 5.6).

2. Plan: circular, oval, or D-shaped (Fig. 2.6).

3. Roof: inseparable from the walls.

Minor features and variations:

1. The floor is normally excavated within the main poles of the framework, to a depth of from 6 to 24 inches (15.24 to 60.96 cm) and sometimes, where timber is scarce, up to 5 feet (1.62 m), creating a dugout hogan or "pit house" (Fig. 5.7). Excavation leaves an earth shelf or "bench" perhaps a foot (.30 m) wide around the interior of the hogan (Hobbs 1942: 152). Peripheral interior benches built up or shored with slabs of rock have also been

Fig. 5.5. Skeleton of an abandoned and eroded conical forked-pole hogan with an extended entry. Note the short logs laid across the upper parts of the south-side leaners. Rock Point, Arizona, 1962.

Fig. 5.6. Interior of the conical forked-pole hogan in Fig. 5.3. Visible are two main poles, leaners, and vegetal covering (appearing to include brush, weeds, maizehusks, and juniper bark). An oil-drum stove stands in the center, carrying a stovepipe made of a smaller drum, a bucket, and a rolled sheet of metal encircled by a wire. Teec Nos Pos, Arizona, 1935; M.S.S. (1070).

recorded archaeologically (Keur 1941: 31; James 1976: 27; cf. masonry benches in Puebloan kivas). The floor is usually simply packed earth, but sand (Brewer 1936) and flagstone (Taylor 1965) floors have been described.[10] Vivian (1960: 17–18) mentioned an archaeological example, the downslope portion of whose floor was built up with earth piled behind a dry-stone retaining wall.

2. If forked poles cannot be obtained, unforked poles may be used; baling wire or barbed wire (and probably formerly yucca fiber) is used to lash these (or forked) poles at the point of crossing (Thomas et al. 1974: 21).

3. Hogans with tetrapod frames have been recorded (Page 1937b: plate 3; Keur 1941: 23; James 1976: 38), and Farmer (1942: 68) reported archaeological hogans with five- and six-forked-pole frameworks in Blanco and Largo canyons, New Mexico. In such cases, distinct entryway poles may be lacking. Keur (1941: 23–24) and Vivian (1960: 9) reported occasional incorporation of living trees in archaeological hogan structures, as do Navajo Land Claim Site Reports.

4. The wall poles directly opposite the doorway may be set 8 to 15 inches (19.32 to 38.10 cm) outside of the general line of the walls to form an interior "mask recess" (Fig. 2.6), which is used to contain masks and other ceremonial objects during the ministrations of a Singer (medicine man), especially during Nightway ceremonies. The mask recess is normally found only in larger hogans (Mindeleff 1898: 493; Ostermann 1917: 26). In a hogan built for Mountaintopway, there is instead a recess in the north wall, to hide one of the characters during rites of the fifth night (Matthews 1887: 418; 1902: 49; Luomala 1938: 84). Possibly, the recess is an analog of the recessed platform in "keyhole-shaped" Puebloan kivas.

5. Carlson (1965: 10) described the following unusual eighteenth-century variant on wall structure in the Gobernador Canyon area

Fig. 5.7. Homestead in a treeless area, with a dugout conical forked-pole hogan in the foreground. Partial erosion of the earth covering reveals brush underneath. Note the canvas (?) doorway curtain, the pelt airing above the entry, and the fragment of a Borden's condensed milk crate on the side to the right. The conical forked-pole hogan in the left middleground has a homemade plank door. Probably between Dinnehotso and Mexican Water, Arizona, 1935; M.S.S. (875).

of New Mexico: "Sticks had then been placed horizontally across this [conical] framework 90 to 120 cm (35.4 to 47.2 in.) above the ground and below them shorter vertical sticks had been placed reaching to the ground." An example of this type of hogan is shown in a photograph by Goddard (1909–10: 14480); its leaners extend only to about one-third of the height of the walls, whose upper parts are made of horizontal logs (see also Fig. 5.5). A 1908 photograph (Museum of Northern Arizona, Earle R. Forrest Collection, plate 136-B) shows a conical forked-pole hogan in which horizontal logs entirely replace leaners.

6. If wood is scarce, short lengths may be spliced together to make leaners (Franciscan Fathers 1910: 330; Haile 1942: 44). Mindeleff (1900: 234) described leaners that were "laced and bound together."

7. A "door slab" or pier of rock, or a pile of stones ("entry marker"), or an extra post, was formerly placed under, against, or next to each of the entry posts so that the east side could always be recognized and to symbolize that the hogan and its songs would endure forever (Fig. 5.2).[11] According to Haile (1937: 3), "present practice largely ignores [door slabs]," and Van Valkenburgh (1940b: 24) wrote that "They are not used by the Navajo of today." Some conical forked-pole hogans, both archaeological and modern, have slabs of stone leaned against the bases of their exterior walls; there may be only a few stones, or slabs may be set around the entire perimeter of the wall.[12] According to Shufeldt (1892: 279), concial hogans built in 1885 near Ft. Wingate, New Mexico, had rocks placed inside and out, at the bases of the less secure timbers; he also mentioned stones sometimes being placed around the smoke hole. Underhill (1956: plate opposite p. 33) reproduced a Ben Wittick photograph of what appears to be conical forked-pole hogan whose exterior is entirely veneered with slabs of stone, and Backus (1854: 213) wrote that "On the outside [of hogans], against the sticks, are placed flat stones and earth, to cover the intervals, and protect them from the weather." Vivian (1960: 14) mentioned two archaeological hogans whose bases were surrounded by a tier or two of horizontal logs, probably to hold the leaners in place and to retard erosion.

8. Mindeleff (1898: 495) described a semicircular hogan, which lacked entry poles and leaners on the entry side; these structures were for summer use. The authors have not observed any of these half-conical hogans.

9. Sometimes the entry poles do not rest upon the ground but have their lower ends supported by vertical posts; this results in a vertical rather than a sloping entryway. Or, more commonly, a vestibule or extended entryway (ch'íládai[gi] = above the exit top) 4 to 6 feet (1.22 to 1.83 m) high may be added (Figs. 5.2, 5.5, 5.8). These are occasionally so large as almost to constitute an added room. Two vertical posts are placed between the inclined entry poles or at their lower ends or some distance beyond them, and a stringer is usually set on or nailed to the forked or unforked ends of these uprights. Two straight or forked horizontal or inclined poles run between this stringer (or the ends of the vertical posts if the stringer is absent) and (1) the middle or upper portions of the main door-frame poles (which may be notched); or (2) the forks of the tripod; or (3) a stringer spanning the entry poles (sometimes supported by two forked poles that lie along the entry poles).[13] Logs (sometimes split), lying either perpendicular or, less commonly, parallel to the above-mentioned horizontal or inclined poles, form the roof of the vestibule ([ch'é'étiin] bikáádéé' nanizhoozhí = [exit trail']s [slender rigid] objects that lie parallel extending across); if parallel, their ends rest on the stringer connecting the vertical posts, and on the horizontal which forms the lower edge of the smoke hole (or, if there are several horizontals, on the lowest). The gap between the entry poles, the verticals, and the vestibule roof are filled by logs and/or planks (ch'é'étiin bighą́ą́déé' bíniizhoozhí = [slender rigid] objects that lean against it lying parallel from exit

Fig. 5.8. Details of extended-entry variants on abandoned conical forked-pole hogans: (left) forked-pole uprights supplemented by square-ended vertical posts (see Fig. 5.4; Artists Point, Monument Valley, Arizona, 1978); (right) complex arrangement of square-ended vertical posts, rabbetted roof beams, and planks (Cedar Ridge, Arizona, 1978).

trail's top). These most commonly lie diagonally, being stacked on the main entry poles (they were occasionally bound to the structure with strips of yucca), but the logs may be leaned against the vestibule roof, or laid horizontally, or palisaded along the sides (combinations of these techniques also occur). The whole entry structure is usually chinked and then covered with earth. Entries range in height from about 3.5 to about 6 feet (1.07 to 1.83 m). Vestibules or passageways of stones and logs, roofed with split junipers, have been reported archaeologically (eighteenth century) in the Gobernador region (Kidder 1920: 325; Carlson 1965: 10, 14) and near Borrego Pass, New Mexico (J. Lee Correll, personal com-

munication). Keur (1944: 76) reported an eighteenth-century hogan with a passageway of "posts set into the ground" that extended 3 feet 10 inches (1.17 m) into the interior of the hogan.

Construction Procedure

Mindeleff (1898: 489–93) gave the most complete description of the construction of the conical forked-pole hogan.[14] When the family head has chosen a suitable site and cleared it of brush, the building materials are gathered, with special attention being given to the three main timbers of the frame, which require substantial forked ends. These poles—typically 8 to 10 inches (20.3 to 25.4 cm) in diameter and 10 to 12 feet (3.05 to 3.66 m) long—are usually cut from living trees, although an old tripod-plus-entry framework may be reused in place. The poles and logs are trimmed of branches and bark, and then, usually, the three forked poles (*tsin halgizhii* = forked timber) and the two entry timbers, which are normally un-forked, are laid down in their approximate future positions, the locations of the butt ends then being marked with stakes. (Or, the south and north timbers alone may be laid down, equal distances being simply paced off in the other two directions.) After post holes are dug, the timbers are removed. A rough circle is drawn well within the line of these holes, and the area thus outlined is excavated.

The principal timbers are carefully positioned, and the butt ends are firmly planted in the ground a short distance back from the rim of the excavation. Two to five or more men raise the poles, often using ropes. One tine of the forked end of the southern pole is placed in the fork of the northern pole, either while the poles are on the ground or after they have been raised. The western pole is considered the main timber (Frisbie and McAllester 1978: 174–75) and may be of somewhat greater diameter. It is raised and receives the interlocked forks of the southern and northern poles (Fig. 5.4), which are often inclined somewhat rearward. These timbers are sometimes bound together near the apex (for framework terminology, see Fig. 2.6). The interlocked apex of the frame may be from 6 to 11 feet or more (1.83 to 3.35 m) above the floor, the taller specimens occurring where relatively long poles are available. Interior diameters range from less than 12 feet (3.66 m) to as much as 30 feet (9.14 m), the average probably being nearer to the lower end of the scale than to the upper. Archaeological examples, especially from pre-Ft. Sumner times, before steel axes were generally available, not infrequently had diameters of less than 10 feet (3.05 m); the average was probably about 12 feet (3.66 m), the minimum 5 feet 6 inches (1.67 m; possibly

a sudatory).[15] The two entry poles are leaned against the tripod on its eastern side, their points placed near its apex; these two poles together are considered to be the eastern pole, although the southern one of these is treated ceremonially as the eastern pole and is the first of the two to be put into position.

The five-pole frame is then buttressed by the leaners, including the branches of the trees that provided the principal timbers (Fig. 5.5). Farmer (1942: 68) recorded twenty-one large and forty-eight small timbers in one eighteenth-century hogan, and no doubt there were originally even more. Shufeldt (1892: 279) estimated twenty to thirty logs, plus branches. Some brush or boughs may be laid on with, and held in place by, the leaners (Hoover 1931: 442–43). In principle, leaners are to be laid on in sunwise sequence (Hill 1938: 178). The entry is completed, interstices are chinked, and the final layer of chips, bark, brush, grass, or whatever, is added (Fig. 5.6). Soil is mixed with water, and the exterior is piled with damp earth to a thickness of about 6 inches (15.2 cm) and smoothed with the hands or, occassionally, a smooth piece of bark or other instrument (Fig. 5.3). Particularly impervious clay may be selected for the exterior coat.

LEAN-TO HOGANS

As discussed in chapter 4, single and double pole-and-brush or -bark or -moss lean-tos are known to the Canadian and Alaskan Athapaskans and to the Western (and probably other) Apache.[16] Eighteenth-century Navajo lean-tos have been recorded, but it is not known whether or not these were earth-covered (Keur 1941: 37). The Navajo may have added their earth covering as a result of Puebloan influence, but the practice may conceivably have had a northern origin; the Kutchin, the Kaska, the Tahltan, the Carrier, and the Chilcotin sometimes covered their lean-tos with sods or earth (Driver and Massey 1957:

295, 308; McKennan 1965: 43; Honigmann 1954: 59, 62).

Hill's informants indicated that lean-tos were sometimes used as permanent dwellings (Fig. 5.9), particularly "during the unsettled period prior to Fort Sumner and before axes became common. According to PP, such houses were still being used in 1933 in the more isolated areas.... SC considered this kind of dwelling a late development" (Kluckhohn et al. 1971: 152). This form now seems to be nearly or completely obsolete as a permanent dwelling. Descriptions follow:

Navajo name: hooghan bijáád t'ááłá'í[ł] (*naaki[ł]*) = [with] one (two) hogan's legs, i.e., one- (two-) legged hogan.

Diagnostic feature: poles leaned against a ridgepole, a boulder, or an earth bank.

Other major features:

1. Wall structure: leaning poles covered with brush, bark, and/or grass, and earth (Fig. 5.9).

2. Plan: semicircular, triangular, subtriangular, rectangular, or subrectangular (Fig. 5.10).

3. Roof: inseparable from walls.

Minor features and variations:

1. The ridgepole may be (1) inclined, one end supported by a vertical or slightly inclined pole, the other end resting on the ground; or (2) horizontal, supported by two verticals (usually forked) or by one vertical and a tree crotch or boulder.

2. Leaners may be placed against either one (usually west) side (single lean-to) or both sides (double lean-to) of the ridgepole, and the end(s) of the structure may be left open or be partly or entirely closed with leaners; the lower ends of the leaners may be set into the ground.

3. Occasionally, where timber was scarce, pits up to 7 feet (2.13 m) deep would be dug; a vertical forked pole was set up in each of the corners at the ends of one wall and were connected by a stringer, against which logs were leaned, either over the pit alone or both over the pit and along the front of the structure.

Fig. 5.9 "Two-legged" double lean-to hogan (hypothetical reconstruction). Two uprights support a ridgepole against which earth-covered poles lean.

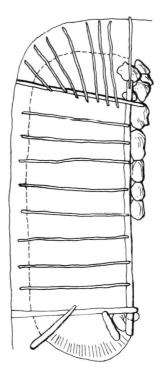

Fig. 5.10. Schematic drawing of the framework and leaners of a "two-legged" single lean-to hogan whose floor has been shallowly excavated into a slope, as seen from above. The open front has a line of stones toward the closed end to give some additional protection from the wind (Mindeleff 1898: 496).

4. Adams (1959) recorded a semicircular lean-to hogan whose leaners stood upon a probably prehistoric crude masonry foundation, their upper ends converging to rest on a boulder.

Use

There are relatively few descriptions in the literature of the now obsolete lean-to hogan.[17] Although we saw no specimens, Kluckhohn et al. (1971: 156) stated that "There was ample evidence of the permanent occupation of the lean-to type of house." Mindeleff (1898: 495) indicated that use at summer farms was typical and that eastward orientation was not required.

VERTICAL-POST HOGANS

Two hogan types—the leaning-log hogan and the palisaded hogan—depend upon four or more vertical posts to support their roofs, which are distinct from their walls.

Leaning-log Hogan

Although more evolved leaning-log hogans and the derivative palisaded hogan are typically round, the earlier form of the former is subrectangular. The subrectangular leaning-log hogan is, in essence, four single lean-to hogans facing a square and provided with a roof (Figs. 5.11, 5.12, 7.1). Thus, it would not have been too great a feat for the Navajo to

Fig. 5.11. Four-sided leaning-log hogan with a flat earth-covered log roof and a homemade plank door with a chain and padlock; most of the earth covering has eroded from the sides. Note the rabetting of the doorway lintel. A ramada stands behind and to the right of the hogan. Southwest of Tsaile, Arizona, 1979.

Fig. 5.12. Flat-roofed leaning-log hogan with a cloth entry-hanging rolled up above the homemade door. The floor is slightly excavated. Note the drying rack at the left, supporting a hide, clothing, and a saddle; post-and-wire fencing forms a corral in the right background. Northern Arizona, 1935; M.S.S. (930).

have invented this form on their own. Nevertheless, as will appear, it seems likely that they were at least influenced by structures of other cultures.

The first observations of leaning-log hogans described in print date from the mid-1880s (Stevenson 1891: 237; Mindeleff 1898: 513; Stephen 1893: 350). Some of Hill's informants considered the "four-legged" hogan to be recent, although others stated that it existed in pre-Ft. Sumner times but was not popular until after that time (Kluckhohn et al. 1971: 152). A subrectangular example with six main uprights and an extended entryway is known archaeologically from the Navajo Reservoir district and dates from the Gobernador Phase, 1696–1770 (Hester and Shiner 1963: 3, 12–14), and other archaeological specimens have also been recorded (Littell 1967-6: Appendix A).

The leaning-log hogan resembles a small, simplified Plains earthlodge, although it is doubtful that the Navajo had contacts with earthlodge builders. The people of the Dismal River Aspect, thought to be Plains Apaches of about 1700, built subpentagonal five- (occasionally six-) post dwellings 12 to 15 feet (3.7 to 4.6 m) wide with extended doorways facing eastward (Gunnerson 1960). All of these leaning-log dwellings are similar to some of the pre-Athapaskan pit dwellings found in the Southwest (Bullard 1962: 133–34; Carlson 1963; Wormington 1947: 154; McGregor 1965: 228, 299, 243, 264), including in Dinétah (Eddy 1966: 320–25). These types of dwellings had a widespread distribution in aboriginal America and Asia, and their ultimate origins are probably undeterminable. Just how late such pit dwellings were still built in the Southwest is uncertain. If they were extinct by the date of Athapaskan arrival, the Puebloan flat-roofed shade, which retained much of the basic construction technique as well as the earth-covered roof, could have provided the primary model for the leaning-log hogan. The Zuni, Santa Ana, and San Ildefonso built ramadas with earth-covered roofs (Gifford 1940: 23). According to Ellis (1960: 11), the Acoma built leaning-log storage structures with earth-covered roofs in historic times, and the Hopi built ramadas of this type (McGregor 1951: 85). The Gila River Yumans also built a house similar to a leaning-log hogan; it was thatched and had an earth-covered roof (Spier 1933: 83–87).

The Northern Athapaskan Kutchin and some Tanana did build moss- and sod- or earth-covered semipit houses with vertical corner posts connected by stringers, but walls were of lashed split vertical poles and the roof was gabled or pyramidal (Vanstone 1974: 34; Clark 1974: 120–24; Driver and Massey 1957: 309). In any case, in view of its rarity in early Navajo archeology and its apparent absence among the Navajo's nearest Northern Athapaskan relatives and among other Apacheans, it seems likely that this type was not brought from the north but was an adaptation of the Puebloan shade, initially as a ceremonial structure (see below). The addition of earth covering to the walls would be a procedure identical with that involving the conical forked-pole hogan (Jett 1981). The relationship, if any, with the Dismal River structures is problematical, but it may be noted that these people seem also to have had considerable contact with Puebloans.

According to Underhill (1953: 195), leaning-log hogans were little used until after Ft. Sumner. In the early days, leaning-log hogans were reportedly of large size and built exclusively for ceremonial use, especially for certain chantways, which require extensive floor space unlike Blessingway rites, which are traditionally held in the less spacious, conical forked-pole hogan; these ceremonial hogans[18] sometimes served later as workrooms or temporary or, occasionally, permanent dwellings but were usually simply left to decay because they were too large to heat efficiently or were in an inconvenient location. Ceremonial use of the earliest known archaeological leaning-log hogan is implied by its having an alcove that apparently served as a sudatory (Hester and Shiner 1963: 13–14). The ceremonial function probably partly accounts for the rarity of this form before relatively recent times (see chapter 13). Its introduction may have coincided with the introduction of some of the Puebloan features of Navajo religion, which often require larger enclosed spaces than afforded by the typical conical hogan.

Through the 1880s, both ceremonial and secular leaning-log hogans remained very uncommon, the conical type being preferred in both contexts unless sufficiently long poles to make spacious conical hogans were scarce (Matthews 1902: 49). Coolidge and Coolidge (1930: 82–83) contended that after about 1890, as steel axes became common, the subrectangular ceremonial leaning-log hogan, which seems usually to have had a flat roof, began to be replaced by larger, circular or subpolygonal leaning-log hogans up to 50 feet (15.2 m) in diameter and employing from six to twelve or more verticals and usually roofed with corbeled logs (Figs. 5.13, 5.16, 1.3; see also Correll 1965: 29). In fact, some four-post hogans seem to have been expanded in size by adding additional verticals, stringers, and leaners (Frisbie and McAllester 978: 30, 106).

Commodiousness, even where few long timbers were available, was probably a significant factor in the adoption of this form for dwellings as well as in its retention as a ceremonial structure. Leaning-log hogans used primarily as dwellings became quite common in the twentieth century, notably in the western Navajo Country, the subrectangular plan gradually being replaced by the more traditional circular plan.

Fig. 5.13. Polygonal leaning-log hogan with a flat, earth-covered roof of boards resting on log beams; homemade plank door with commercial hinges, hasp, and padlock. Note the wire to help hold the southeasterly leaners in place. Most of the sides' earth covering has been eroded. Cedar Ridge, Arizona, area, 1970.

Palisaded Hogan

Palisaded walls are built by setting up posts side by side, usually in a trench. Palisade construction was utilized in pre-Navajo Dinétah about A.D. 500–1000, for stockades around dwellings (as in the prehistoric Great Plains) and to reinforce the earthen walls of pit dwellings (Eddy 1966: 203, 218–19, 228, 270–71, 293). Too, a 1748 Spanish document reports "palisade-huts" (probably of Spanish derivation) as formerly used by the Jicarilla Apache (Gunnerson 1969: 23). In the western part of Northern Athapaskan country, rectangular houses employing a kind of palisaded construction were built (Vanstone 1974: 33; Clark 1974: 120–24). Despite these precursors, Navajo palisading appears to be relatively modern (Kluckhohn et al. 1971: 150), with the possible exception of an eighteenth-century conical forked-pole hogan whose entryway walls were apparently palisaded (Keur 1944: 76).[19]

Hogans with palisaded walls (Figs. 5.14, 5.15) were thought by Underhill (1953: 206) to have derived from Euramerican palisaded huts built beginning in 1879 in connection with the construction of the Atchison, Topeka, and Santa Fe Railroad. The method is recorded among the Navajo in house construction in the 1880s (see chapter 7) and, subsequently, in the erecting of corrals. Palisaded windbreaks also employ a similar technique. Frank Mitchell, apparently referring to palisaded hogans, said, "It was about 1900 when they started using log

Fig. 5.14. Nine-sided palisaded hogan under construction. The posts—some squared—have been placed upright in a nonagonal trench. A plank lies across the square-sawn ends of the logs of each wall. On each plank lies one of the first-tier logs of the corbeled-log roof. The posts supporting the ends of these logs tend to be stouter than the other posts. (Compare with Figs. 5.15 and 5.18.) Southwest of Piñon, Arizona, 1970; R. F.

posts for hogans" (Frisbie and McAllester 1978: 31). The earliest documentation of such a hogan is a 1904 photograph of an interior; the roof supports are inside the line of the paling. The location is not given, but it is somewhere in the eastern or central Navajo Country (Wyeth 1971: 117). A "medicine hogan" with nearly vertical paling is shown in a ca. 1912–13 photograph taken near Shiprock, New Mexico, by H. S. Poley (National Anthropological Archives, photo 54,495). Verplanck (1943: 7, 42) pictured what probably should be considered a palisaded hogan, although the walls are very slightly battered; the overall earth covering suggests a western Reservation location. The photograph is undated, but Verplanck was in the Navajo Country in 1913 and again in 1925, but not afterward. There are several geographically widely scattered records from the 1930s.[20]

It seems probable that the palisaded hogan evolved from the circular leaning-log type under the influence of the techniques em-

Fig. 5.15. Newly built polygonal palisaded hogan employing squared pales; corbeled-log roof. The fresh mud chinking was apparently applied with a trowel. Note the window, the smoke-hole framing, and the stovepipe emerging from a separate opening. North of State Highway 264, Coal Mine Mesa, Arizona, 1970.

ployed with palisaded houses and corrals, or it may have evolved directly from palisaded houses by a simple alteration in floor plan similar to the change from subrectangular to circular leaning-log hogans. Examples of palisaded hogans are known in which the upper ends of the palisade logs adjoin the outer sides of the stringers rather than being wedged under them or directly supporting the roof; in this respect, the pales differ from the leaners of the leaning-log hogan only in that they are vertical rather than leaning.

Detailed descriptions of vertical-post hogans follow:

Navajo name (for vertical-post hogans in general): *hooghan bijáád hólóní[gíí]* = hogan has its [supporting] legs.

Diagnostic feature: four or more vertical posts or poles provide the structure's support.

Leaning-Log Hogan

Navajo Name: hooghan bijáád łani = its-many-legs hogan (according to the number of supports, the hogan may be designated as "four-legged," (*díí' bijáadi hooghan*) "six-legged," etc.).

Major features:

1. Wall structure: four or more vertical posts or poles are connected by horizontal stringers, against whose outward sides logs or poles are leaned; spaces between logs are chinked, boughs and other materials may cover the logs, and there is usually an overall covering of earth or, rarely, sods (Figs. 5.11, 5.12, 5.13, 5.16, 5.17, 7.1, 8.8).

2. Plan: circular, eliptical, subpolygonal, or subrectangular (Fig. 5.17).

3. Roof: flat (Figs. 5.11, 5.12, 5.13, 5.17), center-beam, corbeled-log (Fig. 5.16), or cribbed-log (Fig. 8.8).

Minor features and variations:

1. Traditionally, the principal vertical posts are forked, but today a saddle-shaped depression may instead be cut into the upper end of each vertical to receive the stringer, or the stringers may be nailed or wired to the square-sawn ends of the uprights (Fig. 4.13).

Fig. 5.16. Interior of Yazhe Clark's abandoned six-legged leaning-log hogan with a low-profile corbeled-log roof. Above Middle Trail Canyon, Canyon de Chelly, Arizona, 1972.

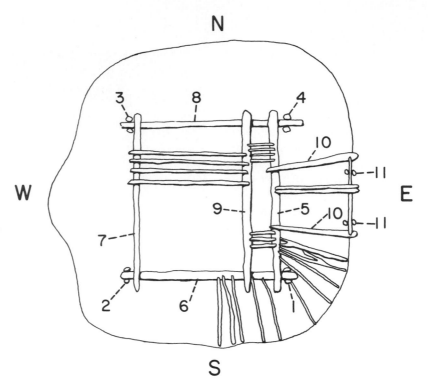

N

W

E

S

Fig. 5.17. Structural diagram of a four-sided lean-ing-log hogan. Shown are the basic framework (*sahdii* = main alone) as seen from above; representative secondary timbers; and the wall outline (modified from Mindeleff 1898).

A. Uprights (*hooghan bijááď* = hogan's legs)
   1. Southeastern post (*ha'a'aahjį' 'íí'áii* = to the east it extends [upright]; *shádi'ááh ha'a'aah-jį' 'íí'áii* = to the southeast it extends [upright]
   2. Southwestern post (*shádi'áajį' 'íí'áii* = to the south it extends[upright]; *shádi'ááh 'e'e 'aah-jį' 'íí'áii* = to the southwest it extends [up-right]
   3. Northwestern post ('*e'e'aahjį' 'íí'áii* = to the west it extends [upright]; *náhookǫs 'e'e'aah-jį' 'íí'áii* = to the northwest it extends [up-right]
   4. Northeastern post (*náhookǫsjį' 'íí'áii* = to the north it extends [upright]; *náhookǫs ha'a'aahjį' 'íí'áii* = to the northeast it ex-tends [upright]

B. Stringers
   5. Eastern stringer (*ha'a'aahjį' naní'áhí[gíí]* = [that which] to the east extends horizontally across; see also, 9, below)

6. Southern stringer (*shádi'áahjį' naní'áhí[gíí]* = [that which] to the south extends horizon-tally across)
7. Western stringer ('*e'e'aahjį' naní'áhí[gíí]* = [that which] to the west extends horizontally across)
8. Northern stringer (*náhookǫsjį' naní'áhí[gíí]* = [that which] to the north extends horizon-tally across)
9. Smokehole stringer (*ch'ílayi' naní'áhí[gíí]* = that which extends horizontally across the smoke hole; name also sometimes applied to 5, above)

C. Entryway (*ch'é'étiin* = exit path)
   10. Entry poles (*ch'é'étiin[jį'] ní'áii* = [slender rigid object] extends horizontally from the exit path; *ch'é'étiin bii' ni'nínilii* = those ly-ing on the ground inside the exit path)
   11. Jamb(s) (*ch'é'étiin 'íí'áii* = it extends verti-cally [at the] exit path; *ch'é'étiin siláii* = a pair lies [at the] exit path
   12. Lintel (*ch'é'étiin siláii naní'áhí[gíí]* = [that which] extends horizontally across exit path a pair there [jambs]; *ch'é'étiin naa dah sitání* = [slender ridgcd object] that lies up across the exit-path opening)

2. The floor may be shallowly excavated, leaving a peripheral shelf or "bench."

3. A mask recess was often constructed along the middle of the rear (western) wall of the hogan (at least in ceremonial hogans) by setting the leaners' ends somewhat outside of the general line of the wall and of the excavated floor (Fig. 5.17). During ceremonies, a skin or cloth curtain would be hung, its lower edge pegged to the bench, to conceal the paraphernalia (Mindeleff 1898: 514).

4. Bailing wire may encircle the walls to enhance their stability (Fig. 5.13).

5. In some areas (such as along the lower San Juan and Little Colorado rivers) where large timber are scarce, the leaning-log hogan's walls are of very light construction, utilizing small poles and brush and even corn and weed stalks, which arc then covered with earth; larger timbers are used only for the supports and the roof (David M. Brugge, personal communication).

6. Two particularly large leaners often flank the entry. Since the sides of the structure are sloping and since a vertical door frame may be used, the entry may be recessed to the line of the eastern stringer. The resulting gaps between door frame and leaners may be filled in with logs, or, rarely, masonry (Loh 1970: 167). Or, especially on larger examples, the entry may be extended outward in a fashion similar to that of the vestibule of a conical forked-pole hogan to a point inside, at, or beyond the outer ends of the entry-flanking leaners. The entry roof is built with horizontal logs, and the sides are closed with leaners (Mindcleff 1898: 513–14; Hester and Shiner 1963: 12–14; Goddard, 1928: 201). (Frank Mitchell called leaning-log hogans with extended entries "the hogans with the big nose"; Frisbie and McAllester 1978: 30.)

Palisaded Hogan

Navajo name: náneeskáál [hooghan], tsin náneeskáalgo hooghan = slender objects were set upright in a circle [hogan], upright-logs-set-in-a-circle hogan.

Major features:

1. Wall structure: a palisade of upright posts is set up, usually in a trench. Mud, sometimes with sticks or boards, is normally used as chinking (Figs. 5.14, 5.15, 5.18, 5.21, 8.7).

2. Plan: circular, subpolygonal, or polygonal (Fig. 5.19).

3. Roof: corbeled-log, cribbed-log, or pyramidal.

Minor features and variations:

1. Upright logs of more or less uniform size may be set in a circle or a polygon and the roof laid on the ends of the uprights or on boards lying across those uprights (Fig. 5.15); or, a number of single or double vertical posts inside or outside of the line of the walls may support the roof (Fig. 8.7). Alternatively, vertical logs (whole, split, or square-sawn, or sawmill slabs) may form walls that connect thicker (and sometimes double) vertical corner posts which, alone or as a supplement to the other verticals, support the roof. When the latter method is used, the tops of the smaller-diameter uprights may be beveled and then wedged under the stringers and sometimes nailed to them; or, the small verticals may also help support the roof, the somewhat uneven line of their tops sometimes being dealt with by laying boards across their ends, in the lines of the walls (Figs. 5.14, 5.21). We have not determined whether the Hispano practice of mortising the wall-top stringer to receive the pointed post ends (Gritzner 1974a: 30) is ever practiced in hogan construction. A polygonal plan is often followed, but if a circular plan is desired, the wall logs must be inclined somewhat in the vicinity of the wall midpoints (Fig. 5.18).

2. One or more strands of wire may encircle the hogan walls for added strength (e.g., Krutz 1974: 115).

3. The rear (western) wall may have a "mask recess" (Seton 1962: 32).

4. Exterior walls may be mud-plastered or entirely buried in earth, sometimes after the addition of a veneer of tarpaper. The earth covering may be sealed with clay. One apparent case of a covering of tarpaper and cement

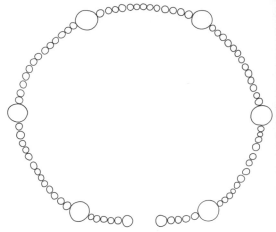

Fig. 5.19. Generalized plan of a palisaded hogan. For emphasis, the six main uprights supporting the roof are drawn somewhat oversized in proportion to the other wall pales.

Fig. 5.18. Detail of a circular palisaded hogan under construction. Corner posts have been set in place and stringers laid to connect their upper ends. A circular trench has been dug just outside of the line of the major uprights, and sawn and debarked juniper logs have been set into it. Since the paling logs' lower ends are in the circular trench and their upper ends lie against the straight stringer, the pales nearest the main posts are vertical but those farther away are slightly inclined. The corbeled-log roof has received a layer of juniper bark; earth will ultimately be applied to the entire exterior. Edge of the Cedars State Park, Blanding, Utah, 1979.

stucco, was observed (Fig. 5.20); McAllester and McAllester (1980: 59, 71) also picture a stuccoed palisaded hogan. An unchinked slab-walled example at Ramah was built purely as a summer hogan (Roberts 1951: 43, figure 1).

5. The floor may be slightly excavated, and a dugout variety of this hogan form has been observed.

6. One example was noted whose doorway was taller than the walls, requiring plank "verge boards" slanting from the top of the doorway to the corner posts at the ends of the adjacent walls; the gaps between the wall tops and the verge boards were filled with horizontal logs.

7. One specimen was seen having masonry flanking the doorway (see corbeled-log hogan, below).

Construction Procedures

The major descriptions of the construction of the leaning-log hogan are by Mindeleff (1898: 509–14) and Ward (1968: 104–05).[21] Four or more stripped and trimmed posts perhaps 8 to 12 inches (.20 to .30 m) in diameter,

Fig. 5.20. Polygonal stuccoed hogan, apparently of palisaded construction; corbeled-log roof. Coal Mine Mesa, Arizona, 1970.

and often forked, are set upright into the earth, their forks perhaps 6 feet (1.83 m) from the ground. Four-post hogans are usually subrectangular (Figs. 5.11, 5.12, 5.17), and sometimes a greater number of uprights is used in building structures of this plan. Gifford (1940: 07) gave the following range of dimensions: 10 by 20 to 15 by 30 feet (3.05 X 6.10 to 4.07 X 9.14 m); however, the examples we have observed were approximately square, not oblong. When more than four verticals are employed, the plan is usually more nearly circular (Figs. 5.13, 5.16); the greater the number of verticals, the more closely the plan approaches a circle. Also, the greater the number of vertical posts, the more spacious the structure can be, and the shorter the stringers required. Leaning-log hogans of up to 50 feet (15.24 m) in diameter and having twelve or more verticals have been recorded (Coolidge and Coolidge 1930: 82–83; Sullivan 1938: 50; Correll 1965a: 29; Frisbie and McAllester 1978: 30).

The main posts (*bijááʼd* = its legs) are usually set into the ground in the following order in the case of four-post examples: southeast, southwest, northwest, and northeast; jewel offerings may be placed in the postholes: white shell (southeast), turquoise (southwest), abalone (northwest), and jet (northeast; Coolidge and Coolidge 1930: 78). According to Mindeleff (1898: 510–13), stringers are laid to connect first the verticals of the southern side and then the uprights of the northern side; the beams of the eastern and western sides are then laid on the stringers already in place, either inside or outside the forks of the uprights (Figs. 5.16, 5.17); this order seems to be confirmed by Stevenson (1891: 237) and Haile

(1942: 55), but the Franciscan Fathers (1910: 332) described the eastern and western beams as being laid first.[22] The roof is normally flat.

In the case of the more nearly circular varieties, the ends of the stringers may or may not abut each other, and the roof is usually of corbeled logs (Fig. 5.16) but is sometimes flat (Fig. 5.13); Wilson (1890: 114) described a six-legged hogan, two of whose uprights were stouter and supported the ridgepole of a center-beam roof. The erection of the roof may precede the emplacement of the walls. The walls (*bighą́ą́dę́ę́' bíniizhoozhí* = [slender rigid] objects that lean against it lying parallel from its top) are formed by (1) leaning poles against the stringers; (2) chinking between the leaners; (3) applying bark, boughs, or cornstalks, and perhaps some stones; and (4) covering the structure with earth. The bases of the leaners lie from 1 to 6 feet (.30 to 1.83 m) beyond the lines of the supporting posts, according to the angle of inclination and the height of the walls. The butts of the leaners may be set into the soil, and the ground within leveled or excavated slightly. These structures average perhaps about 20 feet (6.09 m) across and 7 feet (2.13 m) high, but may be as little as 10 feet by 5.5 feet (3.05 m by 1.67 m; Wilson 1890: 114). The specimen described by Ward (1968: 140, 142) had approximately 129 leaners. After the main walls have been laid, the leaners on the sides of the entryway are installed. The entryway roof poles are set in place next, and then the chinking and earth-covering are undertaken.

The plan of a palisaded hogan may be either polygonal, subpolygonal, or circular (Fig. 5.19). A trench is usually dug, into which the wall logs are set upright (Fig. 5.18). After being chinked the entire structure may be buried with earth (done mainly on the western part of the Reservation). The corbeled-log roof may rest on the ends of the uprights or on boards lying on these ends. However, supplemental uprights with stringers—inside of, within, or outside of the line of the walls—are commonly used to give the roof added support

(Figs. 5.14, 5.18, 5.19, 5.21, 8.7). When the latter method is followed, the corner posts, stringers, and roof (normally corbeled-log) are often constructed first, and then the walls are filled in (Figs. 5.18, 5.21). Seton (1962: 30–32) provided a detailed description of the construction of such a hogan, built for ceremonial use. It used fourteen 7-foot (2.14-m) forked posts to support the cribbed-log roof. The 6-foot (1.83-m) wall logs were set in a foot-deep (.30-m) trench between the main uprights. A puddle was made to mix mud for the chinking and plastering, and earth was banked up against the walls.

Palisaded hogans vary a good deal in size. Some exceed 25 feet (7.62 m) in diameter. The principal limitation on size is the length of available timbers for roof construction. Walls are usually of chest or shoulder height.

STACKED-LOG HOGANS

There are three basic forms of hogans whose walls are constructed of stacked horizontal logs. The oldest is the corbeled-log hogan, a dome-shaped structure in which the logs are even-tiered, the logs ends of each tier meeting at the midpoints of the logs of the previous tier. The second type is the polygonal cribbed-log hogan, whose logs are alternate-tiered, the ends interfingering. Finally, there are a few polygonal abutting-log hogans, in which the even-tiered logs' ends abut posts or each other at the corners.

Corbeled-log Hogan

Despite one Navajo tradition placing its origin around the beginning of the nineteenth century near Navajo Mountain, Utah (Coolidge and Coolidge 1930: 81–82), Navajo Land Claim site records indicate use of log corbeling for hogans by the late 1720s.[23] Early so-called cribbed-log hogans appear to be what we have called corbeled-log hogans (Figs. 5.22, 5.23). Informants agree that the origin of this type was in the pre-Ft. Sumner period

Fig. 5.21. Polygonal palisaded hogan (with a corbeled-log roof) under construction; vertical-plank facade. The first tier of roof logs lies atop the square-sawn ends of the very carefully selected and prepared wall logs (compare with Fig. 5.15). Note door, window, and smoke-hole framing, and homemade ladders. Cedar Ridge, Arizona, 1970.

(Kluckhohn et al. 1971: 150). The earliest identifiable historical reference which we have found refers to 1891 (Nordenskiöld 1893: 58; see also Mindeleff 1898: 498, 500).

The corbeled-log method of dwelling construction was not known to pre-contact Northern Athapaskans.[24] In Dinétah, and seemingly only in that region and in adjacent Colorado, structures very similar to corbeled-log hogans were built during the Los Pinos Phase (A.D. 1–400), and corbeled-log roofs were used contemporaneously. These dwellings are not recorded for after the Los Pinos Phase (Eddy 1961: 14–58; 1966: 271–73, 304–07, 320–25, 329, 351, 506; Bullard 1962: 127; Earl H. Morris, quoted in Wormington 1947: 35–36; Carlson 1963; McGregor 1965: 173–74), but the technique was retained in the

Fig. 5.22. Abandoned corbeled-log hogan utilizing rather large-diameter logs (see Fig. 5.36); the earth covering has eroded away. Note the plank door frame and homemade door. U.S. Highway 89, between Cedar Ridge and The Gap, Arizona, 1978.

Fig. 5.23. Corbeled-log hogan used for storage. Note the plank door framing, the homemade door and handle, and the hasp and padlock. Tree branches have been leaned against the hogan sides to protect the earth covering, which is separated from the entry area by an arrangement of logs. Chauncey and Dorothy Neboyia's main homestead, north of Canyon de Chelly, Arizona, near the head of Beehive Trail, 1972.

Southwest, primarily or exclusively to roof kivas in pueblos of the Mesa Verde area of Colorado. The Developmental and Classic Mesa Verde kiva was round, with stone pilasters supporting a roof "formed by placing poles across them [the pilasters] from one to another. Additional poles were placed across the angles thus formed until a dome-shaped roof was constructed" (McGregor 1965: 287). However, this type of roof is not characteristic of Rio Grande Puebloan kivas (Alfonso Ortiz and Steward Peckham, personal communications), nor of late prehistoric and historic kivas in general. Although the Navajo might have learned the technique from observation of Mesa Verdean ruins, the probability is diminished by the Navajo's to some extent avoiding ruins as ghost-infested. Further, almost no even partially intact kiva roofs exist in Mesa Verde (Nordenskiöld 1893: 57–58). Another

possibility is that the corbeled-stone oven introduced into the Southwest by the Spanish (see chapter 10) was the model for larger, corbeled-*log* structures.[25] (The corbeling technique, using slabs of sheep dung, was also employed for firing pottery at Ramah; Tschopik 1941: 38.)

David M. Brugge (personal communication) has suggested that stacked-log hogans may have evolved independently among the Navajo through development of circular horizontal-bough windbreaks; Rice (Dillon 1970: 68) described one with "a slight bough roof." Theoretically, this evolution would seem simple enough and may well be how the construction technique first evolved. Yet the almost complete lack of the corbeled-log dome at any time anywhere in the world other than the American Southwest leaves a nagging doubt respecting Navajo reinvention; were it not for the apparent absence of the technique between ca. A.D. 1300 and 1726, we would not hesitate to attribute the corbeled-log hogan to adoption from Puebloans. Possibly Ellis' (1960: 4–5) Acoma and Laguna "cribbed-log" storage structures were actually corbeled-log and do represent a Puebloan survival of the technique.

"Stone hogans" of only a few courses of stone, reported archaeologically, probably represent foundations to raise the height of corbeled-log structures as is sometimes done in modern examples (e.g., Platero 1967: 67). The height of wall necessary for a hogan to be considered a stone hogan rather than having a stone foundation cannot, of course, be precisely stated; there is a complete transition between the two forms.

Fig. 5.24. Cribbed-log hogan with a corbeled-log roof. The log ends have sloping-sided box notches on their upper sides. Poles and boards have been nailed on as chinking. Northwest of Lukachukai, Arizona, 1970; R.F.

Cribbed-Log Hogan

Cribbed-log walls were unknown to Northern Athapaskans prior to European contact, although cribbed roofs were constructed over Eskimo (Inuit) and Ingalik Athapaskan rectangular men's houses in western Alaska (Driver and Massey 1957: 295–97; Osgood 1940: 291, 294–95, plate 7; Vanstone 1974: 36).[26]

Underhill (1956: 191) suggested that the development of the hexagonal cribbed-log hogan (Figs. 5.24, 5.25, 5.26, 1.4, 1.5) dated to the period of railroad building during the 1880s, when pre-cut railroad ties became available to the Navajo. However, both corbeled-log and cribbed-log hogans were built by the Navajo prior to 1864. An apparently cribbed example from near Canyon de Chelly, Arizona (Hurt 1942: 91, plate 3), dates to about 1860 (Brugge 1967: 397), and Correll (1965a: 30) gave a date of 1866 for a polygonal hogan. A sampling of unpublished Navajo Land Claim data indicated that the earliest well-dated hogans that can be called truly cribbed were built during the 1840s.[27] Although horizontal-log—mostly corbeled-log —hogans seem to be relatively common archaeologically (Littell 1967-6: appendix 1; James 1976), they are rarely mentioned in

Fig. 5.25. Cribbed-log hogan with a pyramidal plank roof covered with tarpaper. The dormer window over the homemade door has a projecting roof supported by brackets and is flanked by an unused electric light socket. Note the stone foundation and the flagstones in front of the entry, the small spacer logs in the chinks at either side of the doorway, and the mud chinking. Southeast of Tse Bonito, New Mexico, 1970; R.F.

Fig. 5.26. Hexagonal cribbed-log hogan with a pyramidal roll-roofing-covered plank roof and cupola. The logs have been well hewn and full-dovetail-notched (Fig. 5.32). Note the stone foundation, the plank door and window frames, and the commercial (?) louvers in the cupola (see Fig. 2.5). Near Mexican Springs, New Mexico, 1972.

early sources (see Mindeleff 1898: 498, 500). Ben Wittick photographed a cribbed hogan about 1882. The earliest published description seems to be that of Stephen (1893: 350). Too, Matthews (1897: 14) described a cribbed-log hogan; the logs were not notched. Hollister (1903: 68–69) reproduced what he considered to be the first description (1900) of cribbed-log hogans, stating that the ends of the logs were "morticed"; a similar, 1902 example was noted near Shiprock by Forrest (1970: 95–96). Schwemberger (1938) photographed one in 1906, probably in the St. Michaels, Arizona, area. The type is not documented archaeologically for the del Muerto rim area until toward 1900 (James 1976: 61).

The rarity of pre-1900 cribbed-log hogans may reflect the possibility that before wide availability of steel axes, the difficulties of building this relatively commodious hogan type resulted in its construction being confined largely to ceremonial occasions. In fact, Haile (1942: 54–55; see also, Coolidge and Coolidge 1931: 82–83; Wilmsen 1960: 18) categorized this type as primarily ceremonial in function.

The step from corbeling logs to crude cribbing is small—in fact, a complete gradation exists between hogans of these two types. It is possible that a spontaneous evolution occurred, but northern New Mexican Hispanos have long had a cribbed-log housing tradition (Gritzner 1971) introduced from Mexico, where Silesian miners apparently imported it in early colonial times (Winberry 1974). The technique dates to at least the mid-eighteenth century in Santa Fe (Gritzner 1974b: 518), and very likely influenced the emergence of cribbed-log hogans. It is certain that Anglo-

American cabin-building techniques have also strongly influenced more modern examples. Saddle-notching, for example, is typical of the Deep South (Kniffen and Glassie 1966: 61), although it is also practiced by Hispanos (who more commonly employ single or double box-notching). Another possible Hispano influence is the peeling and occasional hewing of logs (Gritzner 1971: 58, 60). Corner-squaring may be an Anglo influence. Certainly, the increasing availability of steel axes at the end of the nineteenth century made possible the spread of corner-timbering and hewing of logs and contributed substantially to the ascendency of cribbed-log hogans (cf., Boyce 1974: 65).

Supportive of the idea of influence from cabin-building is the fact that during the latter nineteenth century, cribbed-log houses seem to have far outnumbered cribbed-log hogans (Mindeleff 1898: 486–87). However, that the idea of true cribbing *could* have been derived from Puebloans is suggested by the following: (1) a form of true cribbed-*roof* construction existed in a kiva at Aztec Pueblo in prehistoric times (Vivian 1959: 72–73); (2) a rectangular cribbed-log roof dating to 1750 occurred on a pueblito with Navajo-Puebloan associations in the Gobernador district (Carlson 1965: 8, 12); and (3) Ellis (1960: 4–5) attributed "cribbed-walled" storage structures (of Hispano derivation?) to the Acoma and Laguna.

An additional possibility is that the polygonal cribbed-log hogan began as a substitution of horizontal logs for the leaning logs of the leaning-log hogan; some cruder cribbed-log hogans have walls that pitch slightly inward as they rise, and evidence exists of former use of interior verticals to support the roof, rather than letting the walls bear its weight. However, although such substitution may have occurred, and although the pitch of the walls may have been influenced by leaning-log hogans, it seems more plausible that the cribbed-log hogan evolved directly from the corbeled-log type, under the influence of Hispano and Anglo cabin-building methods. Relevant to all of this is the other area of the world where cribbed-log "hogans" exist: Siberia. There, by the eighteenth century (but much later in some areas), polygonal cribbed-log dwellings began to be constructed, apparently adapting Russian structural methods to the circular native dwelling form (Levin and Potapov 1964: 217, 265, 314, 316, 353).

Abutting-Log Hogan

The abutting-log method of construction, which employs nails, is certainly of Anglo-American origin among the Navajo, although the technique was to a certain degree anticipated in a number of eighteenth- and nineteenth-century stacked-log hogans in which single living trees were incorporated into the walls; the wall logs abutted these trees. The abutting-log hogan (Fig. 5.27) is presumably much more recent among the Navajo than are

Fig. 5.27. Chauncey Neboyia's abutting-log hogan, with five sides plus a doorway and a pyramidal plank roof (see Fig. 5.40). The basal logs are embedded in the earth on the upslope (right) side and supported by stones on the downslope (left) side. The corner posts are commercially square-sawn. Note the window in the northeastern wall, the plank door frame with a padlock, and the stovepipe. Chinle, Arizona, 1972.

other stacked-log hogan forms; the earliest published record appears to be by Page (1937b: plate V). The presence of other, earlier stacked-log types as well as the use of vertical posts to support the roof would have made the adoption of the abutting-log hogan relatively easy. Whether Navajo use of the abutting-log technique was earlier for hogans or for houses is not clear, but we would guess that houses had priority (see chapter 7).

Descriptions of stacked-log hogans follow:

Navajo name (for stacked-log hogans in general): *tsin hatł'in bee hooghan* = with-stacked-up-logs hogan.

Diagnostic feature: walls of horizontal logs.

Corbeled-Log Hogan

Navajo name: tsin nástl'ingo [bee] hooghan = [with]-circularly-piled-logs hogan; *hooghan dijoolí* = globular hogan; *hooghan yistł'óní* = woven hogan.

Major features:

1. Wall structure: a number of fairly short logs are placed end-to-end in a roughly circular plan, and successive tiers containing progressively shorter logs are stacked on top of one another. The ends of the adjacent logs in each tier meet at the approximate midpoints of the logs upon which they rest. Because the logs of each tier lie somewhat nearer the center of the circle than those of the tier below, the walls gradually converge toward the top, forming a more or less hemispherical building (Fig. 5.22); an opening (usually square) is left at the top to serve as the smoke hole. The logs are chinked, and the whole is covered with earth (Figs. 5.23, 5.28, 5.29).

2. Plan: polygonal, approaching circular (Fig. 5.35), D-shaped.

3. Roof: corbeled-log or inseparable from the walls.

Minor features and variations:

1. Stone foundations are sometimes present.

2. Piles of stone or short sections of masonry walls are often found applied to the hogan walls at either side of the doorway (Fig. 5.28), especially in the far western Navajo Country; these are probably cognate with the "door slabs" and stone piles formerly associated with conical forked-pole hogans; however, they also serve to separate the hogan's earth covering from the entry. Vertical posts next to the doorposts have also been observed (McGowan 1979: 31), and although in some cases these may serve to brace the wall ends or keep the earth covering away from the entry, in other instances they do not (Fig. 5.29). Van Valkenburg mentioned that "door slabs" are sometimes found archaeologically with "the basic 'Round Roof' type" (quoted in Haile 1952: 6), perhaps meaning the corbeled-log (or leaning-log) hogan. James (1976: 25–28, 30–31) reported apparently late-eighteenth-century corbeled-log hogans with pole-roofed masonry entryways up to 1.5 meters long and 0.5 meter wide (4.9 X 1.6 ft) on the Canyon del Muerto, Arizona, rim.

3. Hillside dugout varieties of this hogan have been reported (Kluckhohn et al. 1971: 152).

4. Land Claims records show an eighteenth-century specimen built against a cliff.

5. Wilmsen (1960) pictured an example on whose summit stood a huge, windowed plank cupola with a pyramidal roof.

Cribbed-Log Hogan

Navajo name: tsin ([dah] diitł'in) bee hooghan = with-[stacked-alone]-logs hogan; *hooghan dah diitł'iní* = stacked-alone hogan; may also be designated according to the number of sides, e.g., *tseebíigo dah'adiitł'in* = eight walls, or *tseebíigo 'aháąh déníł* = joined on eight sides.

Major features:

1. Wall structure: logs of approximately equal length are stacked on a polygonal plan, the ends of each log normally being interposed between the ends of the inferiorally and superiorally adjoining logs of adjacent walls. Interstices, if present, are chinked with the usual materials, although cement is occasionally used (Figs. 5.24, 5.25, 5.26).

Fig. 5.28. Corbeled-log hogan with stone-masonry facing flanking the doorway. Note the plank smoke-hole and doorway frames, and the homemade plank door. Cedar Ridge, Arizona, 1970.

Fig. 5.29. Corbeled-log hogan whose entry is flanked by squared vertical posts. Much of the earth covering has eroded away. Note the rocks to the left of the entry, the plank door frame, and the homemade door. The wires projecting from the smoke hole probably once supported a flue or a stovepipe. Cedar Ridge, Arizona, 1970.

Fig. 5.30. Flat-roofed cribbed-log hogan. Between Steamboat and Lizard Springs, Arizona, 1971.

2. Plan: polygonal (Figs. 5.35, 5.38).

3. Roof: corbeled-log (Fig. 5.24), pyramidal (Figs. 5.25, 5.26, 5.34), hipped-with-ridge, beam (Fig. 5.30), or conical-forked-pole(?).

Minor features and variations:

1. In modern examples, the logs are usually corner-timbered by being singly or doubly saddle- or box-notched or, rarely, full-dovetailed at or near their ends (Figs. 5.31, 5.32, 7.7). Square notching has recently been reported from Rock Point (Thomas et al. 1974: 24) and Chinle (McAllester and McAllester 1980: 99). (V-, half-, half-dovetail-, and semilunate-notching have not been observed.) Thus, when the logs are stacked, they fit into notches in the tier of logs on which they rest, thereby minimizing the gap between the logs in each wall. Log ends may be ax-cut and more or less pointed, or sawed square, or sawed at an angle parallel to the wall. Corners may be squared (boxed; cut more or less flush with the walls) or overlapping (projecting beyond the wall ends). Nails may be used at the corners to further strengthen the structure.

2. Logs may be unshaped or crudely or well squared with an ax on four sides, on the interior and exterior sides only, or on the interior only. (For a discussion of timber-shaping, see Jordan 1980: 156–57.) If round logs are used (as is usual), vertical posts may (rarely) be erected at either side of the exterior wall corners to provide stability. Commercially squared timbers (including railroad ties) are

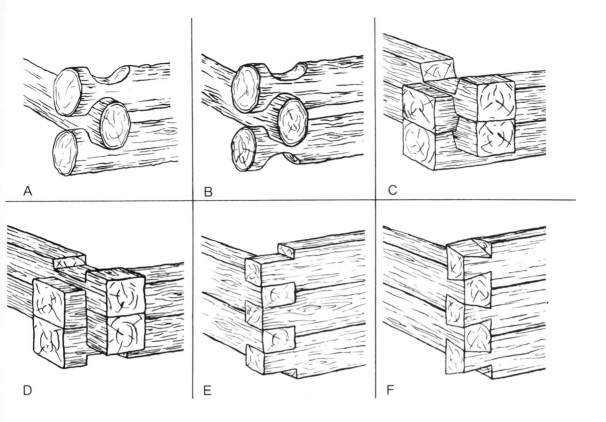

A   B   C

D   E   F

Fig. 5.31. Forms of corner-timbering (notching) used among the Navajo. (*a*) Single saddle-notching on upper surface (squared corner; can be overlapping). (*h*) Double saddle-notching (slightly overlapping corner; can be squared). (*c*) Single box-notching on upper surface (squared logs, slightly overlapping corner; logs can be unsquared). (*d*) Double box-notching (squared logs, slightly overlapping corners). (*e*) Square notching (squared logs and corners). (*f*) Full dovetail notching (squared logs and corners).

Fig. 5.32. Detail of full-dovetail corner-timbering on the cribbed-log hogan in Fig. 5.26 (the only case observed). Inaccuracies in cutting the notches have required insertion of supplemental bits of board between the ends of the timbers. The notches were cut with a saw plus, apparently, an ax. The timbers were well squared with an ax. Note the supplemental nail in the second log end from the top. Near Mexican Springs, New Mexico, 1972.

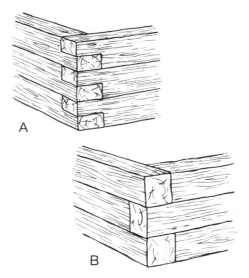

Fig. 5.33. Forms of false corner-timbering used among the Navajo. (*a*) Half-lap or rebate joint (squared logs and corner). (*b*) Full-lap or butt joint (squared logs and corner; logs can be unsquared and corners overlapping).

occasionally used; the ends of these are usually butt- (full-lap) jointed (Fig. 5.33). Fig. 5.34 shows a variation using thick sawed timbers whose ends are half-lapped (rebate-jointed; dimensions of timbers are 8 by 2.5 in., 20.32 by 6.35 cm). Butt jointing, with corner squaring, is said to be a common new technique around Rock Point, Arizona (Thomas et al. 1974: 24; see also Luckert 1979), although Aberle (1966: figures 1–3) pictured an early 1950s example. Since these methods are false-corner timbering, the wall logs are even-tiered (Figs. 2.8, 5.33, 5.34, 5.35), making these forms transitional between fully cribbed-log hogans and abutting-log hogans, although they are classed with the former herein.

3. The walls are normally vertical, but inward-inclining walls also exist, each log being slightly shorter than the underlying log or being notched somewhat farther from its end (Page 1937b: plate 8; Perceval and Lockett 1962: 18).

Fig. 5.34. Cribbed-log hogan made with even-tiered, half-lap-jointed, unchinked, commercially planked logs; the corners have been strengthened with nails. The walls have been covered with brick-pattern roll siding (missing from the right-hand wall). The roll-roofing-covered roof is pyramidal, with eave boards. East of Ft. Defiance, Arizona, 1968.

4. The lowest logs of the walls may lie in a shallow trench, or directly on the ground, or on a partial or complete stone-masonry, cemented cinder-block, concrete, or plank foundation, or have stones and/or earth piled against them (in some instances, the stones may be considered "door slabs").

5. The floor may be shallowly excavated, and dugout cribbed-log hogans occur occasionally.

6. Pieces of wood may be inserted between the ends of the logs on either side of the entry to maintain the same separation as at the cribbed ends (Fig. 5.25). In more traditional examples, vertical posts are set on each side of the wall ends at either side of the entry, to support the wall-ends (Franciscan Fathers 1910: 334; Haile 1937: 3). A specimen whose entire doorway wall was palisaded has been seen. In most modern examples, the rigidity of the entry wall ends is entirely or further maintained by nailing plank doorjambs to the ends of the logs. A log lintel connects the vertical posts at either side of the entry, or the top wall log simply continues unbroken above the doorway. When plank jambs are used, a plank lintel and sill are the rule. The doorway is normally in the center of the eastern wall of the hogan, but sometimes the entry forms one entire (though shorter) side of the polygon; the latter configuration is known both archaeologically (David M. Brugge, personal communication) and ethnographically (Leighton and Leighton 1941a; Newcomb 1966: plate opposite p. 87; Steen 1966: 117; Looney and Dale 1972: 746), and also occurs with abutting-log hogans (see below; Page 1937b: plates V, VI). Haile (1937: 3; 1942: 55) reported extended doorways on cribbed-log hogans; the authors have not seen examples, but a photograph of about 1882 (Museum of New Mexico, Ben Wittick Collection, vol, 2, no. 102V) shows a cribbed-log hogan with a doorway forming one of the sides, the entry being somewhat extended with palisading.

7. Haile (1937: 3), Haile and Wheelwright (1949: 87), and Kluckhohn and Leighton (1962: 44–45) reported, and Kluckhohn et al. (1971: 147) implied, the occasional use of four vertical posts at the interior corners of six-sided cribbed-log hogans to support the roof (see also abutting-log hogans, below). A 1901 Vroman photograph shows what appears to be such a post (Webb and Weinstein 1973: 180, 187).

8. A gable ("cap"), with or without a small window, is sometimes built over the doorway (Fig. 5.25), normally in association with frame roofs (Spencer and Jett 1971: 167; Noble and Geib 1976), especially in the Gallup, New Mexico–Ft. Defiance, Arizona, area (Jett 1976). Also known, with corbeled-log roofs, is a horizontal log above the doorway; this log is held up by short lengths of wood nailed vertically to the walls, and it supports the earth of the roof and the ends of adjacent eave logs (Mooney 1970: 20–21).

9. Logs and/or mortar may be painted, though very rarely.

10. An exterior covering of tarpaper (sometimes mineral surfaced) is occasionally applied, and one instance of stuccoing was seen.

11. McAllester and McAllester (1980: 38, 43, 54) picture a cribbed-log hogan whose interior walls are covered with wallboard.

Abutting-Log Hogan

Navajo name: tsin bee hooghan = with-logs hogan [not distinguished from cribbed-log hogan].

Major features:

1. Wall structure: Stacked horizontal logs or railroad ties whose ends abut each other or vertical corner posts, to which they are normally nailed(Figs. 5.27, 5.40).

2. Plan: polygonal (Fig. 5.35).

3. Roof: hipped or corbeled-log.

Minor features and variations:

1. Cinder-block foundations have been recorded (Anonymous 1972).

2. Log ends may abut (1) corner posts, (2) each other, on the outsides of corner posts, or (3) each other, with no corner posts present.

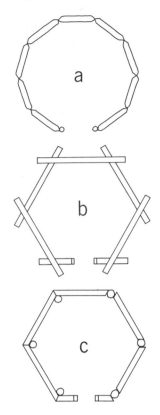

Fig. 5.35. Generalized plans of stacked-log hogans. (*a*) The corbeled-log hogan is even-tiered; (*b*) the cribbed-log hogan is alternate-tiered (corners may be overlapping, as shown here, or squared); (*c*) the abutting-log hogan is even-tiered (two alternative construction methods are shown: posts are at the interior corners in the left half and within the line of the walls in the right half).

3. In one specimen, the peeled logs were stained, and cement chinking was used. In this example, the logs under the window were set vertically (Anonymous 1972).

Construction Procedures

The corbeled-log hogan is not well described in the literature (but see Coolidge and Coolidge 1930: 81–82; Crampton 1975: 45). Kluckhohn et al. (1971: 150–51) termed this the "conical cribwork hogan," and it is sometimes referred to as the "round cribbed-log hogan." Its construction is begun by placing a tier of fairly short logs end to end on the ground in as nearly a circular plan as possible (Fig. 5.35). A second tier is built by laying logs more or less from midpoint to midpoint of the logs of the first tier, across the angles formed by the abutting ends of the first-tier logs (Fig. 5.36). Successive tiers are laid in the same fashion, with increasingly shorter logs, so that the walls are gradually drawn inward, forming a dome (Fig. 5.22). In principle, such hogans' walls are even-tiered, but in practice, the logs or snags used are usually sufficiently uneven in length as seldom to result in a neat, even laying of tier after tier (Figs. 5.36, 5.37). A smoke hole is left at the top of the dome or slightly toward the doorway from the top. The logs are chinked, and the whole is covered with tamped moist earth (Figs. 5.23, 5.28, 5.29). Although corbeled-log hogans are neither as high nor as commondious as other types, they can be constructed with relatively short logs and snags (probably usually juniper), which frequently gives them a rather irregular, randomly built appearance (Fig. 5.37). They appear to have increased in size with the introduction of steel axes (Kluckhohn et al., 1971: 150). James's (1976: 26, 29, 31, 42–43, 46) sample near Canyon del Muerto, Arizona, showed this trend, with diameters ranging from 3.5 meters (11.5 ft) in a pre-1800 example to 5.7 meters (18.7 ft) in the early 1940s. Sharlot Hall mentioned a specimen seen in 1911 estimated to be 15 feet (4.57 m) in diameter (Crampton 1975: 45).

Fig. 5.36. Detail of the corbeled-log hogan employing thick logs shown in Fig. 5.22. Log ends of each tier abut each other at the midpoints of the logs of the preceding tier. Contrast the neat construction with that of Fig. 5.37. Route 89, between Cedar Ridge and The Gap, Arizona, 1978.

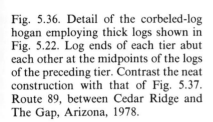

Fig. 5.37. Detail of a ruined corbeled-log hogan constructed of small-diameter logs and snags, many retaining their bark (contrast the irregular construction with the neat construction in Fig. 5.36). Between Canyon de Chelly and Slim Canyon, Arizona, 1971.

Adams (1963: 77) reported that in the Shonto area, corbeled-log hogans were used mainly for storage and as periodic or subsidiary dwellings.

Leighton and Leighton (1941a) published a photo essay on the construction of a cribbed-log hogan (their description was expanded in Kluckhohn et al. 1971: 146–47).[28] Two men did the work, with minor assistance from two women. Gathering of materials and preparation required about 2.5 days, actual construction about 3.5. In building a cribbed-log hogan, the logs, all of approximately the same length, are first gathered and peeled; ideally, they are allowed to dry over the summer before being debarked. They may be roughly or neatly squared, by nicking and trimming and, sometimes, by splitting. They are usually notched, with an ax and/or saw, so that the ends will fit fairly snugly together, imparting stability to the walls and minimizing the gaps between logs. The most common kind of notching (corner-timbering, keying) seems to be single saddle- or box-notching, on top of each log; notching may be done before or after the log is set in place. The ground is cleared, smoothed, and sometimes slightly excavated (in one example, to a depth of about 7 in., 17.8

Fig. 5.38. Ten-sided cribbed-log hogan in an early stage of construction. More than a hundred logs (some reused) and many large rocks have been assembled, a trench has been dug to receive basal logs on the structure's upslope side, and rocks have been set as corner piers on the downslope side. The logs of the first three tiers have been placed, the third tentatively, since notching of the second-tier logs remains to be done (note the single box notching on the reused upper log at the left and the wide chinks between logs). The remaining foundation stones will be emplaced later, and the entry will be at the right. North of lower Canyon de Chelly, Arizona, 1971.

cm). Foundation stones may be put in place, and the logs are stacked (Figs. 5.38, 5.39) in either a sunwise or antisunwise direction (usually the former). The chinks are normally filled, with sticks, juniper bark, and/or mud. The plan is polygonal, the number of sides ranging from five to ten. Six and eight sides are particularly common,[29] but the larger the diameter desired, the greater the number of sides. Walls are from about five to twelve logs tall. They average perhaps 5 to 6 feet (1.52 to 1.83 m) high but range up to 9 feet (2.74 m).[30] Some archaeological examples are less than 10 feet (3.05m) across. However, where long logs, notably ponderosa pine, are available, contemporary cribbed-log hogans may be quite large, with diameters of 25 feet (7.62 m) or more. Shorter logs, such as from pinyon pines, junipers, or smaller cottonwoods, yield smaller structures.[31] If available logs are less than a

Fig. 5.39. Cribbed-log hogan with a corbeled-log roof (see Fig. 8.4), under construction; some of the logs are reused. Note the plank door frame. Between Canyon de Chelly and Monument Canyon, Arizona, 1962.

minimum length, the construction of this kind of hogan is not practicable. The thickest logs are set at the base—in a shallow trench, on the surface, or on a foundation. The logs often diminish slightly in diameter toward the top (Newcomb 1966: 66).

The technique of cribbing differs from corbeling in that the log ends rest on or near the ends, not middles, of the logs of the underlying tier. Thus, unless false corner-timbering is employed, the cribbed-log hogan has alternating, not even, tiers (see Kniffen and Glassie 1966: 49), and the number of logs in each tier is one-half the number of sides of the hogan (ignoring the break of the doorway), if the number of sides is even. Too, the cribbed-log walls are vertical or only slightly battered,

while corbeled-log walls usually curve imperceptibly into the roof.

Typically, after the first three or four tiers of logs are laid, the lower part of the doorway is sawed out (the basal log is sometimes left as a sill). The windows, if any, are sawed out as well (Thomas et al. 1974: 22–23).

Kniffen and Glassie (1966: 48–49) wrote that when considering horizontal-log structures, "The fundamental distinction is the manner in which the horizontal members are joined at the corners. . . . A basic difference distinguishes two all-inclusive groups—the utilization or nonutilization of corner posts or supports to which the horizontal timbers are attached." The abutting-log hogan is built on a polygonal plan (usually hexagonal), usually

Fig. 5.40. Southern corner of Chauncey Neboyia's abutting-log hogan (see Fig. 5.27). The ends of the roughly even-tiered logs are nailed to the commercially square-sawn vertical corner post. Note the foundation stones. Chinle, Arizona, 1972.

Fig. 5.41. Frame house with a gabled roof joined to a stacked-log hogan combining abutting logs (left-hand corner) and butt-jointing (right-hand corner). Note the television antenna and the bottled gas. Black Creek Valley, Arizona, 1968; V.E.S.

with a vertical or slightly inwardly inclined post set up at each corner, about 2 feet (.61 m) of its lower end buried. The horizontal logs or ties do not overlap each other. They tend to be even-tiered, and their ends abut either the corner posts (Fig. 5.40) or, more commonly, the ends of the logs of adjacent walls, on the outsides of the corner posts (Page 1937b: 48, plates V, VI; Link 1968: 50–51); in a few cases, corner posts are dispensed with (Luckert 1979). Unlike early Franco- and Anglo-American examples, nails are used rather than wood joinery or multiple corner posts (see Kniffen and Glassie 1966: 49–50). Walls are vertical or have a slight batter. A few hogans combine the techniques of cribbing and of abutting logs, some of the corners employing one of these methods, some the other (Fig. 5.41).

Horizontal-log hogans frequently have stone-masonry or cemented cinder-block foundations. In the case of corbeled-log hogans, foundations may be useful for increasing the wall height; in all cases, foundations serve to reduce the rate of decay of the logs.

PLANK HOGANS

The final—modern—evolution of the wooden hogan was the emergence of a type with walls of commercially cut planks (Figs. 5.42, 5.43, 5.44, 5.45; 7.12). Although split and hewn planks were used in very limited quantity in the tenth century in the Flagstaff, Arizona, area, and slightly later at Chaco Canyon as well as on the Northwest Coast, Navajo use of planks is indisputably of recent origin and a consequence of the influence of Anglo-American frame-house-building techniques (see chapter 7). Since plank hogans are essentially ignored in the literature, the time and place of their origin is difficult to ascertain; we would guess the Ft. Defiance, Arizona, area during the 1930s. Frank Mitchell termed stuccoed plank hogans "really modern" (Frisbie and McAllester 1978: 31). According to

Fig. 5.42. Leaning-plank hogan with slightly inclined log corner posts and walls and a corbeled log roof; the relationship to the leaning-log hogan is clear. Note the homemade window and the boards bounding the smoke hole. A cut-stone house with a hipped-with-ridge roof stands to the right, behind the hogan. South of Tuba City, Arizona, 1970.

Fig. 5.43. Western-Reservation-style post-and-plank hogan with a corbeled-log roof. There appear to be internal corner posts; the board-capped external posts support the eave logs, which aid the retention of the roof's earth covering. The hogan exterior was once at least partially earth-covered. The doorway is taller than the walls. Note the boards surrounding the smoke hole. Cedar Ridge, Arizona, 1970.

Fig. 5.44. Stuccoed plank hogan with a stone foundation, a pyramidal plank roof, and a large flat-roofed front porch with a plank balustrade. Note the commercial windows with glazing bars; the polygonal, roll-roofing-covered arrangement of boards surrounding the smoke hole; the flagstone walkway; and the electrical connection. Chinle, Arizona, 1971.

Fig. 5.45. Frame hogan with a roll-roofing-covered pyramidal plank roof; probably used for storage. Plank sole plates are visible. Part of the vertical-plank walls' tarpaper covering has been removed. Note the homemade window and the "hatch cover" for the smoke hole. Tuba City area, near the junction of U.S. 89 and Arizona 164, 1969.

McKelvey (1969: 56), plank hogans became popular when the Tribe established its own lumber mill and made cut boards available to all its members. "Many took advantage of the opportunity and built new hogans based on the traditional styling but made of pine planks and roofed with tar paper instead of sod and dirt." Although government sawmills preceded it, the Tribal sawmill at Sawmill, Arizona, northwest of Ft. Defiance, was begun in 1939; it was superseded by the Navajo, New Mexico, mill in nearby Black Creek Valley in 1963 (Anonymous 1969b: 4, 13; Link 1968: 91, 93). Black Creek Valley does, indeed, appear to have a higher frequency of this hogan type than do other portions of the Navajo Country (Spencer and Jett 1971: 170). Because of far poorer insulation properties than log-and-earth hogans, the plank-hogan's popularity probably was dependent upon the adoption of wood-burning stoves (see Franciscan Fathers 1952 on heating). Vertical-post hogans were presumably the forebears of leaning-plank hogans. The abutting-log hogan may have provided the model for the usual, post-and-plank, technique of plank hogan construction, in which the planks are nailed to corner posts, but the influence of Anglo house-framing techniques is also very strong, its ultimate manifestation being the frame hogan.

For a brief period during the late 1960s, the Tribe made available prefabricated hogans. McAllester and McAllester (1980: 14) noted that

Four dwelling-house plans are [presently] available from the tribal housing authority for those who wish assistance in putting up a house. One, a popular one, is a one-room dwelling of the same shape as the cribbed-roof hogan. But it has windows and electricity, and the sparkproof roof around the stovepipe is of roll roofing rather than of earth.

Detailed descriptions of the aforementioned varieties of plank hogans follow:

Navajo Name: tsin neheshjíí' bee hooghan = with-sawed-wood hogan.

Diagnostic feature: walls of planks.

Leaning-Plank Hogan

Major features:

1. Wall structure: slightly inwardly inclined planks nailed to stringers supported by slightly inclined corner posts (Fig. 5.42).

2. Plan: polygonal.

3. Roof: corbeled-log.[32]

Variation:

1. An earth covering is probably sometimes applied.

Post-And-Plank Hogan

Major features:

1. Wall structure: axially horizontal planks nailed between vertical or slightly inclined corner posts (Figs. 5.43, 5.44, 5.46, 5.47).

Fig. 5.46. Detail of the doorway of a western-Reservation-style post-and-plank hogan with a corbeled-log roof, under construction (see Fig. 8.5). Note the doorpost, the slightly inclined log interior corner post, the plank interior midwall post, the exterior nailed-on tarpaper and chickenwire lath to receive stucco. Between The Gap and Willow Springs, Arizona, 1970.

Fig. 5.47. Post-and-plank hogan under construction. Note the windows and the corner and mid-wall posts, some yet to be trimmed to the proper height. Gaps beneath walls may ultimately be filled in with stones. Ft. Defiance, Arizona, 1968; V.E.S.

2. Plan: polygonal.

3. Roof: pyramidal (Figs. 5.44, 7.12), hipped-with-ridge (Fig. 5.49), or corbeled-log (Fig. 5.42, 5.43, 5.46, 5.48, 5.50).

Minor features and variations:

1. Horizontal planks connect and are nailed to the exterior (occasionally interior?) sides of five or more vertical or inward-inclined corner posts and two doorposts (usually commercially cut if vertical, logs if inclined) set into the ground in a circle; vertical posts, usually of lesser thickness, to which the planks are also nailed, may be set midway between the corner posts to stiffen the walls (Figs. 5.46, 5.47), in a fashion similar to studs. Although plywood could be substituted for planks, and may well have been in some structures, we have not observed such practice.

2. A form intermediate between abutting-log and horizontal-plank hogans is shown in

Snow photos 929 and 2225. In addition to some thick planks, railroad ties are apparently used. Some of their ends have been ax-cut to about half-thickness, to allow their being nailed to abutting plank ends (Fig. 5.48).

3. A masonry or poured-concrete foundation may be present (Fig 5.49).

4. Front porches (*chaha'oh* = shade) are sometimes seen in the Chinle, Arizona, area (Fig. 5.44), and a rectangular, plank-sided extended entry may be present, especially in the Gallup, New Mexico–Ft. Defiance, Arizona, area. Sometimes a vestibule is large enough to be essentially an extra room (Fig. 5.49).

5. Vertical corner boards have been noted (Fig. 5.49).

6. A "skin" of tarpaper (sometimes patterned, mineral-surfaced asphalt paper) is usually nailed onto the exterior walls and is occasionally held in place by wooden strips.

Fig. 5.48. Hogan intermediate between an abutting-log hogan and a post-and-plank hogan. It is walled with very thick horizontal planks (possibly including railroad ties) whose ends at the corners have been thinned with an ax to enable nails to be used to affix them to slightly inclined corner posts. The lower part of the roof is corbeled-log; the upper part is flat. Note the metal drum "chimney" encircling the smoke hole, the homemade door with hasp and leather-strap handle, and the canvas door curtain. Various possessions lie outside the hogan, including a crate marked "Armour Star Ham and Bacon" and a saddle. Red Lake (Tolani Lakes), Arizona, 1935; M.S.S. (929).

After the planks are tarpapered, cement stucco may be applied to the hogan over nailed-on chicken-wire lath (Figs. 5.44, 5.46, 5.49, 7.12, 8.5).[88] Sometimes these stuccoed plank hogans are painted. Interior stuccoing is known (Loh 1971: photo). Veneers of sheet metal, of natural or artificial stone (Fig. 5.50), and of fired bricks have also been observed, rarely.

7. In the case of hogans with inclined corner posts and sloping sides, the exterior is sometimes piled over with earth, at least in the far western Navajo Country (Fig. 5.43).

8. A gable or "dormer," with or without a small window, may be built over the door-way (Fig. 5.49), especially in the Gallup–Ft. Defiance area (Spencer and Jett 1971: 167, 169; Noble and Geib 1976; Jett 1976).

Frame Hogan

Major features:

1. Wall structure: horizontal or vertical planks nailed to a frame consisting of horizontal head (top) and sole (sill) plates nailed to vertical corner posts (Fig. 5.45).

2. Plan: polygonal.

3. Roof: pyramidal.

Variations:

1. In a very few cases, exterior battens are nailed over the interstices between vertical planks.

2. Tarpaper is usually nailed over the exterior walls (Fig. 5.45), which may be stuccoed.

3. Cinder-block foundations are usual.

Fig. 5.49. From left: frame garage with hipped-with-ridge roof, stuccoed frame house with gabled roof, plank hogan with extended entry and hipped-with-ridge roof, clothesline, and post-and-wire fence. North of Ft. Defiance, Arizona, 1968.

Construction Procedures

Leaning-plank hogans (Fig. 5.42) may be the earliest of the plank hogans; except for the use of nails and planks instead of logs, they are constructed in a fashion similar to that of lean-ing-log hogans, although the batter of the walls of the former tends to be less. Such ho-gans have previously been ignored in the liter-ature, perhaps because they may often be earth-covered and superficially indistinguisha-ble from other earth-covered, corbeled or cor-beled-log-roofed hogans.

Post-and-plank hogans, although far more prominent, are also almost undescribed in the literature (Spencer and Jett 1971: 166–67, 169; Jett 1981). The types typical of the western Reservation have inwardly inclined corner posts and are similar to abutting-log hogans except that nailed-on planks replace the stacked logs. Exteriors may have earth piled over them (Fig. 5.43) or be stuccoed (Fig. 5.46). The vertical-walled post-and-plank ho-gans common in the central Navajo Country are presumably a later development; their cor-ner posts are of sawn lumber (Fig. 5.47), they normally have hipped, not corbeled-log, roofs, and they are nearly always tarpapered and usually stuccoed. They also often exhibit more elaborate, modern details (Figs. 5.44, 5.49).

Numbers of sides vary from five to twelve. Wall height probably normally ranges from about 5 to 6.5 feet (1.52 to 1.83 m); diameters are variable but are usually comparable to those of other moderate- to large-sized hogans.

Fig. 5.50. Probable post-and-plank hogan with stone veneer, and a flat-roofed plank building of unknown function. The hogan has a corbeled-log roof with eave boards. Planks presumably run between the interior sides of the corner posts, and siltstone slabs set on edge have been cemented onto the walls' exterior. A pole-and-rod drying rack stands at the far right. Near the junction of U.S. 89 and Arizona 164, Tuba City area, 1969.

Frame hogans were rare at the time of the authors' field work but seem to have become more common since (McAllester and McAllester 1980: 21, 23, 27, 73). Their external appearance is similar to that of vertical-walled horizontal-plank hogans, and we may not have adequately distinguished the two in the field. Frame hogans are the type most nearly akin to frame houses, having a true frame including corner posts, head and sole plates, studs, and sometimes cats (see "Frame Houses," chapter 7). (Figure 5.51 pictures a unique, truly "house-sized" structure of basically polygonal plan.)

Planks for construction are obtained from the Tribal sawmill or are purchased in border towns, as are nails and other commercial materials. They are normally brought to the construction site in pickup trucks (Liebler 1962: 307). Plank-hogan roofs are usually of frame construction in the central and eastern areas, corbeled-log in the west. At one time, the Navajo Forest Products Industry (at Navajo, New Mexico) experimented unsuccessfully with the marketing of prefabricated hogans of this general type (Martin Link, personal communication, 1971).

Fig. 5.51. Hogan or house? A polygonal, multiroom, board-and-batten frame dwelling with a pyramidal roof and an attached pyramidal-roofed garage. Commercially made doors and aluminum-frame windows are employed. A corral and barn (?) stand at the right. Between Sanders and Chambers, Arizona, 1968.

Fig. 5.52. Old subrectangular hogan of uncoursed sandstone; logs supplement the stones of the left-hand wall. Four very slightly inclined external corner posts carry four stringers, upon which a corbeled-log roof has been erected. Most of the roof's earth covering and the walls' mortar (if any) have eroded away; there are a few stone slabs on the roof. Above Wild Cherry Canyon, Canyon de Chelly, Arizona, 1978.

MASONRY HOGANS

Stone-masonry hogans are fairly common. Rare and modern are hogans employing cinder blocks or adobe bricks.

Stone Hogan

Hester (1962: 72) wrote, "the circular stone-walled hogan can be considered to be an adaptation of Puebloan masonry to the hogan style, as it post-dates Puebloan contact;" Vivian (1960: 160) concurred, and Brugge (1972b: 13) gave evidence showing that Puebloan-influenced Navajos fleeing the Dinétah dispersed this form southwestward into less Puebloan-influenced areas. The Huschers (1942; 1943: 7), on the other hand, believed the stone hogan to be a very old and widely distributed house type. They considered the surviving Navajo form (Figs. 5.52, 5.53, 5.54, 5.55, 1.3) to owe nothing to Puebloans other than a limited use of mud mortar and the adoption of the corbeled-log roof in place of an original conical brush-covered roof. The Huschers maintained that in the Southwest the circular stone dwelling is confined to the Navajo and that it is nearer the true ancestral

Athapaskan house type than is the conical forked-pole hogan; they also pointed out that shelters resembling the conical forked-pole hogan have been reported for the Hopi (Huscher and Huscher 1943: 53). Stone dwellings are not reported for Northern Athapaskans, however; nor are they characteristic of other Southern Athapaskans. As discussed above, it appears likely that the original Navajo dwellings were conical forked-pole structures and lean-tos and that the Navajo acquired the technique of stone masonry after contact with Puebloans, and probably after 1692. Jett (1964: 294) considered the Huschers' "hogans" to be of Puebloan origin; some workers believe them to be Ute structures (Ellis 1974: 77; Hester 1962: 72).

The recently excavated Cerrito Site in the Rio Chama drainage northwest of Abiquiu, New Mexico, has raised some questions regarding the date of Navajo adoption of masonry. This site of the so-called Piedra Lumbre Phase contains single- and multi-unit circular and subrectangular stone structures and is tentatively attributed to the Navajo. It is dated between about 1640 and 1710, with 1660 suggested as the peak period of occupation (Schaafsma 1979). If these suppositions are

Fig. 5.53. Abandoned circular hogan of uncoursed sandstone; most of the mud mortar has eroded away. The interior was mud-plastered. Erosion has exposed the log corbeling of the roof. The stones flanking the entry have been selected for larger size and for squareness and may have been roughly shaped; part of a plank door frame remains. Canyon Bonito, west of Ft. Defiance, Arizona, 1968.

Fig. 5.54. Circular hogan of roughly coursed uncut stone, with a corbeled-log roof. Note the stone stoop, the plank door and door frame, and the arrangement of logs over the doorway. A post-and-wire fence with a post-and-wire gate stands in the foreground. Near Twin Trail, Canyon del Muerto, Arizona, 1972.

Fig. 5.55. Polygonal hogan of partly coursed, partly uncoursed stone masonry, with a corbeled-log roof and a homemade plank door with commercially made hinges. The stones have been carefully selected and perhaps shaped. A collapsed homemade hibachi is seen to the left of the entry. The stake-and-rail community livestock corral and rodeo grounds (?) stands in the right middle ground. The Gap, Arizona, 1970.

correct, Navajo use of masonry would have begun somewhat earlier than formerly believed, prior to the Refugee Period beginning in 1692. Ceramics at Piedra Lumbre sites are mostly Tewan, and it is possible that these sites are Puebloan. Of interest are circular stone structures of Pueblo III age occurring in the Lower Chaco River area, New Mexico (Reher 1977: 79, 82).

Despite a dearth of early reports in the literature (see also "Stone Houses," chapter 7) and despite many informants' belief that the stone hogan is relatively recent (Kluckhohn et al. 1971: 152), stone masonry is first encountered in unequivocal hogans in Dinétah, during the Gobernador Phase (1696–1770), sometime before 1752 (Brugge 1972b: 6).[34] Stone hogans were common among the eastern Navajo during the succeeding Cabezon Phase, 1770–1863 (Vivian 1960; Hester 1962: 67). Frank Mitchell surmised that stone hogans "in canyons and different places" built during the era of intertribal warfare were built for defense (Frisbie and McAllester 1978: 31); they would have been more bullet- and fireproof than log structures.

In view of the early use and persistence of stone hogans, it is surprising that they were not mentioned by nineteenth-century observers other than Robinson (1848: 33), Ricc (Dillon 1970: 71), Schoolcraft (1853: 70), Bourke (1936: 87, 236), and Stephen (1893: 350). In fact, the use of stone hogans is specifically denied by Letterman (1856: 289) and the Franciscan Fathers (1910: 63). Apparently, most of these observers did not visit the tree-poor areas where stone hogans were common. The earliest photograph of a stone hogan we have discovered dated from 1901, at Ft. Defiance (National Anthropological Archives, No. 54744).

Adobe-Brick, Fired-Brick, and Cinder-Block Hogans

The use of adobe brick in hogans is extremely rare. It is not described in the literature and is in all probability modern. Such hogans are known to us only through published photographs taken near Shiprock (Stirling 1961; Cummings 1964: 8) and through an oral communication from David M. Brugge (1968), respecting Tuba City. There is no evidence that Navajos used adobe brick before the early twentieth century, although adobe hogans obviously would not be well preserved in the archaeology. Navajo use of adobe brick is confined mainly to houses (see chapter 7), and, even in the case of these nontraditional dwellings, its use is very uncommon.

No examples of fired-brick hogans have been recorded, although brick-veneer hogans are known. Cinder-block hogans (Fig. 5.56) are very rare, and the use of this material is

Fig. 5.56. Cinder-block hogan with cut-stone foundation, quoins, door trim, and window sill; corbeled-log roof with eave boards. The window is commercially manufactured. Dinnebito Wash drainage, north of Arizona Highway 264, 1970.

clearly recent and dependent upon Anglo-American manufactured materials and building methods. Recent Navajo Tribal housing programs that have included the gratis distribution of cinder blocks to interested Navajos probably account for the occasional occurrence of cinder-block hogans. Such structures are not noted in the literature outside our own work (Spencer and Jett 1971: 172; Jett and Spencer 1971; Jett 1973), and are undoubtedly quite recent in origin.

Descriptions of masonry hogans follow:
Diagnostic feature: masonry construction.

Stone Hogan

Navajo name: tsé ([nás] tł'in[go]) bee hooghan = with-([circularly]-piled)-rocks hogan.
Major features:
1. Wall structure: stone masonry (Figs. 5.52, 5.53, 5.54, 5.55).
2. Plan: circular (Figs. 5.53, 5.54), elliptical, subpolygonal, polygonal (Fig. 5.55), subrectangular (Fig. 5.52), D-shaped (Fig. 5.57), or irregular.
3. Roof: corbeled-log (Figs. 5.52, 5.53, 5.54, 5.55), flat (Fig. 5.57), center-beam, pyramidal, or conical forked-pole(?).[35]

Minor features and variations:

1. The floor is sometimes shallowly excavated (Vivian 1960: 31; Page 1937: 47), and dugout stone hogans (*łeeh hoogeedgo tsé bee hooghan*) have been reported (J. Lee Correll and William Morgan, personal communications).
2. The masonry may be coursed or uncoursed, with or without spall chinking, and with or without adobe or cement mortar; the stones may be small or large, dressed or unworked (see "Construction Procedures," below).
3. Walls are normally vertical, but Jett has observed an old hogan in Canyon de Chelly whose walls are slightly battered (*i.e.,* there is a small degree of corbeling).
4. Archaeological examples (to as late as ca. 1920) have been recorded in which a natural boulder or cliff forms part of the hogan wall (Fig. 5.57). Archaeologically known unroofed semicircular stone walls which, with the rear walls of natural rock shelters or boulders, form rooms, may also be classified as stone hogans.[36]
5. Occasionally, one or a few courses of logs are laid atop the stone walls, beneath the lowest roof logs (Fig. 5.52).

Fig. 5.57. Remains of an archaeological D-shaped stone hogan built against a cliff base at the top of a talus slope. Note the stone slabs on top of the beams of the flat roof as well as the remnants of an apparent parapet. Above Crack Trail, Canyon de Chelly, Arizona, 1971.

6. One specimen with an exterior masonry bench about 1 foot wide and 1 foot high (.30 X .30 m) was observed. Jerrold E. Levy (personal communication) reported a cement floor near Tuba City, Arizona, dating from the 1930s (the builder had Civilian Conservation Corps experience).

7. The interior walls may be mud-plastered.

8. The doorway may be a simple opening in the wall or may form one side of a polygonal plan, but various types of short masonry vestibules were formerly sometimes added.[37] Plank doorjambs are the rule today. Vivian (1960: 32) recorded instances of monolithic columns or slabs flanking the entries of some archaeological hogans.

Adobe-Brick Hogan

Navajo name: hashtł'ish dik'ání bee hooghan (?) = with-mud-cubes hogan.
Major features:
1. Wall structure: adobe-brick masonry.
2. Plan: circular?
3. Roof: pyramidal?

Cinder-Block Hogan

Navajo name: tsé nádleehé bee hooghan, tsé dik'ání bee hooghan = with-to-rock-transforming [i.e., cement] hogan, with-rock-cubes hogan.
1. Wall structure: cinder-block masonry, cement mortar (Fig. 5.56).
2. Plan: polygonal or circular.
3. Roof: pyramidal (other types may also exist).
Minor features and variations:
1. One example noted by the authors had decorative cut-sandstone quoins, window sills, doorway trim, and foundation (Fig. 5.56).

Construction Procedures

Within the category of stone hogans, there is considerable variation, particularly in archaeological examples.[38] Recorded interior diameters range up to 17 feet, 3 inches (5.93 m).

Archaeological hogans are smaller than modern ones. The average diameter of those studied by Vivian was 9.5 feet (2.90 m), and the minimum was 4.5 feet or 1.37 meters (suggesting that this may have been a storage hogan; Vivian 1960: 29; see also, Malcolm 1939: 6; Farmer 1947: 18; De Harport 1959–4: 1598–1600). In 1846, Robinson (1848) estimated diameters to be about 8 feet (2.44 m), height of walls 4 feet (1.21 m). Maximum wall height today is probably about 6 feet (1.83 m). Gifford (1940: 107) listed typical dimensions as 10 by 20 to 15 by 30 feet (3.05 X 6.10 to 4.07 X 9.14 m), giving the erroneous impression that the usual plan was an ellipse. The masonry may be dry-laid or set in mud or, occasionally nowadays, cement. Keur (1941: 26) described various masonry types in archaeological hogans at Big Bead Mesa, New Mexico, including:

1. Large irregular or rounded uncoursed boulders (see also, Keur 1944: 76; Vivian 1960: 31, 37). Walls of this type are sometimes only two or three stones high, indicating that these were either windbreaks or hogans whose roofs gave the structures most of their height; these would then be considered stone foundations rather than true walls.

2. Long, thin slabs or thick blocks of sandstone (occasionally of up to 1.5 by 2.5 ft, i.e. .46 by .76 m) or a combination of these, with a semblance of coursing or, sometimes, well coursed; spalls are sometimes inserted in the interstices, occasionally with the addition of adobe mortar.

3. Roughly rectangular blocks of stone, coursed or uncoursed, usually set in mud mortar. Wall height was probably from 3.5 to 4 feet (1.07 to 1.22 m).

Masonry types 2 and 3 above are still encountered in hogans (Figs. 5.53, 5.54), and type 1 occurs in windbreaks (Fig. 4.2). Reher (1977: 38, 45) found that in the lower Chaco River area, the bases of hogans often consisted of quite large, angular "boulders," overlain by masonry of medium-sized blocks. Some more modern stone hogans, particularly polygonal

Fig. 5.58. The only poured-concrete hogan recorded. The contact between the two tiers of concrete is visible. Note the roughly cut stone foundation with mud mortar, atop which boards were laid to receive the concrete; the board-framed window opening with a side-hinged, inward-opening window; and the roll-roofing-covered pyramidal roof with stovepipe. A conical firewood pile stands at the right. On Black Mesa, Arizona, 1959; Editha L. Watson.

ones, use carefully selected or very well dressed stones, both of uniform rectangular shape and of less regular form, often set in cement mortar (Fig. 5.55). The plans of archaeological and most contemporary stone hogans are circular (Figs. 5.53, 5.54) or, at least, with rounded corners (Fig. 5.52), unless a cliff or boulder is incorporated to form one wall (Fig. 5.57). However, a significant number of modern stone hogans are polygonal (Fig. 5.55).

Construction involves the finding of, quarrying, transporting, sometimes shaping,

and laying up of the stones on a cleared patch of ground. If mortar is used, as is usual, the clay or cement and sand must be mixed with water in advance of laying the stones (see also, "Stone Houses," chapter 7). The roof is added when the walls have been erected and the mortar has dried.

Adobe bricks are homemade, in forms (see "Adobe-brick Houses," chapter 7). Hogans using this material are exceedingly rare, and we have never encountered one. A few published photographs have appeared (Stirling 1961; Cummings 1964: 8).

Cinder-block hogans are rare; we know of only two passing references (Nielson 1967: 37; Spencer and Jett 1971: 172). Standard, commercially produced blocks are purchased or obtained gratis from the Tribe and are laid up with cement mortar, usually on a polygonal plan (Fig. 5.56). A standard block measures 7.5 by 7.5 by 15.5 inches (19.05 × 19.05 × 39.37 cm).

POURED-CONCRETE HOGAN

Only one example (previously unpublished) of a poured-concrete hogan, on a stone foundation, is known (Fig. 5.58). The material is, of course, modern and is based upon commercially manufactured cement. The technique—employing forms—is presumably an adoption of an Anglo-American construction method, although the somewhat similar practice of building with coursed adobe, sometimes on stone foundations, was common among Rio Grande Puebloans (McGregor 1965: 387, 416; Wendorf 1954: 218) and Jicarilla Apaches (Gunnerson 1969: 23, 25) into early historic times. It is surprising that the one record of this technique is from the isolated Black Mesa area of Arizona (Editha L. Watson, personal communication, 1968).

A description follows:

Diagnostic feature: walls of poured concrete.

Other major features:

1. Wall structure: two courses of concrete poured into a 2- to 3-foot-high (.61 to .91 m) wooden frame, which was moved up to receive the upper course after the lower had set; a space was left for a window (Fig. 5.58).

2. Plan: polygonal.

3. Roof: pyramidal.

Minor feature:

1. A stone foundation supported the single example known (Fig. 5.58). As far as the present authors are aware, this hogan is unique.

Stone house, Canyon de Chelly, Arizona, 1972.

Chapter 6

ADOPTION OF HOUSES

DATE OF ADOPTION OF HOUSES

Although some eighteenth-century Navajos used houses (see below, under "Stone Houses"), house use was discontinued during the latter part of that century, as archaeology shows. Navajo use of houses is specifically denied by certain mid-nineteenth-century commentators. Backus (1854: 213) wrote

> I once endeavored to persuade a rich Navajoe to build a house, and to live in it. He replied, "A house will be of no use to me. I cannot live in it. I must follow my flocks and herds, where I can find grass and water." He was then asked where he slept. He replied, "Just like a dog—on grass or chips."

Eaton (1854: 217) declared that "They do not live in houses built of stone, as has been repeatedly represented. . . ."

In the Ft. Defiance area, headmen are said to have encouraged the building of houses—presumably cribbed-log and stone ones—during the 1880s (Dyk 1947: 19). Although this trend was apparently accelerated under the influence of Agent Dennis M. Riordan during his brief tenure in 1883–84, even by 1881 headman "Manuelito was getting modern ideas and

asked the government to supply him with glass windows, door frames, nails, etc., for a modern house" (Van Valkenburgh n.d.: 27–38). On July 28, 1881, the Agent requested permission to loan wagons to headmen to aid them in house building (Brugge 1968b: 160). In October of 1883, Agent Riordan asked for funds to repair the government sawmill (established in 1880), citing "the growing desire of the Navajoes for modern houses" (Van Valkenburgh n.d.: 9, 38, 60). According to Dunn (1886: 406), "About fifty of the men were induced to build houses, in 1884, but the vast majority still adhere to their temporary hogans. . . ." The Agency contributed materials for these houses (Underhill 1953: 208). When Riordan resigned as Agent in June 1884 (to manage a lumber company), Manuelito asked, in a farewell speech, "Who will teach the Navajo how to build houses, dig ditches, and generally improve themselves?" (Van Valkenburgh n.d.: 94).

The first explicit description of a Navajo house is that of Shufeldt (1892), which documents the construction of a one-room palisaded house at Ft. Wingate in 1888. A different tradition seems to have developed at this post, stressing Hispano *palisado* techniques (see below). Mindeleff (1897: 152; 1898:

503–04), writing in the mid-1890s and drawing upon field experience commencing in 1881 (Judd 1967: 63–64), noted that rectangular Navajo houses were recent and rare. Specifically,

Up to ten years ago there was so little change in the [traditional dwelling types built] that it might be said that there was none.... As a collateral result of the [increased emphasis on farming] ... an effort is now sometimes made to build [permanent] houses on the American plan.... They are rectangular in plan, sometimes with a board roof, and occasionally comprise several rooms.... they are constructed of stone, regular walls of masonry ... [or] of logs, often hewn square....

The log houses referred to ... ordinarily are covered with flat earthen roofs.... Sometimes door and window frames are procured from the sawmill or from the traders ... while nearly always one or more glazed windows occupy the window openings and board doors close the entrances.

Walter G. Marmon (1894: 157), writing of the 1890 census, noted that:

Many [Navajos] are building good storehouses, particularly in the farming localities. This is nôtably so in the Chuski, Lu-ki-chu-ki, and Chinlee valleys and Canyon de Chelly. The generally accepted idea that the Navajos, on superstitious grounds, will not live in houses is fallacious. Many of them are anxious to build houses and live like white people.

Wrote Alexander Stephen (1893: 362), who lived among the stone-house-building Hopi,

But perhaps the most promising indication of their [Navajos'] steady advance toward civilization is displayed in their growing desire to possess permanent dwellings, and many of them already built for themselves comfortable two-roomed stone cabins.

J. W. Powell (1895: 53) wrote, "Originally they dwelt in [conical] hogans ... now they are copying the dwelling places of civilized men." Platero (1967: 167) termed a stone house built in the Cañoncito area in the 1890s

"one of the earlier houses" of the region, and small stone houses appear to date from about 1900 in the lower Chaco River area (Reher 1977: 39). The Franciscan Fathers (1910: 327) noted that "At a very recent date ... the old type of dwelling is being partly displaced by a more commodious log or stone structure [house] of the flat roof type."

According to Ostermann (1917: 26–27),

During the past fifteen or twenty years quite a number of Navajos have built for themselves rectangular houses of stone or logs, having sometimes, two, or even three rooms, with a flat, or occasionally a slant gabled roof, glazed windows, wooden doors, boarded floors, and regular chimneys. Such houses, as a rule, belong to the richer and more progressive Navajos, and are furnished....

Fraser (1919: 205) wrote,

In the vicinity of Chin Lee,—indeed all the way after we had gone about 35 miles [southeast] from Kayenta,—... the customary type of hogan is rare.... Many of the Navajo occupy houses built on the plan of the white men's, some of them have an improved type of hogan with some carpentry work and a little masonry thrown in.

The houses described by Fraser must have been mostly of logs, for Reagan (1919: 246) wrote that there was only one stone house within 60 miles (97 km) of Kayenta. Speaking of the Gallup area about the same time period, Brink (1947: 191) wrote that "The Navajos had a very few one or two room cabins."

Thus, it appears that "modern" log and stone houses first began to be adopted during the early 1880s, and became well established (partially independently) in several areas during the 1890s and early 1900s. Adoption was much later in many areas, however (see chapter 13). These early houses were presumably mostly one-room structures, although Navajo leaders sometimes had more than one room. By the early 1930s, leader Henry Chee Dodge had a large, multiroom house north of Ft. Defiance (Frisbie and McAllester 1978: 252), although he normally dwelt in a hogan (Robert W. Young, personal communication).

FACTORS INFLUENCING ADOPTION OF HOUSES

Mobility and Dwelling Form

The late nineteenth-century emergence of houses among the Navajo was certainly a result of intensive Anglo-American (and, to some degree, Hispano) contact, which familiarized Navajos with new forms, materials, and methods. Further, the termination of hostilities and the availability of wagons and then pickups—for hauling building materials, firewood, and water, and for commuting to fields—have certainly contributed to the trend toward more permanent settlement (which has also been promoted by the government). Rapid population growth and the consequent reduction in per capita grazing area, plus some use of hay, have also reduced grazing-related movements. Writing of the 1880s and '90s, Mindeleff (1898: 482, 503) contended that grass and water scarcity required frequent translocation of the flocks, and that "This condition more than any other has worked against the erection of permanent houses." He felt that an increasing emphasis on agriculture was tending to encourage the adoption of substantial houses. Schmedding (1974: 163), drawing upon experience terminating in 1923, attributed to a mobile lifeway the fact that "The white man's house has found small favor among the Navajo." Despite a decline in transhumant movements, use of modern transport for access to central places and for visiting has also accelerated contact and acculturation and the diffusion of innovation (Tremblay et al. 1954: 213–14).

There is one case in the literature in which competition for resources with Anglos provided a motive for house building. On February 1, 1885, wrote a Joseph City, Arizona, Mormon, "There was two Navajos here today wanting me to put up houses on their spring as the Americans are threatening to Jump them" (Tanner and Richards 1977: 71).

Physical Efficiency and Dwelling Form

The adoption of houses represented first the alteration of the round or polygonal plan, and gradually many Navajos have abandoned the single-room tradition in favor of multiple-room houses, although problems of heating still militate against the latter.

As Vogt (1951: 110), Kluckhohn and Leighton (1962: 45), and Rapoport (1969b: 75) have observed, the trend toward the replacement of the hogan form by the house form cannot be attributed to ease of construction or to any superior qualities of houses in protecting the inhabitants from the elements. The hemisphere is the most efficient enclosure of space in terms of the amount of building materials used and is the most efficient form to heat. The cone and the cylinder follow, while the rectangular house, especially with a steeply pitched gabled roof, is the least efficient form. This order also applies to relative lack of wind resistance. Traditional logs, bark, earth, and stone also result in better insulation than do commercial planks, tarpaper, and stucco.

A further point is that houses have larger surface areas than hogans of comparable volume, leading to houses' greater potential for air and rain leakage as well as heat conduction. One Rock Point resident observed that he "is more comfortable in a hogan than in a square house. He says it has more room and it's easier to arrange the furniture for his own convenience" (Thomas et al. 1974: 23). Navajo/Ute Irene Smith stated, "We always had a traditional hogan of mud and sand [rather than a plank structure] because it stayed warm in winter once the fire was going and cool in summer" (Anonymous 1974b: 128). Another writer, speaking of a "sand-covered" hogan, stated that "Sand makes good insulation, keeping the inside of the hogan cool in summer and warm on colder days ... " (Anonymous n.d.b.). The reasons for adopting houses were, then, cultural and not physical-environmental. The phenomenon of alterations of dwelling type in response to new religious and esthetic values, status considerations, novelty, and other cultural factors is well documented throughout much of the world (Rapoport 1969a: 21–24), and the Navajo follow that pattern.

Religion and Ghost Fear

These changes in housing may seem somewhat strange in view of the Navajo's well-known pragmatism. Further, the hogan is sanctioned by religion and is a symbol of cultural identity. The conical forked-pole hogan was created at the Emergence Place by First Man, according to the Emergence myth (Goddard 1933: 25, 133), and there appear to be specific traditional religious prohibitions and social sanctions against living in houses (Brugge 1963: 22; Fishler 1953: 34; Tremblay et al. 1954: 217–18). Certainly, hogan use is reinforced by its required role in Blessingway and chantways (Haile 1942).

Further, Dunn (1886: 217–18, 406) and Ostermann (1917: 9) suggested that one reason Navajos did not adopt houses earlier was that since their beliefs required at least the abandonment and perhaps the partial or complete destruction of a dwelling if anyone died therein, it would have been foolish to build substantial buildings if there was a risk that they would eventually have to be deserted. This idea is supported by headman Armijo's statement to Navajo Agent John Greiner (Abel 1916: 208) in the 1850s that Navajos would not live in houses because "whenever a head of a family dies [the custom is] to destroy all his property and burn the houses, [and] it would keep them building all the time." Lockett (1952; Jones et al. 1939: 83–84) also mentioned this as a disincentive toward investing in an expensive dwelling. However, many of the small, early houses required little more labor to construct than a hogan, and to avoid having to abandon a dwelling ". . . the sick are often cared for at some distance from the home, precautions which are always taken for modern dwellings" (Haile 1954: 12). Too, Tremblay et al. (1954: 215–16) suggested that at Fruitland the question of what to do in case of a death in a house is often not considered prior to construction. Nevertheless, a 1974–75 survey of residences in Navajo Housing Authority/Housing and Urban Development (NHA/HUD) houses in Window Rock re-

vealed that half the respondents thought they would move if a death occurred in their house (Snyder et al. ca. 1976: 12).

Acquisition of New Skills and Materials

We must again raise the question as to why, among such pragmatists as the Navajo, the physical advantages of hogans are being given up. The answer may in part also be pragmatic: the increased heating efficiency of stoves as compared with hearths may compensate for the relevant advantages of hogans, and overall construction labor is less with modern materials than with logs, earth, and stone, especially where logs or stone must be hauled long distances. Availability of free or low-cost lumber, cinder blocks, and manufactured doors and windows from the Tribe and through government housing programs often offsets the significant cash outlay ordinarily required for commercially manufactured building materials (e.g., Wilmsen 1960: 19). Accessibility of these supplies has greatly increased as a consequence of improved roads and increased motor-vehicle use (e.g., Coolidge and Coolidge 1931: 84). Additional housing subsidies in the form of labor and loans have also contributed importantly to many Navajos' decisions to build houses (see "Frame Houses" and note 4, chapter 7).

Gradual increase in carpentry and other contemporary building skills, plus increased cash income usable for purchase of commercial materials not supplied by housing-assistance programs have undoubtedly contributed importantly to the ability to build houses (Coolidge and Coolidge 1931: 84; Kluckhohn and Leighton 1962: 45), as has availability of new tools (steel axes, saws, hammers). Modern methods and materials tend to be associated with nontraditional dwelling forms in the minds of many.

A considerable number of Navajos gained experience in modern construction methods through employment on government, Tribal, and mission projects such as administrative buildings, schools, chapter houses, chapels, etc. The teaching of "industrial arts" in schools contributed too; for example, carpentry was being taught from at least the beginning of this century (Johnston 1972: 282) and was one of the vocational skills taught in the Special Navajo Education Program commencing in 1946 (Boyce 1974: 202; Thompson 1975: 59, 101; see also, Schmedding 1974: 174).

Influence of Anglo Values

Despite all the above considerations, it is doubtful that the hogan form would be giving way to the house form were it not for the strong influence of changes in values.

The values of the dominant culture have long been taught in government schools and religious missions, and they have been promoted by the Bureau of Indian Affairs, the Public Health Service, and other agencies. To a considerable extent, too, such values have been adopted because of contact with Anglo-American culture through traders, military service, wage work, the tourist trade, and the mass media. These acquired values—which include not only hygiene, comfort, and convenience but also ideas such as "progress," privacy, and status as reflected in one's house and its furnishings—certainly have, in many cases, stimulated Navajos to construct prestigeful (at least to the more acculturated), "progressive" dwellings with at least some of the amenities valued by Anglos (c.f. Haile 1937: 4; Tremblay et al. 1954: 211–13, 217–18; Hannum 1958: 104–08). Utilities were highly valued as amenities among Window Rock Navajos in 1974–75 (Snyder et al. ca. 1976: 13), although these are still not available in most areas.

Lockett (1952: 137; Jones et al. 1939: 82) wrote in 1939,

Actually, Navajos prefer to live in hogans. There are instances where Navajo men with means have built houses near their hogans. This apparently was done primarily to gain more prestige. In reality, the houses were used for storage and for warehouses and the family lives most of the time in the hogan.

Haile (1954: 11) wrote, "The idea of the modern house is, of course, better living accommodations in imitation of whites. But frequently the modern building is used for storage purposes [Fig. 6.1], while the hogan is the preferable dwelling and always the place for the ceremonials" (see also Haile 1937: 4; Hardwick 1970a: 6). According to Kluckhohn and Leighton (1962: 45), "The supplementary cabin is increasingly popular as a place where women can weave or sew when it is raining hard and whither they can withdraw for tasks requiring concentration when the weather is neither so hot nor so cold as to make the cabin uncomfortable." Haile (1942: 56) and Kluckhohn and Leighton (1962: 45) noted that even when a house was the preferred dwelling, typically the occupant also built a hogan, because only there may all ceremonies be performed. A Navajo informs us that in this situation, the hogan is still considered *ghan,* home. To the extent that Navajo religion is no longer observed, individuals may build only houses (Haile 1952);[1] in fact, this seems to be the current trend (Adams and Ruffing 1977: 61–62). Platero (1967: 164–65) wrote that in the mid-1960s, most people in the Cañoncito area wanted houses rather than hogans. Some desired more than one room in the dwellings, and some even dreamed of a private room (see also Mitchell and Allen 1967: 212). Although some older people preferred to remain living in hogans (see also Hardwick 1970), some wanted a house too, for their more acculturated children who had become accustomed to modern conveniences. However, many of those preferring houses wished to retain hogans for ceremonies. Woods (1952: 6) quoted a Navajo: "At Indian school they told us to go home and make our houses like the white people's. My wife and I did this. Now our children with good educations like to come home to see us." Helmut Kloos (unpublished data) found that in 1969 two-thirds of his interviewees in the Aneth area expressed a preference for houses over hogans. He attributed this attitude primarily to school experience and the efforts of the county welfare department. A local welfare caseworker said that many local parents had told him that their children had written

Fig. 6.1. Cribbed-log storage house with an earth-covered center-beam roof; the family lives in a hogan. Some of the storehouse's logs have been planked and all have been debarked. They are singly box-notched and rest on large foundation stones at the corners. Some board chinking is visible, and earth has been piled along the wall bases. Chauncey and Dorothy Neboyia's main homestead, north of Canyon de Chelly, Arizona, near the head of Beehive Trail, 1972.

indicating that they would not come home unless houses with floors and windows were provided (see also, Nielson 1967).

Many of the more acculturated Navajos are ashamed to live in hogans (e.g.,Tremblay et al. 1954: 217–18). At Ramah, in the late 1940s, eleven out of fifteen Navajos expressed a strong preference for houses, and seven actually lived in houses—but all families retained a hogan for supplemental living quarters and for ceremonies. Vogt (1951: 110) observed that "The motive for building them [houses] apparently springs from a desire to live in a house

in the manner of white people. . . . To the Navajo . . . a house . . . is a symbol of acculturation." The work of David Stea (personal communication, 1978) in Black Creek Valley in 1968 suggested that houses also symbolized a steady income (pragmatic success) as well as utilities and their associated comforts, although preference for houses seemed to be largely practical rather than symboblic (Snyder et al. ca. 1976: 17). The hogan, on the other hand, was explicitly contrasted to Puebloan houses in the Navajo Emergence Myth (Goddard 1933: 23–25, 132–33) and thus from a remote period has been a symbol of ethnic identity, a role that has persisted to a fair degree (Tremblay et al. 1954; Crumrine 1964: 41–46) but which appears to be declining (Snyder et al. ca. 1976: 17–18; Jett 1981). Hogans today also symbolize traditionalism and are still preferred by some individuals. Navajo-/Ute Irene Smith remarked, "If we built a house or modern hogan of lumber, which my [Ute] mother likes, we always had to have our traditional hogan alongside for my [Navajo] father" (Anonymous 1974b: 128).

In the fairly acculturated Fruitland community in 1952, negative sanctions no longer existed against house use. Almost everyone was considering improving their old homes or building "better" ones (Tremblay et al. 1954: 217–18). A 1958–59 study of the Ft. Defiance area elicited the information that of the Navajo residents of that community, more than 93 percent of those that responded to a questionnaire preferred to live in houses hav-ing four or more rooms (Young 1961: 306, after Bosch 1961).

A 1974–75 study at Window Rock, Arizona, showed that 47 percent of the residents of NHA/HUD houses would, if given the choice, prefer the "fanciest, largest, most modern" houses, and only 6 percent would prefer to live in a hogan. Further, there was a clear correlation between degree of acculturation and degree of preference for nontraditional housing (Snyder et al. ca. 1976: 11–12).

What may be yet another, incipient, stage in the sequence of dwelling types was observed on the Alamo Reserve. There, large mobile homes comprised 19 percent of all dwellings observed in 1974. The local trader (personal communication) stated that no one lives in hogans any more and that prosperity consequent upon the development of the jewelry business has resulted in many Navajos eschewing tribally provided buiding materials and buying mobile homes instead.

Adobe-brick and frame houses, south of Lupton, Arizona, 1972.

Chapter 7

NAVAJO HOUSE ORIGINS, EVOLUTIONS, AND FORMS[1]

PALISADED HOUSE

Although not particularly common, palisaded buildings have occasionally been built by Anglo-Americans in various regions, including the Southwest. They have a very long history and wide distribution in Europe and were used in early New England (Kniffen and Glassie 1966: 43, 46–47), French Canada (Wonders 1979: 195–96), and in French-influenced areas of the Mississippi drainage. Old photographs show flat-roofed examples at Ft. Sumner, New Mexico (Underhill 1953: 171, 206; Bailey 1964: 160), and at Arizona forts (Horan 1966: 276, 279, 280), and the original trading posts built in the 1870s at Ganado, Arizona, used this technique, as did Red Lake Trading Post at Tonalea, Arizona (1879; Lee and Richardson 1974: 10–11), Suplee's store (1880s) near Ft. Wingate, New Mexico (Packard and Packard 1970: 30, 32), Tsaile Trading Post, Arizona (Before 1886; Amsden 1934: plate 85), the Meadows post at Shiprock, New Mexico (1900; Forrest 1970: 25–26, 52), Oljeto Trading Post, Utah (ca. 1906; McNitt 1962), and a portion of the Cross Canyon, Arizona, trading post (1904 photograph). In reference to the Ganado structure, Bourke (1884: 67)

said that it "is of the Arizona order of architecture—a single-storied, long, low building of 'jacal' or palisade, filled in with mud chinking, and roofed with a covering of earth and brush." Structures like these certainly provided models for the Navajo palisaded house (Figs. 7.1, 7.2), as suggested by Underhill (1953: 206), who believed that the new availability of railroad ties in 1880 triggered such construction.

On the other hand, Tschopik (Kluckhohn et al. 1971: 148) and Leighton and Leighton (1949: 94) termed palisaded Navajo houses "Spanish-" or "Mexican-style." *Jacales* or *palisados* (palisaded houses) have long been built in Mexico northward to the Pima Alto country, and are common among Rio Grande Hispanos (Driver and Massey 1957: 295, 301–02; Pennington 1969: 222; Gritzner 1969: 34; 1974a: 29–31, 39; Torrez 1979). The relationships between the Anglo, Hispano, and Navajo versions are obscure, but the Hispano structures may well have influenced both Anglo and Navajo ones. This form may, in fact, have been adopted by Navajos at several times and places, but we can document one occurrence, certainly among the earliest. In 1885, Shufeldt (1892) noted that several Navajo families settled in the vicinity of Ft. Wingate built conical

Fig. 7.1. Structures, from left: drying rack, with palisade-fenced corral in background; two palisaded houses with center-beam roofs (the paling of each wall is surmounted by a horizontal plank, atop which lies the roof's log sole plate); a flat-roofed subrectangular leaning-log hogan from which most of the earth covering has been eroded (the wall materials have been supplemented with a few sheets of pasteboard and flat stones; the door of the slightly extended entry is made from Arbuckle Roasted Coffee crates). A trash heap shows at the lower right. Dinneh Chille's homestead. Six miles east of Steamboat, Arizona, 1935; M.S.S. (1075).

Fig. 7.2. Palisaded house with a tarpaper-covered gabled roof. The logs have been debarked and their ends sawn square. Note the masonry chimney, the commercially made window set to slide open horizontally, and the sawbuck. Dinnebito Wash drainage, north of Arizona Highway 264, 1970.

forked-pole hogans exclusively. In 1886, some of these Navajos removed to a more sheltered area and built a dwelling that was a hybrid between a leaning-log hogan and a palisaded house, with the western and northern sides battered but the eastern and southern sides vertical. A third type of dwelling was built nearby in 1888, this time a house with all four sides made of palisaded logs. The roof was of earth-covered boards set on rafters sloping away from a center beam. A few planks were used over the door, which was of planks and hung on hinges. A Ben Wittick photograph of Ft. Wingate (Link 1968: 18–19) shows a number of beam roofed structures, set apart from the main buildings, which appear to be Navajo palisaded houses. Shufeldt did not say whether there were Anglo-built palisaded structures at the fort in the 1880s, but 1893 and 1896 photographs show a palisaded outbuilding there (James 1967: 152, 157). The small, one-room Navajo examples of this house type are,

in effect, square palisaded "hogans," except that the walls are taller and usually support beam roofs. However, the apparent recency of the palisaded hogan suggests influence from the palisaded house rather than the reverse.

A detailed description of the palisaded house follows:

Navajo name: tsin náneeskaalgo bee kin = with-upright-logs-set-in-a circle house.

Diagnostic feature: walls of vertical logs.

Major features:

1. Wall structure: line of adjacent, vertical logs (Figs. 7.1, 7.2, 7.3).

2. Plan: rectangular.

3. Roof: beam (Figs. 7.1, 7.3) or gabled (Fig. 7.2).

Minor features and variations:

1. Logs may be unshaped or squared.

2. The vertical logs may be set in a trench or may rest on a stone foundation or on a plank foundation and floor.

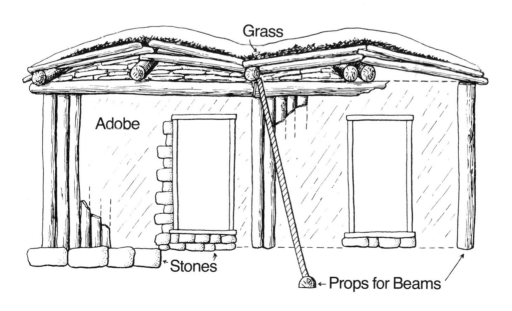

Fig. 7.3. Structural diagram of the facade of a two-room palisaded house with an earth-covered center-beam roof over each unit. Facade length is about 33 feet. Ramah, New Mexico, 1937 (Kluckhohn et al. 1971: 149).

Fig. 7.4. Palisaded dugout house with plank (?) gabled roof whose earth covering is retained by rocks laid along the eaves and by verge boards. Note the fresh mud chinking, the commercial window with glazing bars and screening, the homemade door of narrow boards, and the overturned wagon seat. Big Belly's homestead, Dinnehotso (?), Arizona, 1935; M.S.S. (926).

3. The spaces between logs may be chinked with smaller poles or stones and/or mud (Figs. 7.1, 7.2), and the exterior and interior may be liberally daubed with mud (Figs. 7.3, 7.4).

4. The walls may be surmounted by horizontal logs and/or boards, which act as the roof's sole plates (Figs. 7.1, 7.2).

5. Dugout palisaded houses are known (Fig 7.4).

Construction Procedures

Palisaded houses (Figs. 7.1, 7.2) are not common in the Navajo Country. Brief descriptions appear in Shufeldt (1892), Page (1937b: 48), Corbett (1940: 104, 106), and Tremblay et al. (1954: 197–98). Reichard (1938: plates opposite pp. 78, 79) pictured an interior and an exterior of one specimen. The construction technique is similar to that of the palisaded hogan, except that in a few cases the log ends rest on a foundation. Kluckhohn et al. (1971: 148–50) presented H. S. Tschopik's descriptions of two- and three- room palisaded houses (Fig. 7.3):

[One] house . . . was eleven yards by six yards [10.06 by 5.49 m.] and had two rooms of equal size connected by a door[way]. An exterior door[way] in each room faced east. The walls were of upright pinyon logs plastered [inside and out] with adobe. Other logs [apparently unmortised,] were placed horizontally across the top[s] of the walls. . . . The logs were caulked with adobe and small pieces of sandstone. At the south end of the house the corner posts rested on large stones, and others were placed against the base of the wall to prevent erosion. . . .

Door sills were set on stones, and stone ma-

Fig. 7.5. Cribbed-log house. Although some of the logs appear to be simply saddle-notched, others seem to have more V-shaped notches to receive the V-trimmed lower sides of certain logs and, in a few cases, to have been partly grooved along their upper sides to receive the ridges of the Vs (such a system is otherwise unknown; Phleps 1942). The logs are chinked with sticks and mud and rest on a high stone foundation. The roof is center-beam, with purlins; *latías* are visible, and the earth covering is retained by eave and verge logs. The doorway is plank-framed, and there are commercially made double-hung windows with glazing bars. Note the stovepipe; the pelt, saddle, and other items hung from nails in the exterior wall; the water (?) barrel; and the Navajo saddle blanket on the folded bedspring. The dugout behind the figures is shown in Fig. 7.4. "Big Belly's house. Left to right: Big Belly's son-in-law, Big Belly, Dannie Bia," probably Dinnehotso area, Arizona, 1935, M S.S. (925).

sonry bounded one side of one of the doorways. There was a window on the south side, and a filled-in window on the west. Hispano-style adobe fireplaces had been built in the northwestern and southeastern corners of the house. The packed-clay floors of the two rooms were on slightly different levels. The roof was a variant of the center-beam type.

STACKED-LOG HOUSES

Cribbed-Log House

The cribbed-log house or cabin is an ancient northern and central European house type and was introduced into the Delaware Valley of eastern North America in the seventeenth century by Swedes and Finns, and later (early eighteenth century), but more influentially, into Pennsylvania by German-speaking Central Europeans, especially from the hill country along Czechoslovakia's northern border (Jordan 1978: 23–24; 1980). "Anglo" log cabins eventually reached the Southwest (for example, in Utah in the mid-nineteenth century; Spencer 1945: 447), apparently initially with unpeeled logs, a flat or center-beam earth-covered roof, and the doorway in the gable end. Although it has usually been supposed that Navajo cribbed-log houses (Figs. 6.1, 7.5, 7.6, 1.4, 1.5) derive from Anglo ones,

Fig. 7.6. Cribbed-log house with a tarpaper-covered shed roof of planks. The logs—set on a stone foundation—are debarked, saddle-notched, and chinked with boards, sticks, and mud. Note the use of planks for the door, the door frame, and window frame, the device to close off the window, and the stoop. Spring Canyon, Canyon de Chelly, Arizona, 1971.

cribbed-log hogans were built before the Mexican War and a New Mexico Hispano cribbed-log tradition can be documented from the mid-eighteenth century onward, indicating the possibility of some Hispano influence (see "Cribbed-log Hogans," chapter 5). In fact, most early Navajo log houses differ from typical Western Anglo ones and resemble Hispano ones in that Navajo houses use debarked and often squared logs, utilize almost exclusively saddle- and box-notching, have flat or (later) gabled roofs, have their doorways in one of the long sides, lack fireplaces and chimneys, and have their woodburning stoves in corners rather than at the midpoint of a wall (Gritzner 1971: 58–61). (Beginning in the late 1800s, when boards became available, gabled roofs were added to many Hispano—but fewer Navajo—log houses in snowy areas.) Still,

U.S. government efforts to encourage house adoption beginning in the 1880s were probably the major factor leading to Navajo adoption of the beam-roof log cabin. Many Hispanos were employed by the military in nineteenth-century New Mexico, and this could account for the seeming Hispano elements in Navajo log houses. Consideration also needs to be given to the reported issuance to the army in 1870 of a book of instructions on log-cabin building for frontiersmen (Henry Glassie, personal communication).

Many potential models for cribbed-log houses can be cited. The early (1851) buildings at Ft. Defiance were of cribbed-log construction, except for one stone building (Frink 1968: 7, 21, 24). Photographs show stacked-log houses, with low gables, at Ft. Sumner (Bailey 1964: 160), but although many Navajos became aware of such buildings at that time, they did not adopt them themselves. Underhill (1953: 206–07) suggested that cribbed-log railroad section houses (1879–81) and trading posts (e.g., at Chinle, Arizona; Packard and Packard 1970: 33) served as the immediate models for the Navajo cribbed-log house, which seems first to have become somewhat common during the 1890s (Mindeleff 1898: 503–04). However, application of the cribbed-log hogan construction technique to the plan of the rectangular Euramerican building form (irrespective of the latter's original materials) is also entirely possible. And, direct instruction by men such as Agent Riordan was no doubt involved as well.

Abutting-Log House

The rare Navajo abutting-log house is undoubtedly more modern than the cribbed-log house and is also a type built by Anglo-Americans. Its origins in North America are traceable to French Canada (Wonders 1979), whence it spread into the northern United States and beyond. Its American history is preceded by a long history in Europe (Kniffen and Glassie 1966: 50, 58). No data are available regarding the time of its adoption by Navajos, but it seems likely to postdate the ready availability of nails, since the Navajo version uses nails instead of mortising to secure walls to corner posts.

A description of Navajo stacked-log houses follows:

Navajo name (for stacked-log houses in general): *tsin bee kin* = with-logs house; *tsin haatł'in kin* = stacked-up-logs house.

Diagnostic feature: walls of horizontal logs.

Cribbed-log House

Navajo name: tsin bee kin = with-logs house; *tsin haatł'in* [*bee*] *kin* = [with]-stacked-up-logs house.

Major features:

1. Wall structure: horizontal stacked logs whose end sections are interposed at right angles between the end sections of the inferiorly and superiorly adjoining logs of adjacent walls (Figs. 6.1, 7.5, 7.6). Interstices, if present, are chinked with the usual materials, although cement is occasionally used.

2. Plan: rectilinear.

3. Roof: flat, center beam (Figs. 6.1, 7.5), shed (Fig. 7.6), gabled (Fig. 7.9), or cribbed-log.

Minor features and variations:

1. The logs are usually at least roughly shaped, and may be well squared. They are normally saddle- or box-notched[2] at or near their ends (Figs. 5.31, 7.7), to create a rigid,

Fig. 7.7. Saddle-notched logs of the corner of a cribbed-log house under construction; some of the logs have been squared. South of Canyon de Chelly, Arizona, 1973.

Fig. 7.8. Cribbed-log dugout house with a center-beam roof. The logs are single saddle-notched. Note the small logs and boards nailed on as chinking, the plank-framed doorway, and the wooden-slab stoop. The additional logs and stones on the roof's margins are to retain the earth covering (see Fig. 8.2). South of St. Michaels, Arizona, 1968.

interlocking structure and to cause the logs to fit together snugly with minimal gaps between successive tiers. Log ends may be ax-cut or sawn, and corners may be overlapping or square. Nails are sometimes used for added strength. On a long wall, logs are occasionally spliced by rebate-joining their ends.

2. The ends of the logs at the corners of the house are occasionally masked by vertical planks, presumably to protect them from the weather, and perhaps to present a neater appearance.

3. Chinks, if present, are filled with sticks, boards, mud, or (occasionally) cement. The walls are occasionally plastered with mud or covered with tarpaper or other material(s).

4. The logs are only rarely painted, although if cement chinking is used, it is sometimes painted.

5. Stone foundations are frequent (Fig. 7.5), and earth and/or stones may be piled against the bases of the walls.

6. Floors are sometimes slightly excavated (Leighton and Leighton 1949: 94), and dugout cribbed-log houses occur (Figs. 2.9, 7.8).

Abutting-Log House

Navajo name: tsin bee kin = with-logs house; *tsin haatł'in [bee] kin* = [with]-stacked-up-logs house.

Major features:

1. Wall structure: horizontal logs whose ends abut each other or a vertical corner post rather than overlapping; in the former case, the logs are nailed to vertical interior corner posts.

Fig. 7.9. Cribbed-log house with a gabled roof, under construction by the Draper family for a cattle camp. The logs flanking the window have yet to be trimmed to length. The roof employs poles instead of planks; a ridgepole, two pairs of rafters at either end and two ridgepole struts are in place. Note the rocks beneath the downslope corners. Upper Canyon del Muerto, Arizona, below Bird Head Trail, 1972.

2. Plan: rectilinear.
3. Roof: shed, flat, or frame.
Minor features and variations:
1. Similar to those of cribbed-log houses.

Construction Procedures

Although references to cribbed-log houses are common in the literature, detailed descriptions are lacking (see Mindeleff 1898: 503–04; Tremblay et al. 1954: 197–99). Stacked-log houses are constructed in a fashion similar to that of stacked-log hogans (Figs. 7.7, 7.9).

They vary greatly in size and quality of construction. Roberts (1951: 43) measured a one-room house at Ramah, New Mexico, 12 feet by 10 feet 2 inches (3.6 X 3.1 m), and 6 feet 8 inches (2.0 m) high. Examples studied by Jett from photographs and in the field in the Canyon de Chelly, Arizona, area averaged eleven logs high. Newcomb (1966: plate opposite p. 166) pictured one 15 and 16 logs high; corners were squared after construction. The plan of a cribbed-log house is usually oblong, but L-shaped and even cruciform houses exist.

FRAME HOUSE

Navajo frame houses are clearly completely derivative from Anglo-American building styles and methods. Underhill (1953: 208) contended that in Arizona in the 1880s, "Indians near Fort Defiance and along the valley were building little frame houses like those of the whites," with lumber supplied from the Agency sawmill, established in 1880 (Van Valkenburgh n.d.: 9, 38, 60; Frisbie and McAllester 1978: 156–57). However, although lumber was used in these houses for door and window frames, and sometimes roofs, the structures were probably largely constructed of logs; frame houses (Figs. 7.10, 7.11, 7.12, 7.13) seem to be almost entirely a twentieth-century phenomenon among the Navajo.

We have little good information as to the date of adoption of frame houses by Anglos in New Mexico and Arizona, but in southern Utah they became popular during the first quarter of the twentieth century (Spencer 1945: 452–53). Earlier use is indicated in northern Arizona; in fact, Joseph City, Arizona, Mormons built a 12 X 14 ft. (3.7 X 4.3 m) shingled frame house for a Navajo convert in the fall of 1883, installing a fireplace in 1884 (Tanner and Richards 1977: 70–71). Shufeldt (1892: 281) described the use of some planks in an 1888 Navajo palisaded house at Ft. Wingate, where frame outbuildings were to be found (James 1967), but plank houses were not mentioned by Mindeleff (1898)—although he illustrated a plank roof on a stone house—nor by the Franciscan Fathers (1910). Fraser

Fig. 7.10. Early frame house with ramada. The tiny house—which may be primarily for storage—is sided with boards from crates and has a tarpapered gabled roof. Attached to it is a shade employing poles, boards (including part of an Arbuckle's Coffee crate), brush, and tarpaper. At the entry to the shade is a taller-than-usual rectangular stone-masonry summer fireplace. Between Dinnehotso and Kayenta, Arizona, 1935; M.S.S. (847).

Fig. 7.11. Neatly constructed early frame house, with clapboard siding (rare) and a roll-roofing-covered hipped-with-ridge plank roof. Note the corner boards, the stone foundation, and the concrete stoops; the facade's two paneled, commercially made doors and frames; the commercially made double-hung windows with glazing bars; and the fired-brick chimney just behind the roof peak. "Built under government reimbursement plan," and therefore perhaps not folk housing. Polacca Wash near Tovar Mesa (?), Arizona, 1935; M.S.S. (939).

Fig. 7.12. A modern Navajo homestead, containing a stuccoed plank hogan with a roll-roofing-covered pyramidal roof (note the gable over the entry with its commercially made door); a frame house with a roll-roofing-covered gabled roof, a porch, and commercially made doors and windows (note the louvered vent and the two stovepipes); and a flat-roofed tarpaper-covered frame house. Other structures include a plank doghouse, a wire clothesline, and a plank privy. Ft. Defiance, Arizona, 1968.

Fig. 7.13. Two views of a unique three-story frame house with a broken-profile gabled plank roof, under construction. Unusual features include a veranda, a crude third-story balcony, and a second-story door to a porch roof (which carries a basketball backboard), a chimney, a kind of skylight where the stovepipe projects from the roof of the shed-roofed kitchen addition, and commercially made casement and double-hung windows (one surmounted by a bracket-supported projecting board, two with screens, one with a storm window). Note corner, eave, and verge boards; stucco; and artificial-brick roll siding. This is easily the most unusual Navajo house we have recorded; clearly, its builders were ambitious and creative. Route 12, west of Crystal, New Mexico, 1970; R.F.

(1919: 221) noted houses, possibly of planks, at the Agency sawmill on the Defiance Plateau, and Coolidge and Coolidge (1930: 84) observed that some houses were made of "boards and timbers from the Government sawmills near Fort Defiance"; Reichard (1939: 7) also noted examples in the region around the sawmill, and Haile (1942: 40) mentioned "sawed lumber" houses. A November 1935 Snow photo (Fig. 7.11) depicts a two-room frame "house built under government reimbursement plan," apparently near Red Lake (Tolani Lakes), Arizona. Boyce (1974: 119) stated that Navajo laborers erected "flimsy shacks" at the Ft. Wingate munitions depot during World War II; subsequently, the gov-

ernment built the first public housing project for Navajos, at nearby Church Rock (the Tribe later took over administration of the village).

Frame houses, frequently stuccoed, are extremely common today. Frame and other houses using commercially manufactured materials at least initially reflected both acculturation and the higher-than-average income needed to purchase these materials (Spencer and Jett 1971: 171),[3] although frequency of such dwellings is also correlated with lack of timber (see chapter 13). It seems certain that school instruction as well as employment on Anglo-directed public and private construction projects has in many cases provided expe-

rience which has been significant in the adoption of both frame and cinder-block houses by Navajos (see chapter 6). Occupancy of a frame house is not necessarily an indication of a high degree of acculturation, however. In 1956, the Tribe initiated the Welfare Housing Program, to supply lumber and cinder blocks to needy Tribe members and to provide standardized prefabricated houses to the needy, disabled, and aged (Young 1961: 341; Shepardson and Hammond 1970: 107); this program may, in fact, have been among the most important reasons for the initial acceleration of spread of frame houses. Also significant have been house-building projects using natural or commercial materials and Navajo work crews subsidized by the office of Navajo Economic Opportunity (ONEO), which was funded by the federal Office of Economic Opportunity.[4]

A detailed description of frame houses follows:

Navajo name: tsin neheeshjíí' bee kin = with-planks house.

Diagnostic feature: a wooden framework, based on vertical corner posts and including head (top) and sole (sill) plates, to which an exterior covering is nailed to form the walls.

Major features:

1. Wall structure: a wooden framework, including studs, with nailed-on plank, plywood, wallboard, or sheet-metal covering (Figs. 7.10, 7.11, 7.12, 7.13, 7.14, 7.15).

2. Plan: rectilinear

3. Roof: flat (Fig. 7.12), shed (Fig. 7.16), gabled (Figs. 7.10, 7.12, 7.13, 7.14, 7.15, 7.16, 7.17), pyramidal, or hipped-with-ridge (Fig. 7.11).

Minor features and variations:

1. Horizontal, vertical, or diagonal planks, and plywood, alone or in combination, constitute the major types of wall covering; clapboard (lap siding) is very rarely used (Fig. 7.11). One specimen, at The Gap, Arizona, had composition wallboard facing the interior of the frame and sheet metal on the exterior, in imitation of nearby Anglo buildings (Fig. 7.15).

2. The interstices between vertical planks are occasionally filled with adobe (Corbett

Fig. 7.14. Another unusual frame house, at the same location as Fig. 7.13. A gabled-roof two-story central section is flanked by one-story wings with roll-roofing-covered partial hipped-with-ridge roof. The house is set on a foundation, requiring the wooden steps to the doorway in the nearer wing. A porch topped by a balustrade-girt deck contains a stairway giving access to the upper level. The porch's log floor joists rest on a board atop a heavy beam supported here and there by cinder blocks. Note the commercially made doors and double-hung windows, and the bottled gas. The device attached to the nearer wing is of unknown function. Route 12, west of Crystal, New Mexico, 1970; R.F.

1940: 105) or covered by battens (Fig. 7.16). Corner boards are known (Figs. 7.11, 7.13).

3. The planks or other exterior covering may be painted or, occasionally, plastered with adobe (Corbett 1940: 105). More common are "skins" of tarpaper (Fig. 7.12), canvas (rare), or tarpaper that is subsequently stuccoed using chicken-wire lath (Figs. 7.12, 7.13). The tarpaper is usually simply nailed directly to the planks, but use of thin strips of wood to hold the sheeting down has been observed. Mineral-surface roll siding (Fig. 7.13) is rare. Stone-slab facing is rarely applied (Fig. 7.17; Anonymous 1972).

4. Frame houses are frequently set on stone (Fig. 7.11) or cemented cinder-block foundations. Wooden floors may be installed.

5. Unlike other modern Navajo houses, a very few two-and three-story Navajo frame houses are known (Figs. 7.13, 7.14).

6. Ramadas are occasionally attached to frame houses, and small porticos or overhangs over the door are not uncommon (Figs. 7.12, 7.14). Other sorts of porches and verandas are also known (Fig. 7.13).

7. Plank dugout houses have been seen.

Construction Procedures

Navajo-built frame houses are, unlike most plank hogans, built with frames consisting of posts, heads, sills, studs, and struts, after the fashion of Anglo-American frame construction. Since construction techniques are the same as for the latter (see, for example, Mix and Cirou 1963), no further description is given herein.

MASONRY HOUSES

Stone House

Stone houses seem to have been adopted by the Navajo at two separate periods. Puebloans built stone houses and pueblos long before the Navajo are known to have been in the Southwest, and various considerations lead to the conclusion that the Navajo first learned to build stone dwellings from them (see also, "Stone Hogans," chapter 5): (1) the masonry and other construction techniques of early

Fig. 7.15. Unfinished frame house, presumably Navajo, employing sheet metal on its sides and gabled roof, in imitation of nearby Anglo buildings. Note the studs, cats, and diagonal bracing; the electrical wiring; the commercially made windows hinged at the top; the door frame with hinges, and the louvered gable vent. The old earth-scraper in the foreground may have been used to flatten the sloping site. The Gap, Arizona, 1970.

Fig. 7.16. Frame house sided with vertical boards and battens; roll-roofing-covered gabled roof. Note the picket fence at the left. East of Ft. Defiance, Arizona, 1968.

Fig. 7.17. Frame house with stone-slab veneer and a roll-roofing-covered gabled roof. It has horizontally placed commercially made windows, a commercially made door, and an adjoining ramada employing boards and sheet metal on one side. Note, from left, a post-and-wire-fenced area, individual trees fenced with boards and a bedspring, and an oil drum (perhaps for water). The Gap, Arizona, 1970.

Navajo stone dwellings are quite similar to, though usually of poorer quality than, those of Puebloans; (2) the rectilinear plan, flat roof, and frequent multiroom layout are Puebloan and not, originally, Navajo traits; in fact, rooms of ostensibly Navajo houses of this period usually have rounded corners; (3) the earliest apparently Navajo houses occur at times and places where there is abundant historical and archaeological evidence of Navajo-Puebloan contacts which resulted in the fusion of many aspects of Puebloan and Athapaskan cultures.

Puebloan refugees lived with the Navajo during the half-century or so following the reconquest of New Mexico in 1692 and the abortive Pueblo revolt of 1696 but apparently were eventually entirely absorbed (see chapter 1). Detailed assessment of the archaeological evidence relating to the problem of Puebloan versus Navajo contributions to post-1692 masonry structures in Dinétah and elsewhere is beyond the scope of the present work,[5] but it seems likely that Navajos built small, subrectangular stone dwellings—sometimes with more than one room—at this time, and they may at least have participated in the construction of the small pueblos known as "pueblitos," built in defensible locations and found especially in the Dinétah region (Figs. 7.18,

Fig. 7.18. Ruins of a defensively sited early-eighteenth-century, Refugee Period, pueblito made with good-quality, roughly coursed stone masonry with spall chinking. Note the balcony on the right-hand unit and the log platform spanning the gap between the two units. The architecture is typically Puebloan. Crow Foot Canyon drainage, Canyon Largo area, New Mexico, 1972.

Fig. 7.19. Probably eighteenth-century stone-masonry structures, on a knob of rock at the base of Spider Rock. The left-hand unit is supported by logs spanning a gap in the rock, and a log is incorporated into the wall. The site was probably used as a defensive retreat and for storage. Junction of Monument Canyon and Canyon de Chelly, Arizona, 1957.

7.19, 7.20). However, as Keur (1944: 78) observed, "The [pueblito] structures are typically puebloid." Carlson (1965: 103, 105) wrote,

The idea of building with stone and adobe quite probably came to the Navajo with the influx of Refugees during the Gobernador phase. The construction techniques, roofing of vigas and wooden slabs, cribbed log roofs, bins, loopholes [Figs. 7.22, 12.4], wooden lintels, rectangular rooms, notched log ladders, hatchways and stone towers are generically Puebloan.[6] What are decidedly non-Puebloan are the random arrangement of rooms and the entrance passageways into many rooms. The random arrangement may be explained by accretion and the passageways as defensive in nature. The hooded fireplaces are of Spanish derivation. . . . The forked stick hogan and the sweat lodge structures associated with many

pueblito sites seem to be the only structures of this period relating specifically to the earlier Navajo cultural tradition. . . . Large masonry units with Navajo associations ceased to exist in Navajo culture after the Gobernador phase possibly because defensive citadels were no longer required, although Brugge (1963: 22) has presented a good case for a revivalistic movement inherent in the Blessingway tabus as causative in the decline of masonry structures. . . .

Brugge (1963: 22) noted that "pueblitos and painted pottery . . . are the two elements most specifically prohibited by Blessingway, the basic ceremony of modern Navajo religion." It seems possible, too, that whereas pueblitos were initially useful for defense against Utes and other Amerind enemies, they lost much of

Fig. 7.20. Entrance to an early-eighteenth-century, Refuge Period, pueblito. The opening has been partially filled in to make access more difficult. The stone-and-mud masonry and pole lintel are typically Puebloan. Crow Foot Canyon drainage, Canyon Largo area, New Mexico, 1972.

Fig. 7.21. Walled-up former entry to an early-eighteenth-century, Refugee Period, stone-and-mud pueblito. Two loopholes have been left. Note the old entry's stone lintel. Crow Foot Canyon drainage, Canyon Largo area, New Mexico, 1972.

their utility when the enemy, Spaniard and Amerind, became equipped with firearms (Brugge 1963: 23; 1964a). Brugge (1968a: 17–18) also suggested another possibility:

It is generally supposed that the pueblitos were occupied by refugee Pueblo Indians and the [associated] hogans by Apaches [proto-Navajo,] and this was probably true in the early years of the half century of intensive occupation. It might not be too far from the truth to suggest that the refugees first built their highly defensive homes as much because of distrust of their Athapaskan hosts as from fear of alien enemies. There is good evidence of increasing amalgamation of the two peoples, however, brought about probably by in-termarriage, economic interdependence, and the pressure of external attacks. . . .

Pueblitos began to be built about 1700[7] and seem to have reached their peak in the 1740's. After about 1753 no new construction took place in the pueblitos of the Dinétah. A few were built to the southwest, notably near Wide Ruins [Arizona], Coyote Canyon [New Mexico], and Nazlini [Arizona], in the 1760's. Tradition suggests that these very late pueblitos served as community structures rather than as family dwellings.

Vivian's (1960: 49, 54–78, 156–57) work at Chacra Mesa, New Mexico (see also: Bannister 1965; Brugge 1976: 42–44) suggests that pueblito-type structures were modified as a

Fig. 7.22. Abandoned stone house with a beam roof. The rear portion was built first and was later extended by construction of the post-and-lintel arrangement whose walls were filled in with stone masonry and debarked horizontal logs. A log door frame was built and a stone-slab stoop installed. Opposite Beehive Trail, Canyon de Chelly, Arizona, 1978.

consequence of the Athapaskan tradition of round dwellings. At Chacra, Refugee Period sites include structures intermediate between houses and hogans; there are single and double circular stone hogans; single-room, subrectangular or oval masonry structures; two-room subrectangular or oval masonry structures; and three-room masonry structures with more or less subrectangular rooms. After the mid-eighteenth century one-room, circular stone hogans seem to have been the only survivors of these various forms.

There are a few early- to mid-nineteenth-century references to Navajo stone houses. In 1824, Nathaniel Patten wrote that Navajo "houses are built of stone, some one, and others two stories high" (quoted in Van Valkenburgh 1938a: 7). Drake (1841: ix) declared

that Navajos "live in stone houses," and in 1846 Sage asserted that "Most of them live in houses built of stone. . . ." (Haffen 1956–2: 94). Some of these statements probably represent confusion with Puebloan dwellings, although they could reflect local recollection of eighteenth-century pueblito use. Or, in some instances, stone hogans may be being alluded to. In any case, stone houses of modern times (Figs. 7.22, 7.23, 7.24, 7.25) appear to represent an entirely new introduction of masonry housebuilding as a consequence of late nineteenth-century Anglo-American influences. Many Anglo structures of this period in "border towns" and at military posts were built of dressed or undressed stone (for Ft. Wingate in the early 1890s, see James 1967: 156; for Ft. Defiance, Frazer 1963: 21 and Frink 1968: 20,

Fig. 7.23. House of roughly coursed uncut or roughly cut stone masonry with spall chinking. The exterior may once have been covered with mud plaster. The roof is flat, supported by log beams. Around the edge of the roof, resting on horizontal boards, are two courses of apparently dry-laid stones, presumably intended to retain the roof's earth covering. Doorway and windows have plank frames. The house resembles a Hopi dwelling. Black Mountain area, Arizona, 1970; R.F.

34). Mormon houses at Tuba City and many trading posts were built of stone (Lee and Richardson 1974: 8, 10, 15, 38). Navajo labor was used in the constructing of many of these buildings.

In addition to imitation of the above-mentioned structures, often because of official encouragement, Navajos learned to build even better masonry houses through direct experience (for a similar trend among the Hopi, see McIntire 1971). Coolidge and Coolidge (1930: 84) mentioned "houses [built] by young stonemasons trained in the schools" (see also, Schmedding 1974: 174). It is not clear how early such training was available. Wilken (1955: 121) wrote, "Through experience gained while at St. Michaels, Arizona [mission and school], and by their work at quarrying,

dressing and laying stone for St. Isabel's Chapel [1910], many Indians of the Lukachukai area become fairly adept at stonework as evidenced by the stone houses they have since raised in that community." However, the principal Navajo mason involved in the Chapel project was already skilled, having built a stone house in 1903 and having the Navajo name *Kin 'Íít'íní,* "Housebuilder" (Anonymous 1972). Navajo stone houses were certainly being built by 1890 in some areas (Mindeleff 1898: 487).

Navajos were (and are) often employed and trained as masons in the restoration of prehistoric ruins (e.g. Page 1937b: 48), and many have learned masonry skills as employees on government and private construction projects.[8]

Fig. 7.24. House of coursed, uncut or roughly shaped stone with mud mortar; the corner stones have been carefully selected. The roof is center-beam, with purlins; *latía* ends are visible, overlain with earth (see Fig. 8.1). The stone chimney connects with a corner fireplace (Fig.2.10). The doorway and window are plank-framed. The dark material at the right is the remains of a coal pile. Burnham, New Mexico, 1935; M.S.S. (1006).

Fig. 7.25. Very neatly constructed house of uncoursed cut sandstone, with roll-roofing-covered plank gabled roof. Gable ends are walled with vertical planks. Note the commercially made sliding windows with glazing bars, surmounted by stone lintels; the plank-and-plywood door; and the eave and verge boards. The drum at the right may be for water. Rainbow Lodge, Utah, 1970; R.F.

Adobe-Brick Houses

Adobe-brick houses are rare, except where recent government-directed projects have encouraged their construction (Fig. 7.26). Hand-formed adobe bricks ("turtlebacks") were used sparingly by some prehistoric Puebloans, but in the Rio Grande region coursed adobe was the rule until about 1700, when Spanish influence resulted in frequent use of mold-formed adobe bricks (Wendorf 1954: 218). Adobe brick has continued to be used by many Hispanos and was commonly employed by Anglos during the Territorial period (Bunting 1970; Spencer 1945: 449). Navajo use seems relatively late and a result of Anglo and Hispano impact (for an apparent eighteenth-century exception, probably due to Puebloan influence, see Hester and Shiner 1963: 67–68).[9] Many of the post-1863 buildings at Ft. Defiance (Agency headquarters beginning in 1886), were built of adobe (Frink 1968: 80; Link 1968: 12; Horan 1966: 282, 293), as were many of the buildings at Ft. Wingate (James 1967) and Ft. Sumner (Bailey 1964: 174, 184). At the latter post, Navajos

were hired to make and lay adobes (Stewart 1971: 3). Shufeldt (1892: 281–82) noted that in the 1880s most of Ft. Wingate's buildings were of adobe brick and that Navajos were employed to make the bricks but that no Navajos expressed any intent of copying this technique. The earliest recorded definitely adobe Navajo house is that mentioned by Forrest (1970: 115–16) for 1902 east of Shiprock, New Mexico, which also seems to be almost the only area for which adobe-brick hogans are reported (see chapter 5). The fact that the early dewllings at the government settlement at Shiprock were of adobe brick (destroyed by flood in 1911) is probably significant (Dyk 1947: 156; for other apparent uses of adobe brick near Shiprock, see Mitchell and Allen 1967: 30, 96, 196). Most adobe-brick houses appear to date to after World War II.

Fired-Brick and Cinder-Block Houses

Only one modern, fired-brick Navajo house is known to us, at Cañoncito, New Mexico (Fig. 7.27), although Tremblay et al. (1954: 207) found two at Fruitland (note that

Fig. 7.26. Adobe-brick house with a frame annex, under construction. Note the numerous windows, with board lintels. Cañoncito Reserve, New Mexico, 1970.

Fig. 7.27. The only fired-brick Navajo house (not inhabited) observed. It has a low-pitched (center beam?) tarpapered plank roof; windows; and two chimneys, one for a fireplace, the other for a stovepipe. A pair of clothesline poles and a gabled-roof brick outbuilding stand to the right. Cañoncito Reserve, New Mexico, 1970.

Fig. 7.28. The most elaborate Navajo rural residence observed; a professional builder may have been involved. The house and garage are of cinder blocks, with vertical planks filling the gable ends. Note, from the left, the piles of sand and gravel (with wheelbarrow) for concrete mixing; the commercially made aluminum garage door; the cinder-block retaining wall (and sawhorses); the attached ramada and barbecue; the louvered vent in the gable of the wing; the stone-and-concrete foundation with vents; the television antenna; the exterior window sills and the aluminum-framed commercially made windows; the chimney and stovepipe; the ventilator dormer on the pyramidal-roofed two-story main section; and the fancy two-story front porch with balustrades and decorative wagon wheels. Lupton, Arizona, 1972.

the adobe buildings destroyed at Shiprock in 1911 were replaced by fired-brick and lumber structures; Correll 1965b). They also occur on the Colorado River Indian Reservation (George Roth, personal communication, 1973). In contrast, cinder-block houses (Fig. 7.28) have become relatively common in parts of the Navajo country. Both of these materials are of Anglo-American introduction. Tremblay et al. (1954: 201) did not describe cinder-block houses but stated that some Navajos at Fruitland were thinking of building with cinder-blocks. Adams (1963: 77) recorded one cinder-block house near Shonto, in the late 1950s, and Downs (1965: 1391) noted the type at Piñon in 1960. It is also alluded to by Young (1951: 367). We believe cinder-block houses to be essentially a post-World War II phenomenon among the Navajo. Some Navajos gained

direct experience with cinder blocks through laboring on construction projects. An early case was the building of the Shiprock chapter house in 1934; Navajos provided the labor and even made the concrete blocks (McClellan 1935). Under the Navajo-Hopi Rehabilitation Act, the tribe manufactured cinder blocks for a short time during the 1950s at Shiprock (Robert W. Young, personal communication).

Descriptions of masonry houses follows:
Diagnostic feature: masonry walls.

Stone House

Navajo name: tsé bee kin = with-stone house.
Major features:
1. Wall structure: stone masonry (Figs. 7.22, 7.23, 7.24, 7.25).
2. Plan: rectilinear (Fig. 2.7), trapezoidal

(rare), subrectilinear, D-shaped, oval with a dividing wall, or conformable to the shape of the landform upon which it is built or to which it is attached (all but the first two are mainly or entirely eighteenth-century forms).

3. Roof: flat (Fig. 7.23), shed (Fig. 7.22), center-beam (Fig. 7.24), gabled (Fig. 7.25), pyramidal, hipped-with-ridge, cribbed-log.

Minor features and variations:

1. The masonry may be of unshaped (Fig. 7.22), roughly shaped (Figs. 7.23, 7.24), or neatly dressed (Fig. 7.25) blocks or slabs of stone, with or without adobe or cement mortar, coursed or uncoursed, with or without chinking of spalls and small pieces of wood.

Stones of different sizes, set in patterns, have been observed (Forrest 1970: 198). Stones are usually laid horizontally, but Reher (1977: 38, 46) found a house with many vertical slabs set into the exterior of horizontal-slab walls.

2. One example was seen in which an open-fronted (?) stone structure's shed-roof beam was supported by two vertical posts at the front wall ends; the building was later extended, resulting in these verticals being incorporated into the walls (Fig. 7.22).

3. The interior of walls are sometimes plastered with adobe (Fig. 2.10).

4. Dugout stone houses are not uncommon (Fig. 7.29).

Fig. 7.29. Stone dugout house with a gabled, earth-covered roof protected by tree branches. Note the log-and-plank door frame and the homemade door. The structure is currently used for storage. Chauncey and Dorothy Neboyia's main homestead, north of Canyon de Chelly, Arizona, near the head of Beehive Trail, 1972.

Adobe-brick House

Navajo name: hashtł'ish dik'ání' bee kin = with-mud-cubes house
Major features:
1. Wall structure: adobe-brick masonry with mud mortar (Fig. 7.26).
2. Plan: rectilinear.
3. Roof: frame, flat, or center-beam.
Minor features and variations:
1. Wall exteriors are sometimes adobe-plastered or stuccoed.

Fired-Brick House

Major features:
1. Wall structure: fired brick-and-cement masonry (Fig. 7.27).
2. Plan: rectangular.
3. Roof: center-beam (?); other types may exist.

Cinder-Block House

Navajo name: [hashtł'ish] tsé nádleehí [dadik'ání(gíí)] bee kin = with [mud-] to-rock-transforming-[i.e., cement] [many-cubes] house.
Major features:
1. Wall structure: cinder-block masonry with cement mortar (Figs. 7.28, 7.30).
2. Plan: rectilinear.
3. Roof: pyramidal (Fig. 7.28), hipped-with-ridge, gabled (Fig. 7.28), shed (other types may also occur).
Minor features and variations:
1. The exterior walls may be stuccoed, and the stucco may be painted.

Construction Procedures

Although they are rather common in the Navajo Country, modern stone-masonry houses (Figs. 7.22, 7.23, 7.24, 7.25) are not well described in the literature (see Mindeleff 1898: 503; Tremblay et al. 1954: 199–201; Navajo Environmental Protection Commission Staff 1980).One ruined house, dated no more precisely than the first half of the twentieth century, was excavated (Cassidy 1956: 77–78). It was 16 feet (4.88 m) in its east-west dimension and 13 feet (3.96 m) in its north-south dimension, and the slabs of its wall masonry averaged 8 by 10 by 18 inches (20.3 X 25.4 X 45.7 cm). (For other plans and dimensions, see Fig. 2.7.) Early Navajo houses had earth-covered beam roofs (Figs. 7.22, 7.23, 7.24), as did Puebloan, Spanish, and early Anglo-American houses in the region. With the increasing availability of lumber, frame roofs (Fig. 7.25) have largely replaced flat roofs among Anglos and Navajos. Stone houses, particularly newer ones, tend to use dressed stone (Fig. 7.26) more frequently than do stone hogans. Stones are shaped with steel hammers and chisels, and levels are sometimes used in laying the stonework (Loh 1971: plate).[10]

Adobe for house-building is usually mixed in a pit in clayey soil; to the earth are added variable quantities of sand and binding material (such as straw), according to the nature of the local soil (Boyd 1974: 5, 27–28). Adobe-brick houses under construction were observed on the Cañoncito and Alamo Reservations (Fig. 7.26). Bricks (blocks) were molded in rectangular board frames, each

Fig. 7.30. Cinder-block house under construction. Note the stone foundation and the plank window frames. A ramada stands at the right. The Gap, Arizona, 1970.

frame having two, three, or four sections. Bricks at Cañoncito measured 4.75 × 10 × 15.75 inches (12.4 × 25.4 × 41.0 cm), which does not correspond exactly to other Southwestern brick sizes. Modern Hispano adobes —usually made two at a time—measure about 4 × 9 × 14 inches (10 × 25 × 36 cm; Boyd 1974: 5). Spanish-period adobes averaged about 4 to 6 × 10 × 18 inches (10.2 to 15.2 × 25.4 × 45.7 cm), and nineteenth-century Utah Mormon adobes were 4 × 6 × 12 inches (10.2 × 15.2 × 30.5 cm; Fairbanks 1974: 199–200).

Nothing is known of the history or construction procedures associated with the one fired-brick house seen (Fig. 7.27). We are not sure whether the walls are entirely of masonry or are masonry veneer on a plank frame.

Cinder blocks are purchased or are obtained from Tribal self-help sources. They are standard commercial products. Cement is used in the laying up of the courses of blocks (Figs. 7.28, 7.30).

HOUSE TRAILERS

House trailers (Fig. 7.31) are entirely modern—probably post-World War II—and are commercially manufactured by non-Navajos. Apparently the first—and one of the very few—published references is in our own work, for Black Creek Valley, Arizona–New Mexico, in 1968 (Spencer and Jett 1971: 166).

Descriptions of house trailers follow:

Navajo name: kin naadzízí = towed-here-and-there house.

Diagnostic feature: commercially constructed, originally mobile dwellings.

Major features:

1. Wall structure: bolted sheet metal and/or plywood, on wooden or steel frames (Fig. 7.31).

2. Plan: rectangular.

3. Roof: flat or slightly curved.

Variation:

1. The original wheels may be removed, and the structure set on blocks.

Use

House trailers are not, of course, folk architecture, but they do represent a significant form of rural dwelling in some areas. On the Alamo Reservation, according to the local trader (personal communication), there are no sewage hookups, and so mobile-home residents cut a hole in the floor for the toilet; when too much excrement is accumulated, the trailer is moved to a new site.

Fig. 7.31. Navajo homestead, late twentieth-century style. From left: mobile home with steps and railings and a fenced yard; house trailer; privy; rectangular corral fenced with post-and-wire and post-and-rail fencing (note the steel water tank); plank storage shed with a shed roof, covered with tarpaper. Northeast of Ft. Defiance, Arizona, 1968.

Underside of corbeled-log roof on palisaded hogan, near Houck, Arizona, 1970; R.F.

Chapter 8

ROOF FORMS

In the case of conical, domical, and wedge-shaped hogans and other structures, "walls" and "roof" are part of a continuous surface and so are inseparable. For purposes of this book, these surfaces are treated as walls, although an equally good case could be made for considering them as wall-less roofs (see chapter 3). Other structures have distinct roofs (Table 8.1).[1] Since the authors have classified dwellings on the basis of wall structure and materials, a discussion of roof types has been deferred up to this point. However, now that basic dwelling forms have been defined, we may now proceed to roofs.

CONICAL FORKED-POLE ROOF

Keur (1941: 26) felt that the evidence from Big Bead Mesa, New Mexico, indicated that conical forked-pole roofs were the rule on the eighteenth-century stone hogans there (see also Huscher and Huscher 1942; 1943: 7). We have seen no extant examples, nor are any reported in the literature. The construction of such a roof would be similar to that of a conical forked-pole hogan, but neither entry poles nor doorway would be present. This roof type would represent the combination of an Athapaskan dwelling form and the Puebloan idea of a roof distinct from the walls.

BEAM ROOFS

Several Navajo nearly flat or low-pitched roof types exist. We have termed these collectively "beam roofs." Subdivisions of this category are described below.

TABLE 8.1.
Roof Classification

1. Conical forked-pole roof
2. Beam roofs
   A. Flat roof
   B. Low-pitched roofs
      1. Shed roof
      2. Center-beam roof
3. Stacked-log roofs
   A. Corbeled-log roof
   B. Cribbed-log roof
4. Frame roofs
   A. Gabled roof
   B. Hipped roofs
      1. Pyramidal roof (square or polygonal)
      2. Hipped-with-ridge roof (four or more faces)
5. Tent roof

---

[143]

Flat Roof

Horizontally laid logs or commercially cut beams or, rarely, lengths of steel piping rest, at intervals, on top of the walls or are set into the wall tops, spanning the interior of the structure (Fig. 5.17); occasionally, one or more interior vertical posts are erected for added support. If log beams (*vigas* in Spanish) are used, they may all be laid parallel to each other; on larger structures, several main beams (occasionally paired) may support a tier of smaller beams (*viguetas*) more or less equivalent to ceiling joists. Parallel split or unsplit logs or poles (*latías* in New Mexico Spanish) are laid continuously, at right angles (rarely diagonally) to the beams. Beams are normally laid at right angles to the walls; but when long logs are difficult to obtain, *vigas* are apparently sometimes laid diagonally across the room corners, the central gap being spanned by additional logs, all beams then being covered by *latías* (see photograph in Barnes and Snow 1948: 8); this is a step in the direction of the corbeled-log roof (see below). Small poles and /or brush, juniper bark, or other vegetal material, may be used to fill the interstices and to cover the logs, although planks or plywood sheets may supplement (or occasionally replace) the poles and/or logs. The entire surface of the roof, or a portion thereof, may be covered with earth, sods, and/or tarpaper, mineral-surfaced roll roofing, sheet plastic, or sheet metal. The interlog spaces of a ceiling may be filled with mud. If sheeting is used, it may be nailed onto the beams or boards, or held in place by stones or other materials (such as old automobile tires). Flat stones lying directly atop the beams are commonly seen in roofs of storage structures in Canyon de Chelly (Figs. 5.57, 10.16), and Eaton (1854: 217) mentioned "flat stones for small roofs." (Flat roofs on ramadas may be seen in Figs. 4.8, 4.9, 4.10; on hogans in Figs. 5.11, 5.12, 5.13, 5.30, 5.57, 7.1; on houses in Figs. 7.12, 7.23.)

An opening may be left in the roof as a smoke hole or to admit a stovepipe. This and most of the following roof types may or may not have overhanging eaves and/or verges. Slightly sloping "flat" roofs using logs and poles are of Puebloan derivation, although they are also used by Hispanos. Among the Navajo, they probably date to the Refugee Period (see Mindeleff 1891: 149–51; Vivian 1960: 160; Boyd 1974: 7,9). Sawn planks and sheeting are an Anglo-American introduction, apparently dating, in the case of planks, to the 1880s.

Low-Pitched Roofs

1. *Shed roof.* The shed (one-shed, lean-to) roof is similar to the flat roof. However, for a shed roof the facade of the structure is built a foot or two higher than the opposite wall, so that the roof of earth- or tarpaper-covered planks or logs spanning the structure's interior has a pitch of a few degrees (Fig. 7.6). In some cases, the basic side walls of the structure are even in height, in which case the triangular spaces between the tops of these walls and the verges are filled in with plank construction, typically horizontal, the planks being sawn diagonally where necessary to conform to the slanting roof line. This roof form as used today is an Anglo-American introduction, but Vivian (1960: 31–32) described a semicircular hogan (probably of the eighteenth century), built against a cliff, whose roof poles slanted downward from the overhanging cliff to the wall top. Eagle-trapping pit blinds (chapter 9) and some early dugout dwellings apparently employed shed roofs, which are akin to lean-tos.

2. *Center-beam roof.* One large beam (or sometimes two adjacent or closely parallel beams) extends the length of the dwelling (usually parallel to the facade), its ends resting on the centers of the tops of facing walls. A vertical post in the interior of the dwelling may be added for further support. Other logs and/ or planks are laid at right angles to the ridgepole, one end of each resting on the pole, the other end on the top of the wall or on a head plate; there may be supplemental beams (purlins) between center beam and walls (Fig. 8.1; see also, Figs. 7.5, 7.24). The roof is otherwise finished in the fashion of the flat roof (Fig. 8.2).

Fig. 8.1. Underside of the center-beam roof of the stone house in Fig. 7.24, showing one purlin and a number of *latías* (a board at right angles supports some of the smaller *latías*). A bit of the overlying brush and earth is visible. Burnham, New Mexico, 1935; M.S.S. (1007).

Fig. 8.2. The center-beam roof of the cribbed-log dugout house in Fig. 7.8, seen from above. Logs and a few boards and stones have been placed around the roof edge to retain the now partially eroded earth covering. Note the homemade stovepipe or flue. South of St. Michaels, Arizona, 1968.

(For additional examples of center-beam roofs, see Figs. 7.1, 7.8). On modern houses, the low gable produced by this type of roof is usually filled in with vertical planks (sometimes with battens) or horizontal planks, although the main wall structure may rise to the roof line. A hole for a stovepipe may be left on either side of the main beam(s). An occasional variant of this type involves the use of two parallel main beams set to either side of the centers of opposing walls; this results in a flat central strip from which the flanks of the roof pitch gently, although an earth covering may give the roof a curving profile. The center-beam roof appears to date as early as the eighteenth century among the Navajo (Vivian 1960: 31), but it is also characteristic of Anglo-American cabins of the Rocky Mountains and West Texas, where it is termed "Anglo western" (Grizner 1971: 60–61; Jordan 1978: 84–85, 184, 205). Recent Navajo use is probably largely due to Anglo influences. If a Navajo house has two rooms, each room may be spanned by a center beam (Fig. 7.3; Kluckhohn et al. 1971: 149–52).

STACKED-LOG ROOFS

Corbeled-Log Roof

Often referred to as the "cribbed-log" roof, the corbeled-log roof (Figs. 8.3, 8.4, 8.5, 5.21, 5.39) is usually built in essentially the same fashion as is the corbeled-log hogan, and its logs are even-tiered (e.g., Ward 1968: 140). Rot-resistant juniper is the preferred wood. Roberts (1951: 30, 40) mentioned an example eleven tiers high, the upper three tiers consisting of split logs. McAllester and McAllester (1980: 29) show a thirteen-tier roof, and examples with as many as fourteen tiers are known. Several variants occur in which tiers of logs are fewer in number than in the typical form, and the profiles flatter; in extreme cases, each tier consists of sets of five or six parallel logs, each set covering a relatively large portion of the interior (Fig. 5.16), unlike the extreme domelike examples of corbeled-log roofs, in which each log of a tier has a different orienta-

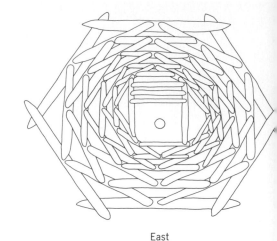

East

Fig. 8.3. Diagram of a corbeled-log roof, as seen from above.

Fig. 8.4. Corbeled-log roof under construction, seen from the interior of a cribbed-log hogan (see Fig. 5.39). The essential logs have been debarked and set in place, the log ends of each tier resting on the midpoints of the logs of the tier below; the uppermost logs bound the rectangular smoke hole, which is off-center, toward the entry. Shorter logs parallel to the principal ones will eventually fill the gaps. Between Monument Canyon and Canyon de Chelly, Arizona, 1962.

Fig. 8.5. Post-and-plank hogan under construction (see Fig. 5.46), showing a partially completed corbeled-log roof. The roof slopes more steeply at the rear than at the front. Between The Gap and Willow Springs, Arizona, 1970.

tion and each covers a relatively small area. The number of tiers, the number of logs per tier, and the profile of the roof depend upon the diameter and number of sides of the hogan and the lengths and diameters of available logs. (For examples of corbeled-log roofs, see Figs. 5.14, 5.15, 5.20, 5.24, 5.42, 5.43, 5.52, 5.53, 5.54, 5.56.) Or, the roof may be corbeled up to a certain height and the gap spanned by parallel horizontal logs. Figure 8.6 shows a roof similar to the last-mentioned variant except that the gap was spanned from east to west by two beams; across the spaces between these beams, *latías* were laid at right angles; additional *latías* covered the spaces between the beams and the corbeling (for a similar but more elaborate example, see McAllester and McAllester 1980: 39, 43, 107). In all varieties, the smoke hole is usually square and may be

Fig. 8.6. Composite roof on a cribbed-log hogan. Upon the corbeled-log lower part of the roof rest two tiers of beams, at right angles to one another. The two uppermost beams are bridged by the smoke-hole logs. From these and from the upper beams, sets of parallel logs slope in four directions. The roof was once earth-covered. Note the saddle-notched corner-timbering and the homemade plank door and frame with lock and chain. Southwest of Tsaile, Arizona, 1972.

Fig. 8.7. Circular palisaded hogan with a corbeled-log roof. Several vertical posts standing away from the walls around the hogan's perimeter support squared stringers which served as eave logs to retain the now eroded earth covering of the roof. Note also the juniper bark and sticks exposed on the roof, the wire reinforcement around the upper part of the walls, the partially eroded mud chinking, the window closed with a plywood sheet, and the homemade door. U.S. Route 66 (I 40) southeast of Burnt Water, Arizona, 1970; R.F.

either central or located somewhat off-center toward the entryway. Low cribbed-log, plank, or other "chimneys" are known but are not common.

The roof logs are chinked with sticks and some or all of the following: juniper bark (Fig. 5.18), greasewood, rabbitbrush, sagebrush, tumbleweeds, other vegetal material, burlap. The roof is then plastered with adobe, and additional damp earth is then applied, before the adobe dries (Newcomb 1966: 67). Today, tarpaper or plastic sheeting is commonly laid under the earth covering to prevent leaking; rarely, a coating of cement—sometimes on chicken wire—is put over the roof (e.g., McAllester and McAllester 1980: 58, 71). Stones, pieces of fabric, sheet metal, and the like are occasionally thrown onto the roof, pre-

sumably to protect it from the weather. The earth covering usually must be renewed once a year, or more often if rains have been heavy. In order to help support the earth covering of this type of roof, a retaining log or plank is frequently nailed or wired horizontally onto the exterior of each wall, at the top (Thomas et al. 1974: 22–23). These horizontals (which may be termed eave logs or boards) may be supported by the hogan's cribwork corners or by vertical logs or squared posts adjacent to the corners (Fig. 8.7), or, occasionally, by wooden brackets. The corbeled-log roof rests either directly on the walls or on vertical posts within or inside or outside the line of the walls (usually only at the corners in the case of polygonal vertical-post hogans, but occasionally also at the midpoints of the walls). The logs of

Fig. 8.8 Abandoned subrectangular leaning-log hogan with a cribbed-log roof (collapsed since photographed). The sides and rear of the roof are covered with small logs laid at right angles to the logs of the cribwork; the structure was originally earth-covered. Note the flue suspended from the smoke hole by wires, and the broken plank door with a hasp. South side of the Canyon de Chelly, Arizona, rim road, 1971.

the lower tiers must be strong, since they support the entire weight of the superior tiers and their covering. Single vertical posts inside a hogan to support a roof log that has shifted position or proven to be a little too short are sometimes seen.

The date of origin of this roof type is unknown, but it seems likely to have first been applied to stone hogans; and in effect, it represents the placing of a corbeled-log hogan on the walls of a stone-hogan, stone hogans having previously utilized only conical forked-pole or beam roofs. Brugge (1972b: 6–7) mentioned a corbeled-log roof at a site of the period 1771–1821. For a discussion of origins of this construction technique, see "Corbeled-log Hogans" in chapter 4.

Cribbed-Log Roof

A few truly cribbed roofs, with alternate-tiered logs, are known. They are set on rectangular or subrectangular dwellings and are roughly pyramidal in form since the logs (purlins) of each tier are shorter than the equivalent logs of the preceding, lower tier. A quadrilateral, truly cribbed roof, supported by corner posts, occurred on a room in a Gobernador Canyon, New Mexico, pueblito dating to approximately 1750 (Carlson 1965: 8, 12; Hannah 1965: 111). A photograph of what seems to be a cribbed-log roof on a subrectangular leaning-log hogan appears in Curtis (1907, opposite p. 82). Figure 8.8 shows an abandoned structure of this type near the

Fig. 8.9. A frame house under construction. Wall studs are visible where exterior boarding has not yet been attached. The unfinished gabled plank roof leaves visible the ridgepole, rafters, collar beams, and queen posts. Presumably, there are tie beams as well. Note the overhanging eaves and verges, the windows, and the presumably homemade sawhorses and ladder. South of Navajo, New Mexico, 1970; R.F.

south rim of Canyon de Chelly, the only one the authors have seen. A 1905 Charles F. Lumis photograph shows what appears to be a "four-legged" hogan near Ganado whose earth-covered roof consists of several tiers of cribbing topped by parallel horizontal logs (Southwest Museum archives). Seton (1962: 32) gave a description of a palisaded hogan with fourteen main forked uprights; seven stringers were installed, followed by a second tier of seven logs laid from end to end of the first-tier logs, and so forth. Such a roof would be cribbed, not corbeled, and these roofs may be more common than casual observation would indicate. However, as Figure 5.16 shows, once the first two tiers of logs are in place, corbeling can be used to finish the roof.

A truly cribbed roof was built on a prehistoric kiva at Aztec Pueblo (Vivian 1959: 72–73), indicating that this trait among the Navajo is probably of Puebloan origin. Nevertheless, it is of interest that this very rare roof type was also used among southwest Alaskan Eskimos (Inuit) and their Athapaskan neighbors, the Ingalik (Vanstone 1974: 36; Osgood 1940: 291, 294–95).

Navajo cribbed-log roofs seem to owe nothing to the Scandinavian gabled ridgepole-and-purlin roof, a cribbed type found occasionally in Texas and elsewhere (Jordan 1978: 84–85).

FRAME ROOFS

A number of roof types of Euramerican origin among the Navajo are largely based upon frame construction techniques, usually employing nails (most exceptions involve dugout roofs). Sawn lumber is normally employed, although occasionally peeled poles are used, particularly for ridgepoles.

Gabled Roof

The gabled (two-shed) roof has a frame-work consisting of a horizontal ridgepole parallel to the building's long axis, from which inclined rafters run to the wall tops (plates). These members are sometimes simply peeled poles but usually are of sawn lumber. In larger dwellings, tie-beams, collar beams, etc., supplement the rafters (Fig. 8.9). (It is not clear whether Navajos ever built gabled roofs lacking ridgepoles, as was standard on log cabins in Texas and the eastern United States [Jordan 1978: 84–85; 1980: 164].) The frame is covered with planks or plywood (Fig. 8.9), which in turn are usually covered with tarpaper or mineral-surfaced roll roofing or, very occasionally, commercially made shingles. The roof pitches in two opposing directions (Fig. 8.10), leaving gables at the two ends of the structure, which in the case of masonry houses may be filled in with horizontal or vertical planks (sometimes with battens). Some overhang is usual. (For examples of gabled roofs, see Figs. 7.2, 7.4, 7.10, 7.12, 7.13, 7.14, 7.15, 7.16, 7.17, 7.25, 7.28).

Hispanos often employed gabled roofs (Gritzner 1979, 1971); but as far as the Navajo are concerned, this and all other frame roofs were introduced by Anglo-Americans during the 1880s. A well-made specimen appears in a pre-1893 Mindeleff (1898: plate 88) photograph (see also, Ostermann 1917: 27).

Hipped Roofs

1. *Pyramidal roof.* Four or more inclined hip rafters (poles or, far more commonly, precut lumber, typically 2 × 4s or 2 × 6s) radiate either from an apex or from a small square, oblong, or polygonal horizontal-plank apical frame, ordinarily a smoke hole (e.g., McAllester and McAllester 1980: 19); the hip rafters (sometimes notched) rest, toward their lower ends, on the tops of the wall corners. The hip rafters may be braced with pieces running diagonally from the wall tops to some point on the ridgepoles, or they may be supplemented by common and jack rafters running from wall tops toward or to the apex or to the

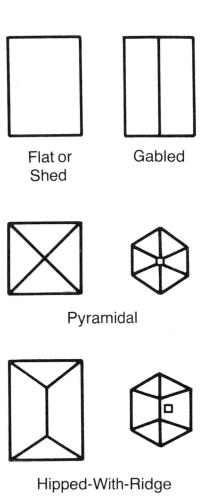

Flat or Shed

Gabled

Pyramidal

Hipped-With-Ridge

Fig. 8.10. Diagrams of roof types made with planks, as seen from above. (*a*) Flat or shed; (*b*) gabled; (*c*) pyramidal; (*d*) hipped-with-ridge. Lines represent eave and verge edges, ridgepoles, and hip rafters.

hip rafters. Planks (typically, 1 X 12s) are laid across the rafters, forming a square or polygonal pyramid which overhangs the walls somewhat (Fig. 8.11). Eave boards (fascias) may be added. The planks are normally covered with mineral-surfaced roll roofing, sometimes underlain by tarpaper or roofing felt (Thomas, Johnson, and Yazzie 1974: 22–23). For hogans, the small frame at the top provides a smoke hole, or if there is an apex instead, a framed opening is often constructed on one face of the pyramid slightly below the apex and usually on the face nearest the doorway. (For examples of pyramidal roofs, see Figs. 5.25, 5.26, 5.27, 5.34, 5.44, 5.58, 7.12.) A frame cover—hipped-with-ridge or gabled—is sometimes set over the smoke hole to wholly seal the opening when a hogan is used exclusively for storage, or to partially seal the opening when a stovepipe is used (Fig. 5.45). A few examples of truncated pyramidal roofs have been observed (e.g., Spencer and Jett 1971: 170); in these cases a flat area, considerably larger than the smoke hole, terminates the pyramid some distance below the projected apex. Occasionally, in the Ft. Defiance-Gallup area, a small, gabled, dormerlike projection of the roof is built over the doorway, and a small window may be set in the gable (Fig. 5.25; Jett 1976).

A pyramidal hogan roof with a cupola atop was observed near Round Rock. Space for hogan ventilation was left beneath the cupola roof. A similar cupola, but with louvered ventilators, was seen near Mexican Springs, New Mexico (Fig. 2.5). Others have been seen at Chinle, Arizona. One case of a corrugated sheet-plastic skylight on one face of a roof has been recorded (Anonymous 1971: 13).

The date of Navajo adoption of the pyramidal roof has not been determined. A Georgian English type, it was especially popular in the southeastern United States (Lewis 1975: 20–21). It was common on Anglo structures in the Southwest around the turn of the century and later, and Navajo use was probably first on houses. A 1930s photograph (2601) in the collection of the Franciscan Fathers, St.

Michaels, Arizona, shows an apparently Navajo house with a pyramidal roof. Armer (1935: 109, 171, plate opposite p. 112) described the construction of a pyramidal roof on a cribbed-log hogan built for her and her husband in the early 1930s at Black Mountain, Arizona. The hip rafters were peeled poles, abutting an apical block of wood which was held up during construction by a vertical pole. There was no smoke hole since a chimney was used. Each ridgepole was braced by a pair of short logs running from the tops of the adjacent walls to a point toward the middle of the pole. The framework was covered with sawmill slabs (flat sides out), which in turn were covered with shingles. This type of roof was a novelty to the local Navajos, who could not understand how it stayed up. The Navajo builder may have gotten the idea of the pyramidal roof at Chinle, where he had a farm. That he was interested in new building methods is indicated by the fact that he took a correspondence course in chimney construction (Armer 1962: 105). Fraser (1919: 205) wrote of hogans in the Chinle Valley "with some carpentry work," which may refer to plank roofs. Fryer (1942: 414) published a photo of a stone hogan with a pyramidal roof. The first appearance of this roof form at Ramah was in 1949, on a hogan; the roof was copied from a pyramidal roof on a house at Lupton, Arizona, and the form has since become common at Ramah (Kluckhohn et al. 1971: 148, 156). Downs (1972: 129) attributed adoption of such roofs at Piñon, during the early 1960s, to the construction of houses and of larger hogans, which supposedly require lumber roofs.

2. *Hipped-with-ridge roof.* This roof is similar to the pyramidal hipped type except that it has a horizontal ridge rather than an apex; it may have four or more faces (Figs. 8.12, 8.13, 5.49). Very rarely, the main ridge ends in gablets. An occasional variant, on hogans, has a narrow flat top in place of the usual ridge (Fig. 8.12). Mineral surfaced roll roofing is the usual covering, but wooden shingles have been observed.

Tremblay et al. (1954: 201) attributed the

Fig. 8.11. Underside of a hexagonal pyramidal hogan roof of planks, with a hexagonal cupola (see Figs. 2.5, 5.26), showing radiating hip and common rafters. Mexican Springs, New Mexico, 1972.

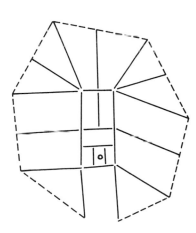

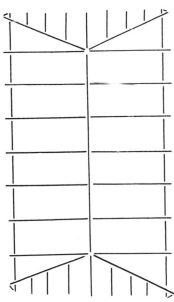

Fig. 8.12. Sketch plan of the disposition of ridgepoles and rafters of an eight-sided (including entry) stone hogan's truncated hipped-with-ridge roof. The circle represents the stovepipe emerging from the smoke hole, the dashed line the roof's lower edge (line omitted over entry). Chauncey and Dorothy Neboyia's summer-farm homestead, Zuni Trail, Canyon de Chelly, Arizona, 1971.

Fig. 8.13. Sketch plan of the disposition of ridgepoles, rafters, and spacers of a cribbed-log house's hipped-with-ridge roof. Chauncey and Dorothy Neboyia's summer-farm homestead, Zuni Trail, Canyon de Chelly, Arizona, 1971.

Fig. 8.14. Wall tent and ramada. The tent has an internal frame, and sits atop horizontal-plank lower walls from which tarpaper is peeling; perhaps the tent should be considered a tent roof. The ramada is roofed with poles and sawmill slabs; logs are leaned against three sides. Note the stovepipe and the home-made table. Cedar Ridge area, Arizona, 1968.

use on houses of this and the preceding roof type to a desire on the part of Navajos to emulate the form of hogan roofs. However, hipped roofs seem actually to be directly derived from identical roofs that were rather popular among Anglo-Americans, particularly around the turn of the twentieth century (for example, at Ft. Defiance; Link 1968: 18–19). A 1935 Snow photograph shows a frame Navajo house with a hipped-with-ridge roof (Fig. 7.11), and the use of hipped roofs on houses probably preceded their use on hogans.

TENT ROOF

This roof consists of a canvas wall-tent surmounting the walls of a rectangular struc-

ture (Fig. 8.14). We have seen only a few examples, probably temporary. One was described for a pinyon-gathering camp north of Red Mountain (Hill), Coconino National Forest, Arizona (Gumerman and Euler 1976: 14). Robert W. Young (personal communication) wrote of "tent houses" (*níbaal kin*):

In the 1930's the Government made wide use of these structures at various work sites (WPA, CCC, etc.) on the Reservation, and at places like the Southwestern Range & Sheep Breeding Laboratory.... They had plank floors and walls, and mine was heated by a stove made out of steel drum. They used to be more common on the Reservation in the past than they are at present, but I suspect that those used by Navajos were patterned after those introduced(?) by the Gov't in the 1930's.

Chapter 9

SUBSISTENCE-ACTIVITY STRUCTURES

As discussed in chapter 1, Navajo subsistence activities have changed over time, and with these changes have come changes in structures related in making a living. As hunting and gathering gave way to farming and herding, new structures were added to the Navajo repertory and old ones were adapted to conform to the changing economy.

ANIMAL SHELTERS

Barns and Sheds

Livestock—especially sheep but also goats, cattle, horses, and burros—has played a vital role in Navajo subsistence for over two centuries. Traditionally, little or no shelter was provided for stock. Old dwellings are, on occasion, used to shelter animals (McAllester and McAllester 1980: 14), but true barns for livestock and for hay storage (*tł'oh bighan* = hay's house), are rare and nontraditional in the Navajo Country, and the use of stables was specifically denied by the Franciscan Fathers (1910: 335). One modern example of a barn (Fig. 9.1) is of vertical-plank, frame construction on its sides, with a stacked-log half-wall at its end. It has a gabled roof. A frame

Fig. 9.1. One of the few Navajo barns observed, apparently used primarily for hay storage. The log-frame structure has vertical-plank walls except on the end, which is partly closed with horizontal logs (note the ladder). The gabled plank roof has log rafters and is covered with tarpaper held down by boards. Black Creek Valley, southwest of Navajo, New Mexico, 1968; V.E.S.

barn covered with corrugated sheet metal was noted between Page and Kaibito, Arizona. Barns have also been recorded in the Ramah, New Mexico, district (Roberts 1951: 41) and in Black Creek Valley, Arizona (Fig. 9.2; Spencer and Jett 1971: 168).

Crude sheds, usually of leaning or horizontal logs or planks, with shed or flat roofs of logs or planks (Fig. 9.3), or ramadalike structures, are fairly commonly seen in association

Fig. 9.2. We call this a "barn" because of its adjacency to the corral and presumed relation thereto, but some nonfarm items are stored in the recessed entryway (the hinges no longer perform a function). The interior is divided into more than one unit. The plank roof is center-beam. The corral fence is post-and-rail, with boards instead of poles. Black Creek Valley, Arizona, 1968.

Fig. 9.3. Sheep shed at the side of a corral. The rear portion is built in lean-to fashion and is earth-covered. Presumably, a flat roof once extended to the forward stringers. Chauncey and Dorothy Neboyia's principal homestead, north of Canyon de Chelly, Arizona, near the head of Beehive Trail, 1972.

with corrals, at least in more acculturated areas. A stone shed with a flat, dirt-covered roof was observed at Alamo, New Mexico. Sheds usually serve as sheep shelters (Spencer and Jett 1971: 168; Olson 1970: 34–35) but sometimes also for the storage of feed (Landgraf 1954: 48–50; Roberts 1951: 42; Kluckhohn et al. 1971: 78).

Barns and sheds are of European, probably Anglo, derivation among the Navajo.

Small-Animal Shelters

The Navajo construct a number of types of small-animal shelters. These do not require eastward orientation (David M. Brugge, personal communication).

Although infrequent, doghouses are sometimes seen. Kluckhohn et al. (1971: 80) mentioned pole-and-earth-roofed hillside dugouts floored with juniper bark (łééchąą'í bá hahoogeed=dog dugout place), brush shelters, and masonry structures built for dogs, but

noted that they were rare. Plank doghouses
(*łééchąą'í bighan* = dog's home) are also occasionally seen (Fig. 7.12; Hannum 1958: 160;
Spencer and Jett 1971: 167–68). Doghouses
have been recorded for Northern Athapaskans, although their precontact use is ques-
tionable (McClellan 1975: 235). In the
Southwest, the sixteenth-century Piro Puebloans were reported as housing dogs in "un-
derground huts" (Hammond and Rey 1966:
83).

Pigpens were noted near Ramah by Roberts (1951: 41) and Landgraf (1954: 48).

Plank and plank-and-chicken-wire coops
and roosting platforms of various forms (Fig.
9.4), for chickens (*naa'ahóóhai bighan* =
chicken's home) and perhaps sometimes for
ducks, geese, or turkeys, are occasionally seen
(Kluckhohn et al., 1971: 80–81; Spencer and
Jett 1971: 167–68). Jett has observed, in the
Canyon de Chelly region, Arizona, dugout
poultry shelters with flat pole-and-earth roofs
(Fig. 9.5), and Downs (1972: 57) mentioned
such structures as being used around Piñon,
Arizona. Hannum (1958: 160) wrote of a
miniature hogan being built for chickens, and
stone-and-mud ovenlike structures (see below)
are occasionally used to shelter poultry (cf. a
similar practice among the Hopi; Mindeleff
1891: 167). A possible archaeological poultry
pen was described by Keur (1941: 35). It was
about 2 feet (.6 m) square and consisted of
vertical stone slabs around a tree, roofed with
poles and floored with slabs. Two contiguous
slab-sided and -roofed coops measuring 0.7 by
2.9 meters (2.1 × 9.3 ft) were described by
James (1976: 52–54) and dated to the 1950s;
they were floored with juniper bark and cloth.
One of the structures functioned as a doghouse
after its use for chickens.

Fig. 9.4. Gable-roofed plank chicken house
on a pole-and-plank platform supported by
cottonwood trunks and vertical posts. A
homemade ladder provides access. In the
background is a cribbed-log storage hogan
with a roll-roofing-covered pyramidal roof.
Chauncey and Dorothy Neboyia's summer
farm homestead, Zuni Trail, Canyon de
Chelly, Arizona, 1971.

Fig. 9.5. Flat-roofed dugout leaning-log
chicken houses. Chauncey and Dorothy Neboyia's main homestead, north of Canyon de
Chelly, Arizona, near the head of Beehive
Trail, 1971.

Fig. 9.6. Cribbed-log pen with a removable flat roof of planks, for confining kids overnight to permit milking of the mother goat in the morning. In the background are a stake-and-rail-fenced corral against the cliff and a stone house with a center-beam roof (see Fig. 7.22). Opposite Beehive Trail, Canyon de Chelly, Arizona, 1978.

A small, square, cribbed-log structure with a roof of loose boards around a rectangular hatchway in Canyon de Chelly was identified by Chauncey Neboyia (personal communication) as a pen to segregate kids from their mothers overnight so that the nanny goats could be milked in the morning (Fig. 9.6.).

FENCES AND ENCLOSURES

Fences are used primarily to control livestock, either by confining them or excluding them. Fences were formerly also used in the capture of certain large game animals.

Fence Types

The following forms of fencing (*'aná'áz-t'i'* = extends in an encircling line) have been recorded among the Navajo and observed by the authors:

1. *Deadwood fence.* A line of piled boughs and brush (*'ił názt'i'* = conifer boughs extend in a circle), or piled pinyon and juniper snags, or both brush and snags (Fig. 9.22).

2. *Leaning-log fence.* A spaced series of single vertical posts, often forked, connected by stringers against which lean, or on which hang, poles or branches (Fig. 9.7; Anderson 1973: 15).

3. *Palisade fence.* Logs, poles, planks, or boughs are planted vertically in the ground (Fig. 9.8); these contiguous uprights may be reinforced with wire or by lashing them to horizontal poles running below the top of the fence.

4. *Stake-and-rail fence* (*tsin bee 'ańt'i'* = logs extend in a line; *tsin 'alkáá'* = logs atop

one another). A spaced series of pairs of vertical posts, each pair holding in place the ends of horizontal rails which connect the pairs of posts (Fig. 9.9, 9.11, 9.12). The logs are usually alternate tiered in adjacent sections of fence.

5. *Post-and-rail and -plank fence.* A spaced line of single vertical posts connected by nailed- or wired-on horizontal poles, slabs, or planks (Figs. 9.2, 5.51, 7.31).

6. *Post-and-wire fence.* Spaced single vertical posts supporting strung or woven wire (Figs. 9.18, 5.54; *béésh 'álts'óózígíí ńt'i'* = iron-that-is-slender [wire] extends in a line; *béésh 'adishahí ńt'i'* = iron-that-snags [barbed wire] extends in a line). Field-corner posts are sometimes braced with single forked poles or by horizontal poles nailed to nearby posts, or with wires or cables attached to buried logs or rocks, as a result of government influence (Roberts 1951: 18, 42–43; McAllester and McAllester 1980: 97).

7. *Stake-and-rider* (*pitchpole, ripgut*) *fence.* A fairly closely spaced series of pairs of poles, each pair planted so as to cross in scissors fashion at right angles to the line of the fence; each fork thus formed supports one or more inclined poles whose lower end(s) rest(s) on the ground beneath an adjacent set of shear poles (Fig. 9.10).

8. *Picket fence.* Thin, very closely spaced vertical strips of wood are nailed to horizontal boards which connect the tops and bases of spaced single vertical posts (Fig. 7.16). These fences are very rare in the Navajo Country and occur only in association with houses (e.g., McAllester and McAllester 1980: 59).

9. *Stone fence* (*wall*). A line of stone masonry, normally of unshaped, uncoursed, dry-laid, tabular stones. Occasionally, logs are laid along the wall top to add height. Stone walls are built particularly in treeless areas and are unknown in some wooded regions.

10. *Tire fence.* Old automobile tires set vertically and wired together (rare; Spencer and Jett 1971: 168).

11. *Wire-spool fence.* Garrick Bailey (personal communication, 1979) reported a

Fig. 9.7. Leaning-log corral fence. Forked corner posts support stringers, against which logs are leaned. The principal timbers and many of the leaners have been debarked. Most were ax-cut. The fence's overhang affords some shelter from snows. Near Black Rock, north of Canyon de Chelly, Arizona, 1972.

Fig. 9.8. Beehive oven and palisaded corral. North of Arizona Highway 264, 1972.

Fig. 9.9. Section of a stake-and-rail corral fence, supplemented by boughs leaned against the outer side. Chauncey and Dorothy Neboyia's main homestead, north of Canyon de Chelly, Arizona, near the head of Beehive Trail, 1972.

Fig. 9.10. Stake-and-rider fence. Inclined poles rest on pairs of shear poles. There are also some horizontal poles. Between Cow Springs and Marsh Pass, Arizona, 1935; M.S.S. (1011).

corral near Fruitland, New Mexico, constructed of the wooden spools used to hold electrical-transmission wire.

12. *Auto-body fence.* Garrick Bailey (personal communication, 1979) has seen two corrals made of wired-together pre-1954 car bodies set on their sides, plus car doors and bed springs, near the west branch of Gallegos Canyon near Carson, New Mexico.

Because of their resistance to rotting, posts and poles of juniper wood are preferred for fencing, but pinyon, ponderosa, oak, and probably other woods are also used (Elmore 1943: 19; Vestal 1952: 12, 14, 72; Roberts 1951: 30). They are usually debarked before use. Miscellaneous other objects, such as wagon tires, sheet metal, bedsprings, old pick-up-truck doors, and almost anything else, including living trees, are also sometimes incorporated into fences. Pieces of fabric, cans, and bottles may be attached, too, to frighten animals and keep them from crossing the fence line.

Fence Origins

Fence types 1 and 2 have eastern, Anglo equivalents (Hart and Mather 1957: 6) but may possibly be of Hispano origin in the Southwest.

"Informants agree that corrals formed of upright pickets or posts [type 3] were a comparatively recent innovation. Presumably they were coincident with the introduction of the axe" (Kluckhohn et al. 1971: 78). Bandelier's 1883 statement that Ft. Wingate-area Navajos had corrals "of brush, not stakes," implies that palisade corrals were common in the Rio Grande area but not yet adopted by the Navajo (Lange and Riley 1970: 60). Palisade fences used for combination corral and fortification enclosures at some forts and early trading posts (cf. Frink 1968: 20; Packard and Packard 1970: 32; Forrest 1970: 25, 67) may have been the models for this sort of Navajo fence, which today is the usual type for corrals in more conservative areas that are also tree-poor (see Franciscan Fathers 1910: 335; Ostermann 1917: 29; Forrest 1970: plate 112), although stake-and-rail fencing is common in more acculturated areas.[1] On the other hand, palisade fences are also used by Puebloans; they appear in pictures of Zuni and Rio Grande pueblos beginning in the 1840s and 1850s (Abert 1962: 67, 69; Sitgreaves 1962: plates 2, 3; Schoolcraft 1854: plate 2; see also Gregg 1968: 50, 54, 59), and were probably introduced there by the Spanish; an 1801 document mentions such a fence in the Rio Arriba area of New Mexico (Boyd 1974: 25). Fence types 4 through 8 and 10 are presumably of Anglo-American derivation.[2] Types 4 through 6 are common, but 7, the rigput fence, is rare; it was brought from the East by Mormon pioneers (Fife and Fife 1956: 260 and plate) and perhaps others. Stone-walled corrals and pens (type 9) are not uncommon in areas where stone is easier to obtain than wood (cf. Vivian 1960: 103; Franciscan Fathers 1910: 63), and are also constructed by Puebloans. They may be of Hispano or Anglo origin in the Southwest. They occur at the supposedly Navajo Cerrito site in the Chama Valley, New Mexico, dating from the latter seventeenth to the early eighteenth century (Schaafsma 1979).

Fencing Fields and Pastures

Fencing of grazing land was still rare in the 1970s, although sometimes a narrow pass or canyon was fenced to confine stock to a particular range. Still, by 1941 range fencing was occasionally used around Ramah (Landgraf 1954: 49, 52), and beginning in 1958 the U.S. Agricultural Conservation Program, among others, has encouraged range fencing (Jeffers and Davis 1967: 37), and the practice is becoming more common. Cases of fencing to confine ghosts to infested canyons have also been recorded (Fonaroff 1963: 222). But in the 1970s fences were not common other than for corrals and surrounding cultivated fields, and the latter fences were restricted in extent in most areas. The authors have also seen a number of cases of young trees, usually cottonwoods, planted for shade near dwellings and protected by fences (Fig. 7.17; see also "Agricultural Structures," below). Roberts (1951:

35) reported this practice for Ramah. Gifford (1940: 101) mentioned an anti-coyote fence of Spanish bayonet around a maize field.

Jett has observed in Canyon de Chelly simple stiles consisting of a rock on either side of the fence, and "baffles" of posts and wire or old wagon wheels for passing through.

[Field] fences are of late introduction. They date from the introduction of stock [by A.D. 1700], when it became necessary to protect the fields from the herds. . . . A difference of opinion exists as to who first suggested the idea of fences [for protection of cultivated fields] to the Navajo . . . the Pueblos and Mexicans . . . or Americans. The earliest types were merely limbs piled one upon the other, or rested on upright forked posts. [Hill 1938: 24; see also Kluckhohn et al. 1971: 78]

These crude fence types seem to survive today mainly in the remote far western areas of the Reservation (Kluckhohn et al. 1971: 76; and personal observations), although Roberts (1951: 18, 41) stated that the piled-brush sheep-corral fence was usual at Ramah and Landgraf (1954: 50, 52) reported its use for field fencing there, when scrub timber was immediately at hand (Map 1.3).

Corrals

Livestock corrals (*'aná'ázt'i'*, or *dibé* [*béégashii, łíí'*] *bighan* = sheep [cow, horse]'s home) are very common features of camps, and sometimes circular ceremonial enclosures (see "Windbreaks," chapter 4) and game corrals (see "Hunting Structures," below) are seen. Corrals are traditionally more or less circular (Fig. 9.8, 9.11; cf. Kluckhohn et al. 1971: 76–78), but rectangular ones have also been built for many years. Keur (1941: 21) recorded a recent (?) rectangular stone corral at Big Bead Mesa, New Mexico, that measured 40 by 75 feet (12.2 X 22.9 m) and was 3 feet (.9 m) high. Arcuate or rectangular stone corrals utilizing cliff sides and cliff shelters are seen, but log fencing is more common (Fig. 9.12); stones from Anasazi ruins are sometimes used to build such enclosures. Palisaded corrals (Figs. 9.8, 9.13) were usual at the turn of the

Fig. 9.11. Corral. The nearer side is fenced with stake-and-rail technique, the log ends of adjacent sections stacked side by side rather than interfingered. The far side of the corral employs palisaded fencing. Below Red Clay Canyon, Canyon de Chelly, Arizona, 1971.

century (Franciscan Fathers 1910: 335) and are still fairly common. Roberts (1951: 41), reporting on three Ramah camps, noted separate sheep and horse corrals, the former usually being made with piled brush, the latter with stakes and rails. (Fields were fenced with post-and-barbed-wire or deadwood fences; Map 1.3.)

Eastward orientation is not considered necessary for corrals (David M. Brugge, personal communication). Piled brush, vertical poles (*náneeskáál* = they stand circularly), horizontal entry bars (*dáádíljah* = close with bars), or Anglo-style gates (*dáádi ńt'i'* = close extending line) are used to close corrals (Figs. 5.55, 9.14, 9.15). Gates are of planks, or of posts and wire, closed by means of wire loops or wire-and-toggle devices (e.g. Roberts 1951: 42–43).

Fig. 9.12. Oblong sheep and goat corral and lambing pen built against a cliff. The corral fencing is crude stake-and-rail, supplemented with boughs leaned against the outside. Piled boughs continue the fence up the rocks at the cliff base. The lambing-pen fence employs posts and both horizontal and vertical boards; the beams suggest that some sort of roof—probably of boughs—is constructed when the pen is being used. Spring Canyon, Canyon de Chelly, Arizona, 1971.

reject their offspring together with their lambs (Kluckhohn et al. 1971: 78). Separate lamb corrals are sometimes used to segregate young lambs in the morning to preclude their being trampled when the flock is taken out to graze; the lambs are then returned to the main corral (Jerrold E. Levy, personal communication, 1978).

According to David M. Brugge (personal communication):

> Regarding lamb pens, there are really two forms, the old style big enough for only one or two lambs used when the rams were run year 'round with the herds and lambs born throughout the year and the modern larger structure[s] perhaps better called lamb corrals that are sometimes used for the herd of lambs that is born all in the spring. The pen to force a ewe to accept and nurse her lamb . . . is an old Spanish type called *hijadero*. . . .

Guernsey (1931: 3–4) described a lamb pen in a rock shelter in Tsegi Canyon, Arizona. It incorporated two adjacent boulders, from which two curved, piled-stone walls extended, converging toward an opening opposite the boulders. (A similar structure, in the open, is pictured in Fig. 4.2; its opening is protected by a nearby arcuate length of wall. However, this structure may well be a windbreak rather than a lamb pen.) De Harport (1959–4: 1597, 1600) described U-shaped lamb pens without entries, built against rock-shelter walls at Canyon de Chelly. They were four to five paces across. Similar pens occur in the lower Chaco River area, New Mexico (Reher 1977: 51–52, 57, 63). James (1976: 48) measured an oval, log-fenced pen (ca. 1954) near Canyon del Muerto, Arizona; it was 7.2 by 11.0 feet and 5.5 inches deep (2.4 by 3.6 by .2 m). At Chauncey and Dorothy Neboyia's summer-farm homestead in Canyon de Chelly in the early 1970s there were two abandoned cribbed-log lamb pens next to the sheep corral (Map 1.4). The currently used pen was not far away. It was small and rectangular, with horizontal-plank sides. A cloth-swathed stringer supported on two vertical poles spanned the structure; in the lambing season the cloths were soaked with kerosene to keep away flies.

Fig. 9.13. Palisade-fenced sheep corral, at a saddle in Comb Ridge, Monument Valley, Arizona, 1935; M.S.S. (830).

Downs (1972: 64) mentioned that, near Piñon, stiles are sometimes built to allow goats to leave and enter sheep corrals at will.

Lamb Pens

Lamb pens (*dibé yázhí bighan* = little sheep's home) are somtimes built, frequently adjacent to or near the sheep corral but also often away from the camp. They may be built of brush, rocks, or vertical or horizontal logs or planks (Figs. 9.14, 9.15), and they sometimes have partially excavated floors, which may be lined with juniper bark or cloths (James 1976: 4, 47–48). They serve to confine and to shelter newly delivered lambs, especially in bad weather, and to keep ewes who

Fig. 9.14. Lamb pen, consisting of a small, polygonal, stake-and-rail-fenced corral sheltered by a flat-roofed shade; the homemade plank gate has fallen. The bundle of cloths hanging at the left are presumably soaked with kerosene during the lambing, to discourage flies. Sliding Rock Ruin alcove, Canyon de Chelly, Arizona, 1971.

Fig. 9.15. Oblong palisade-fenced lamb pen. Note the wired-together double posts at the entry, holding two horizontal poles in place; the pieces of wood on the ground may be for further closing off this entry. The poles atop the fencing suggest a sometime pole-and-brush roof. Sliding Rock Ruin alcove, Canyon de Chelly, Arizona, 1971.

(By the late 1970s, the pen had been dismantled.) Downs (1972: 61–62) mentioned pole-and-earth-roofed dugouts used around Piñon to shelter lambs in bad weather.

Community Livestock Facilities

Sheep-dipping is referred to by the Franciscan Fathers (1910: 259). In the 1970s, sheep-dipping pens, chutes, and tanks were regularly encountered (see Downs 1964: 44–45; 1972: 34–36). They were introduced through government efforts and are usually community facilities. Community corrals, stock-loading chutes, and rodeo grounds (Fig. 5.55) occur in many chapters but will not be given detailed treatment herein.

Wool-packing Stage

After the spring sheep-shearing, the fleeces are typically packed in 6-foot (1.8-m) commercial sacks. Artificial stages or platforms are built from which to suspend the sacks during packing. Roberts (1951: 34, 36, Fig. 2) pictured two examples. One consisted of a triangular (?) pole frame supported by vertical posts. The other used tree crotches instead of posts, and the apparently triangular frame supported an iron hoop which held the mouth of the sack open; the stage was reached by a homemade runged ladder. These homemade devices were no doubt inspired by similar structures routinely used at trading posts.

FIELDS AND FIELD STRUCTURES[3]

Farming has for centuries been a principal contributor to Navajo livelihood. Some of the resulting landscape alterations can be considered architecture only by stretching the definition of that term and therefore are only touched upon here. However, there are a few farm-related constructions which deserve somewhat expanded description.

Clearing, Planting, and Marking

Areas to be devoted to cultivation are cleared of trees, brush, and smaller rocks.

Field shape conforms to that of the plantable space, such as a floodplain or fan; if plenty of arable land is available, as on well-watered mesas, fields are square or oblong or otherwise angular (Map 1.3; for published maps of fields and cultivated areas, see Bryan 1929: 450–51; Landgraf 1954: 48–50; Spencer and Jett 1971: 164–65). Cultivated areas are frequently fenced, often with posts and wire (see "Fences and Enclosures," above). Fields are seldom large; the largest at Piñon in 1962 was 20 acres (8.1 ha; Downs 1965: 1369). At Ramah in the 1940s they were generally small, ranging from less than 1 to more than 100 acres (.4 to 40.5 ha). A field may be divided into as many as six or more sectors of up to 20 acres' (8.1 ha) size which are cropped by different family members (Landgraf 1954: 58). Different crops are usually planted in separate plots, although watermelon and squash may be intercropped. Crop rotation and fertilization were seemingly not practiced before modern times. Traditionally, maize was planted with a dibble in a sunwise helical pattern beginning at the center of the plot, a practice apparently shared only with the Northern Tonto Apache. Today, planting is done in straight rows, often along plowed furrows. Piles of stones may be set up to guide the plowman.

Protection

In dry areas, lines of brush are sometimes erected windward of melon and squash plants to afford protection from the hot afternoon sun and from windblown sand (cf. a similar Hopi practice; Hack 1942: 33). Small fences, or "tipis" of brush or sticks, sometimes with cloth covering (Fig. 9.16), are erected in Canyon de Chelly to protect fruit-tree seedlings against livestock and wild mammalian pests; cloths, sheets of plastic, and cans are often tied to mature trees to frighten livestock and wild pests, and rams' horns may be hung in trees "to give them strength" (Jett 1979b: 299–300, 302–03). Hill recorded the practice of stringing a yucca cord around a cornfield on 2-foot (.6-m) poles, to exclude coyotes; to frighten crows, yucca cords (sometimes with rags attached) were strung above the corn between

Fig. 9.16. Fences and tipiform arrangements of sticks, boards, and cloths protecting peach-tree seedlings from mammalian pests. At the left, two adult trees are individually fenced with posts and wire. Chauncey and Dorothy Neboyia's summer-farm homestead, Zuni trail, Canyon de Chelly, Arizona, 1971.

Fig. 9.17. Scarecrow of poles and old clothing. Phillip Draper orchard, Big Flow Canyon, Canyon del Muerto, Arizona, 1974.

8-foot (2.4-m) poles. Effectiveness is dubious. Scarecrows (*yadíníilzhin*) have long been used as protection against birds, rabbits, and coyotes. These are humanlike figures of poles, clothing, weed-and-grass stuffing, and other materials (Figs. 9.17, 9.18), or simply rags, plastic sheeting, cans, bottles, or dead crows hung on tree limbs, poles, or fence wires (James 1976: 56). Bourke (1884: 78, 98) recorded "vicious-looking scarecrows" in 1881 among both the Navajo and the Hopi; and in 1882 in the Hopi Buttes, Arizona, area, Cushing (1965: 16) observed Navajo pole-and-clothing scarecrows with "deer-bones and clattering sticks." Downs (1972: 93) wrote:

> The Navajo are apt to display considerable ingenuity and wit in constructing human figures by using sticks and old clothes. Often family groups—men, women, and children—will be placed in the fields in attitudes of work or waving at passersby. They seldom discourage birds but they add an element of whimsy to an otherwise tedious, hot, and not too rewarding activity in an often bleak landscape.

There is a taboo against putting eyes on scarecrows, lest the maker go blind (Bulow 1972: 57).

Fig. 9.18. "Michelin Tire Man" scarecrow made of old furniture springs wrapped around a framework of poles. At the mouth of Spring Canyon, Canyon de Chelly, Arizona, 1972.

WATER SUPPLY AND CONTROL

Water Control

Where precipitation is insufficient for crop growth, earth-rimmed water-holding basins may be built around individual plants, which are then hand-watered. Small earth, earth-and-brush or earth-and-log, and masonry or concrete dams (*dá'deestł'in* = walled-up to dam)—occasionally fenced—are sometimes thrown across arroyos and set in rock clefts to form stock ponds (Fig. 9.19)[4] and for diversion of irrigation water. Low earthen dikes to prevent flooding, runoff-spreading weirs, and small flood-control and irrigation ditches (*tó haageed, tó yigeed* = water was dug out, water-furrow dug), up to several kilometers long in the last case, are also built, and fields and field segments may be partially or wholly diked for water retention (Dyk 1947: 34–36, 58, 69; Roberts 1951: 29, 36; Jett 1979b: 300–01).

According to Hill (1938: 24–25), dams and spreading devices were early adopted from Puebloans (Refugee Period?), whereas true ditch irrigation from streams is a post-Ft. Sumner practice (for additional evidence on the antiquity of these practices, see Kluckhohn et al., 1971: 72–74; Bourke 1884: 73, 345–46). However, a large Navajo *acequia* (irrigation ditch) was reported on the Rio Prieto (San Francisco), New Mexico, in 1851, and irrigation was also mentioned for the Mt. Taylor,

Fig. 9.19. Earthen dam. A pipe provides for overflow. Above Fork Rock, Canyon del Muerto, Arizona, 1976.

New Mexico, area, in 1852 (Correll 1976: 265, 288). Further, Letterman (1856: 288) said that some areas were irrigated, and Captain Albert H. Pfeiffer reported irrigation ditches in Canyon del Muerto in 1864 (Kelly 1970: 104; see also, Gwyther 1873: 130). A dam and an irrigation ditch are mentioned in the Origin Legend as having been built by First Man and First Woman (Matthews 1897: 70).

Accelerated government programs beginning in the 1930s have led to construction of many check dams, stock ponds, irrigation projects, bank stabilization structures ("spider jetties"), etc., using Navajo labor.[5]

Wells and Tanks

Particularly from the 1930s onward, many true wells (*tó hahadleeh* = water pulled up repeatedly by rope) of Anglo type, with hand or power water pumps (*tó hahalt'ood* = water is sucked up out) and windmills (*níyol tó*

hayiiłeehí, níyol tó hayiiłt'oodí = wind draws out water repeatedly; *béésh náábałi* = metal whirls rapidly) and tanks, etc., have been installed near or away from habitations. Normally, these are built under government or tribal auspices (Boke 1934; Young 1961: 1974–76; Kluckhohn et al. 1971: 74–76). However, shallow (ca. 2 ft, .6 m) hand-dug wells in washes (e.g., Beadle 1877: 260; Blackwood 1927: 225; Reher 1977: 62) are still excavated (e.g., in Canyon de Chelly), for both domestic and stock water (Fig. 9.20). These have long been used. For example, Kern (1849) mentioned "Indian wells" near Naschitti, New Mexico, and their use no doubt extends back centuries. Springs are sometimes improved as well (Landgraf 1954: 51; Downs 1965: 1395; Neely and Olson 1977: 67), and Leighton and Leighton (1944: plate) picture a spring in a crevice which is fronted by a masonry wall with a door and door frame.

Fig. 9.20. Well for livestock, dug by hand in the dry bed of Wheatfields Creek, above White House Trail, Canyon de Chelly, Arizona, 1979. (Wells for domestic water suppy are at most a few feet in diameter.)

Fig. 9.21. Log watering trough. North of middle Canyon de Chelly, Arizona, 1977.

Troughs

Stock-watering troughs (*tsin bii' ha'ootséél* = log's interior is chopped hollow) are sometimes made by partially hollowing a log for most of its length, with an ax (Fig. 9.21). The only published descriptions are those of Roberts (1951: 16, 36) and Kluckhohn et al. (1971: 76), for Ramah. "They are about two and one half feet [.8 m] long and six to eight inches [15.2 to 20.3 cm] wide and deep. They were made only by men [and] . . . are now common . . ." One stone trough was seen at Ramah (Kluckhohn et al. 1971: 76). Log troughs were considered "modern contrivances" by the Franciscan Fathers (1910: 268–69). Such artifacts have precedents among Euramericans of the region (e.g., James 1913: 45), as well as in Europe itself (Jordan 1980: 161). Jett has seen longer troughs, of planks, north of Canyon de Chelly (Fig. 9.22). Modern troughs of concrete or steel also exist.

Logs are sometimes also grooved shallowly to make salt troughs for livestock (Reichard 1939: 39, plate; Roberts 1951: 16). Jett has observed them south of Lupton, Arizona, and in the Canyon de Chelly region, where they were perhaps 8 feet (2.4 m) long, in one case supplemented by boards, and supported at each end by short forked posts (Fig. 9.23). Salt troughs are a European-introduced trait.

HUNTING STRUCTURES

Although commonly used in former times, hunting structures are now rare or obsolete, for not only are larger quarry animals rare or extinct in the Navajo Country but firearms long ago replaced most of the more primitive hunting weapons and techniques (Franciscan Fathers 1910: 325, 475). Larger

Fig. 9.22. Plank stock-watering troughs; deadwood-fenced sheep corral in the background. North of middle Canyon de Chelly, Arizona, 1979.

Fig. 9.23. Grooved-log salt trough. South of Canyon de Chelly, Arizona, 1972.

game was apparently already uncommon by the late nineteenth century (Parsons 1936: 149), and most traditional big-game-hunting traits were obsolete by shortly after 1900 (Kluckhohn et al. 1971: 440). Some hunting is still done, but food from other sources has minimized the importance of this once very significant economic activity (Downs 1964: 95).

Deadfalls, Pitfalls, and Snares

Since these devices can be considered architecture only by using the broadest definition of that term, descriptions herein are brief.

Deadfalls. Stone-slab deadfalls (*bee' aljizhí* = with which crushing is done) of various

types were used for killing or disabling coyotes, foxes, bobcats, and rodents (see Franciscan Fathers 1910: 322–23; Hill 1938: 168–74; Kluckhohn et al. 1971: 17–19; Gifford 1940: 5, 82 for descriptions and diagrams). The earliest record is 1881 (Bourke 1936: 231–32).

Pitfalls. Pitfalls (*chák'eh* = fell in) were mainly used for deer, particularly in the mountainous regions during November and December. Game trails were sometimes fenced across, leaving a gap where the pit was to be dug, and pit-front log-and-brush hurdles were occasionally placed in the gap. Four pits would sometimes be built in a deer trail. They were usually slightly longer and wider than a deer, and 4 to 9 feet (1.2 to 2.7 m) deep. Forked poles were sometimes set up at either end of the pit to suspend the entrapped deer above the floor, and a sharpened stake was sometimes set in a position to penetrate the animal's heart. Occasionally, four or five sharpened stakes would be used instead, or a straddling bar, or no stakes at all. Ledges were left near the top of the pit, to receive the collapsible roof of twigs or sunflower stalks covered with juniper bark and earth (Hill 1938: 131–32; Gifford 1940: 6, 82; Kluckhohn et al. 1971: 11–12; Franciscan Fathers 1910: 475, 477).

Snares. Bird snares (*tsídii [ɫtsoii] bee wódleehé* = catches [yellow] bird with a cord) were used (Hill 1938: 174–75; Franciscan Fathers 1910: 323–24; Kluckhohn et al., 1971: 14–16; Gifford 1940: 6–7, 83).

Blinds

Hunters sometimes built blinds ('*adááд* = at the away entrance) at waterholes used by game.

Pit-blinds ('*ood* = pit) were also constructed; in them a man could hide in order to catch eagles (by the legs) for ceremonial uses. Pit blinds varied somewhat in form. One described in the legend of the Eagle-Catching-way was dug in four days and was about 4 feet deep, 6 feet long, and 4 feet wide (1.2 X 1.8 X 1.2 m). It apparently had a shed roof of poles covered with earth and camouflaged with grass; a grass-covered yucca mat hung over the entrance (Hill and Hill 1943: 35–36). A similar structure was described in another version of the same legend (Newcomb 1940b: 63, 74). The higher side of the shed roof was supported by five vertical stakes set into the pit floor. The roof of poles, brush, and earth opened toward the east; the opening was covered with a "trap door" of reeds and sticks bound with yucca fiber. A pen confined a rabbit prior to its being staked out as bait. Newcomb (1940b: 70–71) also mentioned the early use of natural crevices as hawk-catching blinds; poles would be used for the roof and sides, and a stuffed squirrel as bait. These were later tabooed. Hill (1938: 160–64) stated that pit-blinds were dug

at night, and averaged about 6 by 3 feet and 4 feet deep (1.8 X .9 X 1.2 m). Sometimes a recess was dug at one end to hold captured eagles, or the hunter occupied a niche in the pit side (Fig. 9.24). Roofs were flat or slightly pitched and were made of poles, bark, and camouflaged earth. The opening was in the center or at one end of the roof.

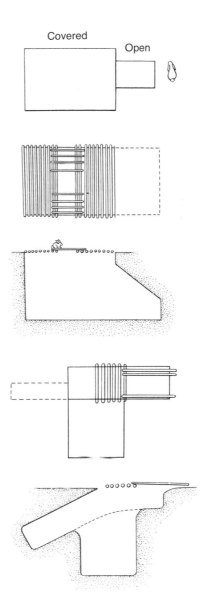

Fig. 9.24. Structural diagrams of eagle pit blinds, as described to W. W. Hill and H. S. Tschopik, Jr., by informants (Kluckhohn et al. 1971: 13).

Tschopik described the entry as being toward the east and being a narrower extension of the main pit (Kluckhohn et al. 1971: 13–14). A live rabbit or stuffed skin was staked by the pit as bait, and a tame eagle (or the first caught) sometimes served as a decoy. The eagles were trapped only during November and December (Franciscan Fathers 1910: 476; Sapir and Hoijer 1942: 316–19; Watson 1968: 23–24; Gifford 1940: 7, 84).

Eagle Cages

Kluckhohn et al. (1971: 80) reported the occasional use of stone or cribbed-pole cages with roofs of horizontal poles, to confine captive eagles kept for ceremonial feathers. Van Valkenburg (1941: 22) mentioned an old stone specimen in Bat Canyon, Canyon de Chelly, and Gifford (1940: 21, 107) referred to eastern Navajo use of domed willow cages.

Game Corrals

The chute-and-pound system was used to capture ungulates, especially antelope (pronghorn) but sometimes also deer and elk. This was done particularly in the southwestern portions of the Navajo Country, preferably in February. Typically, antelope traps were hidden by being built beyond a low ridge or around a valley bend from where the drive began. Each trap (*needzįį* [*n*]) consisted of a large, high-walled, circular corral of piled pinyon and juniper boughs or, rarely, a pitch-pole- or palisade-fenced corral, having an eastern and a western entrance; the latter was closed by a bar with hanging boughs. Haile (1950: 247) also referred to a stone deer corral (*tsé bee needzį[n]į*). Corrals averaged perhaps 300 feet (91.4 m) in diameter. Walls were about 10 to 12 feet (3.1 to 3.7 m) high and were built from the outside after the hunt leader had marked an outline on the ground. The right-hand half (looking toward the entrance from the interior) was constructed first, and the growing tips of the branches pointed toward the rear of the enclosure or were laid sunwise. The driven game was forced into the enclosure by way of a chute consisting of two deadwood fences or, if wood was scarce, fences of verti-

cals, stringers, and hanging boughs, or, occasionally, stone walls. These wings converged toward the eastern entrance of the corral. Annell (1969: 58) claimed palisade fences were used, but this seems doubtful. The chute fences (*'adátł'óól* = at the away entrance string, drawstring) were usually straight, though one might be curved near the corral (Fig. 9.25). They ranged from about 1200 feet (.37 km) to as much as a mile (1.6 km) long and were extended perhaps 2 or 3 additional miles (3.2 to 4.8 km) by lines of brush piles (*'aneelzhiin* = black objects in a line), set at increasingly great intervals (15 to 90 ft, 4.6 to 27.4 m); trees were sometimes incorporated. The farthest pile was built first, then the nearer ones. The right-hand wing was the first built, and both were built from the outside, usually somewhat lower than the corral walls. Bough tips pointed toward the corral. Each major component required about a day to build, totaling some six days. Antelope traps have not been built for many years.[6] Early Land Claim tree-ring dates from game corrals are 1710, 1806, and 1825. Bourke (1884: 72) described an antelope trap seen in 1881.

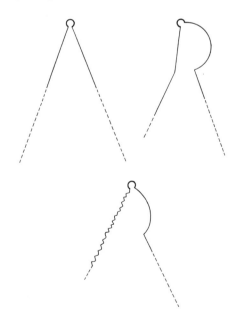

Fig. 9.25. Plans of chute-and-pound antelope traps, as described to W. W. Hill by informants (Kluckhohn et al. 1971: 9).

Origins of Hunting Structures

Northern Athapaskans used snares, deadfalls, pitfalls, eagle pit-blinds (oriented east-west among the Sarsi), and chutes-and-pounds for caribou, mountain sheep, and bison.[7] Pitfalls, deadfalls, eagle pit-blinds, and antelope traps were also known to the historic (and probably prehistoric) Puebloans (Fewkes 1906b: 374; Peckham 1965). Corral traps were, in fact, common in western North America from southern Canada to the southern Southwest (Anell 1969: 120, 123). Deadfalls, pitfalls, snares, and blinds are also very widespread (*e.g.* Lowie 1924: 197–99; Gifford 1940: 5–7, 81–85; Steward 1941: 218–24; 274; Stewart 1941: 366, 368, 422–24; 1942: 240–43). The proto-Navajo probably possessed most or all these devices before their southward migration, although Navajo game corrals were more like southern ones than northern ones.

Beaming Post

The beaming post (*bik'i' 'aldzééh* = on which hides are scraped), described by Kluckhohn et al. (1971: 211; see also Hill 1938: 113), is a post leaned against a tree (which is notched to receive one end) and set into the ground away from the tree base (this end is occasionally forked). Hides, particularly those of deer, are laid across the post for scraping. The earliest description is that of Shufeldt (1889: 60–61), from 1887. The authors have seen only one example, in woodland near Canyon de Chelly, but such an inconspicuous sort of artifact is easily overlooked.

A "scraping frame" is also mentioned, by Kluckhohn et al. (1971: 211) and Haile (1951: 256).

STRUCTURES FOR CRAFT ACTIVITIES

The Navajo have long been known for, and continue to use and profit from, various arts and crafts, including basketry and pottery-making (both uncommon today), weaving, and metal-working (especially for jewelry-making). Craft activities usually occur in dwellings or outdoors and almost never have special buildings exclusively devoted to them. Nevertheless, a few other kinds of structures of a minor nature are created in connection with craft industries.

Pottery-Making

Small stone and clay quarries (*tsé* [or *dleesh*] *hahan'iłígi* = where stones [clay] are repeatedly removed) are known (James 1976: 56; Reher 1977: 62, 68) and supply building and pottery-making materials. Navajo pottery-making does not employ ovens. In most areas, pottery is (or was) fired with wood. In the west, a shallow pit received the pots and the coals. In the east, a ring of four or more stones enclosed the coals or supported the pot. Only at Ramah was a Puebloan-style corbeled dome of slabs of sheep manure built over the pots; this presumably represents an influence from nearby Zuni (Tschopik 1941: 38, 70).

Forges and Smithies

Although now replaced by mobile equipment, forges (*'atsi*[*d*]*k'eh* [*dah 'aznil*] = pounding place) were constructed by silversmiths around the turn of the century (Adair 1974: 16–17, plate 3). Matthews (1883: 172) described these. A rectangular crib consisting of two logs laid at right angles across two others was filled and overtopped with mud, making a platform about 23 × 16 × 5 inches (58.4 × 40.6 × 12.7 cm), into which a 3-inch-deep (7.6-cm) depression 8 inches (20.3 cm) in diameter was sunk. A hole was made from the depression to one end of the platform, to receive the wooden nozzle of the leather bellows. A 4-inch-thick (10.2-cm) slab of rock was laid between the fire bowl and the bellows. Sometimes, the forge was made mainly of masonry and built up quite a bit higher. A photograph in Kluckhohn et al. (1971: 145) shows a forge constructed atop a board platform supported by two stringers laid in the forks of four vertical posts. A 1935 photograph (Fig. 9.26) shows a Navajo blacksmith with an anvil

Fig. 9.26. "Hostin Bekini's blacksmith shop at his winter camp. Bekini's son and Buddy Smith posing." Plows, wagon parts, and other metal items lie on a platform of poles built in a fashion similar to that of low drying platforms. An anvil, held in place by large, bent nails, sits atop a post. Dinnehotso, Arizona, area, 1935; M.S.S. (879).

(*bik'i'atsidí* or *bikáá'atsidí* = on it pounding is done) on a vertical post as well as various items of steel lying atop a low platform supported by vertical posts.

Looms

Rug and belt looms (*dah 'iistł'ǫ́* = up-tied one after the other) are usually in the hogan, on the northern side, in wintertime. They may be erected under the shade or tent or beneath a tree during summer. Looms are occasionally located completely in the open—particularly in areas frequented by photographically inclined tourists (Fig. 9.27). Rug looms are set up vertically, and belt looms are usually somewhat inclined (for descriptions, see Amsden 1934; James 1914; Reichard 1936). Pinyon is the usual wood used for loom uprights "because it is so easily carved" (Elmore 1943: 22). Jerrold E. Levy (personal communication, 1978, and photograph) has observed at a winter camp on Mormon Ridge, Arizona, a unique longish, narrow, horizontal-log weaving shelter with a flat roof in which there was a slot through which the loom poles projected.

Fig. 9.27. Rug loom and ramada. The ramada has walls of leaning poles and cottonwood boughs held in place by a diagonal log. The loom was erected outside to attract model-fee-paying tourists. South of West Mitten Butte, Monument Valley, Arizona, 1962.

Bread ovens north of Canyon del Muerto, Arizona, 1971.

Chapter 10

FOOD-PROCESSING AND STORAGE STRUCTURES

FUEL

Firewood Piles

Firewood is gathered for space heating and for cooking (for hearths and stoves, see chapter 2). Conical firewood (*chizh*) piles of logs leaned together (Figs. 4.15, 5.58) are usual. Rarely, logs are leaned against a stringer supported by a pair of forked poles. Aberle (1966: figures 1–3) pictured logs piled on a pair of boards laid across a pair of logs. These arrangements minimize wetting and rot. Occasionally, wood is simply thrown together in a heap. Quantities of wood chips indicate an established wood-chopping area (Fig. 4.17). According to Haile (1942: 51) wood piles and ash dumps are commonly located slightly north of eastward of the hogan, so that when a person approaches from the east no obstruction intervenes, and when he approaches from the west he may pass unimpeded via the southern (sun) side.

Wood preference varies. Juniper yields cooking coals, but pinyon burns hotly even when wet. Ponderosa, oak, cottonwood, and other woods are also used (Vestal 1952: 13–14; Kluckhohn et al. 1971: 171–72). Aspen is tra-ditionally avoided because it "causes. thunder and lightning" (Bulow 1972: 14). Steel axes and D-saws are employed for wood-cutting.

Coal Mines

Although coal mining was denied by the Franciscan Fathers (1910: 66), small-scale coal mines (*łeejin haagééd* = it is black [i.e., coal] dig out) have supplied domestic fuel in parts of the San Juan Basin since before 1900 (Hoover 1931: 437; Kluckhohn et al. 1971: 171; Huse et al. 1978: 109; cf. the Hopi practice: Colton 1936; Brew and Hack 1939: 12–14). Both small pit mines and shaft mines up to 6 meters (19.7 ft) deep were reported from the lower Chaco River area (Reher 1977: 62, 68). Figure 7.22 shows the remains of a household coal pile at a Burnham, New Mexico, house in 1935.

Bottled Gas

Many contemporary dwellings use bottled gas as a fuel source (e.g., Spencer and Jett 1971: 163). The steel gas cylinders are often seen outside of dwellings.

Fig. 10.1. Navajo woman and girl grinding maize with manos and metates in mealing bins (rare), beneath a cottonwood tree. The bins are of vertical stone slabs on three sides, boards on the fourth. Note: the grass-bundle whisk, in the center; and the screening for sifting, at the left. "At Hattie's summer hogan," south of Comb Ridge and Tyende Wash, east of Kayenta, Arizona, 1935; M.S.S. (833).

MEALING BINS AND MAIZE-GRINDER SHELVES

Although Navajo mealing bins seem to have been primarily indoor features, used mainly during the eighteenth century (see chapter 2), Snow photographs (833, 2229) taken near Dinnehotso in 1935 show the outdoor use of metates (*tsé daashzhéé'* = several-lie-atop stone) placed in adjacent bins made with vertical rock slabs and boards (Fig. 10.1). One of Hill's informants stated that "when green corn was ground, several metates were customarily placed side by side, after the manner of the Pueblos. Slabs of rock were placed around three sides, since the ground material was too liquid to be held on the [usual] goatskin." Gifford's eastern informant said that "four stone slabs were set on edge around the metate but not actually against it; hardened clay on the floor inside the slabs kept the food clean. . . ." (Kluckhohn et al. 1971: 119, 121). Hester and Shiner (1963: 15–16, 36) described two probable metate rests in their excavations in the Navajo Reservoir district. One was simply a flat rock in a small, circular pit; the other consisted of a flat slab of rock surrounded by a ring of cobbles set on edge. A mealing bin was also discovered, the side slabs set 0.5 foot (15.2 cm) into the ground and projecting an equal distance above the surface; the floor was excavated to a depth of a couple of inches.

Today, hand-cranked commercial grinders have largely replaced metates for maize-grinding (other than for ceremonies). "Hand gristmills were introduced by the traders about 1900" (Kluckhohn et al. 1971: 118). Grinders may be attached to tables (often homemade), or special plank shelves may be constructed. In one case, two vertical posts supported the shelf. In another, one end of the shelf was set into a notch in a living cottonwood tree and the other was supported by the stub of a cutoff branch of the tree (Fig. 10.2).

Fig. 10.2. Maize-grinder shelf, consisting of a board nailed at one end to the cottonwood trunk and in the middle to the stub of a branch. Chauncy and Dorothy Neboyia's summer homestead, Zuni Trail, Canyon de Chelly, Arizona, 1972.

OVENS

Earth Ovens

Bowl-shaped, shallow cylindrical, and jar-shaped cooking pits or earth ovens are known, both ethnographically and archaeologically.[1] Food is baked by (1) building and then removing a fire in the pit, inserting the food, and refilling the pit (*łee' ná'álbish 'a'áán* = cooked-in-soil hole; for green corn and corn breads); or (2) leaving the coals in the pit (for meat; Fig. 10.3); or (3) by burying the food with heated stones (for porcupine, prairie dog, and yucca shoots); or (4) mounding hot stones and earth on the surface (for porcupine); or (5) for corn and cornbread, by maintaining a fire on the ground for many hours, after which the hot earth is dug out, the food put in, and the earth replaced. Maize-leaf coverings for the pits were common. Sometimes, another fire would be built atop the refilled pit. Earth ovens using hot stones are widespread in aboriginal North and Middle America, including a few northern Athapaskan groups, all Southern Athapaskans, all Puebloans, and many Shoshoneans (Driver and Massey 1957: 233–34; Gifford 1940: 15, 18, 98, 103; Stewart 1942: 254). Baking pits may be of northern origin among the Navajo but seem equally likely to have been adopted in the Southwest or en

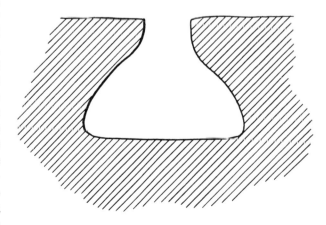

Fig. 10.3. Cross-section of an earth oven, as described to Flora Bailey by an informant. Dimensions are about 5 feet 4 inches deep (1.6 m) and 18 to 20 inches (50 cm) in diameter at the top (Kluckhohn et al 1971: 130).

Fig. 10.4. Corbeled-stone beehive bread oven on a low masonry plinth. Note the stone slabs framing the opening. The stone on the ground at the right is probably for closing the opening while baking is in progress. Cañoncito, New Mexico, 1970.

route thereto. The authors have observed contemporary examples only of the wide, shallow, cylindrical pits made in connection with the girls' puberty ceremonial (*kinaaldá*). Pits of this form have been found archaeologically in the Navajo reservoir district (Hester and Shiner 1963: 14).

"Beehive" Ovens

Outdoor surface ovens (*bááh bighan* = bread's home) of relatively crude stone-and-mud construction are found with moderate frequency near habitations (Figs. 10.4, 10.5), though occasionally located in a sheltered spot several hundred meters from the dwellings (Reher 1977: 43, 48–52, 56–57, 61–63). There appears to be some regional variation in these ovens. Those noted at Cañoncito, New Mex-

Fig. 10.5. Crudely built beehive oven. Large stones and much mud mortar have been used. Instead of the usual round or flattened dome shape, this oven's form is that of a truncated cone with slightly concave sides. Standing Cow Ruin alcove, Canyon del Muerto, Arizona, 1971.

ico, in Black Creek Valley, and near Rock Point, Arizona, were of roughly to rather neatly corbeled stone construction, and more or less beehive-shaped (Figs. 10.4, 10.6), in the fashion of (though smaller than) New Mexico Hispano and Puebloan ovens (which often employ adobe brick or coils of adobe instead of stone); whereas west of the Hopi Country, Navajo ovens appear to be more nearly like Hopi ovens—vertical-walled, with nearly flat tops usually supported by steel rods, pipes, old wagon springs, etc. (Fig. 10.7; such objects may also be used to strengthen corbeled-stone ovens).[2] Both types occur in the Canyon de Chelly area, and James (1976: 3) also reported vertical-slab ovens for this region. Jett saw a square, flat-topped masonry oven near Klagetoh, Arizona, and was informed by David M. Brugge that these are not uncommon (for rectangular masonry fireplaces associated with ramadas, see chapter 4). The oven floor may be somewhat excavated, but at least east of the Chuska Mountains a slightly built-up sand-covered masonry floor may be constructed

Fig. 10.7. Cylindrical, flat-roofed beehive bread oven. Most of the roof has collapsed, revealing the lengths of steel used to support it. Note the large stones capping the walls, the slabs flanking the opening, and the closure stone on the ground at the right. Mouth of Monument Canyon, Canyon de Chelly, Arizona, 1971.

Fig. 10.6. Beehive oven: (left) some erosion of the mud covering reveals the stone corbeling; flat slabs frame the entry. (Note the borrow pits in front of and behind the oven.); (right) detail of the square apical opening, which is the smoke hole when the fire is in the oven but which is covered with a mud-sealed slab during baking. Near Rock Point, Arizona, 1970.

(Kluckhohn et al. 1971: 133–34). In all cases, an opening is left in the structure's top and another, larger, one at its base, preferably toward the east.[3] The stones are chinked, and the whole is covered or plastered with earth, usually obtained from a nearby borrow pit; a slightly raised lip may be built up around the apical opening. At Cañoncito, the oven was set on a masonry plinth (Fig. 10.4), in New Mexico Hispano and Puebloan fashion. Navajo ovens average perhaps about 2.5 to 3 feet (.8 to .9 m) in height and are usually of slightly greater diameter.

Use and Origin of Beehive Ovens

Navajo use of ovens is similar to that of Hispano and Puebloan ones and is particularly to provide bread during large ceremonials. The oven is heated by building a fire in its interior, and then the fire is cleaned out, the dough or other food put inside, the orifices covered with flat stones or sheets of metal and sealed with mud (usually obtained from a shallow pit more or less in front of the oven). The food is allowed to bake for up to 12 hours or more (Mindeleff 1891: 164; Chauncey Neboyia, personal communication). Although these ovens are used primarily for wheat-flour bread baking, they are sometimes used for baking, and perhaps drying, maize.[4] The authors know of no description of Navajo stone ovens in the literature, other than in their own article (Spencer and Jett 1971: 168) and in Kluckhohn et al. (1971: 133–34), although a few brief references and photographs have appeared.[5]

The beehive-shaped bread oven or *horno* was introduced to Spain by the Arabs, and to the New World by the Spanish (Boyd 1974: 15–17; Chavez 1977). It could have been adopted by the Navajo directly from the Spanish, perhaps as a consequence of slave-taking by both cultures. The derivation of the Navajo word for wheat bread, *bááh,* from the Spanish *pan* might be thought to support this hypothesis, but *bah* or *pah* is also the word for bread at a number of New Mexico pueblos (McNitt 1964: 248). Ovens could have been introduced by Puebloan refugees about 1700, or through

the taking of Puebloan slaves; Puebloans early adopted the oven and still use ovens of this general type which are larger and better built than Navajo ones (e.g., Mindeleff 1891: 163–66; Stirling 1940: 567). There are some reasons to question early introduction, however. There is a conspicuous absence of early archaeological beehive ovens. Possible exceptions have been mentioned for the late seventeenth-early-eighteenth-century supposedly Navajo Cerrito site in the Rio Chama, New Mexico, area. However, there is no clear evidence that these circles of burned stones were more than two courses high (Schaafsma 1979: 85, 94–96). The earliest written description of an oven dates from 1851 (Dillon 1970: 70); one informant even stated that such ovens are post-Ft. Sumner (Kluckhohn et al. 1971: 133). The Franciscan Fathers (1910: 218) noted that "*in modern times* ovens, similar to those in use among the Pueblos, have been introduced for baking purposes" (italics added). Kluckhohn et al. (1971: 442) also stated that the oven has increased in use since the 1930s (however, few of the ovens we observed appeared to be much or recently used).

The apical aperture suggests the possibility of adoption from the Zuni (see footnote 3), whose reservation is adjacent to Navajo-occupied lands, and Kluckhohn (1966: 342) attributed the oven among the Ramah Navajo to this source. Or, Spanish-American settlements on the eastern border of the Navajo country may have been a source, during the nineteenth century. In this connection, the setting of the Cañoncito oven on a plinth may be significant, since this is the easternmost area of Navajo occupance. Note, too, that a beehive-shaped oven appears in a Ben Wittick photograph (1880s) of the original Hubbell Trading Post at Ganado, Arizona (Packard and Packard 1970: 30).

DRYING AND STORAGE STRUCTURES

Among Navajo structures, both the most and least prominent in the cultural landscape are in the category of storage structures.

Drying and Storage Racks, Platforms, and Floors

Drying racks (or frames; *dah ná'ázhoozh* = raised bridge; *daht'oh* = raised nest) are frequently erected, to allow the drying of strips of meat, bundles of maize ears, strips cut from melons, or other produce. These structures are also used to air sheep pelts and other bedding and to store objects (e.g., Johnson 1977: 57). Drying racks usually consist of a pair (or more) of vertical (often forked) poles, boards, or trees, and a pole, plank, or pipe stringer(s) (Fig. 10.8; also 5.12, 5.50, 7.1). A single vertical forked pole was occasionally used (Keur

1941: 37; Hill 1938: 41, 112, 127–28; Underhill 1953: 75; Gilpin 1968: 52; Johnston 1972: 1), and tripod meat-drying racks (as used among Northern Athapaskans) were mentioned by one informant (Kluckhohn et al. 1971: 70–71). Wires or ropes tied between trees may serve the same function. Pole-and-wire or -rope clothesline arrangements are also sometimes employed (Figs. 5.1, 5.49, 7.12).

Storage and/or drying platforms are occasionally constructed, in a fashion similar to the wall-less flat-roofed shade, as among Puebloans (Kluckhohn et al. 1971: 70–71). These platforms range from a few feet high (Fig.

Fig. 10.8. Sheepskins on a drying rack consisting of three vertical posts to which are wired two stringers. In the background are a cribbed-log house with a two-doorway facade and a roll-roofing-covered hipped-with-ridge roof, plus a pile of ponderosa pine logs for future house construction. Chauncey and Dorothy Neboyia's main homestead, north of Canyon de Chelly, Arizona, near the head of Beehive Trail, 1972.

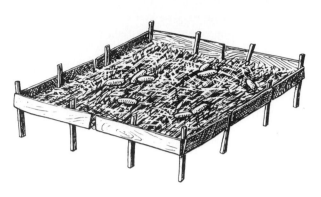

Fig. 10.9. Diagram of a drying platform with maize. Straw lies atop the platform poles to support the maize ears. Ramah area, New Mexico (Kluckhohn et al. 1971: 71).

10.9) to well above head height (Fig. 10.10; cf., Northern Athapaskan platform food caches; Morice 1909: 594). Snow photographed a shadelike structure about 7 feet (2.1 m) high. A vertical post was set outside each corner and extended above the level of the roof; rails connected these uprights to confine the maize fodder and dried squash vines stored on the platform. A homemade rung ladder gave access to the top, and a pole with a cloth tied on was erected on the roof as a scarecrow (Fig. 10.11). James (1976: 5, 49) described platforms of poles set onto the branches of living trees, apparently for hay storage, and Frank Mitchell stated that flat rocks were placed in trees to store cottage cheese (Frisbie and McAllester 1978: 32).

Snow photos of 1935 (see Figs. 5.3 and 9.26) show structures similar to drying platforms, used to keep a variety of possessions above ground level. Ramadas are also sometimes used for meat and produce drying and storage and for storage of fodder and hay, either on the roof (Fig. 10.12) or under it if there are walls to exclude livestock.

Fig. 10.10. Newly constructed hay-storage rack. Stringers rest upon the square-sawn ends of the five uprights and the runged ladder, and support thirteen spaced horizontal logs. Bracing logs are nailed to three of the uprights, whose lower portions are partially debarked. Above Middle Trail Canyon, Canyon del Muerto, Arizona, 1974.

Fig. 10.11. Fodder-storage platform, supported by four uprights. Five taller, supplemental, poles have rails wired to them to retain the maize stalks and other fodder. A homemade ladder gives access to the platform. The manure suggests that livestock seeks the shade beneath the structure. Near Newcomb, New Mexico, 1935; M.S.S. (1003).

Prepared floors of thick, smooth adobe are sometimes made—in a cliff shelter, if available —on which maize is husked and dried and peaches split, pitted, and dried. Their area in Canyon del Muerto was 200 to 300 square feet (19 to 28 sq m), and they were patched each harvest season and used for many years (Steen 1966: 60; Newcomb 1966: plate opposite p. 39).

Storehouses and "Root Cellars"

As has been observed above, hogans— particularly older ones (Fig. 5.23)—and houses (Fig. 6.1) often serve primarily or partially or temporarily as storage structures. Bennett (1975: 10) described her camp as having a cribbed-log hogan, a log storehouse, and a roofless stone hogan used to keep the hay out of reach of the sheep (for hay-storage sheds and barns, see chapter 9). Roberts (1951: 43) mentioned a camp with a frame house, a cabin for storage, and an old hogan for hay storage (see also Landgraf 1954: 50). Downs (1972: 48) stated that many families maintained two hogans—one to live in, one for storage. The aforementioned storage structures are usually distinguishable from dwellings only on the basis of function, although hogans and houses built expressly for storage are probably on the average smaller in size than dwellings. Some storage hogans lack smoke holes (Landgraf 1954: 47, 50) or have had them covered over (Fig. 5.45).

Dugouts (Figs. 10.13, 7.4, 7.8, 7.29, 5.1; see chapter 2), although occasionally inhabited, are today used primarily as "root cellars" for the storage and preservation of perishable foodstuffs (e.g., Johnson 1977: 62). Landgraf

Fig. 10.12. Ramada, with the brush-covered roof projecting outward to the entry; a few leaning poles form open walls. The roof is used to store maize ears; a cloth on a pole serves as a scarecrow. Fields in the middleground are bordered by post-and-wire fences. Comb Ridge (?), east of Kayenta, Arizona, 1935; M.S.S. (829).

Fig. 10.13. Stone dugout storage house. The Gap, Arizona, 1970.

Fig. 10.14. Food-storage pit. The pit appears to have been freshly dug (note the spade at the right) and partially roofed with poles, Russian thistle, and other brush. The cornhusks behind the right-hand melons are for packing and lining. "At Ralph Gray's spring camp," Mexican Water area (?), Arizona, 1935; M.S.S. (2220).

(1954: 50) wrote of "root cellars with earth-covered gabled roofs" used for storage, and Darby et al. (1956: 26) noted that "Root cellars are in fairly common use" for root crops, melons, and pumpkins. Reichard (1934: 6–7 and plate) described one used primarily to store wool. Its approximate dimensions were 12 by 15 feet by 6 feet high (3.7 × 4.6 × 1.8 m). Kluckhohn et al. (1971: 112) mentioned one with a screen door which allowed air circulation.

Storage Pits

Far less noticeable in the landscape than the structures described above—in fact, intentionally hidden—are, or were, food-storage pits (*nook'eh* [*bii' hahoogeed*] = cache place [hole was hollowed out]). Formerly, every family maintained one to four of these pits (Fig. 10.14), usually near the fields or the summer camp (Franciscan Fathers 1910: 267). Hill (1938: 42–45), Kluckhohn et al. (1971: 111–14), Steece (1921: 423), and Bourke (1884: 78) have described these pits. Reputedly, the most ancient was the globular, jar-shaped pit (Fig. 10.15), which originally was excavated with a digging stick. It was sunk into dry ground, to a depth of 2.5 to 7 feet (.6 to 2.1 m), averaging perhaps 5.5 ft. (1.7 m). The walls were further dried and hardened by building a fire inside, and then scraped to a depth of about 2 inches (5.1 cm). The pit was lined with juniper bark as it was filled with domestic or wild produce (dried maize, beans, squash, melon, peaches, sunflower seeds, pinyon nuts, chenopod seeds, wild potatoes). The

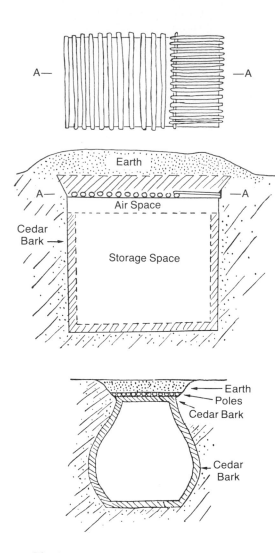

Fig. 10.15. Diagrams of food-storage pits: at-bottom, the jar-shaped type; at top, the rectangular type (Hill 1938: 44).

neck was filled with bark and then covered with sticks if the pit was large, or with a flat rock or weeds or brush, and then with a foot (.3 m) of earth, the first layer dry, the second damp. The surface was convex, for drainage. At canyons de Chelly and del Muerto and near Kayenta (Tyende?) Creek, Arizona, pits were often located in dry rock shelters. A cylindrical wall of stone masonry about 3 feet (.9 m) in diameter was commonly built around the pit's rim; the opening at the top was roofed with poles, rock slabs, vegetal materials or a piece of cloth, and earth (Fig. 10.16). James (1976: 3, 27) reported mud- or stone-lined cists. Anasazi storage cists were sometimes refurbished and used as well.

Rectangular bark-lined pits (Fig. 10.15) were also constructed, particularly for storage of ripe melons. The pits were about 3 by 6 feet (.9 by 1.8 m), and about 5 feet (1.5 m) deep. A 7-inch (17.8-cm) air space was left above the produce. Poles were laid across from one end of the pit to within 1.5 feet (.5 m) of the other end. Sticks at right angles spanned the space between that end and the nearest pole; access

Fig. 10.16. Abandoned storage structure of stone-and-mud masonry, built into a gap in a cliff-shelter ledge; when intact, the structure would have been very inconspicuous. Partial collapse of the flat roof reveals its structure: horizontal poles covered with grass, twigs, and reeds, atop which were placed flat slabs of sandstone, the whole then being covered with mud. Mouth of Spring Canyon, Canyon de Chelly, Arizona, 1978.

was via this space (occasionally, a central hatchway was built instead). Six inches (18.3 cm) of bark and a foot (.3 m) of earth completed the roof. Jett has seen an example sunk into the fill of a prehistoric room in Canyon de Chelly, utilizing the two ancient walls of one corner of the room (Fig. 10.17). A supposedly recent variant similar to early dugout dwellings had a center-beam roof; the beam was supported by an upright at either end of the pit.

In the Canyon de Chelly system, partly or wholly above-ground storage buildings of stone-and-mud masonry—sometimes mud plastered—are built, ordinarily in cliff shelters. They are rectangular or subrectangular (rarely circular) and have flat or slightly sloping roofs provided with hatchways or doors (Figs. 10.18, 10.19, 10.20).

Fig. 10.17. Two storage chambers built into a room in a prehistoric Anasazi ruin. The roof poles are covered with flat stones and mud. Note how straight-edged stones have been selected to bound the hatchways. Spring Canyon Surface Ruin, Canyon de Chelly, Arizona, 1978.

Fig. 10.18. Subrectangular, roughly coursed stone-and-mud-masonry storage building, using the cliff for one wall; beam roof. The stones have been taken from an Anasazi ruin on the site. Note the homemade door with a padlock. The building was refurbished and its walls raised in recent years. Informant Chauncey Neboyia stands beneath the Navajo pictograph of a cow. Standing Cow Ruin, Canyon del Muerto, Arizona, 1971.

Fig. 10.19. Several mud-plastered, stone-masonry storage structures in a cliff shelter. The right-hand structure utilizes a door laid horizontally over its entry. The middle structure is built within a partially collapsed older structure; the ends of the poles of the mud-sealed entry are visible. The other structures are in various states of disrepair. Standing Cow Ruin, Canyon del Muerto, Arizona, 1971.

Fig. 10.20. Stone-and-mud-masonry storage structures in cliff shelters: (left) the hatchway has a board door with commercially made hinges as well as an apparent ventilation opening on the side; (right) the sloping upper front, made of sawmill slabs, is unusual; the plank trap door has a wire handle and a hasp. Near Sliding Rock Ruin, Canyon de Chelly, Arizona, 1971.

Storage pits were indicated in the Rabal document of 1744 (referring to the early eighteenth century; Hill 1940: 397, 402), and Bourke (1884: 78) observed them in 1881. Kluckhohn et al. (1971: 114) noted several late nineteenth- and early twentieth-century references to such structures. Pit storage is very widespread in North America (Driver and Massey 1957: 247–48; Gifford 1940: 16, 20, 99; Stewart 1941: 374, 376; 1942: 250–54; Steward 1941: 280–81, 332–33). The structures described above have prehistoric Anasazi and modern Puebloan equivalents; these were presumably the models for at least the jar-shaped Navajo structures. Northern Athapaskans typically cache their food on platforms (Morice 1909: 594), although rectangular meat-storage pits are reported for Athapaskans of the Koyukuk River, Alaska, (Clark 1974: 132), and the Ingalik of Southwestern Alaska built circular fish-storage pits (Osgood 1940: 334–35). Pits of undetermined shape are recorded for some other Athapaskan groups (Driver and Massey 1957: 248). According to Kluckhohn et al. (1971: 441), storage pits have been more or less obsolete for several decades.

Storage Caves

Storage caves (now largely obsolete) were also used for meat in summertime, for maize in winter; other foodstuffs were also often stored (Kluckhohn et al. 1971: 109–11; James 1976: 33–34). A small cavity (*tséníí' noo'* = rock-nostril [niche] cache) would be sealed with a single, vertically placed flat stone and mud; reeds were sometimes inserted through the mud to provide ventilation. Large cavities were closed with masonry walls, sometimes with square openings (Fig. 10.21); the masonry was at times camouflaged with vertically placed flat slabs rubbed with moss. Flagstone floors were occasionally used, as were slab partitions. Ancient Puebloan masonry storage structures were occasionally refurbished and reused, but this was considered somewhat dangerous (Hill 1938: 43). Objects were also sometimes cached in open crevices and under rocks (e.g., Keur 1941: 34).

Fig. 10.21. Storage structure constructed by walling up a cliff crevice with rocks and mud. Although probably Anasazi (Neely and Olson 1977: 36, 40), this feature is probably similar to those Navajo structures mentioned by Hill (see text). Western Tse Biyi, Monument Valley, Arizona, 1962.

Outdoor Cupboards and Shelves

At some camps, especially those lacking shades, homemade outdoor cupboards for food storage are seen, as are crate shelves for storage of food-preparation, eating, and washing utensils. They may be attached to tree trunks, often some distance above the ground. Food cupboards may have screen doors. Outdoor homemade wooden tables (Figs. 4.14, 8.14) for food preparation and consumption and for dish washing are also used (Jett 1980).

PRIVIES

After food has been processed by the human body, waste is excreted and its disposal becomes an issue. Privies or outhouses (*kin yázhí bii' nii'oh ńda'aldáhígíí* (or *ńda'alyeedígíí*) = little house into which persons go (run) into concealment individually; *chąą' bá hooghan* = feces hogan) had become common in the 1970s in the more densely populated areas but were still uncommon in more remote regions, where feces might be hidden in the brush or buried with the use of shovels, or where dogs might perform the sanitary function, all at some distance from the dwelling (Dyk 1947: 202, Downs 1964: 26; 1972: 53). Privies, which reflect Anglo-American influences, are usually frame structures of square plan, taller than wide, and covered with vertical or horizontal planks (Figs 5.1, 7.12). Through a recent Tribal sanitation program, large numbers of prefabricated plywood privies have been distributed (Spencer and Jett 1971: 168–69). A privy covered with corrugated sheet metal has been noted, as have one palisaded one and one fired-brick probable outhouse (Fig. 7.27) and one of adobe brick (at Alamo, New Mexico). Plank or plywood shed roofs, often covered with tarpaper, are usual; corrugated metal roofs have also been noted.

There is little evidence as to the date of first adoption of privies, but none was present at Ramah in 1941 (Landgraf 1950: 50). A 1943 photo taken near Manuelito, New Mexico, shows a camp with a privy (Gastil 1975: Fig. 23).

Chapter 11

CEREMONIAL AND RECREATIONAL STRUCTURES

SWEATHOUSES (SUDATORIES)

Sweathouses *(táchééh)* for sweat baths are or were used by most aboriginal North American groups (Krickeberg 1939; Driver and Massey 1957: 314–15). Four major forms have been noted for the Navajo.

Conical Forked-Pole Sweathouse[1]

This, the usual Navajo structure, is essentially a miniature conical forked-pole hogan, from 3 to 10 feet (.9 to 3.1 m) in diameter and somewhat less high than wide; but it lacks a smoke hole as well as, usually, the extended entryway (Figs. 11.1, 11.2). Rock slabs sometimes supplement the leaners' vegetal covering (Vivian 1960: 101–102; Thybony 1980: 9), and occasionally brush, pelts, or blankets replace the normal earth covering (see "Construction Procedures and Use," below). The excavation of the floor is proportionately deeper than that of the typical hogan, and there is usually a shallow pit inside and to the right of the entry to receive the heated rocks. The entry may be about 2 feet (.6 m) high and 1.5 feet (.5 m) wide at the base, usually tapering toward the lintel.

The three main timbers have the same names as those of hogans (Mindeleff 1898:

Fig. 11.1. Conical forked-pole sweathouse lacking its earth covering; rocks used for heating are to the right. Across Canyon de Chelly, Arizona, from Chauncey and Dorothy Neboyia's summer-farm homestead at Zuni Trail, 1972.

499–500). They interlock at about a 90-degree angle. Page (1937a) described an example whose main forked poles were about 8 feet (2.4 m) long and were set a few inches into the ground around a 6-foot-wide (1.7-m) circular excavation. Two 4-foot (1.2-m) forked poles sunk 1 foot (.3 m) into the ground and topped by a stringer formed a partially extended entryway. Poles were laid on and covered with

Fig. 11.2. Conical forked-pole sweathouse, with rocks for heating at the right. Chauncey and Dorothy Neboyia's main homestead, north of Canyon de Chelly, Arizona, near the head of Beehive Trail, 1973.

juniper bark and a 6- to 8-inch-thick (15.2 to 20.3 cm) covering of tamped damp earth. Bohrer (1964: 95) described a second example (Fig. 11.3). Its main poles were only about 4.7 feet (1.4 m) long; the western pole was not forked, although the two curved doorway poles were forked and interlocked. The timbers were planted 2 to 8 inches (5.1 to 20.3 cm) from the rim of a 5-foot- (1.4-m-) diameter excavation 9 to 11 inches (22.9 to 27.9 cm) deep.

Tipiform Sweathouse

Two sudatories were described by Olson and Wasley near Prewitt, New Mexico (1956: 329, 358–59). Although otherwise similar to the conical forked-pole sweathouse, one (Fig. 11.5) was peculiar in having a number of unforked juniper poles (set in a shallow trench outside the main excavation) coverging to an apex and secured with bailing wire; upon these were laid pine boards. A lintel was nailed over the entry, and the area above closed with

wired-on boards. A covering of apparently dry earth and stones was added.

Leaning-Log Sweathouse

Hayes (1964: 123) pictured a sweathouse at Mesa Verde National Park, Colorado, which appears to have been built like a square, flat-roofed leaning-log hogan, except that one wall was formed by a large fallen tree, which also supported one end of the roof. The structure was probably built by a Navajo park employee. Huse et al. (1978: 107) described sudatories with four upright poles supporting a flat roof, usually set against a slope or bank.

Dugout Sweathouse

A circular hollow 3 to 6 feet (.9 to 1.8 m) wide is excavated into a bank or slope; a front wall may be raised by laying up logs or branches horizontally, and door posts may be used (Fig. 11.4). The roof is 2.5 to 3.5 feet (.8 to 1.1 m) above the floor and is of earth-covered logs, poles, planks, or sheet metal laid across the slope. The roof rests directly on the soil, or on logs laid at right angles to those of the roof, or on logs laid at various angles around the edges of the excavation. A basin for the heated stones is dug inside and to the right of the entry. A pair of rocks on the roof holds the entryway blanket in place. Exterior rock piles are usually found associated with the structures (Brugge 1956).

In the Nightway myth, fire-heated trenches, for ceremonial sweating, are mentioned (Matthews 1902: 210, 259).

Construction Procedures and Use

Sudatories are built by men. A man can usually erect one in an hour or two; tradition requires that every sweathouse be built in a day's time or less and that a certain song be sung during construction. For structures used in chantways, the growing ends of the framework poles must point upward. Because sudatories are ceremonial, spruce wood, which has religious associations, may be used, although juniper is the typical wood; spruce is proscribed for hogans (Callaway and Witherspoon 1968: 57; Kluckhohn et al. 1971: 318–20, 417). Spruce twigs are also preferred to underlie the earth covering, at least for Nightway, although if scarce they may be augmented by sagebrush or other vegetal material. Matthews (1902: 50–51) described Nightway sweatlodges as employing pinyon for the principal eastern and southern poles, juniper for the western and northern. In the myth of the

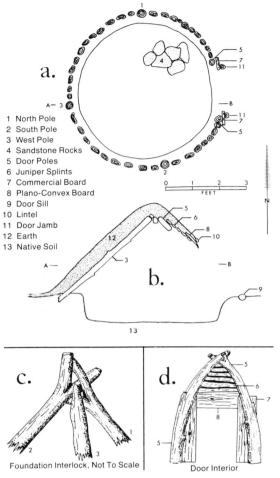

1 North Pole
2 South Pole
3 West Pole
4 Sandstone Rocks
5 Door Poles
6 Juniper Splints
7 Commercial Board
8 Plano-Convex Board
9 Door Sill
10 Lintel
11 Door Jamb
12 Earth
13 Native Soil

Fig. 11.3. Structural diagrams of the (*a*) plan, (*b*) cross section, (*c*) tripod interlock, and (*d*) doorway of a conical forked-pole sweathouse near Window Rock, Arizona, ca. 1962 (Bohrer 1964: 97).

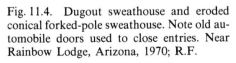

Fig. 11.4. Dugout sweathouse and eroded conical forked-pole sweathouse. Note old automobile doors used to close entries. Near Rainbow Lodge, Arizona, 1970; R.F.

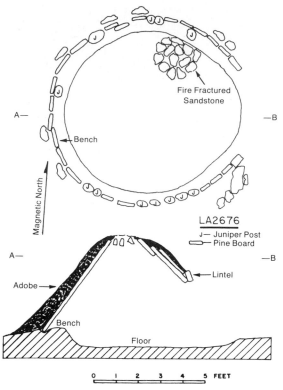

Fig. 11.5. Diagrams of a tipiform sweathouse near Prewitt, New Mexico, 1954 (Olson and Wasley 1956: 359).

Mountaintopway (Matthews 1887: 389), a brush-covered sweathouse built to help on a hunt had poles as follows: east, juniper; south, mountain mahogany (*Cerocarpus* sp.); west, pinyon; north, cliff rose *(Cowania mexicana)*. Oak is also often used for the framework. The butts of the leaners (usually split juniper logs and poles; sometimes cottonwood or other species) may be set in a shallow trench. The floor is usually excavated from a few inches to 2 feet (.6 m), and occasionally is dug partially into a sloping bank. The excavated dirt and other soil from the immediate environs is used to cover the structure. The floor may be lined with juniper bark, spruce twigs, and aromatic plants, or even cardboard. The entrance may be oriented toward any direction but ordi-

narily faces eastward (westward according to the Franciscan Fathers 1910: 341; northward among the eastern Navajo, according to Gifford 1940: 110). When the sudatory is in use, the entry is covered with blankets (ideally, four), canvases, and/or hides. Up to a dozen or so rocks (usually sandstone), preferably more or less spherical and about 1 foot (.30 m) in diameter, are heated in a fire a couple of paces from (i.e., usually eastward of) the entry (the ceremonial minimum number of rocks is four). For ceremonies, the butts of the fire logs, of pinyon and juniper, should point toward the structure. The heated stones are carried between two sticks and are placed in a shallow depression on the north or northeast side (the "cold" side) of the floor (Stevenson [1891: 240] reported the stones being placed toward the south). Heating is usually dry, but sometimes a little water is sprinkled onto the rocks. Afterward, the rocks may be piled to the northeast of the entry for later reuse, and excessively fire-cracked, nonreusable stones are piled beyond or to the northwest. Fresh rocks for future use may be piled farther to the northeast or to the southeast of the doorway. Used sweathouse rocks are sometimes carried to orchards to ward off early frosts (Hill 1938: 49, 58).

Sudatory use is both hygienic and physically and ceremonially therapeutic, as well as social, although utilization has declined in recent years. Sweathouses for ordinary use are commonly located where rocks are available at some 45 to 200 meters (150 to 656 ft) from the dwelling—for privacy and, in the past, so that returning hunters and warriors could purify themselves before entering the camp.[2] If water is available, its proximity is also a prime consideration (Downs 1972: 33), so that the users may bathe after sweating. According to Page (1937a: 19), sweathouses are "built in or near the sandy washes" (users may roll in the sand between uses). When built near the dwelling for rituals related to warfare or epidemic, the sweathouse is normally built some 200 yards (193 m) to the north (Kluckhohn et al. 1971: 318). During certain ceremonials (e.g., Nightway), a sudatory is supposed to be built successively at each of the four cardinal points, some 100 to 200 feet (30.5–61.0 m) from the ceremonial hogan, although often only one is actually erected; each structure may then be decorated with a sandpainting of a rainbow, lightning, or sunbeam figure, and eight plumed wands are set up around the structure. In these ceremonies, pelts and blankets are often used in place of earth covering and may even be used without any superstructure over the excavation. Aaland (1978: 226) described a Navajo on the trail simply sitting on a log, with hot rocks between his feet and a blanket draped over himself and the rocks. In Nightway ceremonies, if no sweatlodge is built a *ko'k'eh* (fireplace) is prepared on the ground. After the fire is cleared away, seven layers of different woods and herbs are piled up, and the blanket-covered patient lies down with his head toward the hogan and pillowed on leaves (Matthews 1902: 53). Blanket-covered sudatories were formerly erected at hunting and other temporary camps (Sapir and Hoijer 1942: 323; Frisbie and McAllester 1978: 83–84).

In 1866, Captain Bristol (1867: 358) quoted informant Jesús [Arviso?] as saying that "sweathouses [are] built of poles covered with grass and dirt, or small excavations in the earth, having been previously filled with red-hot [*sic*] stones." Bourke (1936: 88), in 1881, stated that temporary willow and brush sudatories were usual, with earth-covered ones less common. This seems to have been associated with more frequent changes of residence in the past. A sudatory may be dismantled and re-erected elsewhere.

Sudatories have legendary sanction. An earth-covered one was built by First Man, with the help of Beaver, at the Place of Emergence; by contrasting Puebloans' nonuse of sweathouses, the Emergence Myth made the sudatory a symbol of Navajo ethnic identity (Goddard 1933: 25, 133; Fishler 1953: 35). During Nightway, the four successive sudatories (beginning in the east) are dismantled after use, all traces being obliterated, the components, stones, and ashes being placed under or

in pinyons or other trees, in the direction the sweatlodge was erected vis-à-vis the hogan. Log tips should point away from the hogan and prayersticks be deposited (Matthews 1902: 53; Stevenson 1891: 241).

The sweathouse was presumably brought to the Southwest by ancestral Athapaskans; Navajo tradition confirms this, and both Northern and Southern Athapaskans sweatbathe in special structures (for Western Apache sweathouses, see Hollister 1903: fig. 6; Gifford 1940: 110; Reed 1954; 25).[3] Like the Navajo, most Western Apaches place the hot rocks to the right of the entry; the Southern Tonto entry faced northeast. The earth covering may have been a Navajo innovation following adoption of earth covering for dwellings. However, some Columbia Plateau and California groups, including the Athapaskan Chilcotin, used earth covering (Driver and Massey 1957: 314–15; Krickeberg 1939: 20; Ray 1942: 180).[4]

An apparent sweatlodge was found archaeologically in the Navajo Reservoir district, New Mexico, dating probably to the Gobernador Phase (1696–1770; Hester and Shiner 1963: 50–51), and apparent eighteenth-century sudatories were described by Keur (1941: 37–38; 1944: 77) and Vivian (1960: 101–02; also, Van Valkenburgh 1947b: 17; 1945: 6; Hester 1962: 44–45). Navajo Land Claim records also indicate eighteenth-century use of sweathouses in New Mexico, apparently as early as the 1730s (Navajo Land Claim n.d.b-7: Upper [Canyon] Largo, site T; 9: Cebolleta Mesa, site I). An early documentary reference to the sweathouse is that of Letterman (1856: 289).

SHRINES

Watson (1964: 22) wrote that "an enclosure formed of stones provides a place for prayers and offering ..." but such shrines have otherwise escaped description in the literature. This type of shrine is found among the Puebloans. Farmer (1947: 21) described what may have been an eighteenth-century shrine in the Upper Largo area, New Mexico, consisting of a metate resting on an irregular pile of logs atop a high butte.

Navajo-built cairns presumed to be for ritual use have been reported on Anasazi sites (Ambler et al. 1964: 20; Reher 1977: 82). A 1935 Snow photograph (910) shows a "Navajo shrine at upper end of farming area" near Dinnehotso, Arizona, consisting of a few rocks piled up, with some pebbles on top. (For cairn trail shrines, see chapter 12.)

OTHER CEREMONIAL STRUCTURES

Minor Ritual Structures

As discussed in chapters 4 and 5, ramadas, tipis, and hogans may be built for or temporarily used for ceremonies. Minor temporary ceremonial structures are also built, including sand mounds for sand-paintings, the setting of uprights (such as prayer sticks) on or next to model mountains (*ndii'á dził* = mountain uprights enclosed by a few tiers of logs (Haile 1942: 52–54; Kluckhohn et al. 1971: 363), lines of bent-pole arches in the big-hoop ceremony (Wyman 1966: 12–18), and the sun-house screen (Schevill 1945; McAllester and McAllester 1980: 84).

Dance Grounds

Keur (1941: 38–39; also, Farmer 1947: 21; Hester 1962: 46) described what were apparently eighteenth-century especially prepared dance grounds in the open, somewhat analogous to Puebloan plazas. They were about 25 by from 50 to 75 feet (7.6 X 15.2 to 22.9 m), with boundary stones at the corners and fireplaces along the long sides. (For ceremonial enclosures, see "windbreaks," chapter 4, and "corrals," chapter 9.)

Hitching Posts

The early Navajo are said to have employed hitching posts to which to tether horses for ceremonial purposes.

Holes were dug in the four cardinal directions, approximately fifty feet [15.2 m] from the hogan. In the bottom of each was placed a turquoise, white shell, obsidian and oyster (olivella?) [*Haliotis?*] shell . . . Posts with the figures of the sun and moon carved on each were placed in the holes and the holes filled in with dirt. [Kluckhohn et al. 1971: 91]

Flag Pole

A tall, single pole is sometimes seen next to a dwelling (Fig. 1.2). Some of these may be used to support radio antennas, but Robert W. Young (personal communication, 1980) indicates that most are probably to support flags announcing peyote ceremonies.

RECREATIONAL STRUCTURES

Race Tracks

Circular horse-racing tracks, perhaps of Mormon derivation, were in use in the vicinity of Navajo Mountain, Utah, in the 1930s (Hobler and Hobler 1967), and the authors have reports of one or two other such tracks.

Basketball Backboards

Basketball backboards and baskets (Fig. 7.13) are Anglo introductions and are very popular. One was seen equipped with an electric light, allowing after-dark use.

"Bucking Horse"

Jett has seen, at a Navajo homestead at Chinle, Arizona, a device used to simulate a bucking horse, presumably to provide amusement and to allow practice for rodeo competition. It consists of a horizontal log suspended from trees by means of four ropes, which can then be agitated by someone while the "rider" sits astride the log.

Models

Model hogans, houses (*kįshchíín* = small house facsimile), shades, and corrals (Fig. 11.6) are built by children for amusement, as, for example, when they are herding sheep.

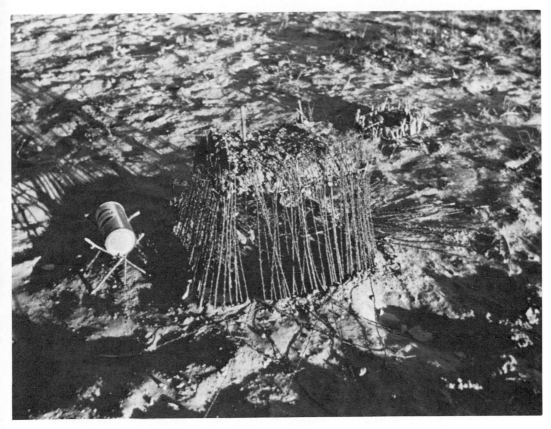

Fig. 11.6. Model of a camp, including a soft-drink-can water tank, an earth-roofed ramada made of tamarisk twigs, and a palisade-fenced corral with horse-manure sheep. Junction of canyons de Chelly and del Muerto, Arizona, 1972.

Models are usually made of twigs or stones. Livestock are represented by stones, pieces of horse manure, or crude clay figurines.[5]

Northeast of Grand Falls, Arizona, are several stone structures identified by local Navajos as parent-built children's play-hogans dating from about 1957 but suggested by more distant informants to have some connection with witchcraft. They are neatly made, shoul-der-height, corbeled-stone-domed structures. They lack apical apertures and thus are not large ovens, although some of them contain a fireplace consisting of a stone slab laid across two rows of flat stones. The doorways extend the full height of the walls, and there is no evidence that the buildings were sudatories (Jerrold E. Levy, personal communication and photographs).

Lowry Ruin fortified crag, Crow Foot Canyon drainage, New Mexico, 1972.

Chapter 12

STRUCTURES RELATING TO TRAVEL, DEFENSE, AND DEATH

TRAVEL STRUCTURES

Trails and Roads

The Navajo have always been a very mobile people (Jett 1978a; 1978b). Their travels have related to hunting and gathering, livestock raising, farming, firewood procurement, raiding, trading, salt gathering, socializing, ritual, and—more recently—obtaining access to employment, education, and health care.

Foot and livestock trails (*'atiin*) were developed by the Navajo, both by repeated use of various routes and by actual construction. Trail improvement is usually done only at steep places. Procedures include cutting or enlarging of hand- and toe-holds or rough steps (the latter usually for livestock) with picks or other tools; making steps by placing logs or rock slabs behind pairs of short posts sunk into rock slopes or by wedging logs across steep-floored crevices and filling in behind them with stones and earth; making of notched-log and pole-and-rung ladders (*haaz'áí* = [rigid object] extends upward); filling small drainages with rocks and earth to form causeways; emplacement of log bridges (*na'nízhoozh*[í] = [rigid objects] lying parallel across), spanning crevices (set into notches in the rock, and roughened or earth-covered for better foot-ing); and construction of log-and-fill ramps and drift fences; bark fragments and wood chips are occasionally laid down over rocky spots.[1] These are all Puebloan traits, but a number are probably also shared with Northern Athapaskans. Trail improvement projects have also been undertaken, especially from the 1930s onward, by the Civilian Conservation Corps, the Indian Service (Bureau of Indian Affairs), and the Tribe.

From the time that Navajos first began acquiring wagons, probably during the 1880s, wagon roads have become established by frequent travel over certain routes. The most important of these seem to have followed well-established horse trails, but new ones came increasingly into being. The acquisition of pickup trucks and other motor vehicles continued this trend, especially after World War II, until now the Navajo Country is laced with "truck trails." Many of these received slight improvement along the lines of trails as described above, and they sometimes required the removal of trees in wooded areas. Too, many miles of truck trails, not to mention true roads, were established or improved by federal, state, county, and Tribal agencies (e.g., Young 1961: 133–43). We shall not endeavor to detail these developments here.

Fig. 12.1 Cribbed-log bus-stop shelter. Black Creek Valley, Arizona, 1968; V.E.S.

Fig. 12.2. Cairn trail shrine along the trail paralleling the south rim of Canyon de Chelly, Arizona, 1973.

Bus-Stop Shelters

In recent years, the Tribe has erected rectangular school-bus-stop shelters (*kį[n] yazhi* = little house) with shed roofs (Fig. 12.1). Horizontal-log, palisaded, and frame construction are common, and adobe brick is used south of Gallup. Doorway orientation is usually eastward or southward, away from storm winds.

Garages

Navajo garages (*chidi bihooghan* = car's home place) are very rare outside of the larger settlements. They are generally of frame construction (Figs. 5.49, 5.51), although cinder blocks are sometimes used (Fig. 7.28), and are imitations of Anglo-American garages (Spencer and Jett 1971: 168–69).

Cairn Trail Shrines

Trail shrines (*tsé ninájihí* = where stones are repeatedly placed)—also known as travel shrines, wishing piles, prayer piles, and wayside altars—are found throughout the Navajo Country. They are roughly conical or columnar cairns of rocks and twigs (Figs. 12.2, 12.3), located along routes of travel, especially at heads of steep trails but also on flats. The traveler typically deposits a green sprig of foliage—usually of pinyon or juniper—on the pile and sets a stone on top to hold the twig in place, reciting a prayer to ensure good luck on, or at the destination of, a journey. The cairns vary in size according to their age and the amount of traffic on the trail, but seem to average 4 to 5 feet (1.2 to 1.8 m) in height.[2] Such shrines appear to be absent among Northern Athapaskans but are ancient and widespread in California, the Southwest, Northwest Mexico, the Central Andes, and Inner Asia (Jett n.d.c). The Apacheans, including the Navajo, presumably acquired shrine use in the Southwest. A travel shrine made of stones from throughout Navajoland was built at the site of Ft. Sumner in 1971, under the auspices of the Navajo Tribal Museum (Anonymous 1971a).

DEFENSE STRUCTURES

Until the end of the Navajo wars in 1864, Navajos raided Puebloan, Hispano, and Anglo settlements for livestock, food, goods, and

Fig. 12.3. Large cairn trail shrine, with recently deposited ponderosa pine boughs. At the head of the trail descending from the Chuska Mountains to Washington Pass, New Mexico, 1972.

slaves, and were in turn raided for similar purposes and in reprisal by Utes, Comanches, Puebloans, Apaches, Hispanos, and Anglos. As a consequence, certain defense-related structures came into use.

Walls and Parapets

Although Hill (1936: 6), describing Navajo warfare, stated that "No type of fortification was employed," defensive masonry walls were in fact formerly constructed to bar access to mesa tops or projecting spurs, or as parapets around such landforms. They ranged from 1 to 12 feet (.3 to 3.7 m) in height (Kidder 1920: 322–23; Van Valkenburgh 1940b: 23–24; Marmon and Pearl 1958: Figs. 1–3; Hester 1962: 45). A probably eighteenth-century wall, at Big Bead Mesa, New Mexico, was 26 feet long, 12 feet high, and 5 feet thick 7.9 × 3.7 × 1.5 m). It had a setback on the inner side,

about halfway up the wall, on which defenders could kneel, to look and shoot through loopholes. The timber-roofed entrance led into a masonry room, from which a short doorway opened onto the mesa top (Anonymous 1940; Keur 1941: 40–43; Van Valkenburgh 1945: 7). In the Lower Chaco River area, a ca. 2-meter-high, 2-meter-thick (6.6 × 6.6 ft) stone-faced, rubble-core wall spans the neck of a cliff spur upon which stands a pueblito of ca. 1750 (Reher 1977: 52, 54). Cliff shelters and structures fortified with masonry parapets (Fig. 5.57) are also known (Brugge 1976: 46).

Constructions of these types undoubtedly represent the influence, and often even the work, of Puebloan refugees and their offspring. Brugge (1972b: 3–4) reported that defensive siting, wall or parapet construction, or both, occurred in 75 percent of dated Navajo sites of between 1700 and 1752, and in 55 percent of

Fig. 12.4. "The shaft," a ladder (not visible) completely surrounded by a shell of uncoursed stone-and-mud masonry. The ladder connects the two ledges upon which is built Shaft Ruin, an early-eighteenth-century Refugee Period defensive site. Note the stone lintels over the doorway and loopholes. Crow Foot Canyon, Canyon Largo drainage, New Mexico, 1972.

dated sites from 1753 to 1770. After 1770, as the influence of the refugees waned and as Ute-owned guns made defensive sites less tenable, the latter become rare. Brugge (1976: 44) did, however, describe log breastworks along the rim of a mesa at a site of about the 1770s near Pueblo Pintado, New Mexico, and a site with a defensive wall (of comparable date) exists northwest of Ganado, Arizona (Robert W. Young, personal communication).

"The Shaft"

Figure 12.4 shows what is, as far as the authors are aware, a unique defensive structure, in the Canyon Largo, New Mexico, drainage. It protects a ladder connecting two ledges upon which are built Refugee Period masonry dwellings (Shaft Ruin). A tapering shell of stone-and-mud masonry surrounds the ladder. It is entered via low doorways and contains loopholes for protection of the lower entry.

Towers

Defensive towers (*yah 'anáhonidzo'* = people repeatedly take refuge inside) were built during the Gobernador and early Cabezon Phases, principally in Dinétah (Hester 1962: 43–44, 64; Keur 1941: 44; Farmer 1947: 18). Jácabo Uguarte y Loyola wrote in 1788 that Navajos had "built ten rock towers within their encampment to safeguard their women and families, from the continuous invasions upon their lands by the Gilenos [Chiricahua Apache]" (Cassidy 1936; Van Valkenburgh 1938b: 155). These particular towers, which were of stone masonry and contained loopholes but no windows, probably had been built earlier but had been refurbished in the 1780s (Brugge 1972a: 98; 1972b: 5). According to Keur (1944: 77–78), towers were typically round or asymmetrical, surrounded by clusters of rooms (such structures are sometimes termed "tower pueblitos"; for a discussion of pueblitos, which also often had defense features and functions, see "Stone Houses," chapter 7). These towers were up to four stories high. Van Valkenburgh (1938b, 1940b, 1947b) described round towers of Navajo construction; one was about 30 feet (9.1 m) in diameter and dated about 1770–1785. Farmer (1942: 69) described one circular example about 14 feet (4.3 m) high and of similar diameter, with two two-room stories and a looped parapet around a stone-slab-covered pole roof. The structure contained a Spanish-style hooded fireplace with chimney. Riley (1954: 51) wrote of a similar specimen, and Kinaazini, near Wide Ruins, Arizona, appears to have been similar, though rectangular; it dates to about 1760 (Brugge 1968a: 17–18; 1972b: 9; Mindeleff 1891: plate LXVI).

Both defensive walls and towers have prehistoric Puebloan equivalents (including in Dinétah; e.g., Mackey and Green 1979), and Puebloan influence—and probably Puebloan refugee construction at least in the case of the earlier specimens—is undoubtedly to be seen in these towers. However, it may well be that Spanish walls and defensive round and square stone-masonry *torreones* provided the primary models (see, for example, Anonymous 1923, 1925; Boyd 1974: 23–26). In any case, traditional and written history indicate that use of defensive sites and structures was mainly in response to Ute attacks (Brugge 1972b: 5).

Watch Pits

Brugge (1972b: 5) also referred to " 'watch pits,' foxhole-like lookouts usually built on the rims of mesas." These are frequently mentioned by informants as having been used in response to Euramerican enemies.

GRAVES

Navajos dispose of the dead in a variety of ways. The following represent traditional graves (*jishcháá*) and other means of disposal.

Rock-Crevice and Slump-Boulder Burials

Corpses are commonly placed in crevices in rocks and cliffs or gullies, or under talus boulders, and sealed in with loose rocks, earth, and/or sticks or brush, to protect the body from coyotes and other scavengers.[3] Ward (1978:332) also recognizes a category "rock-shelter/cave burial" (see also, Van Valkenburgh 1947a: 17). These seem to be southwestern practices, shared by the Hopi and the Chiracahua Apache (Brugge 1978:315), among others.

Covered Surface Burial

A cairn may be built over a body left in an open area (Beadle 1877: 276; De Harport 1959–4: 1598), a common practice in aboriginal western America. A Schwemberger photograph of ca. 1905 shows a grave in which the corpse is laid on a fallen tree and covered with limbs and stones; "such a grave is a rarity," according to the caption. Wilson (1890: 116) noted that if a cadaver is left uninterred, it is covered with stones and brush. Tanner and Steen (1955) described a rock-covered corpse laid to rest in one corner of a prehistoric room in Canyon del Muerto. James (1976: 4, 52, 61) reported a late nineteenth-century "pseudo-hogan" built for a burial. A single course of juniper logs was laid in a circle, the corpse being placed inside the northern portion and covered with two layers of poles at right angles to each other. Bodies are sometimes left in hogans, some or all of the structure sometimes being pulled down and piled upon the corpse (see "Dwelling Abandonment," chapter 2).

Pit Burials

Inhumations are common, especially where rock crevices are not available. Interment is sometimes within the death hogan (especially if the ground outside is frozen) but usually elsewhere, where the ground is soft; the grave is typically about waist-deep. Commonly (at least formerly), the corpse is laid on its side, with its head toward the north, facing westward, or with the head eastward (as among Utes and Paiutes; Stewart 1942; 312), facing toward the north. Sticks, logs, and stones may be mixed with the earth as it is replaced, or piled over the filled grave, to discourage disinterment by scavengers; potsherds were sometimes scattered on the grave.[4] Many

Fig. 12.5. Roofless, horseshoe-shaped, stone-and-mud-masonry grave cist built against the wall of a cliffside cave above Face Rock, Canyon de Chelly, Arizona, 1971.

Northern Athapaskans practiced cremation, and Brugge (1978: 315) attributed an emphasis on inhumation and orientation to Puebloan influences (see Ellis 1968), although Navajo practice also has much in common with that of the Ute and Paiute (Stewart 1942: 312). Albeit that corpse orientation does not seem to be characteristic of most Northern Athapaskans, inhumation *was* practiced, and the Athapaskan Ingalik of southwestern Alaska did orient bodies with their heads westward but facing the sunrise (Osgood 1940: 409).

A pole marker looking approximately like one unit of a pitch-pole fence is occasionally placed near the grave to warn of its contaminating presence (Newcomb 1940a: 76; 1966: plate opposite p. 185).

Since World War II, an increasing number of Navajos have received Christian burials in local cemeteries—not necessarily out of Christian conviction but, frequently, for purposes of neutralization of the contamination that comes from contact with the dead, to honor the deceased, and to afford better protection from grave robbers. Some graves are marked with headstones or wooden crosses, and bodies may be interred in coffins, packing crates, or caskets.[5]

Earth-Oven Burial

According to Ward (1978: 332), old earth ovens were sometimes used for burials.

Cist Graves

Entombment in cists similar to storage structures or ovens occurs or occurred in a few areas. Mindeleff (1897: 167) described the latter as more or less dome-shaped, or partly domed when against a cliff or ruin wall, of crude masonry (horizontally, vertically, or randomly set stones, in mud mortar); the roof was supported on sticks and contained a small opening. Old graves of this type seen by Jett in Canyon de Chelly were vertical-walled and semicircular, built against cliffs or ruin walls, and roofless (Fig. 12.5). Similar former food-storage structures (see chapter 10) were also sometimes used for burials (De Harport 1959–4: 1597–98; Carlson 1965: 25, 102; Hester and Shiner 1963: 38–39). These practices appear to be Puebloan-derived.

Tree "Burial"

A stillborn infant or one dying in its first month or killed by lightning is sometimes wrapped in its coverings and put in a juniper or other tree, sometimes on a platform, and in its cradleboard if one has already been made. It is protected from scavengers by being encased in twigs and branches. Afterbirth is wrapped in the sheepskin upon which the birth took place and is placed in a tree or buried in a pit or under rocks for protection from animals and witches.[6] Tree and scaffold burials were common among Northern Athapaskans (Brugge 1978: 315; Honigman 1946: 86–87; 1954: 140).

Adult outdoor deaths from lightning, tornadoes, or drowning resulted in the bodies simply being left where the individuals died (Newcomb 1940: 78–79).

Broken saddles, dishes, the grave-digging tools, and killed horses or sheep were formerly often seen at graves, and sometimes still are (Franciscan Fathers 1910: 455–56; Young 1961: 530; Leighton and Kluckhohn 1948: 92; Lamphere 1976: 162). Although some graves were hidden to prevent disturbance, others were located in the open (for easier visual detection of graverobbers?). Graves are traditionally avoided by all but practitioners of witchcraft, for fear of ghosts (see "Dwelling Abandonment," chapter 2).

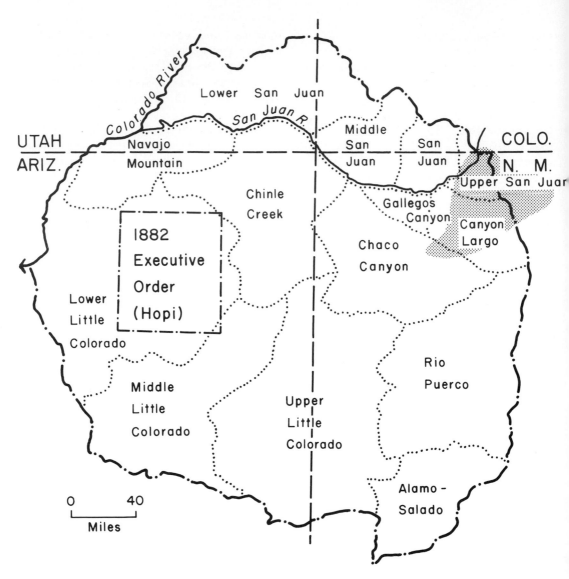

Map 13.1. Boundaries of the Navajo Land Claim and its major subdivisions, showing the approximate extent of Dinétah (stippled), ca. 1600.

Chapter 13

AREAL AND TEMPORAL DISTRIBUTIONS OF DWELLING TYPES

THE NAVAJO TERRITORY

The boundary of the area of maximum areal distribution of distinctly Navajo structures through all periods as given on the unpublished Navajo Land Claim (n.d. a) site map (see also Littell 1967–3: 692–93) is approximately as follows (see Map 13.1): a line running from the mouth of the Little Colorado River, Arizona, southeasterly through Flagstaff to the Mogollon Rim, thence easterly along the Rim, across the New Mexico state line to the Rio Grande at Socorro, thence northerly to the Colorado state line, thence northwesterly through Dove Creek to the Utah state line, thence westerly through Monticello to the Colorado River at the mouth of Dark Canyon, and thence down the Colorado to the mouth of the Little Colorado; an outlier is in Havasu Canyon, Arizona, to which Navajos traveled to trade with the Havasupai.

Hester's (1962) comprehensive study of Navajo territorial migrations, which resulted in this distribution,[2] postulated a gradual spread westward and southwestward from Dinétah. Undoubtedly, however, new and revised tree-ring dates (Stokes and Smiley 1963, 1964, 1966, 1969; Brugge 1967, correcting Hurt 1942) and other data from the Navajo

Land Claim and elsewhere will require revision of at least some details of Hester's reconstruction.

The present area of Navajo occupance and use (aside from localities where Navajos have been relocated outside of the Navajo Country) is considerably smaller than that within the boundary described above. Most of the Dinétah region has long been abandoned by Navajos, as have Colorado and most of that portion of Utah which lies north of the San Juan River and west of Comb Ridge. Outside of "border towns," there are now essentially no permanent Navajo inhabitants south of the southern boundary of the Navajo Reservation in Arizona, nor near the Rio Grande, nor in the mountainous Datil region of west-central New Mexico. In addition to the main Navajo Reservation and the "Checkerboard" of alloted lands in New Mexico's San Juan Basin, there are three small Navajo-occupied areas in New Mexico separated from the main area: the Ramah district, the Cañoncito Navajo Reservation, and the Alamo Navajo Reservation (Map 1.1; Correll and Dehiya 1972).

Naturally, most Navajo dwellings are found within the present or former Navajo territory, and the hogan has not diffused significantly to other tribes, with the exception of

TABLE 13.1.

Relative Frequency of Hogan Forms in Navajo Country-Wide Survey,
expressed as percentages of a hogan sample of 1,222 and of a
permanent-dwelling sample of 4,134; ca. 1969–70

Hogan Form		Percentage of All Hogans		Percentage of All Permanent Dwellings
Conical Forked Pole		2.5		0.7
Vertical-Post	Leaning-log	11.3		
	Palisaded	6.7	20.1	5.9
	Undifferentiated	2.1		
Stacked-Log	Corbeled-log	1.1*		
	Undifferentiated (mostly cribbed-log)	39.5	40.8	12.0
	Abutting-Log	0.2*		
Plank		28.0		8.5
Masonry	Stone	8.0		
	Cinder-Block	0.6	8.6	2.5
	Adobe-Brick	0.0		

Probably an underestimation, because of incomplete differentiation in the field.

the San Juan Southern Paiute and the Havasupai. However, in modern times, hogans have occasionally been built in areas distant from the Navajo Reservation. The existence of hogans in Albuquerque, New Mexico, associated with the Albuquerque Indian School, is documented for between 1908 and 1948 (Hodge 1969: 33–38). Hogans were also built by Navajo railroad workers; we have observed hogans along the Santa Fe line in Arizona and in the Mohave Desert of California, and Chauncey Neboyia recalled that they were built as far north as Stockton, California. Sweathouses were also built by Navajo railroad workers (Brugge 1956). Hogans for exhibit have been built for museums; one conical forked-pole specimen was erected apparently for the 1893 World's Columbian Exposition at Chicago (photo T15462, Tilton Collection, National Anthropological Archives).

Interestingly, "Most of the Navajo and Hopi families remaining [after relocation] on [the] Colorado River [Indian Reservation, Arizona (since 1945)] have acquired standard, and often attractive, housing . . . [with] modern household conveniences. . . . " This phenomenon is partly related to farm-income supplementation through wage work (Young 1961: 202, 207), as well, probably, to relocatees being more innovative than average and being subject to influences from their non-Navajo neighbors. Navajos at Colorado River are said not to build hogans at all but only frame, cinder-block, and fired-brick houses (George Roth, personal communication, 1973).

REGIONAL-VARIATION SURVEY

Within the present-day Navajo Country there is significant regional variation in dwelling-type frequency, but most varieties are found in greater or lesser numbers in all major subregions of Navajoland. Although few studies have been published which give any idea of the frequency of types in specific subregions, field work by the present authors has to a fair degree remedied this lack. Nearly five thousand dwellings throughout the Navajo Country were inventoried, almost entirely during 1969, and frequencies of types were tabulated (Table 13.1). Although the sample is to some extent biased because most observations were made from roads, the general outlines of regional variations in frequency may nevertheless be perceived. (See Appendix).

The existence of these clear regional differences is particularly interesting in view of the conclusion of Kluckhohn et al. (1971: 438) that Navajo material culture is regionally relatively homogeneous. Regional differences were revealed more fully by our study than by theirs for the following reasons: (1) our data-collecting methodology was geographical as well as ethnographic, and (2) we dealt with regional differences in *frequency* rather than simply with presences versus absences. It seems likely that other significant regional differences in contemporary Navajo culture would appear if the relevant data were collected in a similar fashion.

In addition to the survey data, supplemented by published references, a few observations on past dwelling frequencies and distributions are made herein, based mainly on Littell (1967–6: appendix I). However, a more complete picture of the premodern period awaits a more thorough analysis of Navajo Land Claim data.

HOGAN TYPE DISTRIBUTIONS

Conical Forked-Pole Hogan

David M. Brugge, who is familiar with the Navajo Country as a whole, noted (1968) that the conical forked-pole hogan appeared to be nearly extinct east of approximately the line of the Defiance Plateau, Arizona. This view is generally supported by modern published observations. Corbett (1940: 104) found only one of these hogans in the Chaco Canyon, New Mexico, area, and that example was built not by a Navajo but by the local trader. Only one specimen, dating to 1935–40, was found in the lower Chaco River area in 1973–74 (Reher 1977: 38, 47). At Fruitland, New Mexico, Tremblay et al. (1954: 195) observed only one conical forked-pole hogan, which was no longer inhabited but used only for ceremonies. The type was absent in the Prewitt, New Mexico, area (Olson and Wasley 1956: 358–59). Kluckhohn et al. (1971: 147) reported three forked-pole hogans from the Ramah district in the early 1940s, but only one specimen (inhabited) was noted in 1968 in Black Creek Valley, Arizona–New Mexico (Spencer and Jett 1971: 163). In the 1930s, however, Hill's informants stated that such hogans occurred in New Mexico at Crownpoint and Mariano Lake, in Arizona at Red Rock, Lukachukai, Canyon del Muerto, Wheatfields, Crystal, Ft. Defiance, Chinle, Head Springs, and Keams Canyon, and at Aneth, Utah (Kluckhohn et al.

1971: 152). Coolidge and Coolidge (1930: 80), contended that on the "plains east of the Chuska Mountains, where both fuel and building materials are scarce, these [conical forked-pole] houses are often sunk into the ground and so buried in earth on the roof and sides as to make them look like mounds," but these may well actually have been corbeled-log hogans. Correll (1965a: 29) pictured a recently abandoned forked-pole hogan in the Montezuma Creek area, Utah.

For the western Navajo Country, there are more published records. Vogt (1961: 322) wrote that the type was rare except in the Dinnehotso-Kayenta-Tuba City area of Arizona. Page (1937b: plate 3) depicted one from Red Lake (Tolani Lakes), Arizona, and Boyce (1974: 65) stated that in 1939 most of the hogans in Arizona's District 1 (including Red Lake, Kaibito, and Copper Mine) were forked-pole hogans. Adams (1963: 77) noted that about one-quarter of the dwellings in the Shonto, Arizona, area were of this type in the late 1950s; one was built for an Enemyway in 1978 (Laughter 1979: 82–83). Chisholm (1975: 84) stated that in the isolated Navajo Mountain, Utah, area, conical forked-pole hogans were still built by some. About 1970, one was built in the Page-Leche'e, Arizona, area, for peyote ceremonies (Wagner 1974: 333). Scully (1975: 300) pictured one in Monument Valley, Arizona, and Crampton (1960: 26) reported one in Glen Canyon (now Lake Powell) near the mouth of Face Canyon, Arizona. Verplanck (1934: 21) indicated that circular hogans with extended doorways (conical forked-pole hogans?) were usual in the northern part of the Reservation. Snow photographs show a number of forked-pole hogans in 1935–36 in the Leupp-Red Lake, Arizona, and Paiute Farms, Utah, areas, and from Kayenta to Teec Nos Pos, Arizona.

By 1980, McAllester and McAllester (1980: 14) considered the conical forked-pole hogan obsolete. Although this is no doubt an overstatement, even by 1970 our surveys logged only thirty conical forked-pole hogans (2.5 percent of all hogans, 0.7 percent of all

permanent dwellings; ruined examples were excluded). Only a few areas were identified where this hogan type still occurred in significant numbers, although in no case exceeding 21 percent of hogans observed (Appendix). These locales were all in the west. One was the district west of the Echo Cliffs and Ward Terrace, from about Cameron, Arizona, north. Even in this area, conical forked-pole hogans comprised only from 6 to 14 percent of local hogans, and Gumerman and Euler (1976: 15–16) found no currently inhabited examples. Two examples were seen on Route 264 a short distance west of the border of the Hopi Reservation. A third area where some numbers of these hogans occurred was Monument Valley, representing about 12 percent of all hogans (although abandoned examples may have been included). Finally, the area south and east of Navajo Mountain ˜exhibited the highest frequency, 21 percent. A very few conical forked-pole hogans were also noted at other, scattered localities (Map 13.2). Contrary to our expectations, they seemed to be largely absent from at least the southern portion of the conservative Black Mesa, Arizona, area. None were observed by us on the Kaibito and Shonto plateaus, Adams' (1963: 77) findings notwithstanding; however, our data are scanty for that area, and Jerrold E. Levy photos show one east of Kaibito and another south of White Mesa, Arizona. Other extensive areas in which we observed no conical forked-pole hogans were from just east of Kayenta to Chinle via Rough Rock, Arizona; from Black Creek Valley to Round Rock via Lukachukai, Arizona; the entire region east of the New Mexico border; and the whole Reservation in Arizona south of Chinle, west of Black Creek Valley, south of eastern State Highway 264, and southwest of the Hopi Reservation.

The rarity of the conical forked-pole hogan in most regions by the late 1960s contrasts dramatically with the situation in the more distant past, as indicated by nineteenth-century descriptions (chapter 5) and by archaeology (representing predominantly pre-Ft. Sumner sites; Littell 1967–4: 813; Huse et al.

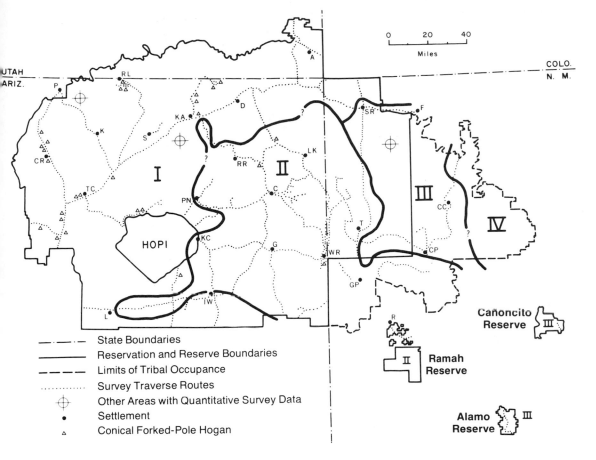

Map 13.2.   The Navajo Country, showing the areas of dominance of different traditional hogan types, ca. 1970, based on detailed analysis of the data summarized in Appendix   and on Huse et al. (1978). Heavy boundary lines (approximate only) divide the region into four major zones of native-materials hogan dominance: I = vertical-post/corbeled-log (west and north); II = cribbed-log; III = stone; IV = vertical-post/corbeled-log (east). Abbreviations stand for the following settlements:

A = Aneth	IW = Indian Wells	RL = Rainbow Lodge
C = Chinle	K = Kaibito	RR = Rough Rock
CC = Chaco Canyon	KA = Kayenta	S = Shonto
CP = Crown Point	KC = Keams Canyon	SR = Shiprock
CR = Cedar Ridge	L = Leupp	T = Tohatchi
D = Dinnehotso	LK = Lukachukai	TC = Tuba City
F = Farmington	P = Page	WR = Window Rock
G = Ganado	PN = Piñon	
GP = Gallup	R = Ramah	

Table 13.2.

Percentages (rounded) of Different Archaeological Hogan Types of All Periods (mostly pre-1864) in the Areas of the Navajo Land Claim (see Map 13.1; adapted from Littell 1967-6: appendix I; the following original categories have been lumped together: "forked-pole" and "forked-pole-cribbed-log"; "cribbed-log" [mostly corbeled-log] and "4-sides + entry").

Hogan Type	Lower San Juan	Middle San Juan	San Juan	Upper San Juan	Canyon Largo	Gallegos Canyon	Chaco Canyon	Rio Puerco	Alamo-Salado	Upper Little Colorado	Middle Little Colorado	Havasu Canyon	Navajo Mountain	Chinle Creek	Lower Little Colorado	1882 Executive Order	Total No. of Hogans	% of All Hogans
Conical Forked-pole	24	26	75	80	55	100	30	15	16	33	41	32	31	40	23	25	718	28
Vertical-Post	3	2	5		2		5	11		1	3		4	10		2	41	2
"Cribbed-Log"	16	16	5		12		11	28	27	27	23	32	18	10	36	41	686	26
Stone	18	32		7	5		11		2	2	8		18	20	10	5	290	11
Stone + Wood Wall	11	6	3	2			11	34	49	21	10		2	10	9	4	375	14
Ring Only (stone foundation?)	11	2	3	4	4		5	8	2	6	7	21	13		3	17	263	10
Dugout	2												2			1	11	<1
In Rock Shelter	9							2	2	1	1	15	2	20		1	41	2
Type Unidentified	6	10	14	7	22	<1	27	2	2	9	5	15	10		19	4	174	7
Total No. Sites	169	34	20	53	59	5	24	151	81	136	81	8	44	12	72	449		
Total Number of Hogans	140	50	37	70	109	4	37	452	166	218	93	19	51	10	162	927	2599	
Percentage of All Hogans	5	2	2	3	4	<1	2	17	6	8	4	1	2	<1	6	36		100

1978: 89, 105). According to tabulations in Littell (1967–6: appendix I; see Table 13.2 and Map 13.1, this book), the traditional conical hogan was the dominant form in all but five of the sixteen areas of the Navajo Country listed, and in none of the latter did its frequency fall below 15 percent. Tradition as well as frequency of mention in legend also indicate that this type predominated in the earliest Navajo periods.

Conical forked-pole hogans have no doubt declined in frequency at least in part because they are less commodious than types with more or less vertical walls (cf. Haile 1942: 53; Downs 1972: 129). A preference for vertical walls and for greater roominess is partly attributable to the adoption of modern furnishings and to larger family size consequent upon the introduction of modern public-health services (although supplemental dwellings may also be built for larger families). More sedentary settlement, beginning in the late nineteenth century, was certainly an important influence, making the building of larger, more substantial dwellings worthwhile. Too, population growth led to smaller per-family grazing territories and thus to less lengthy and frequent movements. Acquisition of steel axes and new building techniques were no doubt of considerable importance as well. Use of stoves for more efficient heating may also have played a significant role.

Lean-to Hogan

There is very little information regarding the former frequency and distribution of lean-to hogans. Mindeleff (1898: 496–97) indicated that such structures were in common use as summer shelters in the 1880s, and Hill described them as having been used during the Navajo wars and as still being utilized in more isolated areas in 1933 (Kluckhohn et al. 1971: 152). Adams (1959) recorded one on Castle Creek, Utah, north of the San Juan River. Since the authors saw no examples in their surveys, they believe the type to be obsolete or nearly so.

Vertical-Post Hogans

The leaning-log hogan, despite its age (Gobernador Phase, ca. 1696–1770), was apparently quite rare until after Ft. Sumner (Underhill 1953: 195) and remained uncommon until the late nineteenth century; before 1890, it seems to have been used primarily as a ceremonial structure for the sand-paintings of chantways (see chapter 5). Archaeology indicates that in past times it was widespread but rare, being absent in several areas and uncommon in all (Table 13.2). After 1890 the form became more common (Coolidge and Coolidge 1930: 82–83). As far as we can determine, the palisaded hogan did not originate before 1900.

The large number of logs needed for vertical-post hogans suggests that availability of steel axes played a significant role in this form's proliferation. For a decade beginning in 1868, Navajos "were issued tools, such as axes, shovels, picks, saws" at Ft. Defiance, to enable them to "build ourselves a home or whatever we wanted to build to live in. In that way we were to improve our living conditions. Later on, leaders from each area went out, got the People together and taught them how to use these tools." Axes remained scarce into the 1890s, however, despite growing numbers of traders, and were frequently borrowed. They seem to have begun to become common during the '90s, at which time tools were issued as inducements to enroll pupils in schools (Frisbie and McAllester 1978: 21, 43, 56, 73).

Despite their rarity before 1890, vertical-post hogans were rather common in the 1970s, and apparently were more so during the earlier twentieth century. They are frequently recorded in the twentieth-century literature. Adams (1963: 77) noted that in the late 1950s approximately three-quarters of the dwellings in the Shonto region were vertical-post hogans. Leaning-log hogans were also recorded in Glen Canyon (Adams et al. 1961: 12), and David M. Brugge (personal communication, 1970) observed that flimsy variants of the leaning-log type were common along the lower

Little Colorado and San Juan rivers. Milton S. Snow photographs show 1935 examples between Kayenta and Mexican Water, Arizona. A typical leaning-log hogan was described in detail from Toonerville, Arizona (Ward 1968: 136–42). The literature gives less evidence of frequent use of this type in most areas further eastward. In Arizona, it is recorded at Wide Ruins, in and near Canyon de Chelly (Sullivan 1938: plates opposite pp. 48, 92; Blackwood 1927: 227), at Rock Point (Thomas et al. 1974: 60), east of Dinnehotso in 1935 (Snow photos 858, 862), east of Steamboat in 1935 (Snow photo 1076), around Tsaile (Frisbie and McAllester 1978: 30), in Black Creek Valley (2), and in the vicinity of Lupton (Spencer and Jett 1971: 163), as well as at Shiprock (Krutz 1974: 115) and near Newcomb, New Mexico (Newcomb 1966: plate opposite p. 103). Palisaded hogans were recorded in Arizona at Lupton (Kluckhohn et al. 1971: 99), Piñon (Downs 1972: 46, 47), and Keam's Canyon, and in New Mexico at Chaco Canyon (Corbett 1940: 105), Seven Lakes (Seton 1962: 30–32), Huerfano Mesa (McAllester and McAllester 1980: 59, 71), and Cañoncito (Platero 1967: 9). Tremblay et al. (1954) mentioned vertical-post hogans at Fruitland, and a few occurred in the Ramah district (Roberts 1951: 43, Fig. 1; Landgraf 1954: 107–14). Leaning-log hogans were common north and east of Chaco Canyon National Monument in the forty-year period following 1935 (Huse et al. 1978: 98, 103–04).

Because both leaning-log and palisaded hogans (as well as corbeled-log and some plank hogans) are usually completely earth-covered in the western and northwestern region and are thus seldom distinguishable from the exterior (Fig. 13.1), the authors were unable adequately to separate these variants in their survey.[3] However, the survey did indicate that vertical-post hogans were the most common hogan forms in several western and west-central Reservation areas, and an important secondary type in certain other areas (Appendix; Map 13.2). Vertical-post hogans proved to be the predominant type or the second most common type after plank hogans

everywhere west and south of the Hopi Reservation as well as in the open country northward from Black Mesa and the Chinle and Lukachukai valleys. It was the second most common hogan form after cribbed-log hogans (discounting plank hogans) in a broad belt from the Defiance Plateau westward to the Hopi Reservation.[4] There were but a few vertical-post hogans between the Defiance Plateau and the Chuska Mountains. Eastward from the Chuskas, we encountered almost none. However, they are apparently common in areas missed by our survey north and east of Chaco Canyon (Huse et al. 1978: 98, 103–04).

Corbeled-Log Hogan

The corbeled-log hogan, though not common today, does occur with regularity in the western part of the Reservation and in the far east, and was much more common in the past. Hall (1975: 45) reported it in the Cedar Ridge, Arizona, area in 1911. Fraser (1916) photographed one on the south rim of Navajo Canyon, Arizona. Bernheimer (1927: 255) recorded one in Tsegi Canyon, Arizona, and Adams (1963: 77) found that it was used in the Shonto area for supplemental dwellings and storage but rarely for principal dwellings, because the structure is very low in average height. We have also seen a number of examples along U.S. Highway 89 in Arizona (Figs. 5.22, 5.28, 5.29) and in the Tuba City area. A Milton S. Snow photograph (803), taken in 1935, shows an old example near Dinnehotso. Other Snow photos from Arizona in 1936 (1091, 1097) show specimens in Marsh Pass and at Kayenta, and a 1935 example from east of Steamboat is also depicted (1076). McGowan (1979: 31) pictured one near White Mesa, Arizona. Frank Mitchell lived in one near Tsaile during the 1880s (Frisbie and McAllester 1978: 30). Jett saw one used as a storehouse (Fig. 5.23), plus several abandoned examples (Fig. 5.37), in the Canyon de Chelly area (see also, James 1976: 46, 103), and an abandoned specimen on the Alamo Reservation. Corbett (1940: 105) found this type at Chaco Canyon, but it was apparently absent at Fruitland (Tremblay et al. 1954) and in Black

Fig. 13.1. Identification problems: is this earth-covered hogan leaning-log, palisaded, corbeled-log, or plank? East of Dinnebito Dam, Arizona, 1970; R.F.

Creek Valley (Spencer and Jett 1971); Oster-mann's (1908: 863) record may refer to this area. Forrest (1970: 96, 98) pictured an apparent example on the San Juan River east of Shiprock in 1902 and another (1907) specimen on the Little Colorado River. A pre-1900 example was described for northeast of Gallup, New Mexico (Hollister 1903: 69), and a specimen with a tree-ring date of 1823 was reported from south of Quemado, New Mexico (Anonymous 1970f). An abandoned corbeled-log hogan on a stone foundation was pictured at Cañoncito by Platero (1967: 167). Huse et al. (1978: 98, 103–04) indicated that since the 1930s corbeled-log and vertical-post hogans have dominated in the San Juan Basin eastward and northeastward of Chaco Canyon National Monument. Farmer's (1942: 70–71) "cribbed-log" hogans, said to be the only contemporary hogan type near Counselors, New Mexico, were probably corbeled.

Corbeled-log hogans did not show up as quantitatively important in any of the authors' survey areas except Monument Valley (Appendix). This may be misleading, however; because of the difficulty of readily distinguishing earth-covered vertical-post hogans from corbeled-log ones (Fig. 13.1), we classed all ambiguous specimens as the former, thus automatically overreporting the former and underreporting the latter. Spot checks plus literature references (especially Adams 1963: 77 and Huse et al. 1978: 98, 103–04) indicate significant occurrences in the west, the far east, and probably the north.

"Cribbed-log" hogans (most are apparently actually corbeled-log hogans), often with stone foundations, are common in the archaeology of most subregions, and many archaeological "stone hogans" consisting of only a few courses of stone are probably better classified as corbeled-log hogans with stone foundations. Archaeological corbeled-log hogans are rare or absent in the Dinétah region and in the Navajo Mountain and Chinle Creek areas (Table 13.2). The corbeled-log form was the most common type during the period 1771–1821 (Brugge 1972b: 6; see also, James 1976: 25–28, 60), but it seems to have declined drastically since earlier times. It may now be nearly extinct in much of the central Navajo Country (cribbed-log and stone hogan regions), although Schmedding (1974: 163), who lived at Keams Canyon and Chaco Canyon, indicated this to have been the usual type during the first quarter of the century, and it was not uncommon in the Canyon del Muerto rim area from before 1800 through World War II (James 1976: 46, 103).

Cribbed-Log Hogan

Among hogans, the cribbed-log type is today prevalent in many districts, notably in wooded areas from the northern fringes of Black Mesa southeastward to Ramah and from Indian Wells, Arizona, to U.S. Highway 666 (Appendix; Map 13.2). Although used as early as the 1840s, cribbed-log hogans remained rare until the twentieth century (see chapter 5). The Franciscan Fathers (1910: 333) described this type as being "occasionally built in mountains and other districts where timber is available"; twenty years later, Coolidge and Coolidge (1930: 83) stated that "Such houses are rapidly supplanting the older forms wherever the timber is plentiful . . . " Verplank (1934: 21–22) indicated that hexagonal log hogans were the common type "in the southern part of the country," and Sullivan (1938: 45) said they were common in timbered areas. According to Leighton and Leighton (1944: plate caption), the cribbed-log hogan was the "common type of hogan in the wooded areas," and Boyce (1974: 65) wrote that it was the usual form outside of the far west.

Cribbed-log hogans occur today mainly in the central part of the Navajo Country, where good-sized trees are abundant. Adams (1963: 77) found no examples in the Shonto area in the west, although an apparent specimen at Kayenta was pictured (Anonymous 1970a: 4). Jerrold E. Levy (personal communication) found this to be a secondary type on northwestern Black Mesa; Looney and Dale (1972:

746, 768, 771) and Anderson (1973: 14, 19) pictured examples near the northern base of Black Mesa. It has been recorded at Chinle (Frisbie and McAllester 1978: 30) and in Canyon de Chelly (Hyde and Jett 1967: 114), where it has, during this century, largely replaced the formerly common leaning-log and stone types (Chauncey Neboyia, personal communication). Published references for Arizona also exist for Lukachukai (Scully 1975: 295, 299), Nazlini (Anonymous 1975: 39), Rock Point (Thomas, Johnson, and Yazzie 1974), Tsaile, and Ganado (McAllester and McAllester 1980: 30, 57, 62, 68, 98). In Black Creek Valley in 1968, about 75 percent of all hogans were cribbed-log (Spencer and Jett 1971:170), and by the 1940s the cribbed-log hogan was the most common dwelling in the Ramah district (Roberts 1951: 40; Landgraf 1954: 107–14, Kluckhohn et al. 1971: 146–47). Elsewhere in New Mexico, specimens are reported for the San Juan River valley west of Shiprock in 1902 (Forrest 1970: 95–96) and for Fruitland (Tremblay et al. 1954: 195), Newcomb (Newcomb 1966: plate opposite p. 87), and Togye (Hollister 1903: 68). However, Corbett (1940) did not record the cribbed-log hogan at Chaco Canyon, and only two were found in 1973–74 in the lower Chaco River area (Reher 1977: 38, 44, 47).

Most published archaeological reports and summaries fail to distinguish between corbeled-log and cribbed-log hogans. Further, since the popularity of the latter is essentially a twentieth-century phenomenon, archaeology is of little help in providing a picture of the form's spread. Examination of Land Claims files does indicate the earliest examples (1840s) to have been built in the southeastern area of Navajo occupance (see chapter 5, note 27). Whether the subsequent spread of the form represents a diffusion from this subregion or whether one or more later, separate, inventions and diffusions of the form occurred is not clear.

Some Havasupai adopted the cribbed-log hogan in imitation of the Navajo (Spier 1928: 178).

Abutting-log Hogan

The abutting-log hogan seems to occur only rarely and sporadically. The very few published references are of little use in defining its geographical range, but a central-Reservation association is suggested. Specific sites include Chinle (Fig. 5.27) and Piñon (Luckert 1979).

Plank Hogan

There appear to be almost no published photographs or descriptions of plank hogans other than in our own study of Black Creek Valley (Spencer and Jett 1971) and McAllester and McAllester's (1980: 21, 23, 27, 73, 93) photographs taken near Valley Store, Arizona, and Shiprock, New Mexico (see also Hyde and Jett 1967: 116 for the Echo Cliffs, Arizona, and McKelvey 1969: 56 for White Mesa). All indications are that these types are quite recent in origin. Our survey indicated that plank hogans had become very popular in a number of areas by 1970. Although they were the predominant form only along routes 89 and 64 in the far western area and on route 15 from west of Leupp to Indian Wells, they were a significant type in most areas. Wagner (1974: 333) reported them as the "standard" type in the Page-Leche'e area. Plank hogans in the far western region usually have corbeled-log roofs, and leaning-plank types seem to be confined to the west. Elsewhere, post-and-plank hogans—normally carrying pyramidal roofs of planks—are the rule; thus, there may well have been at least two separate centers of development and dispersal.

Stone Hogan

Stone hogans have been recorded in the archaeology of all but two (San Juan and Gallegos Canyon) of the fifteen Land Claims subregions of the Navajo Country (Map 13.1), often in moderately large numbers. They were particularly common in the east during the eighteenth century. James S. Robinson (1848:33) recorded them as typical of the Cañoncito band in 1846.

The stone hogan seems to have declined in popularity in more recent times in many areas but to have survived in numbers in the San Juan Basin. Although stone hogans are rather uncommon elsewhere today, they do occur very widely. Most observers (e.g., Haile 1942: 40) have considered them to be most frequent in rocky treeless areas (although modern transport allows logs and other materials to be brought in from a distance if the builder considers it worthwhile). In the west, stone hogans were not recorded at Shonto (Adams 1963: 77), where small timber is available. Kluckhohn (1927: 223) wrote that "one of the very few rock dwellings in the Navajo Reservation" was near Navajo Mountain, and the Franciscan Fathers (1910: 63)—centered at St. Michaels, Arizona—stated that stone was not used for hogans. Stone hogans have, on the other hand, been recorded for Glen Canyon (Adams et al. 1961: 12) and Cummings Mesa, Utah (Ambler et al. 1964: 20), and for Canyon de Chelly (Page 1937b: 48), Many Farms (Sanchez 1948: 50), and Red Rock, Arizona (Werner 1972: 4; Gilpin 1968: 64). Some stone hogans were seen in Nazlini Canyon in 1863 (Lindgren 1946: 242). Four stone hogans were recorded in and near Black Creek Valley (Spencer and Jett 1971: 166; Spencer 1969: 101). In the early 1930s, Hill reported stone hogans from Chinle, Canyon del Muerto, Lukachukai, Crystal, and Ft. Defiance (Kluckhohn et al. 1971: 152). As far as New Mexico is concerned, none was recorded at Ramah (where wood is abundant) except one false start (Roberts 1951: 42; Landgraf 1954: 107–14; Kluckhohn et al. 1971: 143), but Foster (1958: 37) pictured one not far away, between Whitewater and Gallup. A nineteenth-century specimen has been reported on Mesa Gigante (Wilson 1972: 17) and another example noted south of the Laguna Reservation (Kuer 1941: 24). But despite evidence of infrequency elsewhere, the literature indicates that stone hogans are common in the San Juan Basin. They were said to have been the most abundant form at Chaco Canyon (Corbett 1940: 104, 106; see also, Prudden 1906:

plate opposite p. 30) as well as along the lower Chaco River in 1973–74 (Reher 1977: 38, 44) and were also found at Shiprock (Anon. 1970g: 10), Newcomb (Newcomb 1966: plate opposite p. 198), Fruitland (Tremblay et al. 1954: 195), between Burnham and Tseya (C. Kluckhohn, quoted in Malcolm 1939: 10), at Coyote Canyon (Page 1937b: 48), Star Lake (Postma 1947: 163), Torreon (Anonymous 1967); Cañoncito (Platero 1967: 167), Mariano Lake, and Alamo (Kluckhohn et al. 1971: 143, 152).

Our survey showed that although scattered examples occurred throughout the central Navajo Country, stone hogans were found there in significant numbers (maximum: 10 percent of all hogans) only in the southern Black Mesa area (Appendix; Map 13.2); perhaps Hopi influence is to be seen there. In the west, stone hogans comprise from 9 to 17 percent of all hogans in the tree-poor area west of the Echo Cliffs and Tuba City. They also account for from 6 to 19 percent in the generally treeless zone between Black Mesa and the Utah border and between Chinle and Lukachukai washes and the Utah line. However, only in the central San Juan Basin of New Mexico (39 percent), at Cañoncito (86 percent), and on the Alamo Reservation (55 percent) is the stone hogan the predominant form. On route 666 along the western edge of the basin, stone hogans were the second most frequent hogan type (18 percent).

Cinder-Block and Adobe-Brick Hogans

The authors know of cinder-block hogans only south of Chaco Canyon; at Ramah; north of Mentmore, New Mexico; south of Chinle; on Route 89; near Tuba City; and in Dinnebito Valley near Arizona Highway 264. Nielson (1967: 37) mentioned "hogan-like houses made with . . . cinderblocks" in the Aneth area. Only two abobe-brick hogans have been noted, near Tuba City (David M. Brugge, personal communication, 1968) and near Shiprock (Stirling 1961: photos; Cummings 1964: 8), plus a possible example on the Alamo Reservation. Both of these hogan types are presumably quite recent.

EXPLANATIONS FOR HOGAN TYPE DISTRIBUTIONS

On the basis of hogan types (exclusive of plank hogans) tallied mostly in 1969–70, the Navajo Country thus appears to be divisible into four rather clear-cut regions (Map 13.2). In the extreme east, vertical-post and corbeled-log hogans predominate. A stone-hogan region includes the central San Juan Basin in New Mexico plus Cañoncito and Alamo. A cribbed-log-hogan region stretches across the central Reservation from the northern margins of Black Mesa southeastward into New Mexico to include the Dutton Plateau and Ramah, and from Indian Wells to route 666. To the north, west, and southwest of this central area is a vertical-post-hogan zone. Each of these regions can be subdivided. In the far east, stone hogans are a minority type, increasing to the westward. The cribbed-log hogan is an important secondary type in the San Juan Basin but not at Cañoncito or Alamo. In the central region, vertical-post hogans become increasingly common toward the west, so that there is really a broad transition zone between center and west. In the far west, and northeast of Black Mesa, stone hogans are a significant tertiary type but not in the Navajo Mountain and Monument Valley areas nor along the northwestern base of Black Mesa. At Navajo Mountain, in Monument Valley, in the far west, and to some extent east of Tuba City, conical forked-pole hogans still formed a small but significant minority of the hogans in 1970. The west in general appears also to have more corbeled-log hogans than elsewhere, with the possible exception of the far east.

Degree of Acculturation

The selection of raw material(s) employed within any folk architectural tradition is a reflection of several rational factors . . . [including] cultural traditions and preferences, technological skills and available tools, the perceived function of the housing units undergoing construction, the desired degree of comfort and/or durability required, perceived environmental stresses such as extremes of temperature or moisture, and the availability of raw materials within the local environment. . . . [Gritzner 1947a: 25]

All of these factors appear to have influenced the development and distribution of hogan types.

Despite the multitude of factors at work, there seem to be two principal classes of reasons for the distributional patterns described. One of these is the extent of acculturation, which in turn reflects the related variables of (1) regional differences in degree of conservatism and (2) effective distances from centers of innovation. Historically, Reservation Period acculturative influences have come primarily from the south and southeast. Specifically, Ft. Wingate and Gallup, New Mexico, and Ft. Defiance and Window Rock, Arizona, have been the primary foci of Anglo-Navajo contacts and have been the points of origin of Federal and Tribal development programs (Spencer and Jett 1971: 159–60). The canyons of the Colorado and San Juan rivers and the rugged adjacent country have minimized influences from the west and north, and it was this remote, rough country in which hid most of those who escaped the Ft. Sumner confinement and acculturative impact (Sapir and Hoijer 1942: 347–49). Personal observation and conversations with knowledgeable individuals, plus a few hints in the literature (e.g., Chisholm 1975: 84), have led us to conclude that the western Navajo Reservation, especially around remote Navajo Mountain, is generally the most conservative section of the Navajo Country. It seems likely, then, that the survival in the west of old hogan forms which are rare or obsolete elsewhere is related to this greater degree of conservatism and distance from centers of innovation. This would seem largely to account for the significant presence in the northwest of conical forked-pole and corbeled-log hogans and, to some degree, the prevalence of leaning-log hogans and, possibly, the significant occurrence of stone hogans in the west and the far east.

Availability of Building Materials

Degree of isolation and conservatism can only partially explain the distribution patterns of traditional hogan types. Local availability of building materials seems to have exerted an even greater influence. Despite the rather surprising contention of Kluckhohn et al. (1971: 3) that "the ecology tends to be similar throughout the Navaho Reservation," there is very great regional variability in climate, landforms, rock types, soils, and vegetation (see chapter 1). There seems to be no doubt that regional differences in availability of building materials are the primary factor conditioning the distribution of traditional hogan types. Stone hogans, for example, are found in numbers almost only in relatively treeless lower-elevation areas, specifically those in which stone is readily available (cf., Haile 1942: 40; Sullivan 1938: 45); this finding compares with Gritzner's (1974a: 26–27, 33–34) for Hispano folk housing in New Mexico. Although stone hogans last longer than log ones and seem once to have had some prestige value (e.g., Taylor 1965; Hollister 1903: 70–71), they require more effort to build because of the large number of heavy stones that must be collected (Page 1937b: 48; denied by Chauncey Neboyia, a sometime mason), and the insulating quality of stone is poorer than that of logs. These factors probably account for the current lack of popularity of stone hogans in areas where logs are available. The Alamo Reservation is an exception, for junipers are moderately abundant there. The apparent dearth of stone hogans in the southwestern part of the Reservation may reflect the absence, over wide areas, of suitable rocks. Too, there may have been, in the San Juan Basin, more cultural continuity with the stone-construction tradition of Refugee Period Dinétah and parts of the Basin.

Leaning-log and palisaded hogans, as well as corbeled-log hogans, are particularly common in areas poorly timbered or timbered largely with juniper and pinyon pine.

The rapidly tapering and generally gnarled trunks of these species tend to restrict the length of structural members to less than ten feet, thereby placing some limitation on the way in which they may be incorporated as individual members of a wall assemblage. Throughout this [pinyon-juniper] environmental zone [in north-central New Mexico], *jacal* (vertical post) buildings are a common feature [of Hispano villages and farmsteads]. [Gritzer 1974a: 29]

The limited length of these logs—especially juniper—also seems to favor vertical-post and corbeled-log hogans over cribbed-log ones in such environments in the Navajo area. As early as the 1880s, Mathews (1902: 49) recorded an instance near the Chuska Mountains of a leaning-log hogan being built instead of a conical forked-pole one owing to the lack of long timbers. He was informed that the latter type was the easier to build if suitable logs were available. Mindeleff (1898: 498, 500) indicated that corbeled-log hogans were, in the 1880s, "common in the valleys where timber is scarce and difficult to procure."

As noted above, writers have in the past observed an association between frequency of cribbed-log hogans and presence of timber. Our survey confirmed this observation. The areas of predominance of the cribbed-log hogan among traditional hogans are all either largely forested with pinyon or ponderosa pine, or are fairly near such forests, or are adjacent to watercourses along which cottonwoods grow. Most areas within which this form does not predominate are relatively treeless or have mainly only scrub trees such as juniper. Similarly, Gritzner (1974a: 29–30) found that Hispano use of horizontal-log construction was largely confined to the higher-elevation zones in which tall timber was available. Apparent exceptions to the generalization that cribbed-log construction dominates where appropriate timber is available are found on the portions of Black Mesa nearest the Hopi villages and in areas in the northwestern part of the Navajo Reservation. The timber on Navajo Mountain has not been utilized because of the sacredness of this eminence; otherwise, the above-mentioned conservatism and isolation of the northwest,

along with the general paucity of large trees, is probably the reason for the cribbed-log hogan not predominating there. It seems likely on the whole that, given suitable materials and full familiarity with the form, the cribbed-log hogan would everywhere be the preferred hogan type built with native materials.

The distributional pattern of plank hogans was probably initially closely related to degree of acculturation, to availability of lumber from the government and Tribal sawmills near Ft. Defiance, and to local employment opportunities, since money is required to obtain nails, tarpaper, chicken-wire and cement. However, the authors' survey indicated that, although off-the-road areas have fewer plank hogans, there was still no very good region-wide correlation between the above factors and plank-hogan frequency. Most Navajo families today probably have enough cash income to be able to buy the materials needed to build a plank hogan, and the predominance of plank hogans in the far west and southwest appears to be primarily a function of treelessness and lack of stone. Less conservative areas seem to be largely skipping the "stage" of plank hogans in favor of building frame houses.

Summary of Temporal Changes

The earliest periods of Navajo history appear to be characterized by overwhelming predominance of conical forked-pole hogans, and these remained very common until the early twentieth century, after which they rapidly waned in popularity. Stone hogans were becoming common in much of the tree-poor San Juan Basin by the mid-eighteenth century and remained so until very recent times. In areas where some timber was available, the corbeled-log form had gained prevalence by the end of the eighteenth century; although continuing to be built (especially for storage) in the western, northern, and far eastern areas, after 1890 it was increasingly eclipsed in most districts by vertical-post hogans, whose maximum development occurred during the first third of the twentieth century. Both corbeled-log and vertical-post hogans were replaced by cribbed-log hogans during the early to middle twentieth century in areas where longer logs were available.

Some of the changes in the relative overall popularities of the various hogan types relate to the successive development of new forms, which had comparative advantages in certain environmental zones. However, nonenvironmental factors probably also played a major role. Vertical-post, cribbed-log, masonry, and plank hogans contrast with conical forked-pole, lean-to, and corbeled-log hogans in that the former are more commodious and have vertical or nearly vertical walls. Such hogans are harder to heat—especially plank hogans, whose thin walls provide poor insulation. The rise in popularity of these hogans seems closely related to wide availability of steel axes and, to a lesser degree, saws (cf., Coolidge and Coolidge 1931: 82). Not only did steel axes make practical the building of larger dwellings and those employing large numbers of logs, they also made firewood acquisition much easier, thus partially compensating for the greater heating requirements of larger hogans. Another factor was the adoption of flues and then of wood-burning stoves, which increased firing —and, therefore, heating—efficiency. Finally, the increasing adoption of European-style furnishings—especially beds and tables—favored both commodiousness and vertical walls rather than inward-inclining sides.

THE ACCELERATION OF HOUSE ADOPTION

As detailed in chapter 6, house adoption seems to have commenced in the 1880s in areas experiencing relatively intensive contact with Anglos, and house use became well established in these areas during the 1890s and 1900s. Based upon field work ending in 1893, Cosmos Mindeleff (1898: 486) wrote:

The houses of people, the homes "we have always had" . . . are rapidly disappearing, and the examples left today are more or less influenced by ideas derived from the whites. Among the Navajo such contact has been very

slight, but it has been sufficient to introduce new methods of construction and in fact new structures. . . .

By 1930, Coolidge and Coolidge (1930: 78) were able to write that "stone and lumber houses [are] often seen. . . ." Initial adoption was later elsewhere, however, and as late as 1939 the statement could be made that "the hogan is almost the universal type of Navajo home . . ." (Jones et al. 1939: 82). There were only a few houses near Red Rock, Arizona, in 1942, although one had four rooms (Werner 1972: 32, 107). In the Ramah area, the first cabin was built in 1917, but widespread use of houses occurred only after World War II (Vogt 1951: 110). The first Navajo house in the Wide Ruins, Arizona, area seems to have been built in the mid-1940s (Hannum 1958: 104–08). There were some Hispano- and Anglo-influenced houses near Counselors, New Mexico, at the beginning of the 1940s (Farmer 1942: 71). Kluckhohn and Leighton (1962: 45) noted in the early 1940s that "Cabins of wood or stone which follow white prototypes are now common in the regions closest to the railroads, but native dwellings are still in the majority. . . ."

Although many areas remained entirely or largely houseless until the 1970s, adoption continued to spread and accelerate and in some of the late-adopting areas the "stage" of log and stone houses was partly or wholly skipped. By 1960, Vogt (1961: 322) observed, "There has been a strong trend toward White-style [log] cabins or frame or rock houses." Frame-house building had nearly replaced hogan construction at Fruitland by 1952 (Tremblay et al. 1954: 217–18). In the vicinity of Piñon, between 1960 and 1965 "permanently located rectangular houses, which were constructed with pitched roofs and made of logs or cement blocks, had replaced perhaps a quarter of the hogans . . ." (Downs 1972: 129). At Shonto,

the hogan . . . is rapidly giving way to other and more modern forms of housing. In 1955 there was only one Navajo domicile within the entire community which was not a hogan; today [1972] nearly every residence [homestead] group includes at least one rectangular multiroom house of wood, cement block, or stucco. While many of the older hogans still remain in use, and while their aggregate number probably still exceeds the number of more modern dwellings, it is reported that there has been no new hogan construction for the last eight years. [Adams and Ruffing 1977: 61–62]

In the San Juan–Gallegos Mesa, New Mexico, area, houses were increasingly accepted during the period 1935–50. "Since 1910 [and especially since 1965] there has been a definite shift from hogans and single-room dwellings to multi-room houses, and, more recently, mobile homes." In 1978, there were twenty hogans, sixty houses, and eleven trailers (Elyea et al. 1979: 88). When asked whether he knew of anyone under thirty years of age who was building a hogan, John Martin, former Navajo resident of Crownpoint, New Mexico, answered "No" (personal communication, 1978). He said they were thinking in terms of house trailers.

Although our survey suggests a certain correlation between frequency of houses and proximity to major roads and settlements, this was not nearly so marked as we had anticipated. Nor was there a good correlation between frequency of *frame* houses and proximity to highways and towns. To a small degree the latter situation reflects Tribal distribution of frame "welfare houses" during the 1950s and '60s as well as other housing-assistance programs, but to explain the diffusion of houses more fully we would require data on education, employment, income, communications, and so forth, information which we do not have.

Since 1963, the Navajo Tribe has taken advantage of U.S. Department of Housing and Urban Development housing assistance programs, and by 1976 over 1,000 standard Anglo-style houses (Fig. 13.2) had been erected on the Reservation (Snyder et al. ca. 1976: 3). Since these houses are commercial types, built almost exclusively in clusters of from ten to fifty or more in established communities, they

Fig. 13.2. The future? A housing project at Shiprock, New Mexico, 1972.

TABLE 13.3.
Relative Frequency of House Forms in a Navajo Country-Wide Survey,
expressed as percentages of a sample of 2,912 houses and of a sample
of 4,134 permanent dwellings, ca. 1969–70

House Form		Percentage of All Houses		Percentage of All Permanent Dwellings
Vertical Log		1.3		0.9
Stacked-Log	Undifferentiated (mostly cribbed-log)	10.5	10.7	7.8
	Abutting-Log	0.2*		
Frame		76.5		53.3
Masonry	Stone	4.8	6.6	4.9
	Cinder-Block	1.4		
	Adobe-Brick	0.3		
	Fired-Brick	<0.1		
Hybrid		1.5		1.1
Trailer		3.4		2.5

*Probably an underestimation, because of incomplete differentiation in the field.

are not considered in this study of vernacular architecture. Nevertheless, their presence has undoubtedly had an influence on rural Navajos' perceptions of appropriate, "modern," housing. And, the great increase in cash welfare income during the last two decades has vastly increased the possibility of translating these perceptions into practice.

HOUSE TYPE DISTRIBUTIONS

Houses are now found throughout the Navajo Country, and in the areas surveyed they outnumbered hogans more than two to one (Table 13.3). This finding was a surprise to us, and we have some evidence that areas distant from main roads do not exhibit as extreme a house/hogan ratio. Nevertheless, houses were clearly becoming, if indeed they were not already, the predominant dwelling category. Further, three-quarters of the houses surveyed were *frame houses,* which are very clearly quite recent in Navajo culture. This was the predominant house type in almost all areas, ranging from 6 to 100 percent of all houses surveyed. Predominance of frame houses was described by Tremblay et al. (1954: 207) for Fruitland, by Nielson (1967: 37) for Aneth, Utah (he may have considered plank hogans to be houses), and by Spencer and Jett (1971: 170) for Black Creek Valley, but they are seldom explicitly referred to in earlier works. They are indicated during the 1930s around

Polacca Wash (Fig. 7.11), Red Lake (Tolani Lakes), Sawmill, and Lukachukai, Arizona, and Chaco Canyon, New Mexico (Corbett 1940: 105), Ft. Wingate during World War II, and at Ramah (one specimen) in 1946 (Roberts 1951: 18, 43; Kluckhohn et al. 1971: 148; see also, "Frame House," chapter 7). Their spread must have been very rapid, apparently nearly entirely after World War II.

In regard to older house types, there are some clear-cut regional variations in frequency which correspond rather well to the differences in hogan frequency described above (although the literature is of little help in defining house-materials distributions). With few exceptions, the *stone house* is the predominant non-frame, non-trailer house form in most areas in which vertical-post hogans are the primary non-plank hogan type and where stone hogans predominate (western, southwestern, and northern Reservation, much of the San Juan Basin, Cañoncito; see Map 13.2). This is presumably primarily a function of lack of good timber for construction, and Mindeleff (1898: 487) indicated that stone houses were built in the unwooded valleys. In the lower Chaco River area, small stone houses were built as early as 1900; larger ones became common beginning about 1940. Stone houses were found to be the most common Reservation Period type in this area (Reher 1977: 39–52). As early as 1919, an elaborate multiwindowed stone house was seen high on Black Mesa (Johnston 1972: 245). A stone house (apparently the first) was built at Wide Ruins in the mid-1940s (Hannum 1958: 104–08), and another was reported at Piñon (Downs 1965: 1391). Sullivan (1938: plate opposite p. 80) photographed one at Chinle. Snow photographs of 1935–36 (1006, 1106) show stone houses on Douglas Mesa (near Kayenta?) and near Burnham, New Mexico. One was apparently built around the turn of the century near Ramah, where there were four stone houses about 1941 (Landgraf 1954: 107–14; Kluckhohn et al. 1971: 143, 148).

Although they are widely distributed, *palisaded houses* appear to be important only north of Piñon (18 percent) and west and

northwest of Gallup (12 percent). They were described for 1888 at Ft. Wingate (Shufeldt 1892), and a 1935 Snow photo (Fig. 7.1) taken east of Steamboat shows an example. Six were also seen at Ramah in the 1940s (Fig. 7.3; Kluckhohn et al. 1971: 148), and they occurred at Cañoncito by 1890 (Platero 1967).

The *stacked-log house* (almost exclusively cribbed) is the principal non-frame house in most areas where the usual hogan form is cribbed-log. Reichard (1939: 7) observed that in well-wooded localities such as Lukachukai, Arizona, there were a number of log or frame houses built in Anglo style. Hoover (1931: 443) wrote that cribbed-log houses were common from Ft. Defiance north, and this is still an area of high frequency (36 percent of houses), probably because of early acculturation plus availability of ponderosa Pine. They are most common (64 to 86 percent) in the adjacent Chuska Mountains. Hannum (1958: 113–14) recorded a mid-1940s example at Pine Springs, Arizona, and Sullivan (1938: plate opposite p. 45) photographed one in the Chinle Valley (see also, Frisbie and McAllester 1978: 327). A "new" (1977) log house was photographed at Lukachukai by McAllester and McAllester (1980: 97). Another specimen was photographed in 1935 by Snow (Fig. 7.5) in the Dinnehotso area. Examples were also reported for Ramah for 1946 (Roberts 1951: 43; Kluckhohn et al. 1971: 148) and in the lower Chaco River area in a 1973–74 survey (Reher 1977: 39, 44). Boyce (1974: 65) recorded their absence in District 1 (Kaibito, Copper Mine, and Red Lake) in 1939. That these distribution patterns date from the earliest period of modern Navajo house building is suggested by Mindeleff (1898: 486–87): "Many of the modern houses of the Navaho in the mountainous and timbered regions are built of logs, sometimes hewn. These houses are nearly always rectangular in shape, as also are all of those built in stone masonry in the valley regions."

Exceptions to the above patterns include the significant occurence of *cinder-block houses* near Navajo Mountain, east of Kayenta, near Dinnebito Dam, Arizona, and south and southeast of Piñon (assuming these to have been correctly identified by Farber); and the importance of *house trailers* along route 15 westward from Indian Wells and on the Alamo Reservation (for which dates are four years more recent than for most other areas surveyed). The Navajo Mountain case remains unexplained, but the high frequency of cinder-block houses north of the Hopi villages (cf., Downs 1965: 1391; 1972: 129) suggests influence on these areas from the adjacent Hopi Country, where cinder-block houses are the most popular current form (McIntire 1971: 517). Kluckhohn et al. (1971: 442) claimed that "Cinderblock houses are also becoming prevalent, especially in the more populated areas near the trading posts or towns." Our survey found cinder-block houses to be widely distributed, but otherwise very uncommon except in the far west; one was recorded at Shonto in the late 1950s (Adams 1963: 77), with a considerable increase in numbers by 1972 (Adams and Ruffing 1977: 61–62). George Roth (personal communication, 1973) reported their use on the Colorado River Indian Reservation.

Adobe-brick houses attain some local importance only at Alamo, Cañoncito, and, apparently, at nearby [Rincon] Marquez, New Mexico (Platero 1967: 167; Anonymous 1968b), because of federal-Tribal programs encouraging the building of these kinds of houses. Adobe houses are also recorded for Fruitland (Tremblay et al. 1954: 207) and Ramah (Landgraf 1954: 107–14). One house built partially of adobe bricks was recorded west of Round Rock (our survey; there was formerly an adobe-brick flour mill at Round Rock). *Fired-brick houses* are known only from Fruitland (Tremblay et al. 1954: 207), Cañoncito (our survey), and the Colorado River Indian Reservation (George Roth, personal communication, 1973). Tremblay et al. (1954: 201) wrote:

Builders of adobe houses, as they become more acculturated, think of future construction in terms of cement blocks and fired bricks. Adobes appear to be more transitory in the shift toward modern construction than either frame or stone houses. The mud bricks are time consuming in their fabrication and it takes longer to lay them than it does cement [*sic*] or cement blocks. For these reasons the building of adobe houses will probably be curtailed.

In this connection, one may take note of the aforementioned Tribal-federal programs which included teaching Navajos to build adobe-brick houses.

Respecting the distribution of house trailers, they are referred to in the literature for the Page-Leche'e, Arizona, area in 1970 (Wagner 1974: 273), for Black Creek Valley in 1968 (Spencer and Jett 1971: 166), for the San Juan–Gallegos Mesa area (Elyea et al. 1979: 88), and for Cañoncito (Anonymous 1974a).

SHADE AND TENT DISTRIBUTIONS

Most forms of temporary and summer dwellings other than flat-roofed shades are rare or uncommon today, although single lean-to shades seem to have been common, perhaps even predominant, during the nineteenth century. Stephen (1893: 350) stated that there were "many" single, "two-legged," lean-to shades in use, and Curtis (1907: 136) contended that the single lean-to was once the common Navajo summer shelter but had largely been supplanted by the ramada. The latter is not mentioned by Mindeleff (1898) and may have been uncommon before 1900: nevertheless, it appears to have been used by the Navajo as early as the Gobernador Phase (1696–1770), perhaps ceremonially (see chapter 4).

There is some areal variation in the frequency of ramada use, the range being, according to our survey, from none to 30 percent of all dwellings. The authors found no clearcut association between shade frequency and environment or degree of acculturation, and are unable to explain these variations. We also suspect that our sampling of shades may have been less accurate than that of permanent dwellings.

According to Roberts (1951: 41–42), in the Ramah district circular windbreaks of tall, heavily leaved vertical boughs and saplings filled the role played by ramadas in other areas. According to Mindeleff (1898: 494), stacked-bough windbreaks were possible only in wooded areas. Where fewer boughs are available, the palisaded windbreak would be more likely. Stone windbreaks would be largely a phenomenon of treeless areas.

The type of boughs or brush used on the roofs and sides of shades varies areally, according to local availability. Thus, cottonwood (apparently preferred), oak, juniper, or other boughs may be used, or weed and corn stalks, tumbleweeds, or other brush where trees are absent.

Tents have never been extremely common in most areas. Although Kluckhohn and Leighton (1962: 45) wrote that "canvas tents are frequently seen," Page (1937: 48b) stated that well-to-do families usually had tents but that ramadas were more typical. Around Ramah in 1941, tents were usual in warm-season sheep camps (Landgraf 1954: 50). The high frequency of tent bases found in the lower Chaco River area survey (Reher 1977: 39, 43, 49, 51–52, 56–62) suggests that tents are or were more frequently used than ramadas in treeless areas and where sparse forage requires frequent moving of flocks.

Chapter 14

NAVAJO ARCHITECTURE AND ACCULTURATION

There is perhaps no tribal people in the world —and certainly none of such complexity—better documented ethnographically, historically, and archaeologically than the Navajo. Thus, this society provides a unique opportunity for the study of material-culture change.

Change has always been characteristic of much of Navajo culture and has been accelerating ever more rapidly since the Second World War. Most elements of Navajo material culture using native materials have become rare or obsolete in the last few decades, and the most visible aspects of that culture—those of traditional architecture—appear to be on the brink of becoming relict features in the landscape. In many areas, hogans are no longer being built as residences, and native materials are often no longer employed even in owner-built houses. Commercially manufactured house trailers are making major inroads on folk housing in some areas. Perhaps the 1970s was the last decade during which a study of the kind reported in this book could have been made.

The detailed description of the forms and chronologies of Navajo structures is certainly of interest in its own right; the Navajo are, after all, North America's most numerous tribal people, occupying some 16,000,000 acres (2,444,200 ha) of land. But beyond this, the study of Navajo architecture over time can be broadly illuminating of Navajo culture change as a whole and of the attitudes shaping that change. Further, a detailed study of the sources and processes of change in this single sector of one people's culture may contribute to our understanding of culture change in general.

One broad conclusion to which study of Navajo architectural evolution leads is that the origins of innovation are far more complex than might at first be supposed. Jett (1981) has written elsewhere:

If the first migrating proto-Navajo to reach New Mexico a few centuries ago were able to see today's range of hogan types, he would probably not recognize any of them, with the possible exception of the nearly obsolete conical forked-pole hogan, as having any relation to Athapaskan housing. And yet, every Navajo today would unhesitatingly class every one of these structures as a hogan and therefore, by definition, Navajo.

This is because traditional Navajo architecture, *though unequivocably Navajo,* has been significantly shaped by influences from at least four main cultural sources: Athapaskan, Puebloan, Hispano-American, and Anglo-American. The distinction between diffusion and invention becomes blurred. Outside influences were experienced, but those items accepted were reinterpreted to conform to Navajo conceptions of rightness, and the result was a series of hybrid dwelling forms which were significantly different from the parent types. That is, diffusion led to recombination, resulting in something clearly derivative yet at the same time clearly original, the originality lying in the recombination. And perhaps this was the typical course of innovation through human history.

The Navajo (like the Japanese) have often been pointed to as an example of a people who have been successful in adopting (and, often, in elaborating) foreign ideas and techniques while continuing to retain a distinct and distinctive cultural identity.

Evon Vogt (1961: 327–28) termed the Navajo "incorporative":

... elements from other cultures are incorporated into Navajo culture in such a way that the structural framework of the institutional core ... is maintained, and the borrowed elements are fitted into place in terms of the pre-existing patterns. The result has been a steady growth in cultural content ... without important losses—except for fishing ... and ... raiding. ...

Vogt's basic "institutional core" of Navajo culture included: the Navajo language; a farming, sheepherding, and handicraft economy; the concept of harmony; elaborate curing ceremonials; witchcraft; hogans, sweathouses, and sheep corrals, oriented eastward; fear of ghosts and abandonment of dwellings when a death has occurred within; dispersed settlement; matrilocality; the nuclear family and the homestead group; political leadership based upon a local headman; and matrilineal exogamous clans. Many of these traits relate to settlement practices and are basically of Athapaskan (northern) origin, as is the Navajo language. The economy, the religious traits, and clans

are, on the other hand, largely of southwestern origin.

Although by no means devoid of philosophical and esthetic sensibilities, the Navajo are essentially a pragmatic people. Incorporativeness, and the pragmatism which it reflects, appear to be Northern Athapaskan legacies (Wagner and Travis 1979; Vanstone 1974: 125).

Certainly, gradual incorporation did take place over the years. However, the impact of the late seventeenth/early eighteenth-century period of intensive Puebloan-Athapaskan contact was so rapid and so profound, especially in economy, religion,[1] and architecture, that some scholars are of the opinion that fully *Navajo* culture dates only from the time of this interaction and that the ancestors of the affected Athapaskans are properly called Apachaean proto-Navajo but not yet true Navajo. James Hester (1962: 91–92) viewed later cultural adoptions as primarily incorporative, but he felt that the Gobernador Phase or Refugee Period was one of cultural *fusion,* with Puebloan traits at first being dominant although later becoming simplified and, in some cases, eliminated. David Brugge (1968: 19–20) discussed this idea with specific reference to the conical forked-pole, corbeled-log, and stone hogans, which he saw as the blending of aspects of Athapaskan and Puebloan traditions rather than simply the piece-meal addition of a few Puebloan traits to a basically Athapaskan dwelling form. The same can probably be said with respect to the leaning-log hogan (Jett 1981).

The authors concur with Hester's and Brugge's views. However, once the four basic hogan types mentioned above were established, further hogan evolution—the emergence of palisaded, cribbed-log, adobe-brick, and cinder-block hogans—was mainly a matter of incorporation of Euramerican methods or materials. The structural changes were minor or moderate, not major, and were relatively simple extensions of existing forms and practices. An exception is the plank hogan, with its Navajo form but largely Anglo structure and materials; it can be considered an example of true fusion.

James Downs (1964: 94–99) has taken issue with the idea expressed by Vogt and others that Navajo culture history has been characterized by a succession of foreign increments to a continuing, essentially unchanging institutional core rather than the replacement of old elements by new or radical adjustment of the core to accommodate additions.

As has been pointed out above, most or all of the core elements relating to economy and religion are derivative from or were profoundly altered by alien cultures; the same is probably true of the clan system. Most remaining core characteristics that are of northern, Athapaskan, origin are—besides the Navajo language—in the realms of architecture and settlement. These realms reflect not only the means of livelihood of the people but also, importantly, their social values. Individualism, autonomy, and privacy are valued, but so are helpfulness and cooperation within the community. Social interaction, especially along homestead-group and clan lines, is highly valued, and increasingly this is also true at community and even tribal levels. But an aloofness toward outsiders is also characteristic, and personal individualism and autonomy are mirrored in the contemporary tribal preoccupation with Navajo control of Navajoland and non-Navajo's activities therein. Downs (1964: 96–98) felt that the maintenance of social isolation from outsiders (reinforced by language, aloof behavior, and dispersed settlement) has been the key factor in the maintenance of Navajo cultural distinctiveness over the centuries, rather than there being an immutable institutional core that can be added to but not subtracted from.

And yet despite a considerable degree of social isolationism, people of diverse ethnic origins were permitted to join the Navajo. There are, for example, clans of Jemez, Hopi, Ute, and Mexican origin, and slaves taken from other groups sometimes ultimately became men and women of some standing in the community. Perhaps this seeming contradiction is accounted for by these individuals having adapted to Navajo ways (while still, perhaps, contributing useful new ideas). Nevertheless, it would seem that Navajo distinctiveness had a close call during the Gobernador Phase, when it was seemingly very nearly overwhelmed by Puebloan culture. The Athapaskan proto-Navajo were profoundly and for all time changed by that contact, yet their progeny managed, after about half a century, to purge themselves of certain distinctively Puebloan traits, notably painted pottery and pueblo-style architecture. These "are the two elements most specifically prohibited by Blessingway, the basic ceremony of modern Navajo Religion" (Brugge 1963: 22). It may well be that the emergence of Blessingway and its emphasis on hogans was a direct response to the threat of being culturally submerged by aliens. Certainly, the hogan was and is a symbol of ethnic identity (Crumrine 1964). Besides being appropriate to a dispersed and mobile settlement pattern (which became more so after the Gobernador Phase), the hogan stood for both individualism (or, more properly, familyism) and tribal affiliation and, with its central focus and radial and concentric conceptual sectoring, reflected Athapaskan social values. No matter that the structure was a fusion of Athapaskan and foreign elements; it served its practical and social functions better than ever and—despite its mixed origins—remained distinctively Navajo. In other words, all hogan forms, though reflecting fusion, were supportive rather than disruptive of Navajo pragmatic and social values.

And what of the present era of rapid change among the Navajo? Although far from being assimilated into Anglo culture, the Navajo are nevertheless certainly once again in a phase of fusion, even transculturation, with respect to architecture as well as in many other areas of culture. Specifically, symbols of ethnicity are on the wane; for example, distinctive Navajo dress, adornment, and hair styling are disappearing, and most families' principal dwelling is now a house, not a hogan. Does this imply, then, that the Navajo sense of ethnic identity is disintegrating? The answer seems to be a resounding "No." The Navajo language is still spoken (though not always well) nearly universally, and despite inroads by the Native American Church and, to a lesser degree, by Christianity and nonbelief, and despite an insufficiency of Singers, Navajo religion remains extremely powerful. Perhaps because of these things as well as the overwhelming population and territorial-size superiority of the Navajo as compared with other tribes, plus their relative prosperity, the Navajo seem to have a quite secure sense of ethnic identity. The decline of hogan use, then, may be a manifestation not of cultural disintegration but rather of cultural complacency—a sense of Navajoness sufficiently strong to allow the adoption of foreign housing.

Though declining rapidly in numbers and no longer a core characteristic in the guise of a primary dwelling, the hogan will probably continue to be used as a seasonal dwelling in more remote locations. Further, because of its close association with Navajo religion (still a part of the core), the hogan seems destined to endure—though in diminished numbers—for many years to come.

APPENDIX:
Frequencies of Common Hogan and House Forms

The following table summarizes the local frequencies of the more common hogan and house forms as determined by the author's surveys, supplemented by a few published and unpublished data from other workers; information presented pertains to 1970 unless otherwise noted. Dwelling forms accounting for less than 5 percent in any category are excluded. Data from more than one local area were lumped together when there was a high degree of similarity between the samples involved. Frequencies of shades and tents are also indicated but may have been underreported in some cases. Figures in brackets were not included in the totals and averages at the end of the table. The field workers involved are indicated by initials: V.E.S., Virginia E. Spencer; S.C.J., Stephen C. Jett; R.F., Roy Farber; J.E.L., Jerrold E. Levy. The areas surveyed are presented in an approximately west-to-east sequence.

Some caution in interpreting the data is necessary because: (1) most surveying was done from maintained roads; therefore, a probable bias exists toward more recent structures since off-road areas appear to have fewer modern dwellings; (2) some areas (e.g., Black Creek Valley and the Canyon de Chelly system) were completely surveyed, while most areas were merely sampled; this sometimes affects the comparability of data from different areas, and the differences in sample size distort the final totals and averages to a slight extent; (3) although most of the surveys were conducted during 1970, some areas were sampled in other years, again affecting the comparability of the data to some degree. On the whole, however, the survey provides a good general picture of dwelling type distribution ca. 1970. Map 13.2 presents much of this information in graphic form, and the implications of distribution patterns are discussed in Chapter 13.

Route or Area Sampled	Permanent Dwellings, No.	Percentage of Permanent Dwellings — Hogans	Percentage of Permanent Dwellings — Houses	Predominant Hogan (% of all hogans)	Subpredominant Hogans (% of all hogans)	Predominant House (% of all houses)	Subpredominant Houses (% of all houses)	Shades and Tents (% of all dwellings)	Field Worker
W of Cameron, Rt. 64; Gray Mt.–Bitter Sprgs., Rt. 89	297	35	65	plank 39	leaning-log 19, stone 17, conical forked-pole 8	frame 82	stone 7	12	V.E.S.
W of Tuba City, Rt. 160	113	29	71	plank 42	leaning-log 9, stone 9, conical forked-pole 6	frame 78	stone 9, trailer 8	8	V.E.S.
Bitter Springs–Page, Rt. 89	31	42	58	plank 92	vertical post 8	frame 100		0	V.E.S.
Lechee area (1971)	60	10	90	plank 67	vertical-post? 33	frame 78	trailer 20	2	J.E.L.
Page–Tonalea via Kaibito; Shonto–Betatakin	80	44	56	vertical-post 52 (most palisaded)	plank 23, cribbed-log 11, stone 9	frame 78	stone 9	21	V.E.S.
Rainbow Lodge area	30	47	53	palisaded 36, cribbed-log 36	conical forked-pole 21, plank 7	frame 63	cinder-block 5, stone 12	21	R.F.
Tuba City–Kayenta, Rt. 160	164	45	55	vertical-post 59	plank 29, cribbed-log 10	frame 81		18	V.E.S.
NW Black Mesa (1971)	58	53	47	vertical-post? 61	stacked-log (cribbed?) 29, vertical-post? 13	frame 89	trailer 11	16	J.E.L.
Southern Monument Valley, Rt. 163	65	55	45	vertical-post 47	stacked-log (½ corbeled) 29, plank 12, conical forked-pole 12	frame 92		13	V.E.S.
Kayenta–N of Rock Pt. via Mexican Water, Rts. 160, 12	114	40	60	vertical-post 53	plank 26, stone 6	frame 89	cinder-block 7	26	V.E.S.
Red Mesa–Hovenweep Jct. via Montezuma Creek (1978)	41	22	78	vertical-post 56	plank 44	frame 94		16	S.C.J.

[234]

Location									
Mexican Water–Shiprock, Rts. 160, 504	134	28	72	vertical-post 38 (ca. ½ leaning-log)	plank 27 / stone 19 / stacked-log 19	frame 87	trailer 7	14	V.E.S.
Tuba City–Hopi, Rt. 264	72	46	54	vertical-post 47	plank 24 / cribbed-log 12 / palisaded 9 / conical forked-pole 6	frame 67	stone 18	13	V.E.S.
Dinnebito Dam area	43	47	53	vertical-post 80	stone 10	frame 57	stone 26 / cinder-block 13	17	R.F.
W Res. boundary– Indian Wells, Rt. 15; Dilkon–Castle Butte; Rt. 6 S of Bidahochi	155	25	75	plank 55	vertical-post 30 / stacked-log 13 (most cribbed)	frame 87	trailer 6	20	V.E.S., S.C.J.
Rt. 4 and NE of Seba Dalkai (1972)	66	18	82	plank 92	cribbed-log 8	frame 100		6	S.C.J.
Indian Wells–Lizard Springs, Rt. 15	152	12	88	cribbed-log 42	plank 22 / palisaded 8	frame 68	stone 21	12	V.E.S.
Hopi–Ganado, Rt. 264; Lizard Springs–Chinle, Rt. 63	127	22	78	cribbed-log 36	palisaded 32	frame 80	cribbed-log 12	9	S.C.J., V.E.S.
Bidahochi–Rt. 264, Rt. 6 (1971)	28	36	64	stacked-log 60 (most cribbed)	plank 30 / palisaded 10	frame 78		10	S.C.J.
Low Mt. area–Hopi; Piñon–Hopi, via Rts. 67, 65, 4	95	51	49	vertical-post 35 (most palisaded)	cribbed-log 29 / plank 15 / stone 8	frame 64	cinder-block 34 / stone 6	22	R.F.
Chinle–Piñon, Rt. 4; Cottonwood–Black Mt.	130	34	66	cribbed-log 50	plank 23 / vertical-post 18	frame 78	cribbed-log 10 / stone 7	6?	R.F.
Black Mesa N of Piñon	22	50	50	cribbed-log 55	plank 27 / palisaded 18	frame 64	palisaded 18 / cribbed-log 9 / cinder-block 9	21	R.F.
Kayenta–Many Farms, Rt. 18	104	38	62	stacked-log 45 (most cribbed)	plank 33 / leaning-log 13 / stone 8	frame 89	cribbed-log 6	22	V.E.S.
Chinle–Many Farms, Rt. 63	206	27	73	cribbed-log 56	leaning-log 22 / plank 18	frame 84	cribbed-log 7	22 (except field structures)	V.E.S.

Route or Area Sampled	Permanent Dwellings, No.	Percentage of Permanent Dwellings		Predominant Hogan (% of all hogans)	Subpredominant Hogans (% of all hogans)	Predominant House (% of all houses)	Subpredominant Houses (% of all houses)	Shades and Tents (% of all dwellings)	Field Worker
		Hogans	Houses						
Canyon de Chelly system floor (1972)	75	63	47	cribbed-log 55	stone 34, leaning-log 9	frame 47	stone 37, cribbed-log 16	30	S.C.J.
Chinle–Ft. Defiance, Rt. 7	210	31	69	cribbed-log 65	plank 20, leaning-log 11	frame 81	cribbed-log 12	17	V.E.S.
N of Rock Point–Lukachukai, Rts. 63, 12	90	22	78	cribbed-log 70	leaning-log 20	frame 79	cribbed-log 16	22	V.E.S.
Lukachukai–Navajo, Rt. 12	150	30	70	cribbed-log 80	plank 18	frame 57	cribbed-log 36	9	V.E.S.
Black Creek Valley (1968)	744	20	80	stacked-log (most cribbed) 75	plank 5	frame 69	stacked-log (most cribbed) 20	7	V.E.S.
Chambers–Ganado, Rt. 63; Ganado–St. Michaels, Rt. 264	74	29	71	cribbed-log 86	plank 10	frame 81	cribbed-log 11	14	S.C.J.
Cedar Point–Gallup via Burnt Water, Rt. 66; Mentmore–Tse Bonito	67	25	75	cribbed-log 59	plank 24, leaning-log 12	frame 56	cribbed-log 12, palisaded 12, trailer 10	? (present)	R.F.
Chuska Mts. N of Wash. Pass & N of Cottonwood Pass (1972)	46	7	93	cribbed-log 100		stacked-log (most cribbed) 86	frame 6	7	S.C.J.
Chuska Mts. S of Washington Pass (1972)	50	34	66	cribbed-log 100		stacked-log (most cribbed) 64	frame 33	22	S.C.J.

Location	No.	%	%	dominant	%	nondominant	%	dominant	%	nondominant	%	No.	Source
Crownpoint–Navajo Church via Mariano Lake	126	36	64	cribbed-log	56	plank	42	frame	81	cribbed-log / stone	10 / 5	18	V.E.S.
Ramah–El Morro	21	24	76	cribbed-log	80	plank?	20	frame	69	stacked-log (most cribbed)	25	?	R.F.
Rt. 666 on Reservation	474	21	79	stacked-log (most cribbed)	44	plank / stone	36 / 18	frame	77	cribbed-log	16	5	V.E.S.
Fruitland area (1952)	[67]	[21]	[79]	stone	?	stacked-log / vertical-post	? / ?	frame	[32]	stone / cribbed-log / adobe-brick / palisaded	[30] / [13] / [11] / [9]	[9]	Tremblay et al. 1954
Colo. line-Shiprock; Shiprock-Farmington, Rts. 666, 550	12	73	27	plank	37	stone / stacked-log	25 / 25	frame	100			1	V.E.S., S.C.J.
San Juan Basin, Rts. 9, 57; NE of Standing Rock	250	26	74	stone	39	plank / cribbed-log	28 / 25	frame	53	stone	31	10	V.E.S.
Lower Chaco River (1974)	294	66	34	stone	98			stone	79	frame	13	?	Reher 1977
Cañoncito Reserve	64	11	89	stone	86	plank	14	frame	49	stone / adobe-brick / cinder-block	21 / 18 / 6	7	S.C.J., V.E.S.
Alamo Reserve (1974)	97	10	90	stone	55	plank / corbeled-log / adobe-brick	27 / 9 / 9	frame	39	adobe-brick / trailer / cinder-block / stone	26 / 21 / 7 / 6	0	S.C.J.
TOTAL & AVERAGES	5,222	31	69	dominant	61	nondominant	39	dominant	75	nondominant	25	ca. 14	

NOTES TO THE CHAPTERS

CHAPTER 1

1. Principal sources for this section are: Underhill 1956; Young 1958, 1961; Reeve 1959, 1960; Hester 1962; Fonaroff 1963; Shepardson 1963; Christian 1965; Jett 1967: 26–32; Brugge 1964a, 1972a, 1972b; Adams and Ruffing 1977. Additional references for specific facts are included in the text.

2. For phase differentiation in the Canyon del Muerto area during the Reservation Period, see James 1976: 102–06.

CHAPTER 2

1. Also *ch'oh, chaa'oh,* and *chahash'oh.*

2. Eaton 1854: 217, Letterman 1856: 289; Malcolm 1939: 11; Keur 1941: 35–36; Vivian 1960; Hester and Shiner 1963: 27, 41–45, 53–59, 61, 65–69; Frisbie 1968: 28; denied by Stephen 1890.

3. The (more or less) circular floor plan is said to symbolize the sun and moon, and to be a result of imitating the homes of other creatures, especially of the Ant People, who taught First Man and First Woman to build in the shape of the ant hill (Newcomb 1940a: 23–24; 1967: 198; Loh 1971: 4).

4. Shufeldt (1892: 279), however, implies the use of downed timber at Ft. Wingate, New Mexico, in the 1880s, and informants at Ramah and at Red Rock, Arizona, stated that in pre-steel-ax days, dead wood was used (Kluckhohn et al. 1971: 144). Coolidge and Coolidge (1930: 81) were also informed that branches from fallen trees were used before steel axes became available. Correll (personal communication, 1971) noted disagreement in this regard among informants, some of whom consider sound fallen timbers preferable to old living trees since the former are free from tabus such as the possibility of a bear having rubbed against the tree.

5. Among the Northern Athapaskans linguistically most closely related to the Navajo, women build the dwelling, but among many other groups, men do. Chiricahua and Western Apache women do the building, but, among other Apacheans, both sexes participate. Puebloan men tend to do most of the building (Driver and Massey 1957: 315; Opler 1965: 22–23).

6. Woods (1952: 6), in a popular article, quoted a Navajo as saying that during times of war Navajos oriented their structures toward the west. We have no other confirmation, however, and Hill (1936: 12) described windbreaks used by war parties as having their entries toward the east.

7. Gerald 1958: 5, 8; Schaeffer 1958: 17; Tuohy 1960: 28; Baldwin 1965: 71; Vivian 1970: 126–27; Opler 1965: 22–23.

8. Keur 1941: 79–80; Farmer 1942: 68; Vivian 1960: 21, 32; Carlson 1965: 9; Hester and Shiner 1963: 9; Brugge 1976: 43–44.

9. Matthews 1897: 142; Coolidge and Coolidge 1930: 82; Sapir and Hoijer 1942: 425; Haile 1937: 6; 1950: 75; 1951: 105; Kluckhohn et al. 1971: 157.

10. Letterman (1856: 289) mentioned both blankets and sheepskins, and Shufeldt (1892: 280) wrote that "a blanket is invariably hung as a door"; Mindeleff (1898: 516) also mentioned the blanket as the usual entry cover. Navajo Max Hanley recalled that ca. 1902 only blankets were used in the Four Cor-

ners area (Johnson 1977: 18). Schmedding (1974: 163), drawing on experience ending in 1923, stated that a blanket was usual. This was also implied by Coolidge and Coolidge (1931: 78).

Milton S. Snow photographs taken in 1935–36, mostly between Marsh Pass and Teec Nos Pos, Arizona, show primarily doors but also a fair percentage of blankets. According to Sullivan (1938: 44), wooden doors were usual but blankets or sheepskins were sometimes used. Haile (1937: 36) and Luomala (1938: 83) mentioned the blanket as being the normal doorway covering, and Haile (1942: 40), Ickes (1933: 58), and Page (1937b: 49) wrote that blankets were used on some doorways, doors on others. Some areas, closer to centers of Anglo influence, adopted doors earlier; at Crystal, New Mexico, in 1929, doors seem to have been usual (Sapir and Hoijer 1942: 425), and Smith (1933: 60), whose observations were probably largely near U.S. Highway 66, implied that doors were normally used on hogans. Landgraf (1954: 47) indicated that plank doors with padlocks were usual in the Ramah, New Mexico, area in 1941. Observations of Stephen Jett indicated the prevalence of doors in the late 1950s.

11. Keur (1941: 29) mentioned a "peephole" in an eighteenth-century stone hogan, but this was not a true window. Ickes (1933: 58) wrote that hogans had no windows. Informants indicated to David Brugge that the first hogan to have windows in the Cornfields, Arizona, area was built between 1910 and 1920. Page (1937b: 49) stated that "Most hogans do not have windows. However, a few stone hogans [sic], usually of the square or rectangular shape, have small glass windows in frames." Writing in 1939, Lockett (1952: 140; Jones et al. 1939: 84) noted that school programs encouraged the installation of windows and wooden or packed clay floors for health reasons. No hogans in the Ramah area had windows in 1941 (Kluckhohn et al. 1971: 148). Vogt (1951: 110), who worked at Ramah, noted that by 1949 he had observed only one hogan with windows, near Thoreau, New Mexico. There is, however a 1937 record of a hogan with windows at Ramah. Hannum (1958: 109) thought that a hogan with a window at Wide Ruins, Arizona, was worthy of note in the mid-1940s. Some hogans with windows are documented in the 1940s by Boyce (1974: 64, 98).

If a broken window is left unrepaired, some believe, ghosts and other bad things may enter (Bulow 1972: 47).

12. Hester 1962: 47; Hester and Shiner 1963: 12; Keur 1941: 31–32; Vivian 1960: 21, 37; Crampton 1960: 28; James 1976: 4, 26, 29; Newcomb 1966: 87.

13. Goddard 1909–11: 14491; Page 1937b: plate 2; Haile 1942: 51; Leighton and Leighton 1944: 15;

Landgraf 1954: 47; Newcomb 1966: 23; Aberle 1966: Fig. 4.

14. Brugge 1968a: 18–19; 1972b: 9; Vivian 1960: 105–6; James 1976; Yost 1958: 112; Haile 1937: 6; 1952: 5; Reher 1977: 49–52.

15. See also Mindeleff 1898: 516–17, plate 90; Curtis 1907: 76; Haile 1937: 6; 1952: 5; Rapoport 1969b: 75. According to Sprague (1967: 79), sitting opposite the entry "let the warrior husband observe entering visitors and gave him time to reach his weapons if the callers were enemies."

16. See also Haile 1937: 7; 1942: 44; 1952: 5; Leighton and Leighton 1944: 94; Anonymous 1968a; Kluckhohn et al. 1971.

17. Although it might be supposed that the word *kin* derives from some Utaztecan word for house— e.g., *ki* (Hopi, Pima), *kan* (Numic; see also the Zuni *k'ia' kwin ne*)—the existence of Northern Athapaskan cognates—e.g., *kun* (Kutchin for "house"), *koon,* Ingalik for "house," *-kin* (Beaver and Chipewyan for "house")—suggests the word was not loaned (Osgood 1936: 48; 1940: 312; Goddard 1912: 105, 1917: 413). The Navajo *-ghan,* home, may be related. The word *kan,* "lean-to," exists in Western (?) Apache (James 1906: 18–19), and the terms *kongha* and *kozhán* are used by the Jicarilla Apache (Curtis 1907: 54). But note the Numic forms: *kahan* (Uinta Ute), *ka[h]n* (various), *ga[h]n* (Southern Paiute, some Shoshoni; Wheeler 1879: 434; Steward 1941: 334), and the Ouray Ute bark lodge, *mogho'gan* (Lowie 1924: 220). See also the Chipewyan *hoogha'* = he is building houses (Robert W. Young, personal communication).

18. Note, however, that "some [Anglo pioneer] builders preferred a site for their cabins facing east to get the benefit of the warmth of the morning sun at the front door.... [One Ohioan] wrote 'On building our cabin [in 1800] it was set to front north and south ... [with a] compass ... we had no idea of living in a home that did not stand square with the earth itself" (Weslager 1969: 13).

19. After any death, according to Chauncey Neboyia (1971). "The ghosts of the dead are greatly feared, except those of the very old and very young, and even in the case of these the absence of fear is largely verbal" (Dyk 1947: 186).

20. Documentation for these taboos is found in: Backus 1854: 213–14; Letterman 1856: 289; Bristol 1867: 357; Beadle 1873: 559; 1877: 276; John Menard, quoted in Yarrow 1881: 123; Dunn 1886: 218–19, 406; Wilson 1890: 116; Mindeleff 1898: 487; Hollister 1903: 71; James 1905: 648; Curtis 1907: 80–81; Franciscan Fathers 1910: 455–56; Ostermann 1917: 27; Haile 1917; Reagan 1919: 243; Coolidge and Coolidge 1930: 151, 298; Haile 1937: 8; Luomala 1938: 85; Hill 1938: 179; Sullivan 1938;

49; Newcomb 1940a: 21, 78; 1966: 64, 220; Sapir and Hoijer 1942: 431; Kluckhohn 1948; Landgraff 1954: 51; Correll 1965a: 29; Johnston 1972: 230; Werner 1972: 119; Schmedding 1974: 164; Ward and Brugge 1975: 31-33; Gumerman and Euler 1976: 15; James 1976: 54-55; Frisbie and McAllester 1978: 159-60, 332. According to Dyk's (1947: 60) informant, "We always have to move south, four days after a person dies." A tradition "explaining" the haunted hogan idea is given in Hannum (1958: 143-44; see also Hannum 1945: 131).

Keeping dogs or cats in a hogan during a storm is thought to attract lightning (Bulow 1972: 14). Kluckhohn et al. (1971: 332) reported that Ramah Navajos formerly hung large cattail-and-yucca mats in hogans, a round one to the west and a rectangular one to the east, "to scare the lightning so it will not hit your hogan or your sheep or your people." If an owl or a crow alights on a hogan, it must be killed or bad luck will ensue (Hill 1938: 178).

21. Opler 1974: 380; 1975: 189; for the Western Apache, see Lockwood 1938: 45; Gerald 1958: 10; Mails 1974: 181–82; for the Mescalero Apache, see Emerson 1973: 13.

22. Note that ghost fear, removal of the dying, and destruction or abandonment of death dwellings are also characteristic of Utes, Paiutes, and the Wind River Shoshoni (Stewart 1942: 312–13, 319; Lowie 1924: 279–80). Death-dwelling destruction is also practiced by the Pima, Maricopa, Yavapai, and Walapai (Drucker 1941: 147).

CHAPTER 3

1. A dwelling may, however, also serve simultaneously or successively as a place for storage, for ceremonies, for meetings, as a workshop, and for other purposes (Brugge 1968a: 18–19).

2. For an example, with bibliography, see Rickert 1967; see also Noble 1969, Kniffen 1939; 1965; Glassie 1968; Pillsbury and Kardos ca. 1971.

3. However, some writers have used the term "hogan" very loosely, applying it to any type of Navajo dwelling simply because it is Navajo. This does not conform to Navajo usage, although the term *hooghan* is sometimes applied to certain types of shades.

Hogans are sometimes termed "winter dwellings" in contrast to summer shades. However, hogans are also used in summer and may be built and used at summer camps.

4. One basic division in Navajo appears to be between "male" conical forked-pole hogans and "female" *yaadahaskání* hogans; Mindeleff (1898: xx; 1900: 234) wrote of a third category, *'iyada[ha]skání* or flat-roofed hogans, but neither Robert Young, William Morgan, nor ourselves has been able to interpret this alleged term. Nor is it clear how hogans with frame roofs fit into this scheme. Other classifications refer to the materials of the walls, the number of "legs" (vertical posts) that support the structure, and the number of sides a polygonal hogan has. *Yaadahaskání* are also called *yahatso,* "spacious below" (Haile 1942: 53).

CHAPTER 4

1. Dillon 1970: 68; Stephen 1890; 1893: 350; Mindeleff 1898: 494; Franciscan Fathers 1910: 335, Ostermann 1908: 864; 1917: 26; James 1905: 642; Landgraf 1954: 50; Kluckhohn *et al.* 1971: 157, 159–60; Downs 1972: 46; Hill 1938: 146, 148.

2. Legend describes hunters building a shelter consisting of four concentric bough circles as protection against attack by supernaturals; parallel brush walls led from the inner circle to the entry of the outer circle (Luckert 1975: 75–76). Whether any such structure was ever built outside of legend is doubtful.

3. Mindeleff 1898: 497–98, plate 87; Steece 1921: 418; Hayes 1964: 122; Spencer and Jett 1971: 166; Downs 1972: 104.

4. For descriptions, see Stephen 1890; 1893: 350; Mindeleff 1898: 496–99; 1900: 234; Hollister 1903: 65; Ostermann 1917: 25–26; Franciscan Fathers 1910: 334–36; Coolidge and Coolidge 1930: 81; Frisbie and McAllester 1978: 30.

5. Gillmor and Wetherill (1934: 73) referred to an extinct practice of building platforms of poles in tree tops for refuge from wolves. This sounds apocryphal.

6. A photo showing wall tents apparently thus erected at Grand Canyon, Arizona, in the 1880s appears in Hughes (1967: 67), and the tents used by archaeologists in the late 1930s at Awatobi, Arizona, were erected in this fashion (Smith 1952: Fig. 29). Navajo use of this erection technique dates back at least to the early 1930s (Chabot 1936: 9).

CHAPTER 5

1. A summary of the historical portions of this and the following two chapters was presented at the 1971 meetings of the Southwest Anthropological Association and the American Ethnological Society (Jett and Spencer 1971).

2. In the Emergence Myth, First Man built, "a [conical] Hogan of Willow plastered with Earth" at the place of Emergence. Eastern and western poles of big reed were set, upon which were leaned the southern and northern poles, of oak and mock orange, respectively; four layered tiers of willow twigs were then applied (Goddard 1933: 25, 133; Haile and Wheelwright 1949: 32–33; see also Sapir and Hoijer 1942: 109; Thomas et al. 1974: 21). For a mythic explanation of why Navajos build hogans instead of houses, see Fishler (1953: 34).

3. Callaway and Witherspoon (1968: 53–55) recorded another tradition, that conical and dome-roofed hogans were given to the first people simultaneously. Frank Mitchell indicated that the first hogans were: (1) the flat-roofed leaning-log type, and (2) the conical forked-pole type. (Frisbie and McAllester 1971: 171). Coolidge and Coolidge (1931: 78) reported that the first hogan, that of the Hogan Songs, was a leaning-log hogan built in the Underworld. The conical hogan was first built for a Blessingway after the slaying of the Monsters of this world.

4. Driver and Massey 1957: 295, 299; Birket-Smith 1930: 46; Osgood 1936: 54; 1940: 326; Vanstone 1974: 34, 37; Honigmann 1954: 59, 61, 149.

5. For tree-ring dates and discussion, see Hester 1962; Jett 1964: 293–95; Stokes and Smiley 1963, 1964, 1966, 1969. For additional ideas on Navajo entry into the Southwest, see Gunnerson 1956 and Aschmann 1970.

6. Tronosco (orig. 1788; quoted in Worcester 1947: 220); Gregg (1954 [orig. 1844]: 198-99); McNitt (1964: [orig. Simpson 1849]; 73, 95); Simpson (1952: 13); Schoolcraft (1853: plate 17); Backus (1854: 213); Letterman (1956: 289); Cremony (1969 [orig. 1868]: 306); Lange and Riley 1970 [orig. 1883]: 60; Dunn (1886: 217); Matthews (1887: 418, plates 10, 11); Riordan 1890: 377; Garland 1930 [of 1895]: 295; Powell (1895: 53). Cremony wrote that "Long, slender and supple poles are then hooped closely about the stakes . . ." of the framework. This is not verified by any other source, and presumably reflects a gratuitous assumption based on Cremony's familiarity with this practice among the Apache. Robinson (1848: 33) described stone hogans, and Bourke (1936 [orig. 1870s]: 87, 236) mentioned both conical forked pole and stone hogans.

7. David M. Brugge (personal communication) suggested, however, that Western Apache use of forked poles may stem from contacts with the Navajo during the earlier eighteenth century, although he acknowledged that the trait's absence among other Apache groups may represent loss.

Some Southern Paiutes are said to have used three interlocking forked poles as a foundation for conical and half-conical wickiups, which were covered with poles and grass, brush, or bark. Although it is possible that this usage existed among the Paiute prior to contact with Athapaskans, there are indications that it spread from the Navajo to the Southern Paiute: (1) the Kaiparowits Paiute more distant from the Navajo seem not to have used forked poles but instead built dwellings using a foundation of four lashed unforked poles; the Southern Ute also used four-pole frameworks, although land-claims informants indicated that some Utes built three-pole frameworks in the Mancos Creek Area, in imitation of Navajo practice; (2) the Southern Paiutes said to have used three forked poles (Kaibab, San Juan) were adjacent to the Navajo, and a San Juan informant stated that the practice was recent; (3) the San Juan and the Kaiparowits stated that their sweathouses were of Navajo origin (Kelly 1964: 57–58; 158, 172–83); (4) the San Juan Paiute have in various other ways become strongly "Navajoized." Of the Kaibab, Steward (1939: 5) wrote, on the basis of photographs, that their conical and semiconical dwellings were erected "upon interlocking poles," but the photos seem to show only, in a few cases, one forked pole into whose crotch some of the other, unforked, poles are leaned. Although Drucker (1941:105) lists the Shivwits band, west of the Kaibab, as having used "two interlocked forks," photographs indicate one forked pole at the front, to support the other unforked poles (Fowler and Fowler 1971: 58). Ellis (1974: 43) contended that the Shoshoni used interlocking forked-pole foundations, but evidence for this is ambiguous. Steward (1941: 233, 334) and Stewart (1941: 378, 1942: 257) reported the Death Valley Shoshoni using two foundation poles, one forked; they indicated tripod-foundation dwellings using interlocked forked poles among neighboring Northern Paiute groups, the Hamilton, Nevada, Shoshoni, and Southern Paiutes in the Henry Mountains, Utah; some other Shoshoni, Southern Paiute, and Ute groups are listed as using forked poles with four-pole foundations. These attributions are based upon informants' statements, and it may be that typically only one foundation pole had a fork.

Cushing (1965: 51) reported in 1882 that the Havasupai used a "conical, half-underground structure, made by supporting three forks against one another, laying lesser poles around these in a circle, and covering the whole with sticks, flags, grasses, and dirt, extending the front out in the shape of a veranda. . . ." Spier (1928: 173–74, 176, 181; see also, Hoover 1929: 271,275) described a conical, earth-covered structure on a four-forked-pole foundation; two poles were heavier than the other two. Additional poles were leaned on (and sometimes tied to) the forks, leaving an entry and, often, a smoke hole. Horizontal poles were tied around the outside; the outside was then covered with tiers of boughs or weeds. The usual entry was extended, and a blanket door was usual. The exterior was often partially or wholly earth-covered. A typical example of such a structure was 4.6 X 4 meters (15.1 X 13.1 ft) in diameter, with the entry oriented toward the sunrise. This dwelling type appears to represent Navajo and, possibly, Western Apache influence on an older four-lashed-pole conical dwelling form.

Gifford (1940: 108) reported that the Walpi Hopi have a "conical [field] hut like the Navaho hogan . . . 'old Hopi type, not recently from Navaho.' All details of Navaho hogan. . . ." We assume this structure is derivative.

Utes are known occasionally to have constructed hogans, presumably under Navajo influence (e.g., Lowie 1924: 220), and the San Juan Paiute also adopted the practice from the Navajo (Stewart 1942: 257).

8. Rather than building conical dwellings, the more usual Western Apache practice is to bind several curved poles together to form a bowed conical framework (Opler 1936a: 205; Lockwood 1938: 45; Gerald 1958; Schaeffer 1958; Tuohy 1960; Baldwin 1965: 70–71); this may represent influence from Caddoans of the southern Plains, although hide-covered semidomical dwellings of Athapaskans of the northern Alaska-Yukon borderlands have points in common as well (Vanstone 1974: 33). Cremony (1969, originally 1868: 306) attributed the Navajo's use of earth covering to the climate being colder in the Navajo Country than in Apache areas.

9. "The lack of descriptive reports on Apache wikiups probably reflects not only the perishable nature of the structures, but a lack of Apache archaeology, which in turn may be partially explained by the impermanent nature of Apache camps" (Vivian 1970: 129; see, too, Jett 1964: 294).

10. Compare the flagstone floor and peripheral stone bench in the cribbed-log hogan the Armers had built for themselves in the early 1930s (Armer 1935: 109).

11. Haile 1942: 43; 1952: 5; 1951: 91; Keur 1941: 21; 1944: 76; Vivian 1960: 21; Amsden 1939: 127; James 1976: 32.

12. Vivian 1960: 14–15; McGregor 1965: 441;

Palmer 1929: 47; Keur 1941: 21, 27, 30; James 1976: 32–33. Compare rings of piled stone in the San Carlos Apache country (Gerald 1958), and "tipi rings" attributed to Jicarilla and Faraon Apaches in northeastern New Mexico (Gunnerson 1961: 30–35; Gunnerson and Gunnerson 1970: 3) and found elsewhere in the Plains and Rocky Mountains.

13. Stephen 1890; Mindeleff 1900: 233–44; Ostermann 1917: plate; Verplank 1934: 46; Perceval and Lockett 1962: 16; Thomas et al. 1974: 21.

14. See also Matthews 1887: 418; Stephen 1890; Shufeldt, 1892: 279–80; Ostermann 1917: 20–22, 26; Haile 1937: 1; 1942: 42–45; 1952: 3; Brewer 1936; Luomala 1938: 83–84; Gifford 1940: 107; Vivian 1960: 8–23; Taylor 1965; Kluckhohn et al. 1971: 144, 150; James 1976).

15. Littell 1967–4: 813; Vivian 1960: 9; Keur 1941: 28; Stephen 1890; Letterman 1856: 289; Shufeldt 1892: 279; Sullivan 1938: 44. Diameters given for modern Western Apache wikiups are: 7.9 feet (2.4 m) for a temporary structure (Vivian 1970); 12 feet (3.7 m; Curtis 1907: 131); 10.5 feet (3.2 m), 13.4 feet (4.1 m; Gerald 1958); ca. 12 to 25 feet (3.7 to 8.6 m), averaging 15 to 18 feet (4.6 to 5.5 m; Opler 1973: 58–61); and ca. 12 to 15 feet (3.7 to 4.5 m; Schaeffer 1958: 19).

16. Earth-covered double lean-tos among the Havasupai may reflect Navajo influence (Spier 1928: 175–76).

17. Mindeleff 1898: 494–99; 1900: 234; Franciscan Fathers 1910: 335 – 36; Kluckhohn et al. 1971: 152; Keur 1941: 37.

18. Terms applied in the literature include "ceremonial hogan," "Yeibichai hogan," and "medicine lodge"; Navajo designations include *hatáál biniiyé hooghan* = for-sing [ceremonial] hogan, *hooghan bii' hataal* = sing-inside hogan, *hooghan bii' nahaghái i* = ceremonial-performed-inside hogan. For references, see: Stevenson 1891: 237; Mindeleff 1898: 513–14; Mindeleff 1900: 234; Matthews 1902: 49–50; Franciscan Fathers 1910: 333, 380; Haile 1942: 53; Haile 1952; Schmedding 1974: 165; Frisbie and McAllester 1978: 30.

Although leaning-log structures seem to have been common for chantways, especially Mountain-top Way, Barthelmess in 1883 observed a Mountaintop Way "ceremonial lodge" about 20 feet (6.10 m) in diameter with "a pointed roof" (Frink and Barthelmess 1965: 41). In one Navajo legend, a hogan "of the pointed type used in the Night Chant, and much larger than the first round one" was built; the former type was also used for Eagle Catching-way (Newcomb 1940b: 70–71).

19. Powell (1895: 53) pictured a conical forked-pole hogan whose extended entryway exhibits palisading in its sides. An 1882(?) Wittick photo shows

rudimentary palisading in the slightly extended entry of a cribbed-log hogan.

20. Hegemann 1963: 284–85; Hoover 1931: 443, Pospíšil 1932: 63; Newcomb 1934: 7; Seton 1962: 32.

21. See also Wilson 1890: 114; Stevenson 1891: 237; Franciscan Fathers 1910: 332–33; Corbett 1940: 104–05; Coolidge and Coolidge 1930: 83; Kluckhohn et al. 1971: 150, 151–52.

22. For ritual purposes, the stringers in the cardinal directions are equivalent to the poles of the conical forked-pole framework.

23. Full analysis of the vast body of Land Claim information has not been attempted; it is hoped that someone will undertake one eventually. Jett made limited samplings of these records, particularly as regards stacked-log hogans. Data relevant to the dating of corbeled-log hogans are as follows: Navajo Land Claim (n.d.b.), vol. 9, Cebolleta Mesa, N.M., site F, corbeled-log work resting on a stone foundation built against a cliff, dating to about the 1730s; vol. 10, Middle [Rio] Puerco, N.M., site W, two corbeled-log superstructures on low stone walls, last quarter of the eighteenth century (see also sites F and DD); vol. 12, Alamo Salado Alamocito Creek, N.M., site BB, hogan from end of the eighteenth century; vol. 7, Upper [Canyon] Largo, N.M., corbeled-log hogan of probably eighteenth century date. Ellis (1974: 258) cited a hogan from site D, Pitch Paint (J) group, near the Hopi Country, as dating from ca. 1726. An 1823 specimen south of Quemado, N.M., was pictured in Anonymous 1970f. See also, Hester 1962: 63–65; James 1976: 46.

24. An intriguing (and so far unique) ancient dwelling from a site on the Fraser Plateau of British Columbia exhibited remains of logs disposed in a pattern suggesting the possibility of corbeled-log construction, especially since no postholes were found. Ethnic attribution is not possible, although it lies within historic Chilcotin Athapaskan territory. The structure dates from ca. A.D. 700 (Wilmeth 1978: 73–74, 151).

25. Corbeled-log tombs built by ancient Bell Beaker people in the Netherlands (Holwerda 1909, 1912) may represent this kind of substitution of logs for stones in making corbeled structures. This is the only other instance of corbeled-log construction known to us anywhere.

26. Apparent traditional use of crude cribbing is also recorded for Beaver fish traps (Goddard 1916: plate 8) and for Kutchin fireplaces (Osgood 1936: 53).

27. Navajo Land Claim (n.d.b.), vol. 9, Cebolleta Mesa, N.M., site F, two five-sided hogans firmly dated at ca. 1845; vol. 12, Alamo Salado, Alamocito Creek, N.M., site W, hogan with four walls plus an

entry, dated at about 1848. See also Littell (1967-4: 748).

28. See also, Hollister 1903: 69; Franciscan Fathers 1910: 333–34; Ostermann 1917: 22; Roberts 1951: 40, Fig. 1; Thomas, Johnson, and Yazzie 1974: 22–23.

29. "The eight-sided house is a symbol of earth itself, with its eight directions. Its center added to the eight makes the mystic nine so prevalent in Navaho ceremonies" (Armer 1935: 107). In hexagonal hogans, the long axes usually run north-south.

30. One Navajo gave the following formula for hogans of this type: normally, 40 logs—8 sides 5 logs tall, exclusive of the roof; for large hogans, 60 logs (Sapir and Hoijer 1942: 423). Newcomb (1966: 65) mentioned a hexagonal hogan 10 logs high. Two hogans studied in 1971 in Canyon de Chelly had 6 and 8 walls alternately 9 and 10, and 10 and 11 logs high, respectively. Another hogan (Fig. 5.38), under construction in 1971 just north of Canyon de Chelly, was 10-sided; 234 logs of various lengths, some used, had been gathered for walls and roof, plus about 91 blocks of sandstone for the foundation and a pile of gravelly sand (for mortar?). The logs were box-cut, the lowest ones being set on stone blocks, which were set in a trench on the up-slope side. The walls appeared to be intended to be about 12 logs high. The structure's diameter was about 19 feet (5.79 m); interior wall lengths ranged from about 4.7 feet (1.43 m) to 11.7 feet (3.57 m) in the case of the wall with the doorway. An example described by Roberts (1951: 40) as relatively small was 7 logs high and about 17.9 feet (5.43 m) in diameter, with walls ranging from 8 feet 9 inches to 9 feet (2.06 to 2.74 m) long. The smoke hole of the corbeled-log roof was 10 feet 10 inches (3.3 m) from the floor. The hogan built by the Armers (1935: 108–11), with Navajo help, was 11 logs high and 24 feet (7.32 m) across; its external chinking was of cement, and stucco held on by wire lath covered the exterior; it had a stone floor and bench.

31. A Rock Point, Arizona, hogan builder said octagonal hogans are about 20 feet (6.10 m) in diameter (Thomas et al. 1974: 22–23). The following additional diameters have been recorded for modern examples: 11 feet (3.35 m; Kluckhohn et al. 1971: 146); 16 feet (4.88 m; Farmer 1942: 68); 25 feet (7.32 m); 4.0 × 4.4 meters (13.1 × 14.4 ft), 5.1 × 5.9 meters (16.7 × 19.4 ft), 6 meters (19.7 ft; James 1976: 48, 50, 55).

32. Jett has seen a flat, brush roof on such a structure. Whether this was a temporary expedient, or whether the dwelling should be classed as a shade, was not determined.

33. Compare the use of "wire lath" to hold in the

"plaster and cement" chinking of the cribbed-log hogan the Armers had built in the early 1930s.

34. The Rabal document of 1744 mentions masonry, but clearly with reference to pueblitos (Hill 1940). For additional references to masonry, see Chapter 7.

35. There seems no reason to accept as accurate Bourke's (1936: 87) mid-nineteenth-century description of domical corbeled-stone hogans; this may represent a confusion between stone hogans, corbeled-log hogans, corbeled-log roofs, and cor-

beled-stone ovens. (But see "Models," chapter 11).

36. Malcolm 1939: 6; Keur 1941: 24–27; Farmer 1947: 18; Vivian 1960: 29; Bannister 1965: 153–54; Brugge 1976: 45; Reher 1977: 50–51; Hester and Shiner 1963: 43–45, 59, 61.

37. Keur 1941: 29; Vivian 1960: 25, 30, 32, 47; Malcolm 1939: 7, plate I; Hollister 1903: 74; Prudden 1906: plate opposite p. 30.

38. Page 1937b; Malcolm 1939: 5–11; Farmer 1942; Vivian 1960: 25–43; Bannister 1965; Kluckhohn et.al. 1971: 152 – 53.

CHAPTER 6

1. Charlotte J. Frisbie (personal communication, 1971) wrote, "There is evidence for using hogans for Peyote ceremonials as well as for replacing Blessingway (in the form of House Blessing Cere-

monial) with a Peyote meeting, which blesses the hogan." House Blessing Ceremonials are still common as well.

CHAPTER 7

1. For additional history of the details of houses, see Chapter 3.

2. Double box-notching was said by Weslager (1969: 339–40) to be generally rare in the United States but "a prevailing method in northern New Mexico."

3. Hoover (1931: 436) wrote that around Lukachukai, Arizona, where alfalfa was raised commercially, "their greater prosperity is reflected in their houses."

4. Krutz (1974: 116–17) listed the following Bureau of Indian Affairs–Department of Housing and Urban Development joint-financed housing programs available to Arizona tribal members: Mutual Self-Help Program, in which the participant contributes a minimum of 10 percent "sweat equity" (labor), with the Housing Assistance Administration contributing the rest of the construction capital, with repayment based on income level (repayment plus utilities not to exceed 25 percent of gross income); Low Rent and Turnkey programs, involving HAA-built and contractor-built houses, respectively.

5. See Kidder 1920; Van Valkenburgh 1938b; Keur 1941, 1944; Farmer 1942, 1947: 13, 18; Vivian 1960; Dittert et al., 1961; Hester and Shiner 1963; Carlson 1965; Bannister 1965; Brugge 1972b; Wilson and Warren 1974; Brugge 1976: 42–44; Adams 1976; Reher 1977: 52, 54–55.

6. Because these structures appear to be essen-

tially Puebloan in origin, they are not described in detail herein. Note that Northern Athapaskans also used notched-log ladders.

7. The earliest firm date is 1694 (Wilson and Warren 1974: 14).

8. (Cf. Anonymous 1933: 31; Boke 1934; Tisinger 1935; Benton 1936; Kluckhohn et al. 1971: 150). Chauncey Neboyia informed us that his father became a mason through participating in the building of the Chinle boarding school (1910) and later used these skills not only in ruin stabilization but also in constructing a fine, cut-stone hogan. Neboyia was also frequently employed as a mason on ruin stabilization projects prior to 1979. At a schoolhouse project at Burnham, New Mexico, "Practically every adult Indian of this community has helped construct these buildings (Tisinger 1935: 32). During the 1920s, Joe Schmedding (1974: 348) employed Navajos as quarrymen and masons in building Low Mountain Trading Post.

9. An "adobe house" is attributed to Monster Slayer in the legend of the Eagle-Catchingway; houses of jet, abalone, etc., are also mentioned (Newcomb 1940b: 54).

10. Jerrold E. Levy (personal communication, 1978) has observed flat-roofed stone houses in the Kaibito-Cow Springs, Arizona, area built for Navajos by Hopis hired for the purpose sometime between 1920 and 1936. One had a large portico.

CHAPTER 8

1. Roofs are *bikáa'gi, bikáá'déé'* (= on or from its top), modified by *na'nízhoozhí[gíí]* (=[long, ridged objects] lie parallel across) for beam roofs. For cribbed- and corbeled-log roofs there is *hooghan (kin) bighą́ą́' tsin daastł'inígíí* (=logs piled up

on hogan's [house's] top), or *bikáá' dah 'az'ą́* (=roundish thing sits on top). One may also speak of *hooghan bikáá'* or *bighą́ą́'[déé']* (=[from] hogan's [exterior] surface or top). "Ceiling is *wódahdéé' sikaadí* = it spreads up above.

CHAPTER 9

1. It is possible that this represents not only differences in degree of acculturation but also differences in the need to protect corralled animals from coyotes.

2. Undated Simeon Schwemberger photographs of about 1905 show probably Navajo stake-and-rider, stake-and-rail, and wire-net fences, apparently in the St. Michaels, Arizona, area (Museum of Northern Arizona archives). Charles F. Lummis photographs of 1906 show a stake-and-rider fence near Ft. Defiance and a barbed-wire fence in Canyon del Muerto (Southwest Museum Archives). Dyk's (1947: 99, 142) informant referred to using wire for fencing about 1905 and 1909 in the Bluff, Utah, area. Fraser (1919: 210a) shows stake-and-rider and post-and-wire fences, and Hegemann (1963: 212) illustrated a stake-and-rider fence north of Klagetoh in 1928. Ripgut and wire fences were not uncommon in the northern Arizona portion of the Reservation in 1935, as shown in Snow photographs.

3. Taken mainly from Hill 1938: 23, 29–39; also Roberts 1951: 29, 33; Wyatt 1941: 6; Sasaki 1966: 18–33; Gifford 1940: 16–18; 100–02; Johnston 1972: 173; and personal observations.

4. Downs 1965: 1395; Franciscan Fathers 1910: 63; Roberts 1951; 18, 29, 34–35; Johnston 1972: 230; Neely and Olson 1977: 67.

5. Anonymous 1933: 31; Hall 1934; Boke 1934; Wathen 1934; Neuffer 1935; Musgrave 1937; Landgraf 1954: 51.

6. Hill 1938: 98, 148–50, 168–69, 172–73; Sapir and Hoijer 1942: 317–27; Gifford 1940: 7, 85; Franciscan Fathers 1910: 475; Hester 1962: 37; Kluckhohn et al. 1971: 8–9. For a description of a Paiute trap for Bighorn Sheep near Navajo Mountain, see Wetherill 1954. Some known locations of presumed Navajo traps are also given. For other locations, see Hill 1938: 96.

7. Morice 1910: 118–24; Curtis 1928: 13–14, 95–96; Goddard 1916: 214; Birket-Smith 1930: 21–22; Osgood 1936: 25, 33–34; Cooper 1938; Clark 1974: 160–62; Honigmann 1954: 34–35, 37, 41–42, 44, 152.

CHAPTER 10

1. For documentation and descriptions of use, see: Hill 1938: 173–74; Bailey 1940: 285; Steggerda and Eckhardt 1941: 217, 219–20; Wyman and Bailey 1943: 6–7; Gifford 1940: 15, 98; Dyk 1947: 56, 91; Wetherill 1946: 39; Kluckhohn et al. 1971: 130–33; Hester and Shiner 1963: 46; Keur 1941: 32; Reichard 1939: xxiii, 23, 41, 53; Johnson 1977: 62; Dittert et al. 1961: 237–38.

2. Mindeleff (1891: 163–64) did not mention ovens of this type among the Hopi, and Curtis (1922: 21, 44) wrote that "Both ovens and stoves are very recent" at Hopi and that "since about 1910 hemispherical outdoor ovens have become quite common." However, Bourke (1884: 253) wrote that in 1881, "Ovens, shaped like bee-hives, are to be found in every street, and also upon the roofs," and an illustration of Hano, Arizona, in Powell (1972: 1; orig. 1875) appears to show an oven.

3. Except at Zuni, Laguna, and Acoma, the equivalent upper hole in Hispano and Puebloan ovens is usually smaller and somewhat below the apex.

4. Walker 1964: 86; Dillon 1970: 70; Bailey 1940: 283, 285; Dyk 1947: plate 3; Newcomb 1966: plate opposite pp. 103, 198; Gilpin 1968: 52; Boyce 1974: 112; One informant stated that ovens were first used to bake green maize and, more recently, for bread (Kluckhohn et al. 1971: 133). However, the name "bread's home" seems to indicate otherwise. Chauncey Neboyia (personal communication) denied use of the oven for maize. Hispanos made bread, parched and roasted corn, and dried staples in beehive ovens (Boyd 1974: 15–17).

5. The only other relatively unequivocal references or photographs not already cited which we have encountered are: James 1913: 217 (1898 photo of an apparent oven inside a ramada); Franciscan Fathers 1910: 218; Anonymous 1936; Steggerda and Eckardt 1941: 219; Farmer 1942: 71; Correll 1965a: 31; Mitchell and Allen 1967: 30, 96; Bateman 1970: 11; and Huse et al. 1978: 108–09. In 1926, Forrest (1970: 144) noted what he supposed was a masonry sweat lodge. This was presumably an oven; note, however, a legendary sweathouse built of stones by Hogan God (Curtis 1907: 104; see also Mindeleff 1966: 333).

CHAPTER 11

1. This description is derived mainly from Stevenson 1891: 239–40; Stephen 1893: 361; Mindeleff 1898: 499–500; Matthews 1902: 50–53, plates 1, 2; Curtis 1907: 117–18; Franciscan Fathers 1910: 340–43; Ostermann 1917: 28; Coolidge and Coolidge 1930: 78; Page 1937a; Bailey 1941; Leighton and Leighton 1941b; Hurt 1942: 91; Olson and Wasley 1956: 328, 258-60; Bohrer 1964; Callaway and Witherspoon 1968: 58; Kluckhohn et al. 1971: 317–28.

2. Van Valkenburgh 1945: 6; Keur 1941: 37–38; 1944: 20; Vivian 1960: 101; Kluckhohn et al. 1971: 317–18; Aaland 1978: 148–53.

3. Although Morice (1909: 593) attributed the sweathouse to all Athapaskans, and Driver and Massey indicate the presence of sweatbathing among both the Sarsi and the Chipewyan, Curtis (1928: 25) stated that the latter had no sweathouse, though the former did (p. 101). For the Kutchin, see Osgood (1936: 52, 55). For a mythic account of the first Navajo sweathouse, see Fishler (1953: 35).

4. Since at least the 1870s, the Havasupai have covered their sweatlodges with earth (Cushing 1965: 51); previously, blankets and buffalo hides were the usual covering. The hot rocks are placed just south of the entry, which is oriented toward the east. The sweathouse is believed to have been introduced by the Southern Paiute or the Navajo (Spier 1928: 336; Smithson and Euler 1964: 15). Earth-covered sudatories, apparently of fairly recent origin, have also been recorded for the Cocopah, the Yavapai (Drucker 1941: 106, 176), the Southern Ute, and the San Juan Paiute (Stewart 1942: 259). Zuni use of the Navajo-style sweathouse was thought by Gifford (1940: 110) to represent a diffusion, although this was denied by informants.

5. Leighton and Leighton 1941a: 273; Leighton and Kluckhohn 1948: 61, 63; Hannum 1958: 159; Brown 1970: 6; Kluckhohn et al., 1971: 402–03; Reher 1977: 62, 68).

CHAPTER 12

1. Keur 1941: 39–40; Roberts 1951: 54–55; Riley 1954: 51; Crampton 1960: 21–34, 42–44; Adams et al. 1961: 23; Kluckhohn et al. 1971: 105, 162; James 1976: 56–60.

2. Van Valkenburgh 1940a; Watson 1964: 22; McSparron 1950; Wyatt 1941: 39; Downs 1972: 100.

3. Bristol 1867: 357; Yarrow 1881: 123; Dunn 1886: 219; Franciscan Fathers 1910: 453; Bourke 1936: 219; Marmon 1894: 159; Mindeleff 1897: 167; Hill 1936: 16; Dyk 1947: 60: Leighton and Kluckhohn 1948: 92; De Harport 1959: 1597; Ward and Brugge 1975; Reichard 1939: 124.

4. Franciscan Fathers 1910: 454; Haile 1917: 30–31; Sapir and Hoijer 1942: 431; Roberts 1951: 75; Dyk 1947: 61, 168; Young 1961: 529–31; Downs 1972: 109; Ward 1978.

5. Ward and Brugge 1975: 35; Ward 1975, 1978; Griffen 1978, 1979; Shepardson 1978; Frisbie and McAllester 1978: 335; Reichard 1939: 35–36.

6. Bailey 1950: 70–71, 91; Young 1961: 530; Woods 1952; Ward and Brugge 1974: 33; Franciscan Fathers 1910: 451; Frisbie and McAllester 1978: 41; Shepardson 1978: 385–86).

CHAPTER 13

1. A summary of the first part of this chapter was presented at the 1972 meetings of the Association of Pacific Coast Geographers (Jett 1973).

2. See also, Schroeder 1963; Brugge 1972a, 1972b; Ellis 1974; Adams 1976.

3. Such hogans are sometimes referred to as "earth" hogans; in Navajo, the category *łeezh (bis) 'ahidiitł'in[go] hooghan,* "soil-(clay-) stacked-against-one-another hogan," exists (Franciscan Fathers 1910: 337).

4. The testimony of Chauncey Neboyia, as well as personal observations of ruined specimens, indicates that the leaning-log hogan was once a common type in the Canyon de Chelly system. Cribbed-log hogans have now nearly completely replaced it.

5. This despite a statement by Long Mustache of Klagetoh that the type originated at, and diffused from, Navajo Mountain during the nineteenth century, as a defensive dwelling (Coolidge and Coolidge 1931: 82).

CHAPTER 14

1. Note the consistency with Navajo pragmatism and individualism of the Navajo's acceptance of individual-focused nine-day curing ceremonials but rejection of the community-oriented rainmaking kachina cult.

BIBLIOGRAPHY

Aaland, Mikkel. 1978. *Sweat.* Santa Barbara: Capra Press.

Abel, Annie Heloise. 1916. The Journal of John Greiner, 1852. *Old Santa Fe* 3(11): 199–243.

Aberle, David F. 1966. *The Peyote Religion Among the Navaho.* Viking Fund Publications in Anthropology 42.

Abert, James W. 1962. *Report of Lieut. J. W. Abert of His Examination of New Mexico in the Years, 1846–47.* Albuquerque: Horn & Wallace.

Adair, John. 1974. *The Navajo and Pueblo Silversmiths.* Norman: University of Oklahoma Press.

Adams, E. Charles. 1976. Locations of Some Navajo Refugee Period Sites in Southern Colorado. *Awanyu* 4(2): 23–30.

Adams, William Y. 1959. Navajo and Anglo Reconstruction of Prehistoric Sites in Southeastern Utah. *American Antiquity* 25(2): 269–72.

———. 1963. *Shonto: A Study of the Role of the Trader in a Modern Navajo Community.* Bureau of American Ethnology, Bulletin 188.

———, Alexander J. Lindsay, Jr., and Cristy G. Turner II. 1961. *Survey and Excavations in Lower Glen Canyon, 1952–1958.* Museum of Northern Arizona Bulletin, 36.

——— and Lorraine T. Ruffing. 1977. Shonto Revisited: Measures of Social and Economic Change in a Navajo Community, 1955–1971. *American Anthropologist* 79(1): 58–83.

Ambler, J. Richard, Alexander J. Lindsay, Jr., and Mary Anne Stein. 1964. *Survey and Excavations on Cummings Mesa, Arizona and Utah, 1960–1961.* Museum of Northern Arizona Bulletin, 39.

Amsden, Charles. 1934. *Navaho Weaving: Its Technic and History.* Santa Ana: The Fine Arts Press.

———. 1939. The Ancient Basketmakers, IV. *The Masterkey* (13): 125–31.

Anderson, Susanne. 1973. *Song of the Earth Spirit.* San Francisco and New York: Friends of the Earth/McGraw-Hill Book Company.

Anell, Bengt. 1969. *Running Down and Driving of Game in North America.* Studia Ethnographica Upsaliensia, 30.

Anonymous. 1923. Ancient Spanish Torreón at Manzano. *El Palacio* 14(9): 126.

———. 1925. Spanish Torreón at Manzano. *El Palacio* 19(8): 165.

———. 1933. Indian Emergency Conservation Work Pictures *Indians at Work* 1(7): 30–31.

———. 1934a. Indian Architecture and the New Indian Day Schools. *Indians at Work* 1(13): 31–33.

———. 1934b. The First Tribal Capital. *Indians at Work* 1(24): 5–6.

———. 1936. Views from Tohatchi, New Mexico

Anonymous, *continued*
—Navajo Agency. *Indians at Work* 3(16): 51
———. 1938. The House of Navajo Religion. *El Palacio* 45 (24–26): 116–18.
———. 1940. Navajo Had Walled Fort. *El Palacio* 47(4): 96.
———. 1967. Photograph of Hogan. *The Navajo Times* 8(36): B13.
———. 1968a. Hogans Still Used by Navajo Families. *Gallup Independent,* Ceremonial Edition, Aug. 6, Section D: 1
———. 1968b. Rincon Marques Community Seeks Aid from Tribe, ONEO & PHS. *The Navajo Times* 9(41): 14.
———. 1969a. New Housing Concepts Changing Face of Area, *The Navajo Times* 10(34): 29C.
———. 1969b. *Navajo Pine Progress.* Navajo, N. M.: Navajo Forest Products Industries.
———. 1970a. Highlights of Assistant to Vice President's Visit to Navajoland. *The Navajo Times* 11(4): 4–5.
———. 1970b. Savings of School Funds Is Due to Shop Projects. *The Navajo Times* 11(5): 9.
———. 1970c. More Housing To Be Built. *The Navajo Times* 11(31): 18.
———. 1970d. ENA Reports Reservation Home Improvements Program. *The Navajo Times* 11(35): 18.
———. 1970e. Shiprock & Window Rock Slated for Low-Rent Houses. *The Navajo Times* 11(37): 5AA.
———. 1970f. Navajos Who Helped in the Land Claims Research for the Tribe. *The Navajo Times* 11(37): 15A.
———. 1970g. The Navajos Trade Hogans for Air-Conditioning. *Business Week* 2(199): 100, 104.
———. 1970h. Industry Is Dedicated at Mexican Hat, Utah. *The Navajo Times* 11(45): 1.
———. 1970i. Navajoland. *The Orange Disc* 19(6): 15–23.
———. 1971a. Shrine Marks Tragic Years. *The Navajo Times* 12(3): 9.
———. 1971b. Construction Job Training Program Initiated for Navajos. *The Navajo Times* 12(6): 25.
———. 1972. Development in Navajo Hogan Construction. *Padres' Trail,* Nov.: 12–13.
———. 1974a. Tornado Hits. *The Sacramento Bee* 234(38,618), Oct. 11: A8.

———. 1974b. *Sweet Land, Sweet Liberty.* Englewood Cliffs, N.J.: Prentice-Hall.
———. 1975. The Navajo . . . His Land. *Arizona Highways* 51(6): 36–39.
———. n.d.a. *Navajo Adventure.* St. Michaels, Ariz.: Sisters of the Blessed Sacrament.
———. n.d.b. *Monument Valley Tribal Park, The Navajo Nation, Arizona-Utah: Motoring Guide.* [Window Rock]: Department of Parks and Recreation, Navajo Nation.
Armer, Laura Adams. 1935. *Southwest.* New York: Longmans, Green and Co.
Arnberger, L. P. 1962. *Flowers of the Southwest Mesas.* Globe: Southwest Monuments Association.
Aschmann, Homer. 1970. Athapaskan Expansion in the Southwest. *Yearbook, Association of Pacific Coast Geographers,* 23: 79–97.
Ayer, Mrs. Edward, tr. 1916. *The Memorial of Fray Alonso de Benavides, 1630,* annotated by Frederick Webb Hodge and Charles F. Lummis. Chicago: privately printed.

Backus, E. 1854. An Account of the Navajoes of New Mexico. In: Henry R. Schoolcraft, *Information Respecting the History Condition and Prospects of the Indian Tribes of the United States,* 4: 209–15. Philadelphia: Lippincott, Grambo & Co.
Bailey, Flora L. 1940. Navajo Foods and Cooking Methods. *American Anthropologist* 42(2): 270–90.
———. 1941. Navaho Women and the Sudatory. *American Anthropologist* 43(3), Pt. 1: 484–85.
———. 1950. *Some Sex Beliefs and Practices in a Navaho Community, with Comparative Material from Other Navajo Areas.* Papers, Peabody Museum of American Archaeology and Ethnography, Harvard University, 40(2).
Bailey, L. R. 1964. *The Long Walk.* Los Angeles: Westernlore Press.
Baldwin, Gordon C. 1965. *The Warrior Apaches.* Tucson: Dale Stuart King.
Bannister, Bryant. 1965. Tree-Ring Dating of the Archaeological Sites in the Chaco Canyon Region, New Mexico. *Southwestern Monuments Association, Technical Series* 6(2): 116–214.
Barnes, Robert A., and Milton Snow. 1948. Report on the Navajo. *The Desert Magazine* 11(5): 5–8.

Bateman, Walter L. 1970. *The Navajo of the Painted Desert.* Boston: Beacon Press.

Beadle, J. H. 1873. *The Undeveloped West; or Five Years in the Territories.* Philadelphia: National Publishing Company.

———. 1877. *Western Wilds, and the Men Who Redeem Them.* Cincinnati: Jones Brothers & Company.

Bennett, Kay. 1975. *Kaibah: Recollection of a Navajo Girlhood.* N.p.: Kay Bennett.

Bent, Charles. 1853. Indian Tribes of New Mexico. In: Henry R. Schoolcraft, *Information Respecting the History Condition and Prospects of the Indian Tribes of the United States,* 1: 242–46. Philadelphia: Lippincott, Grambo & Co.

Benton, Thomas. 1936. Building for the Navajo. *Indians at Work* 3(17): 27–30.

Bernheimer, Charles, L. 1927. The Fifth Bernheimer Expedition to the Southwest. *Natural History* 27(3): 248–56.

Birket-Smith, Kaj. 1930. *Contributions to Chipewyan Ethnology.* Report of the Fifth Thule Expedition 1921–24, 6(3). Copenhagen.

Blackwood, Beatrice. 1927. An Anthropologist Among the Navajo. *Natural History,* 27(3): 222–28.

Bohrer, Vorsila L. 1964. A Navajo Sweathouse. *Plateau* 36(3): 95–99.

———and Margaret Bergseng. 1963. *An Annotated Catalogue of Plants from Window Rock, Arizona.* Navajoland Publications, 1.

Boke, Richard. 1934. The Mexican Springs Erosion Control Station an Institution of Education and Research. *Indians at Work* 1(13): 13–16.

Bosch, James W. 1961. *Fort Defiance: A Navajo Community in Transition,* 1. Window Rock: Public Services Division, Navajo Tribe.

Bourke, John G. 1884. *The Snake Dance of the Moquis of Arizona.* New York: Charles Scribner's Sons.

———. 1936. Bourke on the Southwest [Lansing S. Bloom, ed.]. *New Mexico Historical Review* 11(1): 77–122; 11(3): 217–44.

Boyce, George A. 1974. *When Navajos Had Too Many Sheep: The 1940's.* San Francisco: The Indian Historian Press.

Boyd, E. 1959. *Popular Arts of Colonial New Mexico.* Santa Fe: Museum of International Folk Art.

———. 1974. *Popular Arts of Spanish New Mexico.* Santa Fe: Museum of New Mexico Press.

Brew, J. O. and John T. Hack. 1939. Prehistoric Use of Coal by Indians of Northern Arizona. *Plateau* 12(1): 8–14.

Brewer, James Jr. 1936. Notes on How to Build a Hogan. *Southwestern Monuments Monthly Report, Supplement,* June: 485–88.

Brink, Mrs. L. P. 1947. Memories. In: J. C. de Korne (ed.), *Navajo and Zuni for Christ,* pp. 191–93. Grand Rapids: Christian Reformed Board of Missions.

Bristol, H. B. 1867. Testimony. *Condition of the Indian Tribes.* Senate Report 156, 39th Congress, 2nd Session: 357–58.

Brown, Donald N. 1974. Social Structure as Reflected in Architectural Units at Picuris Pueblo. In: Miles Richardson, ed., *The Human Mirror: Material and Spatial Images of Man,* 317–38. Baton Rouge: Louisiana State University Press.

Brown, Jo Jeffers. 1970. Navajo Country, Arizona, U.S.A. *Arizona Highways,* 46(7).

Brugge, David M. 1956. Navaho Sweat Houses. *El Palacio* 63(4): 101–6.

———. 1963. *Navajo Pottery and Ethnohistory.* Navajoland Publications, 2.

———. 1964a. Navajo Land Usage: A Study in Progressive Diversification. In: Clark S. Knowlton (ed.), *Indian and Spanish American Adjustments to Arid and Semi-arid Environments.* The Committee on Desert and Arid Zone Research, Contribution 7: 16–26.

———. 1964b. Big Bead Mesa. *Navajo Times* 5(43), Oct. 22: 28

———. 1967. Revised Dates for Navajo Hogans Near Canyon de Chelly. *American Antiquity* 32(3): 396–98.

———. 1968a. Pueblo Influence on Navajo Architecture. *El Palacio* 75(3): 14–20.

———. 1968b. *Navajos in the Church Records of New Mexico, 1694–1875.* Research Section, Navajo Tribe, Research Reports, 1.

———. 1972a. *Navajo and Western Pueblo History.* The Smoke Signal, 25.

———. 1972b. *The Navajo Exodus.* Archaeological Society of New Mexico Supplement 5.

———. 1976. Small Navajo Sites: A Preliminary Report on Historic Archaeology in the Chaco Region. In: Albert E. Ward (ed.), *Limited Activity and Occupation Sites: A Collection of Conference Papers,* Contribution to Anthropological Studies 1: 41–49.

———. 1978. A Comparative Study of Navajo

Brugge, David M., *continued*
    Mortuary Practices. *American Indian Quarterly* 4(4): 309–28.

Bryan, Kirk. 1925. Date of Channel Trenching (Arroyo Cutting) in the Arid Southwest. *Science* 72(1607): 338–44.

————. 1928. Change in Plant Associations by Change in Ground-Water Level. *Ecology* 9(4): 474–78.

————. 1929. Floodwater Farming. *The Geographical Review* 19(3): 444–56.

Bullard, William Rotch Jr. 1962. *The Cerro Colorado Site and Pithouse Architecture in the Southwestern United States Prior to A.D. 900.* Papers, Peabody Museum of American Archaeology and Ethnology, Harvard University, 44(2).

Bulow, Ernest L. 1972. *Navajo Taboos.* Navajo Historical Publications, Cultural Series, 1.

Bunting, Bainbridge. 1970. Take a Trip with NMA: An Architectural Guide to Northern New Mexico. *New Mexico Architecture,* 12(9–10): whole issue.

Callaway, Sydney M., and Gary Witherspoon. 1968. *Grandfather Stories of the Navahos.* Rough Rock: Rough Rock Demonstration School.

Carlson, Roy L. 1963. *Basket Maker III Sites Near Durango, Colorado.* University of Colorado Studies, Series in Anthropology, 8.

————. 1965. *Eighteenth Century Navajo Fortresses of the Gobernador District.* University of Colorado Studies, Series in Anthropology, 10.

Cassidy, Ina Sizer. 1936. Stone Towers of New Mexico and Arizona. *Indians at Work* 3(13): 10.

Cassidy, Francis E. 1956. Navajo Remains in New Mexico. In: Fred Wendorf, Nancy Fox, and Orian L. Lewis, eds., *Pipeline Archaeology,* pp. 77–79. Santa Fe and Flagstaff: The Laboratory of Anthropology and the Museum of Northern Arizona.

Chabot, Maria. 1936. Navajo Blanket Weaving. *Indians at Work* 4(6): 6–12.

Champe, John L. 1949. White Cat Village. *American Antiquity* 14(4): 285–92.

Chavez, Tibo. 1977. In Search of the Horno. *New Mexico Magazine* 55(1): 28–33, 46–47.

Chisholm, James S. 1975. The Social Organization of Ceremonial Practitioners at Navajo Mountain, Utah. *Plateau* 47(3): 82–104.

Christian, Jane. 1965. *The Navajo: A People in Transition, Part Two.* Southwestern Studies 2(4).

Clark, Anette McFadyen. 1974. *Koyukuk River Culture.* Canadian Ethnology Service, Paper 18.

Colton, Harold S. 1936. Hopi Coal Mines. *Museum Notes* 8(12): 59–61.

Cook, Ronald U., and Richard W. Reeves. 1976. *Arroyos and Environmental Change.* Oxford: Clarendon Press.

Cooley, Maurice. 1962. Late Pleistocene and Recent Erosion and Alluviation in Parts of the Colorado River System, Arizona and Utah, *United States Geological Survey, Professional Paper* 450-B: 48–50.

Coolidge, Dane, and Mary Coolidge. 1930. *The Navajo Indians.* Boston: Houghton-Mifflin Company.

Cooper, J. M. 1938. *Snares, Deadfalls, and Other Traps of the Northern Algonquians and Northern Athapascans.* The Catholic University of America, Anthropological Series, 5.

Corbett, John M. 1940. Navajo House Types. *El Palacio* 48(5): 97–108.

Correll, J. Lee. 1965a. The Navajo Hogan. *The Navajo Times* 6(24): 29–31

————. 1965b. Third Annual Shiprock Fair and the San Juan Flood. *The Navajo Times* 6(39): 6B, 10B.

————. 1976. *Through White Men's Eyes: A Contribution to Navajo History.* Window Rock, Ariz.: The Navajo Times Publishing Company.

————and Alfred Dehiya. 1972. *Anatomy of the Navajo Indian Reservation: How It Grew.* Window Rock: The Navajo Times Publishing Company.

————, Editha L. Watson, and David M. Brugge. 1969, 1973. *Navajo Bibliography with Subject Index,* 3 vols. Research Section, Navajo Parks and Recreation, Research Report, 2.

Crampton, C. Gregory. 1960. *Historical Sites in Glen Canyon, Mouth of San Juan River to Lee's Ferry.* University of Utah, Anthropological Papers, 46.

————, ed. 1975. *Sharlot Hall on the Arizona Strip: A Diary of a Journey Through Northern Arizona in 1911.* Flagstaff: Northland Press.

Cremony, John C. 1969. *Life Among the Apaches.* Glorieta, N.M.: The Rio Grande Press (originally published 1868, San Francisco).

Crumrine, N. Ross. 1964. *The House Cross of the Mayo Indians of Sonora, Mexico: A Symbol of Ethnic Identity.* University of Arizona, Anthropological Papers, 8.

Cummings, Violet May. 1964. *Along Navajo Trails.* Washington: Review and Herald Publishing Association.

Curtis, Edward S. 1907, 1922, 1928. *The North American Indian,* 1, 12, 18. Published by the author.

Cushing, Frank Hamilton. 1886. A Study of Pueblo Pottery as Illustrative of Zuni Culture Growth. *Bureau of Ethnology, Annual Report* 4: 437–521.

————. 1965. *The Nation of the Willows.* Flagstaff: Northland Press (originally published 1882, *Atlantic Monthly* 50 [299 and 300]: 362–74, 541–59).

Darby, William J., C. G. Salisbury, and W. J. McGanity, eds. 1956. *A Study of the Dietary Background and Nutriture of the Navajo Indian.* Journal of Nutrition, 60, Supplement 2.

De Harport, David L. 1959. *An Archaeological Survey of Cañon de Chelly, Northeastern Arizona: A Puebloan Community through Time,* 4 vols. Ph.D. dissertation, Harvard University, Cambridge.

Dickey, Roland F. 1949. *New Mexico Village Arts.* Albuquerque: University of New Mexico Press.

Dillon, Richard H., ed. 1970. *Journal of Private Josiah M. Rice, 1851, A Cannoneer in Navajo Country.* Denver: Old West Publishing Company, Fred A. Rosenstock.

Dittert, Alfred E. Jr., James J. Hester, and Frank W. Eddy. 1961. *An Archaeological Survey of the Navajo Reservoir District, Northwestern New Mexico.* Monographs of the School of American Research, 23.

Downs, James F. 1964. *Animal Husbandry in Navajo Society and Culture.* University of California Publications in Anthropology, 1.

————. 1965. The Social Consequences of a Dry Well. *American Anthropologist* 67(2): 1387–1416.

————. 1972. *The Navajo.* New York: Holt, Rinehart and Winston.

Driver, Harold E., and William C. Massey. 1957. *Comparative Studies of North American Indians.* Transactions of the American Philosophical Society, n.s., 47(2).

Drucker, Philip. 1941. Culture Element Distributions: XVII. Yuman-Piman. *Anthropological Records* 6(3): 91–230.

Dunn, J. P. 1886. *Massacres of the Mountains: A History of the Indian Wars of the Far West, 1815–1875.* New York: Harper & Brothers.

Dyk, Walter, 1947. *A Navajo Autobiography.* Viking Fund Publications in Anthropology, 8.

Eaton, J. H. 1854. Description of the True State and Character of the New Mexican Indians. In: Henry R. Schoolcraft, *Information Respecting the History Condition and Prospects of the Indian Tribes of the United States,* 4: 216–21.

Eddy, Frank W. 1961. *Excavations at Los Pinos Phase Sites in the Navajo Reservoir District.* Museum of New Mexico Papers in Anthropology, 4.

————. 1966. *Prehistory in the Navajo Reservoir District, Northwestern New Mexico.* Museum of New Mexico Papers in Anthropology, 15(1).

Ellis, Florence Hawley. ca. 1960. *Acoma and Laguna Hunting Structures, Storage Structures, Windbreak Shelters, and Sweathouses.* Report (Def. Jt. Ex. 529) to Indian Claims Commission, Dockets 227, 229, 266.

————. 1968. An Interpretation of Prehistoric Death Customs in Terms of Modern Southwestern Parallels. In: Albert H. Schroeder, ed., *Collected Papers in Honor of Lyndon Lane Hargrave,* Papers, Archaeological Society of New Mexico, 1: 57–76.

————. 1974. An Anthropological Study of the Navajo Indians. In: *Navajo Indians* 1: 27–609. New York: Garland Publishing.

Elmore, Francis H. 1943. *Ethnobotany of the Navajo.* University of New Mexico Bulletin 392, Monographs of the School of American Research, 1(7).

Elyea, Janette M., Emily K. Abbink, and Peter N. Eschman. 1979. *Cultural Resources of the N.[avajo] I.[ndian] I.[rrigation] P.[roject], Blocks IV and V Survey.* Window Rock, Ariz.: Navajo Tribal Cultural Resources Management Program.

Emerson, Dorothy. 1973. *Among the Mescalero Apaches: The Story of Father Albert Braun, O. F. M.* Tucson: University of Arizona Press.

Euler, Robert C. 1961. Aspects of Political Organization Among the Puertocito Navajo. *El Palacio* 68(2): 118–20.

Fairbanks, Jonathan L. [1974]. Shelter on the Frontier: Adobe Housing in Nineteenth Century Utah. In: Margaret Jupe, ed., *Frontier America: The Far West,* pp. 197–209. Boston: Museum of Fine Arts.

Farmer, Malcolm. 1942. Navajo Archaeology of Upper Blanco and Largo Canyons, North ern New Mexico. *American Antiquity* 8(1): 65–79.

———. 1947. Upper Largo Navaho—1700–1775. *The Kiva* 12(2): 13–24.

Fenneman, Nevin M. 1931. *Physiography of the Western United States.* New York: McGraw-Hill Book Company.

Fewkes, J. Walter. 1906a. The Sun's Influence on the Form of Hopi Pueblos. *American Anthropologist,* n.s. 8(1): 88–100.

———. 1906b. Hopi Shrines near the East Mesa, Arizona. *American Anthropologist,* n.s. 8(2): 346–75.

Fife, Austin, and Alta Fife. 1956. *Saints of Sage and Saddle: Folklore Among the Mormons.* Bloomington: Indiana University Press.

Fishler, Stanley A. 1953. *In the Beginning.* University of Utah, Anthropological Papers, 42.

Fonaroff, Leonard. 1963. Conservation and Stock Reduction on the Navajo Tribal Range. *The Geographical Review* 53(2): 200–23.

Forbes, Jack D. 1960. *Apache, Navajo, and Spaniard.* Norman: University of Oklahoma Press.

Forrest, Earle R. 1970. *With a Camera in Old Navaholand.* Norman: University of Oklahoma Press.

Foster, Roy W. 1958. *Southern Zuni Mountains.* Scenic Trips to the Geologic Past, 4.

Fowler, Don D., and Catherine S. Fowler. 1971. *Anthropology of the Numa: John Wesley Powell's Manuscripts on the Numic Peoples of Western North America, 1868–1880.* Smithsonian Contributions to Anthropology, 14.

Franciscan Fathers, 1910. *Ethnologic Dictionary of the Navajo Language.* St. Michaels, Ariz: St. Michaels Press.

———. 1952. Home Heating Navaho Style. *The Padre's Trial,* Jan.: 11–12.

Fraser, George C. 1916. *Notes of a Journey Taken by George C. Fraser and George C. Fraser Jr., June 24, 1916, to August 3, 1916, to Acoma, Meteor Creator [sic], San Francisco Mountains and through the Navajo Country.* Unpublished m.s. in the Princeton University Library, Princeton, N.J.

Fraser, George C. 1919. *Notes of Journeys into Mississippi, Texas and the Navajo Country, 1919.* Unpublished m.s. in the Princeton University Library, Princeton, N.J.

Frazer, Robert W., ed. 1963. *Mansfield on the Condition of the Western Forts, 1853–54.* Norman: University of Oklahoma Press.

Frink, Maurice. 1968. *Fort Defiance and the Navajos.* Boulder: Pruett Press.

———and Casey E. Barthelmess. 1965. *Photographer on an Army Mule.* Norman: University of Oklahoma Press.

Frisbie, Charlotte Johnson. 1968. The Navajo House Blessing Ceremonial. *El Palacio* 75(3): 26–35.

———. 1970. *Navajo House Blessing Ceremonial: A Study of Cultural Change.* Doctoral dissertation, University of New Mexico, Albuquerque.

———and David P. McAllester, eds. 1978. *Navajo Blessingway Singer: The Autobiography of Frank Mitchell (1881–1967).* Tucson: University of Arizona Press.

Fryer, E. R. 1942. Navajo Social Organization and Land Use Adjustment. *Scientific Monthly* 55(Nov.): 408–22.

Garland, Hamlin. 1930. *Roadside Meetings.* New York: Macmillan.

Gastil, Raymond. 1975. *Cultural Regions of the United States.* Seattle: University of Washington Press.

Gerald, Rex E. 1958. Two Wikiups on the San Carlos Indian Reservation, Arizona. *The Kiva* 23(3): 5–11.

Gifford, E. W. 1940. *Culture Element Distributions: XII, Apache-Pueblo.* Anthropological Records 4(1): 1–207.

Gillmor, Frances, and Louisa Wade Wetherill. 1934. *Traders to the Navajos: The Story of the Wetherills of Kayenta.* Boston: Houghton Mifflin Company.

Gilpin, Laura. 1968. *The Enduring Navaho.* Austin: University of Texas Press.

Glassie, Henry. 1968. *Pattern in the Material Folk Culture of the Eastern United States.* Philadelphia: University of Pennsylvania Press.

Goddard, Pliny Earl. 1909–11. *P. E. Goddard*

Photographs. Unpublished album, Anthropology Department, American Museum of Natural History, New York.

———. 1912. *Analysis of Cold Lake Dialect, Chipewyan.* American Museum of Natural History, Anthropological Papers, 10(2): 67–170.

———. 1913. *Indians of the Southwest.* New York: American Museum of Natural History.

———. 1916. *The Beaver Indians.* American Museum of Natural History, Anthropological Papers, 10(4): 201–94. New York.

———. 1917. *Beaver Dialect.* American Museum of Natural History, Anthropological Papers, 10(6): 399–546.

———. 1928. Native Dwellings of North America. *Natural History* 28(2): 191–203.

———. 1933. *Navajo Texts.* American Museum of Natural History, Anthropological Papers, 34(1).

Gregg, Andrew K. 1968. *New Mexico in the Nineteenth Century.* Albuquerque: University of New Mexico Press.

Gregg, Josiah. 1954. *Commence of the Prairies,* 2, Max L. Moorhead, ed. Norman: University of Oklahoma Press (originally published 1844).

Gregory, Herbert E. 1915. The Oasis of Tuba, Arizona. *Annals of the Association of American Geographers* 5: 107–19.

———. 1916. *The Navajo Country, a Geographic and Hydrographic Reconnaissance of Parts of Arizona, New Mexico, and Utah.* United States Geological Survey Water-Supply Paper 380.

———. 1917. *Geology of the Navajo Country, a Reconnaissance of Parts of Arizona, New Mexico, and Utah.* United States Geological Survey Professional Paper 93.

Griffen, Joyce. 1978. Variations on a Rite of Passage: Some Recent Navajo Funerals. *American Indian Quarterly* 4(4): 367–81.

———. 1979. *Navajo Burials, Anglo Style.* Museum of Northern Arizona Research Report, 20.

Gritzner, Charles. 1969. *Spanish Log Construction in New Mexico.* Doctoral dissertation, Louisiana State University, Baton Rouge.

———. 1971. Log Housing in New Mexico. *Pioneer America* 3(2): 54–62.

———. 1974a. Construction Materials in Folk Housing Tradition: Considerations Governing Their Selection in New Mexico. *Pioneer America* 6(1): 25–39.

———. 1974b. Hispano Gristmills in New Mexico. *Annals of the Association of American Geographers* 64(4): 514–24.

Guernsey, Samuel James. 1931. *Explorations in Northeastern Arizona.* Papers, Peabody Museum of American Archaeology and Ethnology, Harvard University, 12(1).

Gumerman, George J., and Robert C. Euler. 1976. *Papers on the Archaeology of Black Mesa, Arizona.* Carbondale and Edwardsville: Southern Illinois University Press.

Gunnerson, Dolores A. 1956. The Southern Athabaskans: Their Arrival in the Southwest. *El Palacio* 63(11–12): 346–65.

Gunnerson, James H. 1960. An Introduction to Plains Apache Archaeology—The Dismal River Aspect. *Bureau of American Ethnology, Bulletin 173, Anthropological Papers,* 58: 131–260.

———. 1969. Apache Archaeology in Northeastern New Mexico. *American Antiquity* 34(1): 23–34.

———and Dolores A. Gunnerson. 1970. Evidence of Apaches at Pecos. *El Palacio* 76(3): 1–6.

Gwyther, George. 1873. An Indian Reservation. *The Overland Monthly* 10(2): 123–34.

Hack, John T. 1942. *The Changing Physical Environment of the Hopi Indians of Arizona.* Papers, Peabody Museum of American Archaeology and Ethnology, Harvard University, 35(1).

Haile, Berard. 1917. Some Mortuary Customs of the Navajo. *The Franciscan Missions of the Southwest* 5: 29–32.

———. 1937. *Some Cultural Aspects of the Navajo Hogan* (mimeo). Fort Wingate: Ft. Wingate Summer School.

———. 1942. Why the Navaho Hogan? *Primitive Man* 15(3–4): 39–56.

———. 1943. Soul Concepts of the Navaho. *Annali Lateranensi* 6: 59–94.

———. 1950. *A Stem Vocabulary of the Navaho Language,* 1, *Navaho-English.* St. Michaels, Ariz.: St. Michaels Press.

———. 1951. *A Stem Vocabulary of the Navaho Language,* 2, *English-Navaho.* St. Michaels, Ariz.: St. Michaels Press.

———. 1952. *Introduction to Navajo Blessingway.* Galley proofs. St. Michaels, Ariz.: [St. Michaels Press].

Haile, Berard *continued*
———. 1954. *Property Concepts of the Navaho Indians.* Catholic University of America, Anthropology Series, 17.
———and Mary C. Wheelwright. 1949. *Emergence Myth According to the Hanelthnayhe or Upward-Reaching Rite.* Museum of Navajo Ceremonial Art, Navajo Religion Series, 3.
Hall, Edward Twitchell. 1944. Recent Clues to Athapascan Prehistory in the Southwest. *American Anthropologist* 46(1): 98–105.
Hall, Ray Ovid. 1934. One Thousand Charcos. *Indians at Work* 1(10): 12–16.
Halloran, Arthur F. 1964. *The Mammals of Navajoland.* Navajoland Publications, 4.
Hammond, George P., and Agapito Rey. 1966. *The Rediscovery of New Mexico.* Albuquerque: The University of New Mexico Press.
Hannah, John W. 1965. Appendix I: Tree-Ring Dates from the Morris Sites, Gobernador District, New Mexico. *University of Colorado Studies, Series in Anthropology,* 10: 109–13.
Hannum, Alberta. 1945. *Spin a Silver Dollar: The Story of a Desert Trading-Post* New York: The Viking Press.
———. 1958. *Paint the Wind.* New York: The Viking Press.
Hardwick, Dick. 1970. Smoke Signals from Hardwick's Hogan. *The Navajo Times* 11(46): 2.
Harmon, O'Donnell and Henninger, Associates. n.d. *Program Design Study for the Navajo Tribe.*
Hart, John Fraser, and Eugene Cotton Mather. 1957. The American Fence. *Landscape* 6(3): 4–9.
Hayes, Alden C. 1964. *The Archeological Survey of Wetherill Mesa, Mesa Verde National Park —Colorado.* National Park Service, Archeological Research Series, 7-A.
Hegemann, Elizabeth Compton. 1963. *Navaho Trading Days.* Albuquerque: University of New Mexico Press.
Helm, June and Nancy D. Lurie. 1961. *The Subsistence Economy of the Dogrib Indians of Lac la Martre in The Mackenzie District of the Northwest Territories.* Ottawa: Northern Co-ordination and Research Centre, Department of Northern Affairs and National Resources.
Hester, James J. 1962. *Early Navajo Migrations and Acculturations in the Southwest.* Museum of New Mexico Papers in Anthropology, 6.
——— and Joel L. Shiner. 1963. *Studies at Navajo Period Sites in the Navajo Reservoir District.* Museum of New Mexico Papers in Anthropology, 9.
Hill, W. W. 1936. *Navaho Warfare.* Yale University Publications in Anthropology, 5.
———. 1938. The Agricultural and Hunting Methods of the Navaho Indians. Yale University Publications in Anthropology, 18.
———. 1940. Some Navaho Culture Changes During Two Centuries (with a Translation of the Early Eighteenth Century Rabal Manuscript). *Smithsonian Miscellaneous Collections,* 100:395–415.
——— and D. W. Hill. 1943. The Legend of the Navajo Eagle-Catching Way. *New Mexico Anthropologist* 6–7:31–36.
H[obbs], H[uldo] R. 1942. The Navaho Hogan Survives. *El Palacio* 49(7): 152–53.
Hobler, Philip M. and Audrey E. Hobler. 1967. Navajo Racing Circles. *Plateau* 40(2):45–50.
Hodge, William H. 1965. *The Albuquerque Navajos.* Anthropological Papers of the University of Arizona, 11.
Hollister, U. S. 1903. *The Navajo and His Blanket.* Denver: published by the author.
Holwerda, J. H. 1909. Das Alteuropäsche Kuppelgrab. *Praehistorische Zeitschrift* 1(3–4): 374–79.
———. 1912. Neue Kuppelgräber aus der Veluwe (Provinze Gelderland in den Niederlanden). *Praehistorishe Zeitschrift* 4(3–4): 368–73.
Honigmann, John J. 1946. *Ethnography and Acculturation of the Fort Nelson Slave.* Yale University Publications in Anthropology, 33.
———. 1954. *The Kaska Indians: An Ethnographic Reconstruction.* Yale University Publications in Anthropology, 51.
Hoover, J. W. 1929. Modern Canyon Dwellers. *Journal of Geography* 28(7): 269–78.
———. 1931. Navaho Nomadism. *The Geographical Review* 21(3): 429–45.
Horan, James D. 1966. *Timothy O'Sullivan, America's Forgotten Photographer.* New York: Bonanza Books.
Hough, Walter. 1906. Pueblo Environments. *Proceedings, American Association for the Advancement of Science,* 55: 447–54.

Huc, M. 1900. *Travels in Tartary, Thibet and China During the Years 1844–5–6.* Chicago: The Open Court Publishing Company.

Hughes, J. Donald. 1967. *The Story of Man at Grand Canyon.* Grand Canyon Natural History Association Bulletin 14.

Hurt, Wesley R. Jr. 1942. Eighteenth Century Navajo Hogans From Canyon de Chelly National Monument. *American Antiquity* 8(1): 89–104.

Huscher, Betty H., and Harold A. Huscher. 1942. Athapaskan Migration via the Intermontane Region. *American Antiquity* 8(1): 80–88.

———. 1943. The Hogan Builders of Colorado. *Southwestern Lore* 9(2): 1–92.

Huse, Hannah, Bradley A. Noisat, and Judith A. Halasi. 1978. *The Bisti-Star Lake Project—A Sample Survey of Cultural Resources in Northwestern New Mexico.* Bureau of Land Management, Albuquerque District, 1.

Hyde, Philip, and Stephen C. Jett. 1967. *Navajo Wildlands: "as long as the rivers shall run."* San Francisco: Sierra Club.

Ickes, Anna Wilmarth. 1933. *Mesa Land: The History and Romance of the American Southwest.* Boston and New York: Houghton Mifflin Company.

James, Charles D., III. 1976. *Historic Navajo Studies in Northeastern Arizona.* Museum of Northern Arizona Research Paper 1.

———and Alexander J. Lindsay, Jr. 1975. Ethnoarchaeological Research at Canyon del Muerto, Arizona: A Navajo Example. *Ethnohistory*, 20(4): 361–74.

James, George Wharton. 1905. Aboriginal American Homes: Brush, Mud, and Willow Dwellings. *Craftsman* 8(8): 640–49.

———. 1906. Indian Homes. *The Four-Track News,* 11(1): 16–19.

———. 1913. *In and Around the Grand Canyon: The Grand Canyon of the Colorado River in Arizona,* revised edition. Boston: Little, Brown, and Company.

———. 1914. *Indian Blankets and Their Makers.* Chicago: A. C. McClurg & Co.

James, Harold L. 1967. The History of Fort Wingate. In: Frederick D. Trauger, ed., *Guidebook of Defiance—Zuni—Mt. Taylor Region, Arizona and New Mexico,* pp. 150–58. Socorro (?): New Mexico Geological Society.

Jeffers, Jo, and Wayne Davis. 1967. Cultivators of the Soil. *Arizona Highways* 43(10): 34–38.

Jett, Stephen C. 1964. Pueblo Indian Migrations: An Evaluation of the Possible Physical and Cultural Determinants. *American Antiquity* 29(3): 281–300.

———. 1967. *Tourism in the Navajo Country; Resources and Planning.* Navajoland Publications, A.

——— 1973. Traditional Navajo Dwellings: Types and Distributions [abstract]. *Yearbook of the Association of Pacific Coast Geographers,* 35: 185.

———. 1975. The Destruction of Navajo Orchards in 1864: Capt. John Thompson's Report. *Arizona and the West* 16(4): 365–78.

———. 1976. Comments on the Navajo Hogan. *Places* 3(2): 49.

———. 1977. History of Fruit-Tree Raising Among the Navajo. *Agricultural History* 51(4): 681–701.

———. 1978a. Origin of Navajo Settlement Patterns. *Annals of the Association of American Geographers* 68(3): 351–62.

———. 1978b. Navajo Seasonal Migration Patterns. *The Kiva* 44(1): 65–75.

———. 1979a. The Navajo's Canadian Connection: A Reply. *Annals of the Association of American Geographers* 69(3): 482–85.

———. 1979b. Peach-Tree Cultivation and Use among the Canyon de Chelly Navajo. *Economic Botany* 3(33): 298–310.

———. 1980a. The Navajo Homestead: Situation and Site. *Yearbook of the Association of Pacific Coast Geographers,* 41: 101–18.

———. 1980b. Housing Changes among the Navajo of the North American Southwest. In: Maheshwari Prasad, ed., *Selected Readings on Tribes,* in press. New Delhi: Classical Publications.

———. 1981. Cultural Fusion in Native-American Folk Architecture: The Navajo Hogan. In: Jay Edwards, ed., *The Study of Vernacular Architecture,* in press. Baton Rouge: Louisiana State University Press.

———. n.d. Cairn Trail Shrines in the Americas. In preparation.

Jett, Stephen C., *continued*
——— and Virginia E. Spencer. 1971. Navajo Dwellings: Three Hundred Years of Change. *Abstracts of the Joint Annual Meetings of the Southwestern Anthropological Association and American Ethnological Society,* pp. 20–21, 36.

Johnson, Broderick H., ed. 1977. *Stories of Traditional Navajo Life and Culture by Twenty-two Navajo Men and Women.* Tsaile: Navajo Community College Press.

Johnston, Bernice. 1972. *Two Ways in the Desert.* Pasadena: Sociotechnical Press.

Jones, Thomas Jesse, Charles T. Loram, Harold B. Allen, and Ella Deloria. 1939. *The Navajo Indian Problem.* New York: Phelps-Stokes Fund.

Jordan, Terry G. 1978. *Texas Log Buildings: A Folk Architecture.* Austin: University of Texas Press.

———. 1980. Alpine, Alemannic, and American Log Architecture. *Annals of the Association of American Geographers* 70(2): 154–80.

Judd, Neil M. 1967. *The Bureau of American Ethnology: A Partial History.* Norman: University of Oklahoma Press.

Kangieser, Paul C. 1966. *Climates of the States: Arizona.* Climatography of the United States, 60–2.

Kearney, Thomas H., and Robert H. Peebles. 1951. *Arizona Flora.* Berkeley and Los Angeles: University of California Press.

Kelly, Isabel. 1964. *Southern Paiute Ethnography.* University of Utah Anthropological Papers, 69.

Kelly, Lawrence C. 1970. *Navajo Roundup: Selected Correspondence of Kit Carson's Expedition against the Navajo, 1863–1865.* Boulder: The Pruett Publishing Company.

Kemrer, Mead F., and Donald L. Graybill. 1970. Navajo Warfare and Economy, 1750–1868. *The Western Canadian Journal of Anthropology,* 2(1): 204–11.

Kephart, Horace. 1917. *Camping and Woodcraft,* 1. New York: The Macmillan Company.

[Kern, Richard H.] 1849. *Diary* [of Col. Washington's Navajo Expedition]. Manuscript in the Huntington Library, San Marino, California.

Keur, Dorothy Lewis. 1941. *Big Bead Mesa, An Archaeological Study of Navajo Accultura-* *tion, 1745–1812.* American Antiquity 7(2), Pt. 2, Memoirs of the Society for American Archaeology, 1.

———. 1944. A Chapter in Navajo-Pueblo Relations. *American Antiquity* 10(1): 75–86.

Kidder, A. V. 1920. Ruins of the Historic Period in the Upper San Juan Valley, New Mexico. *American Anthropologist* 22(4): 322–29.

Kluckhohn, Clyde. 1927. *To the Foot of the Rainbow.* New York: Century.

———. 1948. Conceptions of Death Among the Southwestern Indians. *Harvard Divinity School Bulletin,* 66: 5–19.

———. 1966. The Ramah Navaho. *Bureau of American Ethnology, Bulletin* 196: 327–77.

———, W. W. Hill, and Lucy Wales Kluckhohn. 1971. *Navaho Material Culture.* Cambridge: The Belknap Press of Harvard University Press.

——— and Dorothea Leighton. 1962. *The Navaho.* Revised by Lucy H. Wales and Richard Kluckhohn. Garden City: Doubleday Anchor Books.

Kniffen, Fred. 1939. Louisiana House Types. *Annals of the Association of American Geographers* 26(4): 179–93.

———. 1965. Folk Housing: Key to Diffusion. *Annals of the Association of American Geographers* 55(4): 549–77.

——— and Henry Glassie. 1966. Building in Wood in the Eastern United States—A Time-Place Perspective. *The Geographical Review* 56(1): 40–66.

Krickeberg, Walter. 1939. The Indian Sweat Bath. *Ciba Symposia* 1: 19–25.

Krutz, Gordon V. 1974. Living Conditions. In: Thomas Weaver, ed., *Indians of Arizona: A Contemporary Perspective,* pp. 112–23. Tucson: University of Arizona Press.

Lamphere, Louise. 1976. *To Run After Them: Cultural and Social Bases of Cooperation in a Navajo Community.* Tucson: University of Arizona Press.

Landgraf, John Leslie. 1950. Land Use in the Ramah Navaho Area, New Mexico. *Transactions of the New York Academy of Sciences,* Ser. 2, 13: 77–84.

———. 1954. *Land-Use in the Ramah Navaho Area, New Mexico.* Papers, Peabody Museum of American Archaeology and Ethnology, Harvard University, 42(1).

Lange, Charles H. and Carroll L. Riley. 1970. *The Southwestern Journals of Adolph F. Bandelier 1883–1884.* Albuquerque: University of New Mexico Press.

Langley, Dama. 1968. The Indestructibles. *Arizona Highways* 44(8): 8–13, 28–35.

Laubin, Reginald, and Gladys Laubin. 1957. *The Indian Tipi: Its History, Construction, and Use.* Norman: University of Oklahoma Press.

Laughter, Albert. 1979. Navajo Ranger Interprets Our People, Our Past. *The National Geographic Magazine* 156(1): 80–85.

Lee, Joe and Gladwell Richardson. 1974. My Wonderful Country. *Frontier Times* 48 (2): 6–15, 29, 33–35, 48–51, 54–56, 58–60, 62, 64.

Leighton, Dorothea, and Clyde Kluckhohn. 1948. *Children of the People.* Cambridge: Harvard University Press.

Leighton, Alexander H., and Dorothea Leighton. 1941a. A Navaho Builds a House. *Natural History* 47(5): 272–73.

———. 1941b. A Navaho Takes a "Turkish Bath." *Natural History* 48(1): 20–21.

———. 1944. *The Navaho Door: An Introduction to Navajo Life.* Cambridge: Harvard University Press.

———. 1949. *Gregorio, the Hand-Trembler: A Psychobiological Personality Study of a Navaho Indian.* Papers, Peabody Museum of American Archaeology and Ethnology, Harvard University, 40(1).

Leopold, Luna B. 1951. Vegetation of Southwestern Watersheds in the Nineteenth Century. *Geographical Review* 41(2): 295–316.

Letterman ["Letherman"], Jonathan. 1856. Sketch of the Navajo Tribe of Indians, Territory of New Mexico. *Smithsonian Institution, Annual Report* 10: 283–97.

Levin, M. G., and L. P. Potapov, Eds. 1964. *The Peoples of Siberia.* Chicago: University of Chicago Press.

Levy, Jerrold E. 1978. Changing Burial Practices of the Western Navajo: A Consideration of the Relationship Between Attitudes and Behavior. *American Indian Quarterly* 4(4): 397–405.

Lewis, Pierce F. 1975. Common Houses, Cultural Spoor. *Landscape* 19(2): 1–22.

Liebler, H. Baxter. 1962. The Social and Cultural Patterns of the Navajo Indians. *Utah Historical Quarterly* 30(4): 298–325.

Lindgren, Raymond E., ed. 1946. A Diary of Kit Carson's Navaho Campaign, 1863–1864. *New Mexico Historical Review* 21(3): 226–46.

Link, Martin. 1968. *Navajo: A Century of Progress 1868–1968.* Window Rock: The Navajo Tribe.

Littell, Norman. 1967. *Proposed Finding of Fact in Behalf of the Navajo Tribe of Indians in Area of the Overall Navajo Claim (Docket 229),* 3, 4, and 6. Window Rock: The Navajo Tribe.

Lockett, H. Claiborne, 1952. Hogans vs. Houses. In: *For the Dean: Essays in Honor of Byron Cummings . . . ,* pp. 137–42. Tucson: Hohokam Museums Association.

Lockwood, Frank C. 1938. *The Apache Indians.* New York: The Macmillan Company.

Loh, Jules. 1970. The Soul of the Navajo. *Esquire* 74(5): 162–67, 176–77, 179–82, 184.

———. 1971. *Lords of the Earth: A History of the Navajo Indians.* New York: Crowell-Collier Press.

Looney, Ralph and Bruce Dale. 1972. The Navajos. *The National Geographic Magazine* 142(6): 740–81.

Lowie, Robert H. 1924. *Notes on Shoshonean Ethnography.* American Museum of Natural History, Anthropological Papers 20(3): 185–314.

Luckert, Karl W. 1975. *The Navajo Hunter Tradition.* Tucson: University of Arizona Press.

———. 1979. *Coyoteway: A Navajo Holyway Healing Ceremonial.* Tucson and Flagstaff: The University of Arizona Press and the Museum of Northern Arizona Press.

Luomala, Katharine. 1938. *Navaho Life of Yesterday and Today.* Berkeley: United States National Park Service (Western Museum Laboratories).

Mackey, James, and R. C. Green. 1979. Largo-Gallina Towers: An Explanation. *American Antiquity* 44(1): 144–54.

Mails, Thomas E. 1974. *The People Called Apache.* Englewood Cliffs, N.J.: Prentice-Hall.

Malcolm, Roy L. 1939. Archaeological Remains, Supposedly Navaho, from Chaco Canyon, New Mexico. *American Antiquity* 5(1): 4–20.

Marmon, L. H., and G. C. Pearl. 1958. A Fortified Site Near Ojo Del Padre: Big Bead Mesa Revisited. *El Palacio* 65(4): 136–42.

[Marmon, Walter G.] 1894. Navajo Reservation. *Report on Indians Taxed in the United States (except Alaska) at the Eleventh Census: 1890.* Washington.

Matthews, Washington. 1883. Navajo Silversmiths. *Bureau of Ethnology, Annual Report* 2: 71–178.

———. 1887. The Mountain Chant: A Navajo Ceremony. *Bureau of American Ethnology, Annual Report* 5: 385–467.

———. 1897. *Navaho Legends.* American Folk-Lore Society, Memoirs, 5.

———. 1902. *The Night Chant, a Navaho Ceremony.* Memoirs, American Museum of Natural History, 6.

McAllester, David, and Susan W. McAllester. 1980. *Hogans: Navajo Houses & House Songs.* Middletown, Conn.: Wesleyan University Press.

McClellan, Catherine. 1975. *My Old People Say: An Ethnographic Survey of Southern Yukon Territory.* National Museums of Canada, Publications in Ethnology, 6 (1 & 2).

McClellan, William W. 1935. Chapters on the Navajo Reservation. *Indians at Work* 3(3): 42–43.

McGowan, Dan. 1979. Land of Red Earth and Blue Sky. *Arizona Highways* 55(8): covers, 1–3, 16–31, 47–48.

McGregor, John C. 1951. *The Cohonina Culture of Northwestern Arizona.* Urbana: University of Illinois Press.

———. 1965. *Southwestern Archaeology,* 2nd edition. Urbana: University of Illinois Press.

McIntire, Elliot G. 1967. Central Places on the Navajo Reservation: A Special Case. *Yearbook of the Association of Pacific Coast Geographers* 29: 91–96.

———. 1971. Changing Patterns of Hopi Indian Settlement. *Annals of the Association of American Geographers* 61(3): 510–21.

McKelvey, Mike. 1969. White Mesa, the Quiet Land That Stands Alone. *Western Gateways* 9(1): 6–10, 56–58.

McKennan, Robert A. 1965. *The Chandalar Kutchin.* Arctic Institute of North America, Technical Paper 17.

McNitt, Frank. 1962. *The Indian Traders.* Norman: University of Oklahoma Press.

———. 1964. *Navaho Expedition.* Norman: University of Oklahoma Press.

———. 1972. *Navajo Wars: Military Campaigns, Slave Raids, and Reprisals.* Albuquerque: University of New Mexico Press.

McSparron, Cozy. 1950. The Wishing Pile. *Arizona Highways* 26(8): 34–39.

Mindeleff, Cosmos. 1897. Cliff Ruins of Canyon de Chelly, Arizona. *Bureau of American Ethnology, Annual Report* 16:78–198.

———. 1898. Navaho Houses. *Bureau of American Ethnology, Annual Report,* 17: 475–517.

———. 1900. Houses and House Dedication of the Navaho. *Scientific American* 82(15): 233–34.

———. 1966. Navajo Sweat Baths. In: Joseph Miller, *Arizona: The Last Frontier.* New York: Hastings House (orig. pub. 1899, *Commercial Advertiser,* repr. *The Phoenix Republican*).

Mindeleff, Victor. 1891. A Study of Pueblo Architecture: Tusayan and Cibola. *Bureau of Ethnology, Annual Report* 8: 3–228.

Minter, Becky. 1970. Navajo College Approves Campus Construction Plans. *The Navajo Times* 11(52): 20.

Mitchell, Emerson Blackhorse, and T. D. Allen. 1967. *Miracle Hill: The Story of a Navaho Boy.* Norman: University of Oklahoma Press.

Mix, Floyd M., and Ernest H. Cirou. 1963. *Practical Carpentry.* Homewood, Ill.: The Goodheart-Wilcox Co.

Mooney, James R. 1970. Navajoland. *The Orange Disc* 19(6): 16–23.

Morgan, Lewis H. 1881. *Houses and House Life of the American Aborigines.* U. S. Geographical and Geological Survey of the Rocky Mountain Region, Contributions to North American Ethnology, 4.

Morice, A. G. 1909, 1910. The Great Dené Race. *Anthropos* 4: 582–606; 5: 113–42, 419–43, 643–53, 969–90.

Musgrave, M. E. 1937. Helping the Navajo Help Themselves. *Indians at Work* 4(12): 35–39.

Navajo Environmental Protection Commission Staff. 1980. *Radiation Uranium Mining Houses.* Briefing paper. Window Rock: unpublished.

Navajo Land Claim. n.d.a. Untitled site map, Navajo Land Claim. Window Rock: unpublished.

————. n.d.b. *Navajo Land Claim Site Reports,* vols. 7, 9, 10, 12. Window Rock: unpublished.

Neely, James A. and Alan P. Olson. 1977. *Archaeological Reconnaissance of Monument Valley in Northeastern Arizona.* M[useum of] N[orthern] A[rizona] Research Paper 3.

Neuffer, H. C. 1935. Navajo Self-Government at the Hogback Irrigation Project. *Indians at Work* 2(12): 14–19.

Newcomb, Franc Johnson. 1934. Doorways Face the Dawn. *New Mexico Magazine* 7(7): 7, 40.

————. 1940a. *Navajo Omens and Taboos.* Santa Fe: The Rydal Press.

————. 1940b. Origin Legend of the Navajo Eagle Chant. *Journal of American Folk-lore* 53(207): 50–77.

————. 1966. *Navajo Neighbors.* Norman: University of Oklahoma Press.

————. 1967. *Navaho Folk Tales.* Santa Fe: Museum of Navajo Ceremonial Art.

Nielson, John Deasy. 1967. *The Geography of Selected Aspects of Cultural Change Among the Navajos of the Aneth Area, Southeastern Utah.* Master's thesis, University of Utah, Salt Lake City.

Noble, Allen G., and M. Margaret Geib. 1976. The Navajo Hogan. *Places* 3(1): 35–36.

Noble, William A. 1969. Approaches Toward an Understanding of Traditional South Asian Peasant Dwellings. *The Professional Geographer* 21(4): 264–71.

Nordenskiöld, G. 1893. *The Cliff Dwellers of the Mesa Verde, Southwestern Colorado: Their Pottery and Implements.* Stockholm: P. A. Nostedt & Söner [reprinted 1979, The Rio Grande Press, Glorieta].

Olsen, Robert W., Jr. 1969. The Powell Survey Kanab Base Line. *Utah Historical Quarterly* 37(2): 261–68.

Olson, Alan P., and William W. Wasley. 1956. An Archaeological Traverse Survey in West-Central New Mexico. In: Fred Wendorf, Nancy Fox, and O. L. Lewis, eds., *Pipeline Archaeology,* pp. 256–390. Santa Fe and Flagstaff: Laboratory of Anthropology and Museum of Northern Arizona.

Olson, John. 1970. Experience Is Their Textbook. *Life* 68(20): 32–37.

Opler, Morris E. 1936. A Summary of the Jicarilla Apache Culture. *American Anthropologist* 38(2): 202–23.

————. 1965. *An Apache Life-Way: The Economic, Social, and Religious Institutions of the Chiricahua Indians.* New York: Cooper Square Publishers.

————. 1973. *Greenville Goodwin Among the Western Apache: Letters from the Field.* Tucson: University of Arizona Press.

————. 1974. Review of Gunnerson's *The Jicarilla Apaches. Arizona and the West* 16(4): 379–81.

————. 1975. Problems in Apachean Cultural History, with Special Reference to the Lipan Apache. *Anthropological Quarterly* 48(3): 182–92.

Osgood, Cornelius. 1936. *Contributions to the Ethnography of the Kutchin.* Yale University Publications in Anthropology, 14.

————. 1940. *Ingalik Material Culture.* Yale University Publications in Anthropology, 22.

Ostermann, Leopold. 1908. The Navajo Indians of New Mexico and Arizona. *Anthropos* 3: 857–69.

————. 1917. Navajo Houses. *The Franciscan Missions of the Southwest* 5: 20–29.

Owen, Blanton, 1980. The Farm Sled of the Southern Appalachian Highlands: Its Construction, Use and Operation. *Pioneer America Society Transactions* 3: 25–45.

Packard, Gar, and Maggy Packard. 1970. *Southwest 1880 with Ben Wittick, Pioneer Photographs of Indian and Frontier Life.* Santa Fe: Packard Publications.

Page, Gordon B. 1937a. The Navajo Sweat House. *New Mexico Anthropologist* 2(1): 19–21.

————. 1937b. Navajo House types. *Museum Notes* 9(9): 47–49.

Palmer, Rose A. 1929. *The North American Indians.* Smithsonian Scientific Series, 4.

Parsons, Elsie Clews. 1923. Navaho Folk Tales. *Journal of American Folk-lore* 36: 368–75.

————. 1936. *Hopi Journal of Alexander M. Stephen.* Columbia University Contributions to Anthropology, 23(1). New York.

————. 1939. *Pueblo Indian Religion,* 1. Chicago: University of Chicago Press.

Paulson, Ivar. 1952. The "Seat of Honor" in Aboriginal Dwellings of the Circumpolar Zone, with Special Regard to the Indians of Northern North America. *International Congress of Americanists* 29(3): 63–65.

Peckham, Stewart. 1965. *Prehistoric Weapons in the Southwest,* Museum of New Mexico Press, Popular Series Pamphlet, 3.

Pennington, Campbell. 1969. *The Tepehuan of Chihuahua: Their Material Culture.* Salt Lake City: University of Utah Press.

Perceval, Don, and Clay Lockett. 1962. *A Navajo Sketchbook.* Flagstaff: Northland Press.

Phleps, Hermann. 1942. *Holzbaukunst: Der Blockbau.* Karlsruhe: Fachtblattverlag Dr. Albert Bruder.

Pillsbury, Richard, and Andrew Kardos. ca. 1971. *A Field Guide to Folk Architecture of the Northeastern United States.* Geography Publications at Dartmouth, 8.

Platero, Dillon. 1967. Naas'ooldah: Forward Together. In: Robert A. Roessel, Jr., *Indian Communities in Action,* pp. 156–79. Tempe: Arizona State University.

Pospíšil, František. 1932. *Ethnologické Materiálie z Jihozápadu U.S.A.* Brno: Published by the author.

Postma, Richard. 1947. Our Semi-Centennial Celebration a Challenge to Youth. In: J. C. de Korne, ed., *Navaho and Zuni for Christ,* pp. 155–63. Grand Rapids: Christian Reformed Board of Missions.

Powell, John Wesley. 1875. The Hopi Villages: The Ancient Province of Tusayan. *Scribner's Monthly,* 11(2): 193–213 (reprinted 1972 by Filter Press, Palmer Lake, Colo.).

———. 1895. *Canyons of the Colorado.* Meadville, Pa.: Flood & Vincent.

Prudden, T. Mitchell. 1906. *On the Great American Plateau.* New York: G. P. Putnam's Sons.

Rapoport, Amos. 1969a. *House Form and Culture.* Englewood Cliffs, N.J.: Prentice-Hall.

———. 1969b. The Pueblo and the Hogan. In: Paul Oliver, ed., *Shelter and Society,* pp. 66–79. New York: Frederick A. Praeger.

Ray, Verne F. 1942. *Culture Element Distributions: XXII, Plateau.* Anthropological Records 8(2): 99–262.

Reagan, Albert B. 1919. The Influenza and the Navajo. *Indiana Academy of Science Proceedings* 29: 243–47.

———. 1930. *Notes on the Indians of the Fort Apache Region.* American Museum of Natural History, Anthropological Papers 31(5): 281–345.

Reed, Allen C. 1954. Apache Cattle, Horses and Men. *Arizona Highways* 30(7): 16–25.

Reeve, Frank D. 1959. The Navajo-Spanish Peace: 1720's–1770's. *New Mexico Historical Review* 34(1): 9–40.

———. 1960. Navaho-Spanish Diplomacy, 1720–1790. *New Mexico Historical Review* 35(3): 200–35.

Reher, Charles A., ed. 1977. *Settlement and Subsistence along the Lower Chaco River: The CGP Survey.* Albuquerque: University of New Mexico Press.

Reichard, Gladys A. 1928. *Social Life of the Navajo Indians, with Some Attention to Minor Ceremonies.* Columbia University Contributions to Anthropology, 7.

———. 1934. *Spider Woman: A Story of Navajo Weavers and Chanters.* New York: The Macmillan Company.

———. 1936. *Navajo Shepherd and Weaver.* New York: J. J. Augustin.

———. 1939. *Dezba, Woman of the Desert.* New York: J. J. Augustin.

Rickert, John E. 1967. House Facades of the Northeastern United States: A Tool of Geographic Analysis. *Annals of the Association of American Geographers* 57(2): 211–38.

Riley, Carroll L. 1954. A Survey of Navajo Archaeology. *University of Colorado Studies, Series in Anthropology,* 4.

Riordan, M. J. 1890. The Navajo Indians. *Overland Monthly* 16(94): 373–80.

Roberts, John M. 1951. *Three Navajo Households.* Papers, Peabody Museum of American Archaeology and Ethnology, Harvard University, 40(3).

Robinson, Jacob S. 1848. *Sketches of the Great West. A Journal of the Santa Fe Expedition Under Col. Doniphan.* Portsmouth Journal Press (republished in microcard, 1960, Lost Cause Press, Louisville. Also, C. L. Cannon, ed. 1932, *A Journal of the Santa Fe Expedition Under Col. Doniphan,* Princeton University Press, Princeton).

Roessel, Robert, and Dillon Platero. 1974. *Coyote Stories of the Navajo People.* Phoenix: Navajo Curriculum Center Press, Rough Rock Demonstration School.

Russell, Scott C. 1977. The Agricultural Field House: A Navajo Limited Occupation and Special Use Site. In: *Center for Anthropological Studies, Occasional Papers in Archaeology and Ethnohistory,* 1: 35–40.

Sanchez, George I. 1948. *"The People": A Study of the Navajos.* Lawrence: United States Indian Service.

Sapir, Edward. 1916. *Time Perspective in Aboriginal American Culture, a Study in Method.* Canadian Department of Mines, Geological Survey, Memoir 90, Anthropological Series, 13.

———— and Harry Hoijer. 1942. *Navaho Texts.* Iowa City: Linguistic Society of America.

Sasaki, Tom T. 1964. Changes in Land Use Among the Navaho Indians in the Many Farms Areas of the Navajo Reservation. In: Clark S. Knowlton, ed., *Indian and Spanish American Adjustments to Arid and Semiarid Environments,* The Committee on Desert and Arid Zone Research, Contribution 7: 34–37. Lubbock.

Schaafsma, Curtis F. [1979]. *The Cerrito Site (AR-4), A Piedra Lumbre Phase Settlement at Abiquiu Reservoir.* Santa Fe: School of American Research.

Schaeffer, Margaret W. M. 1958. The Construction of a Wikiup on the Fort Apache Indian Reservation. *The Kiva* 24(2): 14–20.

Schevill, Margaret. 1945. The Navajo Screen. *The Kiva* 11(13): 3–5.

Schmedding, Joseph. 1974. *Cowboy and Indian Trader.* Albuquerque: University of New Mexico Press.

Schoolcraft, Henry R., ed. 1853, 1856. *Information Respecting the History Condition and Prospects of the Indian Tribes of the United States,* 3, 4. Philadelphia: Lippincott, Grambo & Co.

Schroeder, Albert H. 1963. Navajo and Apache Relationships West of the Rio Grande. *El Palacio* 70(3): 5–23.

Schwemberger, Simeon. 1906(?) Photograph album at Hubbell Trading Post National Historic Site, Ganado, Arizona.

————. 1938. A Navajo Family and Hogan. *El Palacio* 45(21–23): plate opposite p. 102.

Scully, Vincent. 1975. *Pueblo/Mountain, Village, Dance.* New York: The Viking Press.

Sellers, William D., and Richard H. Hill. 1974. *Arizona Climate, 1931–1972.* Tucson: University of Arizona Press.

Seton, Julia M. 1962. *American Indian Arts: A Way of Life.* New York: The Ronald Press Company.

Shepardson, Mary. 1963. *Navajo Ways in Government: A Study in Political Process.* American Anthropologist, 65(3): Pt. 2, American Anthropological Association, Memoir 96.

————. 1978. Changes in Navajo Mortuary Practices and Beliefs. *American Indian Quarterly* 4(4): 383–95.

———— and Blodwen Hammond. 1970. *The Navajo Mountain Community: Social Organization and Kinship Terminology.* Berkeley and Los Angeles: University of California Press.

Shufeldt, R. W. 1889. The Navajo Tanner. *Proceedings of the United States National Museum* 11: 59–66.

————. 1892. The Evolution of House-Building Among the Navajo Indians. *United States National Museum Proceedings* 15: 279–82.

Simpson, James H. 1852. Annual Address. *Annals of the Minnesota Historical Society* 3: 5–19.

Sitgreaves, Lorenzo. 1962. *Report of an Expedition Down the Zuni and Colorado Rivers.* Chicago: The Rio Grande Press (originally published 1853, 32d Congress, 2d Session, Senate Executive Document 59).

Smith, Watson. 1952. *Kiva Mural Decorations at Awatovi and Kaiwaka-a, with a Survey of Other Wall Paintings in the Pueblo Southwest.* Papers, Peabody Museum of American Archaeology and Ethnology, Harvard University, 37.

Smith, Mrs. White Mountain [Dama Margaret]. 1933. *Indian Tribes of the Southwest.* Stanford University: Stanford University Press.

Smithson, Carma Lee and Robert C. Euler. 1964. *Havasupai Religion and Mythology.* University of Utah, Anthropological Papers, 68.

Snyder, Peter Z., Edward K. Sadalla, and David Stea. ca. 1976. *Socio-Cultural Modifications and User Needs in Navajo Housing.* Unpublished ms.

Spencer, J. E. 1945. House Types of Southern Utah. *The Geographical Review* 35(3): 444–57.

Spencer, Virginia Evelyn. 1969. *The Geography of Navajo Dwelling Types, with Special Reference to Black Creek Valley, Arizona-New Mexico.* Master's thesis, University of California, Davis.

———— and Stephen C. Jett. 1971. Navajo Dwellings of Rural Black Creek Valley, Arizona-New Mexico. *Plateau* 43(4): 159–75.

Spicer, Edward, 1954. Spanish-Indian Acculturation in the Southwest. *American Anthropologist* 56(4): 663–78.

———. 1962. *Cycles of Conquest: The Impact of Spain, Mexico and the United States on the Indians of the Southwest, 1533–1960.* Tucson: University of Arizona Press.

Spier, Leslie. 1928. *Havasupai Ethnography.* American Museum of Natural History, Anthropological Papers, 29(3).

———. [1933]. *Yuman Tribes of the Gila River.* Chicago: University of Chicago Press.

Sprague, Marshall, and the Editors of Time-Life Books. 1967. *The Mountain States: Arizona, Colorado, Idaho, Montana, Nevada, New Mexico, Utah, Wyoming.* New York: Time-Life Books.

Steece, Henry M. 1921. Corn Culture Among the Indians of the Southwest. *Natural History* 21(4): 414–24.

Steen, Charlie R. 1966. *Excavations at Tse-Ta'a, Canyon de Chelly National Monument.* U. S. National Park Service, Archeological Series, 9.

Steggerda, Morris, and Ruth B. Eckardt. 1941. Navaho Foods and Their Preparation. *Journal of the American Dietetic Association* 17(3): 217–25.

Stephen, A. M. 1890. Navajo Dwellings. *Our Forest Children* 4(4): 223.

———. 1893. The Navajo. *The American Anthropologist* 6(4): 345–62.

Stevenson, James. 1891. Ceremonial of Hasjelti Dailjis and Mythical Sand Painting of the Navajo Indians. *Bureau of Ethnology, Annual Report* 8: 229–85.

Steward, Julian. 1939. *Notes on Hiller's Photographs of the Paiute and Ute Indians Taken on the Powell Expedition of 1873.* Smithsonian Miscellaneous Collections, 98(18).

———. 1941. Culture Element Distributions: XIII, Nevada Shoshoni. *Anthropological Records* 4(2): 209–360.

Stewart, Omer C. 1941. Culture Element Distributions: XIV, Northern Paiute. *Anthropological Records* 4(3): 361–446.

———. 1942. Culture Element Distributions: XVIII, Ute–Southern Paiute. *Anthropological Records* 6(4): 231–356.

Stewart, Ronald L. 1971. Fort Sumner: An Adobe Post on the Pecos. *El Palacio* 77(4): 12–15.

Stirling, Matthew W. 1940. Indian Tribes of Pueblo Land. *The National Geographic Magazine* 78(5): 549–96.

Stirling, Betty. 1961. *Mission to the Navajo.* Mountain View, Calif., Omaha, Portland: Pacific Press Publishing Associates.

Stokes, M. A. and T. L. Smiley. 1963. Tree-Ring Dates from the Navajo Land Claim, I, The Northern Sector. *Tree-Ring Bulletin* 25(3–4): 8–18.

———. 1964. Tree-Ring Dates from the Navajo Land Claim, II, The Western Sector. *Tree-Ring Bulletin* 26(1–4): 2–11.

———. 1966. Tree-Ring Dates from the Navajo Land Claim, III, The Southern Sector. *Tree-Ring Bulletin* 27(3–4): 2–11.

———. 1969. Tree-Ring Dates from the Navajo Land Claim, IV, The Eastern Sector. *Tree-Ring Bulletin* 29(1–2): 2–15.

Stubbs, Stanley A. 1950. *Bird's-Eye View of the Pueblos.* Norman: University of Oklahoma Press.

Sullivan, Belle Shafer. 1938. *The Unvanishing Navajos.* Philadelphia: Dorrance and Company.

Tanner, Clara Lee, and Charlie R. Steen. 1955. A Navajo Burial of about 1850. *Panhandle-Plains Historical Review,* 28: 110–18.

Tanner, George S., and J. Morris Richards. 1977. *Colonization on the Little Colorado: The Joseph City Region.* Flagstaff: Northland Press.

Taylor, Betty. 1965. The Navajo Hogan. *The Navajo Times* 6(28): 10.

Teit, J. A. 1956. Field Notes on the Tahltan and Kaska Indians: 1912–15. *Anthropologica* 3: 40–171.

Thomas, Alfred Barnaby. 1932. *Forgotten Frontiers.* Norman: University of Oklahoma Press.

Thomas, Peter, Frank Johnson, and Jonah Yazzie. 1974. Hogan Building at Rock Point, Arizona. *Tsa'aszi'* 1(2): 21–26, 60.

Thompson, Hildegard. 1975. *The Navajos' Long Walk for Education: A History of Navajo Education.* Tsaile: Navajo Community College Press.

Thybony, Scott. 1980. The Rediscovery of the Colorado Plateau. *Plateau* 52(1): 2–9.

Tisinger, R. M. 1935. The First Navajo PWA Day School Is Completed. *Indians at Work* 2(14): 31–33.

Torrez, Robert J. 1979. The Jacal in the Tierra Amarilla. *El Palacio* 85(2): 14–18.

Touhy, Donald R. 1960. Two More Wikiups on the San Carlos Indian Reservation. *The Kiva* 26(2): 27–30.

Tremblay, Marc-Adélard, John Collier, Jr., and Tom T. Sasaki. 1954. Navaho Housing in Transition. *América Indígena* 14(3): 187–219.

Tschopik, Harry Jr. 1941. *Navaho Pottery Making: An Inquiry into the Affinities of Navaho Painted Pottery.* Papers, Peabody Museum of American Archaeology and Ethnology, Harvard University, 17(1).

Underhill, Ruth M. 1953. *Here Come the Navaho!* Lawrence, Kansas: Bureau of Indian affairs.
———. 1956. *The Navajos.* Norman: University of Oklahoma Press.

Vanstone, James W. 1974. *Athapaskan Adaptations: Hunters and Fishermen of the Subarctic Forests.* Chicago: Aldine Publishing.

Van Valkenburgh, Richard. F. 1938a. *A Short History of the Navajo People* (mimeo.). Window Rock: Navajo Service.
———. 1938b. A Striking Navajo Petroglyph. *The Masterkey* 12(4): 153–57.
———. 1940a. Sacred Places and Shrines of the Navajos, Part II, Navajo Rock and Twig Piles Call Tsenadjihihi. *Plateau* 13(1): 6–9.
———. 1940b. We found the Ancient Tower of Haskhek'izh. *The Desert Magazine* 3(8): 22–24.
———. 1941. *Diné Bikeyah* (mimeo.). Window Rock: Navajo Service.
———. 1945. Big Bead Mesa—Where Campfires Burned in Ancient Days. *The Desert Magazine* 8(4): 4–8.
———. 1947a. Flint Singer Returns to the Underworld. *The Desert Magazine* 10(7): 15–17.
———. 1947b. Trail to the Tower of the Standing God. *The Desert Magazine* 11(1): 16–18.
———. n.d. *The History of the Navajo Nation,* Chapter IX, "A Period of Dishonor, 1880–1884," based on the letter books of the Navajo Agency at Ft. Defiance, ms. 284–994, in Box 9, the Richard Fowler Van Valkenburgh Collection, Arizona Historical Society, Tucson.

Verplanck, James Delancey. 1934. *A Country of Shepherds.* Boston: Ruth Hill.

Vestal, P. A. 1952. *Ethnobotany of the Ramah Navaho.* Papers, Peabody Museum of American Archaeology and Ethnology, Harvard University, 40(4).

Vivian, R. Gwinn. 1959. *The Hubbard Site and Other Tri-Wall Structures in New Mexico and Colorado.* National Park Service Archeological Research Series, 5.
———. 1960. *Navajo Archeology of the Chacra Mesa, New Mexico.* Master's thesis, University of New Mexico, Albuquerque.
———. 1970. An Apache Site on Ranch Creek, Southeast Arizona. *The Kiva* 35(3): 125–30.

Vogt, Evon Z. 1951. *Navaho Veterans: A Study of Changing Values.* Papers, Peabody Museum of American Archaeology and Ethnology, Harvard University, 41(1).
———. 1961. Navaho. In: Edward H. Spicer, ed., *Perspectives in American Indian Culture Change,* pp. 278–336. Chicago: University of Chicago Press.

Wagner, Marilyn, and Richard W. Travis. 1979. In Search of the Navajo's Canadian Connection. *Annals of the Association of American Geographers* 69(3): 480–82.

Wagner, Roland Marshall. 1974. *Western Navajo Peyotism: A Case Analysis.* Ph.D. dissertation, University of Oregon, Eugene.

Walker, J. G. 1964. Through Cañon de Chelly. In: L. R. Bailey, ed., *The Navajo Reconnaisance: A Military Exploration of the Navajo Country in 1859.* Los Angeles: Westernlore Press.

Ward, Albert A. 1968. Investigation of Two Hogans at Toonerville, Arizona. *Plateau* 40(4): 136–142.
———. 1975. Gravestones for Ganado Mucho: A Contribution to Navajo Ethnohistory. *The Masterkey* 49(3): 94–104.
———. 1978. Navajo Graves: Some Considerations for Recording and Classifying Reservation Burials. *American Indian Quarterly,* 4(4): 329–46.
——— and David M. Brugge. 1975. Changing Contemporary Navajo Burial Practice and Values. *Plateau* 48(1–2): 31–41.

Waterman, T. T. 1925. North American Indian Dwellings. *Smithsonian Institution, Annual Report,* 1924: 461–85.

Wathen, A. L. 1934. The Fruitland Irrigation Project, Northern New Mexico. *Indians at Work* 1(23): 31–33.

Watson, Editha L. 1964. *Navajo Sacred Places.* Navajoland Publications, 5.

Watson, Editha L., *continued*
———. 1968. An Odd Sandpainting Rug. *El Palacio* 75(3): 22–25.
Webb, Wallace, and Robert A. Weinstein. 1973. *Dwellers at the Source: Southwestern Indian Photographs of A. C. Vroman, 1895–1904.* New York: Grossman Publishers.
Wendorf, Fred. 1954. A Reconstruction of Northern Rio Grande Prehistory. *American Anthropologist* 56(2): 200–27.
Werner, Ruth. 1972. *Novice in Navajoland.* Scottsdale: Southwest Book Service.
Weslager, C. A. 1969. *The Log Cabin in America From Pioneer Days to the Present.* New Brunswick: Rutgers University Press.
Wetherill, Louisa Wade. 1946. Some Navajo Recipes. *The Kiva* 12(5–6): 39–40.
Wetherill, Milton. 1954. A Paiute Trap Corral on Skeleton Mesa, Arizona. *Plateau* 26(4): 116.
Wheeler, Geo[rge] M. 1879. *Report upon United States Geographical Surveys West of the One Hundredth Meridian, 7, Archaeology.* Washington: Government Printing Office.
Wilken, Robert L. 1955. *Anselm Weber, O.F.M., Missionary to the Navajo, 1898–1921.* Milwaukee: The Bruce Publishing Company.
Wilmeth, Roscoe. 1978. *Anahim Lake Archaeology and the Early Historic Chilcotin Indians.* Archaeological Survey of Canada, Paper 82[1].
Wilmsen, Edwin N. 1960. The House of the Navajo. *Landscape* 10(1): 15–19.
Wilson, E. F. 1890. The Navajo Indians. *Our Forest Children* 3(10): 113–17.
Wilson, John P. [1972]. *An Archaeological Survey on Pueblo of Laguna Lands.* Archaeological Society of New Mexico, Supplement 2.
——— and A. H. Warren. 1974. LA 2298 the Earliest Pueblito? *Awanyu* 2(1): 8–26.
Winberry, John J. 1974. The Log House in Mexico. *Annals of the Association of American Geographers* 64(1): 54–69.
Wonders, William C. 1979. Log Dwellings in American Folk Architecture. *Annals of the Association of American Geographers* 69(2): 187–207.
Woods, Betty. 1952. We explored the Valley of Thundering Water. *The Desert Magazine* 15(4): 4–9.
Woolsey, Nethella Griffin. 1964. *The Escalante Story.* Escalante: Escalante Camp, Daughters of Utah Pioneers.
Worcester, David E. 1947. *Early History of the Navaho Indians.* Doctoral dissertation, University of California, Berkeley.
Wormington, H. M. 1947. *Prehistoric Indians of the Southwest.* Denver Museum of Natural History, Popular Series, 7.
Wyatt, Charles D. 1941. Canyon de Chelly National Monument. *Arizona Highways* 17(8): 4–9, 37–39.
Wyeth, Betsy James, ed. 1971. *The Wyeths: The Letters of N. C. Wyeth, 1901–1945.* Boston: Gambit.
Wyman, Leland C. 1936. The Female Shooting Life Chant; A Minor Navaho Ceremony. *American Anthropologist* 38(4): 634–53.
———. 1952. Native Navaho Method for the Control of Insect Pests. *Plateau* 24(3): 97–103.
———. 1966. Snakeskins and Hoops. *Plateau* 39(1): 4–25.
——— and Flora L. Bailey. 1943. Navajo Girl's Puberty Rite. *New Mexico Anthropologist* 6–7(1): 3–12.

Yarrow, H. C. 1881. A Further Contribution to the Study of the Mortuary Customs of the North American Indians. *Bureau of Ethnology, Annual Report,* 1: 87–203.
Yost, Billie Williams. 1958. *Bread Upon the Sands.* Caldwell, Idaho: The Caxton Printers.
Young, Robert W. 1958, 1961. *The Navajo Yearbook,* 7, 8. Window Rock: Navajo Agency.
——— and William Morgan. 1980. *The Navajo Language.* Albuquerque: University of New Mexico.
——— and William Morgan. 1980. *The Navajo Language.* Albuquerque: University of New Mexico Press.

INDEX OF
NAVAJO TERMS

GENERAL INDEX

NOTE: Figure captions are indexed only with respect to structures, major structural features, personal names, and places. Italicized page numbers refer to captions or tables *only*.